The Royal Pardon

ACCESS TO MERCY IN FOURTEENTH-CENTURY ENGLAND

This book provides the first comprehensive examination of the use of the royal pardon in fourteenth-century England. The letter of pardon was a document familiar to the king's subjects; imbued with symbolic resonance as the judgement of the king, it also served a practical purpose, offering a last hope of reprive from the death sentence or life as an outlaw. The fourteenth century was a pivotal time of change for the system of English justice, and saw the evolution of a legal structure still recognisable today, yet the role of the royal pardon adapted and endured. This study brings together legal and literary texts, parliamentary records, yearbooks, and plea rolls, in order to examine the full influence of royal mercy.

Chapters analyse the procedures of pardoning, the role of royal mercy at moments of political upheaval (including the 1381 Peasants' Revolt) and the range of views expressed by legal theorists, parliamentary representatives, and by the diverse range of people who, at one time or another, had reason to seek royal mercy. The appendices include full lists of all those who acted as `intercessors' for mercy; comprising c. 1,000 names in total, these lists reveal the role of women and personal servants of the crown, alongside the great nobles of the realm, in providing access to royal grace. The implications of this study on royal mercy go well beyond legal history, encompassing the major political and constitutional debates of the period, the theological underpinnings of royal mercy and the social context of the law.

Dr HELEN LACEY is Lecturer in Late Medieval History at Mansfield College, University of Oxford.

YORK MEDIEVAL PRESS

York Medieval Press is published by the University of York's Centre for Medieval Studies in association with Boydell & Brewer Limited. Our objective is the promotion of innovative scholarship and fresh criticism on medieval culture. We have a special commitment to interdisciplinary study, in line with the Centre's belief that the future of Medieval Studies lies in those areas in which its major constituent disciplines at once inform and challenge each other.

All enquiries of an editorial kind, including suggestions for monographs and essay collections, should be addressed to: The Academic Editor, York Medieval Press, University of York, Centre for Medieval Studies, The King's Manor, York, YO1 7EP (E-mail: gmg501@york.ac.uk).

Publications of York Medieval Press are listed at the back of this volume.

The Royal Pardon

ACCESS TO MERCY IN
FOURTEENTH-CENTURY ENGLAND

Helen Lacey

THE UNIVERSITY *of York*

YORK MEDIEVAL PRESS

First published 2009

A York Medieval Press publication
in association with The Boydell Press
an imprint of Boydell & Brewer Ltd
PO Box 9   Woodbridge   Suffolk IP12 3DF   UK
and of Boydell & Brewer Inc.
668 Mt Hope Avenue   Rochester   NY 14620   USA
website: www.boydellandbrewer.com
and with the
Centre for Medieval Studies, University of York

ISBN 978 1 903153 28 4

The publisher has no responsibility for the continued existence or accuracy
of URLs for external or third-party internet websites referred to in this book,
and does not guarantee that any content on such websites is, or will remain,
accurate or appropriate.

A CIP catalogue record for this book is available
from the British Library

Printed in Great Britain by
CPI Antony Rowe, Chippenham and Eastbourne

CONTENTS

ACKNOWLEDGEMENTS

There are a number of people I should like to thank for the help they have given me during my research for this book. Firstly, Mark Ormrod has given expert advice and encouragement since the beginning of my university career. Mark's insight and commitment have been invaluable, and are truly appreciated. Nick Havely has also provided a constant source of inspiration and assistance throughout my doctoral studies. Thanks also to Shelagh Sneddon for her help with transcribing and translating archival material, to James Bothwell for his advice concerning the holdings of The National Archives and to Gwilym Dodd for his constructive criticism and advice. I would also like to thank my colleagues at York, Durham and Oxford, who always offer friendship and wise advice: Jocelyn Wogan-Browne, Judy Frost, Lucy Sackville, Katy Gibbons, Hannah Greig, Michael Prestwich, Christian Liddy, Lawrence Black, Giles Gasper, Natalie Mears, Tom Pickles, Helena Carr and Kathryn Gleadle.

On a personal note, I would like to thank my family and friends for their constant encouragement and forbearance: David, Briony, Robert, Julia, Catherine, Isla, Abigail, Samuel, Helen, Hannah, Mike, Nicola and Jonny. Kirsty and Victoria deserve special thanks for checking the appendices so diligently. Finally, I should like to thank my parents, who are unfailing in their enthusiasm and support for all my endeavours; it is to them that this book is dedicated.

I must also thank the *Journal of Medieval History* and Boydell & Brewer for allowing me to reproduce extracts from the following articles:

'Grace for the Rebels: The Role of the Royal Pardon in the Peasants' Revolt of 1381', *Journal of Medieval History* 34 (2008), 36–63.
'"Mercy and Truth Preserve the king": Richard II's Use of the Royal Pardon', in *Fourteenth Century England IV*, ed. J. Hamilton (Woodbridge, 2006), pp. 124–35.

ABBREVIATIONS

BL	British Library
BIHR	*Bulletin of the Institute of Historical Research*
CChR	*Calendar of Charter Rolls*
CCR	*Calendar of Close Rolls*
CFR	*Calendar of Fine Rolls*
CPR	*Calendar of Patent Rolls*
EETS	Early English Text Society
EHR	*English Historical Review*
Foedera	Thomas Rymer, *Foedera, Conventiones, Literae et cujuscunque generis Acta,* Record Commission edn, 3 vols. in 6 parts (London, 1816–30)
Foedera [First edition]	Thomas Rymer, *Foedera, Conventiones, Literae et cujuscunque generis Acta* (London, 1704–35)
P&P	*Past and Present*
PPC	*Proceedings and Ordinances of the Privy Council of England,* ed. N. H. Nicolas, 7 vols. (London, 1834–7)
PROME	*The Parliament Rolls of Medieval England,* ed. C. Given-Wilson *et al.,* CD-ROM (Leicester, 2005)
Rôles gascons	*Rôles gascons, 1290–1307,* ed. C. Bémont (Paris, 1906)
RPHI	*Rotuli Parliamentorum Anglie hactenus inediti, 1279–1373,* ed. H. G. Richardson and G. O. Sayles, Camden Society, 3rd series 51 (London, 1935)
RS	Rolls Series
SCCKB	*Select Cases in the Court of King's Bench,* ed. G. O. Sayles, 7 vols., Selden Society 55, 57, 58, 74, 76, 82, 88 (London, 1936–71)
SR	*Statutes of the Realm, 1101–1713,* ed. A. Luders *et al.,* Record Commission, 11 vols. (London, 1810–28)
TNA	The National Archives, London
TRHS	*Transactions of the Royal Historical Society*
Walsingham, *CA*	Thomas Walsingham, *Chronicon Angliae 1328–1388,* ed. E. M. Thompson, Rolls Series 64 (London, 1874)
Walsingham, *HA*	Thomas Walsingham, *Historia Anglicana,* ed. H. T. Riley, Rolls Series 28 (London, 1863–4)

CHAPTER ONE

Introduction

The king's pardon was an important legal document in fourteenth-century England, yet its influence was felt far beyond the confines of the judicial system; it played a part in the major political crises of the period, and carried with it a symbolism that resonated throughout medieval culture. The power to grant mercy was inherited by the monarchs of later medieval England as one of the prerogative rights of the Crown. In practical terms this privilege was extended to supplicants in the form of letters patent of pardon, which were authorised by the monarch or his chancellor and then issued from the royal Chancery. The prerogative was wide-ranging: as ultimate arbiter of the law, the king could intervene at any point in the legal process and pardon all charges brought in his name. From the accession of Edward I to the deposition of Richard II, close to 40,000 of these letters patent are recorded on the patent rolls alone, and numbers were increasing across the period, despite the dramatic fall in population after the mid-century Black Death pandemic.[1] While in many ways the monarchs of the fourteenth century had come to preside over the judicial system as symbolic figureheads, rather than active judges, they still saw fit, on occasion, to personally intervene and grant mercy to one of their subjects.[2]

---

[1] The exact number of pardons issued cannot be calculated, as not all were recorded in the government archives. However, the total figure is substantially higher, when those recorded on the supplementary patent rolls (TNA C 67, commonly referred to as the 'pardon rolls') and those on the Gascon and Scottish rolls (TNA C 61; C 71) are taken into account. The C 67 series records the issue of almost 20,000 pardons by Edward I and his three successors. Many of these were recorded separately because they were issued under the grant of a general pardon. A proportion of these were then duplicated onto the main patent roll (TNA C 66). For further discussion of these records, see below, Appendices: Introduction, p. 183 and Appendix 1.

[2] For legal cases in which the Crown intervened directly, see TNA KB 145/1/18; JUST 1/425, fols. 12v, 13, 21v, 22; SC 1/39/27; SC 1/55/86; *Year Books of the Reign of King Edward the Third, Years XI–XX*, ed. A. J. Horwood and L. O. Pike, RS 31 (London, 1883–1911), III, 196–7; *Calendar of Letter Books of the City of London*, ed. R. R. Sharpe, 10 vols. (London, 1899–1912), G, II, 23. The King's Bench acknowledged the personal influence of the king in its proceedings: *SCCKB*, III, cxxxiii–iv. See also A. Musson, *Medieval Law in Context: The Growth of Legal Consciousness from Magna Carta to the Peasants' Revolt* (Manchester, 2001), pp. 218–64; J. Watts, *Henry VI and the Politics of Kingship* (Cambridge, 1996), pp. 1–80, for discussion of the extent to

The fourteenth century also saw an important innovation in the process of pardoning; in the latter half of Edward III's reign the Crown introduced a new form of comprehensive pardon, enshrined in statutory form and available to anyone who chose to purchase a copy before a stated deadline. These 'general pardons' were negotiated in Parliament, and involved the active cooperation of the Commons in their formulation.[3] Indeed, the use of pardons of all types became a regular feature of parliamentary discussion and debate. The grant of a general pardon, in particular, could play an important political role in symbolising reconciliation between the Crown and the polity in the aftermath of a governmental crisis on the scale of the Good Parliament in 1376, for example, or the 1381 Peasants' Revolt.[4] Moreover, they provided tangible evidence of the Crown's obligation to provide effective justice for its subjects. Accordingly, these public acts of mercy became trademarks of the English Crown in the later Middle Ages, yet their role has received little attention from historians. The purpose of this introductory chapter is to address the major trends and methodological problems of existing scholarship on the subject, and to examine the wider context of discretionary mercy.

Historiographical Debates

One reason for the relative neglect of pardoning in the existing scholarship has been the tendency to dismiss it as a prime example of the corruption and nepotism endemic in the medieval courts of justice. Historians and legal theorists have often struggled with the notion that this kind of personal discretionary judgment could have any legitimate place in a properly functioning legal system. The concept that something defined as a crime might be forgiven without punishment by the power vested in the person of the king carries notions of personal interpretation and modification of the law to its extreme. Pardoning therefore provides an example of law at its most discretionary. Several of the eminent constitutional and legal historians of the nineteenth and early twentieth centuries were scathing about this perceived

which the medieval monarch played an active role in the legal system. For discussion of the associated area of royal arbitration, see E. Powell, 'Arbitration and the Law in England in the Later Middle Ages', *TRHS* 5th series 13 (1983), 49–67; E. Powell, 'Settlement of Disputes by Arbitration in Fifteenth-Century England', *Law and History Review* 2 (1984), 21–43; C. Rawcliffe, 'English Noblemen and their Advisers: Consultation and Collaboration in the Later Middle Ages', *Journal of British Studies* 25 (1986), 157–77; C. Rawcliffe, 'Parliament and the Settlement of Disputes by Arbitration in the Later Middle Ages', *Parliamentary History* 9 (1990), 316–42.

3 For further discussion of general pardons, see below, Part II. 'Commons' is used throughout this book to refer to the representatives in Parliament.

4 For further discussion, see below, Chapters 8 and 9.

defect in medieval law.[5] These scholars contrasted the vagaries of the royal prerogative of mercy with the reliable predictability of English common law, a legal code that had reached its apogee in the Victorian courts of justice. For Bishop Stubbs, the parliamentary Commons of the later Middle Ages were fighting a losing battle against the Crown's exploitation of its prerogative powers, which he castigated in no uncertain terms: 'this evil was not merely an abuse of the royal attribute of mercy, or a defeat of the ordinary processes of justice, but a regularly systematised perversion of prerogative'. It was, he added, manipulated by the 'great people of the realm' to secure an exemption from the law for their retainers, or for those who paid them enough to buy their support.[6] Jean Jules Jusserand concurred, adding that the royal Chancery willingly granted these pardons in order to boost government revenue. As a result, he stated, 'the number of brigands increased by reason of their impunity', and men dared not bring the most formidable criminals to justice for fear of reprisals. The Commons could do little in the face of such corruption, yet they 'unweariedly renewed their complaints against these crying abuses'.[7] It is important to note, however, that not all constitutional historians were so outspoken in their condemnation. Pollock and Maitland took a more measured approach, criticising only the treatment of those who killed in self-defence, or by accident.[8]

It was not until 1969 that a comprehensive study of the origins and use of the royal pardon in England was published. Naomi Hurnard's detailed examination of the role of pardoning in the legal sphere provided a thorough and scrupulous survey of the array of archival material relating to royal mercy, and did much to further the cause of empirical research in the study of this prerogative power.[9] However, Hurnard reiterated the condemnation with which earlier scholars had dismissed royal pardons. Her work sought to drive home the point that royal pardons were responsible for holding back the development of the common law, by substituting 'administrative discretion for judicial decision, uncertainty for the predictability of

5 W. Stubbs, *The Constitutional History of England in its Origin and Development* (Oxford, 1875), II, 582; J. J. Jusserand, *English Wayfaring Life in the Middle Ages: XIVth Century*, 4th edn (London, 1961), pp. 166–7; F. Pollock and F. M. Maitland, *The History of English Law Before the time of Edward I*, 2nd edn (Cambridge, 1911), II, 478–84.

6 Stubbs, *Constitutional History*, II, 582.

7 Jusserand, *English Wayfaring Life*, p. 167.

8 The Anglo-Saxon customs of *wergild* and *wite* addressed the problem of differing degrees of liability, but had been replaced with deferment to the king's mercy in each specific case. This, for Pollock and Maitland, was a somewhat inadequate stop-gap measure: Pollock and Maitland, *English Law*, II, 483–4; J. F. Stephen, *History of the Criminal Law of England* (London, 1883), III, 42–4.

9 N. D. Hurnard, *The King's Pardon for Homicide Before AD 1307* (Oxford, 1969).

punishment'.[10] In medieval England, she asserted, the king's prerogative of mercy was certainly used to excess, and yet was scarcely ever available to those condemned to death in error. While Henry III misused the prerogative in his attempts to appease opposing factions, Hurnard blamed Edward I in particular for taking this corruption to new heights by using pardons as an incentive to enlist military recruits. This 'disastrous expedient' removed all pretence of any equitable motives for pardoning.[11]

Hurnard demonstrated that the royal pardon was an important subject, and one that might be explored beyond the bounds of her work, which focused on the use of pardons for homicide only in the period before 1307. Since her book was published, nearly forty years ago, scholars have generated a huge volume of work on the role of justice, law, kingship and political culture in later medieval society, and this material gives an entirely new context to a study of pardoning. One important conclusion of this more recent work has been that the fourteenth century was a dramatic period of evolution and change in the English legal system. The reasons for this change, and its impact on medieval society, have been the subject of much debate. Several scholars writing in the 1970s and 1980s thought that the fourteenth century witnessed a dramatic decline in public order, as foreign warfare became the priority of the government, to the detriment of domestic stability. Hurnard's views on pardon fitted well with this picture, and historians such as Herbert Hewitt, Gerald Harriss and Richard Kaeuper similarly characterised the use of the royal pardon as a short-term expedient taken to channel resources into the war effort. According to this view pardoning therefore occupied a minor role in the wider debate over public order in the later fourteenth century 'war-state'.[12] An alternative to this view, put forward by Anthony Musson, Mark Ormrod and others, is that there was a perceived deterioration in standards of public order in this period, because medieval expectations had risen in

---

10 Hurnard, *Homicide*, p. vii.
11 For discussion of military pardons, see below, Chapter 7, pp. 100–6 and Appendix 2.
12 Reform of the judicial system had long been on the political agenda of the Commons, echoing the contemporary perception that the quality of the legal system was degenerating. Some historians suggest that this perception reflected a real qualitative slide in the fourteenth century: B. H. Putnam, 'The Transformation of the Keepers of the Peace into the Justices of the Peace, 1327–1380', *TRHS* 4th series 12 (1929), 19–48; H. J. Hewitt, *The Organisation of War under Edward III 1338–62* (Manchester, 1966), p. 173; G. L. Harriss, *King, Parliament and Public Finance in Medieval England to 1369* (Oxford, 1975), pp. 354–5, 516–17; R. G. Nicholson, *Edward III and the Scots: The Formative Years of A Military Career, 1327–1335* (Oxford, 1965), pp. 130, 174, 197; T. F. T. Plucknett, *A Concise History of Common Law* (London, 1956), p. 457; *The Shropshire Peace Roll, 1400–1414*, ed. E. G. Kimball (Shrewsbury, 1959), pp. 43–5; R. W. Kaeuper, *War, Justice and Public Order: England and France in the Later Middle Ages* (Oxford, 1988), pp. 126–7.

line with the expanding legal apparatus, which reached a greater range of the populace than ever before.[13] These historians have, to an extent, moved away from Hurnard's negative stance towards pardons, emphasising the degree to which concepts of pardon and mercy permeated medieval society and were, at various times, both criticised and extolled by supplicants and by those in positions of judicial authority. It is certainly an interpretation that allows for a more nuanced understanding of medieval attitudes to the royal pardon, and it has done much to inform the analysis offered in this book.

This debate on fourteenth-century law and order has not evolved in isolation; much work on the ideology of the law and the nature of political culture, in particular, has changed the intellectual landscape since Hurnard's book was published. In the 1970s the 'Warwick school' of historians, which included Edward Thompson and Douglas Hay, sought to apply Marxist techniques of analysis to the social history of crime in the seventeenth and eighteenth centuries.[14] For Hay, the continued use of the royal pardon in eighteenth-century England served to promote a belief in the fairness and equity of a legal system that upheld the propertied interests of the ruling elite. While the government expanded the number of crimes punishable by death, it mitigated the severity of the law with the use of royal pardons, and therefore kept the populace in a deferential relationship with the ruling class. Although this work has since been modified and challenged, it served to raise awareness of the extent to which the law influenced, and was in

---

[13] A. Musson and W. M. Ormrod, *The Evolution of English Justice: Law, Politics and Society in the Fourteenth Century* (Basingstoke, 1999), pp. 161–93; A. Musson, *Public Order and Law Enforcement: The Local Administration of Criminal Justice, 1294–1350* (Woodbridge, 1996), pp. 189–201; A. J. Verduyn, 'The Politics of Law and Order during the Early Years of Edward III', *EHR* 108 (1993), 842–67; E. Powell, 'The Administration of Criminal Justice in Late-Medieval England: Peace Sessions and Assizes', in *The Political Context of Law: Proceedings of the Seventh British History Conference*, ed. R. Eales and D. Sullivan (London, 1987), pp. 49–59. Musson and Ormrod's stated aim is to 'assess the evolution of justice in an objective manner, free from the moral hyperbole of medieval – and of some modern – commentators'. Musson and Ormrod, *Evolution*, p. 11.

[14] D. Hay, 'Property, Authority and the Criminal Law', in *Albion's Fatal Tree: Crime and Society in Eighteenth Century England*, ed. D. Hay, P. Linebaugh, J. Rule, E. P. Thompson, E. Palmer and C. Winslow (New York, 1975), pp. 17–64; E. P. Thompson, *Whigs and Hunters: The Origins of the Black Act* (New York, 1976). See also J. M. Beattie, *Crime and the Courts in England 1660–1800* (Princeton, 1986); J. A. Sharpe, *Crime in Early Modern England, 1550–1750*, 2nd edn (London, 1998); J. Innes and J. Styles, 'The Crime Wave: Recent Writing on Crime and Criminal Justice in Eighteenth-Century England', in *Rethinking Social History*, ed. A. Wilson (Manchester, 1993), pp. 201–65. K. Kesselring discusses this material, and its relevance to royal pardons in the early modern period: K. J. Kesselring, *Mercy and Authority in the Tudor State* (Cambridge, 2003), pp. 4–7.

turn shaped by social relations.[15] As Krista Kesselring argued in her study of pardoning in sixteenth-century England, the legacy of the Warwick school has been to emphasise the 'links between legal processes and social relations of power'.[16] In recent years this has meant that the scholarship on law and justice has been linked to work on constitutional history and political culture. It prompts questions about how the use of royal mercy reflected or shaped relations between the Crown and its subjects, and how people from all social levels thought about their relationship with government and their interaction with the legal system.

Historians of the later Middle Ages have in recent years become increasingly interested in such questions, in part through the emergence of a 'new constitutional history', which looks to explore the nature of relations between the centre of government and the localities, and emphasises the importance of 'the values, ideals and conventions governing political life'. Edward Powell has argued that these values should be taken to include '... not merely such matters as the inalienability of the royal prerogative or the necessity of parliamentary consent to taxation, but also the advice given to rulers in the "mirrors for princes" literature – for example the exhortation that the prince should cultivate the virtues of justice, piety, mercy, patience and so on'.[17]

---

15 P. King, *Crime, Justice and Discretion in England, 1740–1820* (Oxford, 2000). Kesselring gives a useful survey of the reactions to Hay's work: Kesselring, *Mercy and Authority*, pp. 5–7.

16 Kesselring, *Mercy and Authority*, p. 7.

17 E. Powell, 'After "After McFarlane"', in *Trade, Devotion and Governance: Papers in Later Medieval History*, ed. D. J. Clayton, R. G. Davies and P. McNiven (Stroud, 1994), p. 10. Other works of 'new constitutional history' include: E. Powell, 'Law and Justice', in *Fifteenth-Century Attitudes: Perceptions of Society in Late Medieval England*, ed. R. Horrox (Cambridge, 1994), pp. 29–41; E. Powell, *Kingship, Law and Society: Criminal Justice in the Reign of Henry V* (Oxford, 1989); C. Carpenter, 'Introduction: Political Culture, Politics and Cultural History', in *The Fifteenth Century IV: Political Culture in Late Medieval Britain*, ed. L. Clark and C. Carpenter (Woodbridge, 2004), pp. 1–20; C. Carpenter, *The Wars of the Roses: Politics and the Constitution in England, c.1437–1509* (Cambridge, 1997); C. Carpenter, 'Political and Constitutional History: Before and After McFarlane', in *The McFarlane Legacy: Studies in Late Medieval Politics and Society*, ed. R. H. Britnell and A. J. Pollard (Stroud, 1995), pp. 175–206; J. L. Watts, 'Public or Plebs: The Changing Meaning of "the Commons", 1381–1549', in *Power and Identity in the Middle Ages: Essays in Memory of Rees Davies*, ed. H. Pryce and J. L. Watts (Oxford, 2007), pp. 242–60; J. L. Watts, 'Looking for the State in Later Medieval England', in *Heraldry, Pageantry, and Social Display in Medieval England*, ed. P. R. Coss and M. H. Keen (Woodbridge, 2002), pp. 243–67; S. Walker, M. J. Braddick and G. L. Harriss, ed., *Political Culture in Later Medieval England; Essays by Simon Walker* (Manchester, 2006); S. K. Walker, 'Rumour, Sedition and Popular Protest in the Reign of Henry IV', *P&P* 166 (2000), 31–65; G. L. Harriss, 'The Dimensions of Politics', in *McFarlane Legacy*, pp. 1–20; G. L. Harriss, 'The King and his Subjects', in *Fifteenth-Century Attitudes*, ed. Horrox, pp. 13–28; G. L. Harriss, 'Political Society and the Growth of Government in Late Medieval England', *P&P* 138 (1993), 28–57; W. M. Ormrod, *Political Life in Medieval England,*

Powell argued for a revival of research into the workings of the machinery of law and government, and central to this was the idea that the development of judicial institutions and codes of law inevitably regulated and constrained the exercise of royal power. This 'new constitutional' approach has not neglected the operation of patronage, and has done much to elucidate the way in which the Crown supplemented its authority with patron–broker–client ties, both inside and outside the institutional framework. Thus the interaction between bureaucracy and patronage remains at the heart of our understanding of the exercise of royal authority. The medieval legal system was one area that exemplified such interaction. Powell expressed a concern to set the workings of the law in their social context, but stressed that medieval law could not be reduced merely to the play of patronage: 'It was too open, too complex a system, expectations of it were too high, and its rules and procedures had a logic and momentum of their own which restricted, though it did not exclude, manipulation.'[18] With this approach in mind, Powell examined Henry V's use of the royal pardon against the backdrop not only of the judicial problems that faced the king at his accession, but also the political unrest in the wider community. He persuasively demonstrated that the general pardons issued by Henry V were aimed at reconciling political society to the government, in a public display of their commitment to the regime. Powell also convincingly maintained that the success of Henry V's general pardons, compared to those of other regimes, owed much to his ability to present them as an assertion of royal authority rather than an admission of weakness.[19]

This call to explore the social context of political culture, justice and patronage has been taken up, in recent years, by historians working on the fourteenth and fifteenth centuries. John Watts, for example, has investigated ideas of government, complaint and the use of legal vocabulary in a wide array of later medieval texts.[20] This scholarship has given a new insight into medieval politics and justice and has successfully utilised post-structural techniques of linguistic analysis to examine the rhetoric of all types of source material. Studies of later medieval advice literature, for example, have demonstrated the importance attached to the exaltation of mercy and clemency as royal virtues.[21] Gwilym Dodd's recent work on the place of private

---

c.1300–1450 (London, 1995); C. Carpenter, *Locality and Polity: A Study of Warwickshire Landed Society, 1401–1499* (Cambridge, 1992).

18 Powell, 'After "After McFarlane"', p. 12.

19 Powell, *Kingship, passim*; E. Powell, 'The Restoration of Law and Order', in *Henry V: The Practice of Kingship*, ed. G. L. Harriss (Oxford, 1985), pp. 53–74; Powell's approach is endorsed by Musson and Ormrod, *Evolution*, p. 82.

20 J. L. Watts, 'The Pressure of the Public on Later Medieval Politics', in *Fifteenth Century IV*, ed. Clark and Carpenter, pp. 159–80; Watts, 'Public or Plebs', pp. 242–60; Watts, *Henry VI, passim*.

21 M. Giancarlo, *Parliament and Literature in Late Medieval England* (Cambridge, 2007); D. Grummitt, 'Deconstructing Cade's Rebellion: Discourse and Politics in the Mid

petitioning in the fourteenth century has similarly brought together many of these new techniques, to demonstrate the importance of petitioning, both at a parliamentary level and at a wider social level, among the county communities.[22]

One of the fundamental aims of this book, then, is to further the study of the attitudes to pardoning that prevailed across the whole range of institutions and models of political thought. The role of the royal pardon is ideally suited for such a study: the concept of pardoning generated discussion that spanned a variety of institutions and political modes of thought, while at a practical level it was used on a day-to-day basis in the king's courts and in Parliament itself. This study examines the political ideals laid down in normative tracts concerned with mercy, but it also seeks to elucidate the practical understanding of the role of the prerogative, articulated in parliamentary debates, legal commentaries and literary texts, and by the actions of court officials, royal justices, juries and supplicants, recorded in the judicial and administrative records of government.

In the last twenty years, several studies on French petitions for pardon have been produced that suggest the potential for examining the language and structure of such documents. The work of Claude Gauvard and Natalie Zemon Davis has demonstrated the importance of examining these archives in the light of a variety of source material including chronicles, journals, documents from urban and seigneurial officials, and theoretical treatises on justice.[23] In the English context, the work of Krista Kesselring on sixteenth-century pardons has also done much to elucidate the dramatic and visual impact of pardoning as a public display of reconciliation.[24] She examined the

---

Fifteenth Century', in *The Fifteenth Century VI: Identity and Insurgency in the Late Middle Ages*, ed. L. Clark (Woodbridge, 2006), pp. 107–22; P. Strohm, *Politique: Languages of Statecraft between Chaucer and Shakespeare* (Notre Dame, 2005); R. F. Green, *A Crisis of Truth: Literature and Law in Ricardian England* (Philadelphia, 1999); J. Ferster, *Fictions of Advice: The Literature and Politics of Counsel in Late Medieval England* (Philadelphia, 1996); P. Strohm, *Hochon's Arrow: The Social Imagination of Fourteenth Century Texts* (Princeton, 1992); P. Strohm, *Social Chaucer* (Cambridge MA, 1989); P. McCune, 'The Ideology of Mercy in English Literature and Law 1200–1600' (unpublished PhD thesis, University of Michigan, 1989); M. Stokes, *Justice and Mercy in Piers Plowman* (Cambridge, 1984); A. P. Baldwin, *The Theme of Government in Piers Plowman* (Cambridge, 1981); R. F. Green, *Poets and Princepleasers: Literature and the English Court in the Later Middle Ages* (Toronto, 1980).

22 G. Dodd, *Justice and Grace: Private Petitioning and the English Parliament in the Late Middle Ages* (Oxford, 2007).

23 C. Gauvard, '*De grace especiall': Crime, etat et société en France à la fin du Moyen Age* (Paris, 1991); C. Gauvard, 'Résistants et collaborateurs pendant la guerre de cent ans: le témoignage des lettres de rémission', *Actes du 3e congrès national des sociétés savantes (Poitiers, 1986): section d'histoire médiévale et de philologie, 1: la 'France anglaise' au moyen âge* (Paris, 1988), pp. 123–38; N. Z. Davis, *Fiction in the Archives: Pardon Tales and their Tellers in Sixteenth-Century France* (Cambridge, 1987).

24 Kesselring, *Mercy and Authority, passim*; K. J. Kesselring, 'To Pardon and to Punish:

'scaffold speeches' of leading members of the Tudor polity, and concluded that mercy functioned alongside punishment to articulate and construct royal authority.[25]

However, such conclusions cannot simply be transposed on to the political circumstances of the fourteenth century. In the case of the general pardon issued in the wake of the 1381 Peasants' Revolt, to take one example, new questions are raised by the grant of mercy to all of the king's subjects free of any requirement to purchase individual pardons. Even more pressing than the need to examine the specific political circumstances of the fourteenth century, however, is the need to address the process of pardoning that lay behind them. A detailed analysis of pardoning procedure remained absent from the revisionist approach that Powell pioneered, and the assumptions about the workings of the general pardon that underlie his conclusions have yet to be elucidated. This book therefore addresses both the established procedures of pardoning that lay behind grants of royal mercy, and their more immediate significance in promoting reconciliation in the aftermath of political crises. It also seeks to elucidate the role of pardoning in the lives of the king's subjects, and in so doing looks at the interaction between the Crown and the local communities. A study of the role of the royal pardon in fourteenth-century England thus brings together much of the recent scholarship on later medieval law, justice and political culture and draws on the historiographical developments in linguistic analysis and new constitutional history.

The structure of this book reflects my aim to examine the role of individuals who were involved in the pardoning process, and to elucidate the link between the Crown and its subjects that the royal pardon provided. Different types of pardon emerged during the fourteenth century, and so the book is divided into two main parts, the first dealing with individual pardons, and the second with group and general pardons. Chapters 3, 4 and 5 focus on the involvement of different groups of people in the pardoning process; firstly, those supplicants who sought individual grants of mercy; secondly, the 'intercessors' who helped others secure a royal pardon; and thirdly, the personal role of the monarch. Part II examines the evolution of the general pardon. Chapter 7 examines the use of 'group' pardons, which increased throughout the fourteenth century, and Chapters 8, 9 and 10 then examine the role of the general pardon at key moments of political instability, focusing on the interaction between the Crown and it subjects in the wake of crises on the scale of the Good Parliament of 1376, the 1381 Peasants' Revolt and Richard II's Revenge Parliament of 1397. The concluding chapter seeks to set

---

Mercy and Authority in Tudor England' (unpublished PhD thesis, Queens University, Ontario, 2000); K. J. Kesselring, 'Abjuration and its Demise: The Changing Face of Royal Justice under the Tudors', *Canadian Journal of History* 34 (1999), 345–58.
[25] Kesselring, *Mercy and Authority*, pp. 1–22.

the pardon in a wider cultural context and to review the attitudes towards the royal pardon that were expressed in fourteenth-century England.

These chapters seek to draw together a range of medieval texts, from the administrative records of government to vernacular protest literature, parliamentary rolls and legal treatises. The legal and governmental texts, including the patent rolls of Chancery, the receipt rolls of the exchequer, the letters and ancient petitions to the Crown, the records of Parliament, the Year Books and the eyre, Gaol Delivery and King's Bench rolls, give some insight into the practical processes of pardoning.[26] Opinions on pardoning were expressed by a wide range of writers; legal theorists such as the authors of *Bracton* and *Fleta* were prominent authorities, but several chroniclers, including Walsingham, Froissart, Knighton and Usk among others, also gave their views.[27] Common petitions to Parliament sought remedies to perceived abuses of the system of pardoning, but at other times requested a grant of mercy from the monarch. Still other attitudes towards the royal pardon are conveyed in the advice literature of John Gower, in outlaw romances such as the *Tale of Gamelyn*; in the visionary–political discourse of *Piers Plowman*; and in the didactic drama of Corpus Christi plays including *The Killing of Abel*.[28] Finally,

---

26 TNA C 67/26–37; C 237; C 81; C 49; C 266; C 66; E 401; JUST 1; KB 27. The bails on special pardons contained in C 237 provide valuable information concerning the legal procedures surrounding pardoning. Several privy seal writs warranting letters under the great seal relate to pardons, C 81; as do the king's remembrancer rolls, C 49; cancelled letters patent, C 266; and patent rolls, C 66. Information about the financial aspect of pardoning is contained in the exchequer receipt rolls, E 401. Petitions concerning pardons can also be found in the SC 8 class of ancient petitions to the Crown. Of the court rolls, the eyre and Gaol Delivery records, JUST 1, have been sampled to provide evidence for the use of royal pardons, as have the King's Bench rolls, KB 27. Further evidence has been drawn from the Year Books.

27 *Fleta*, ed. H. G. Richardson and G. O. Sayles, Selden Society 72, 89, 99 (London, 1955–84); *Britton*, ed. F. M. Nichols (Oxford, 1865); *Bracton on the Laws and Customs of England*, ed. S. E. Thorne (Cambridge MA, 1968–77); *The Treatise on the Laws and Customs of the Realm of England commonly called Glanvill*, ed. G. D. G. Hall (London, 1965); *The Chronicle of Adam Usk 1377–1421*, ed. C. Given-Wilson (Oxford, 1997); *Historia Vitae et Regni Ricardi Secundi*, ed. G. B. Stow (Philadelphia, 1977); *Knighton's Chronicle, 1337–1394*, ed. G. H. Martin (Oxford, 1995); *Concordia: The Reconciliation of Richard II with London*, ed. A. G. Rigg and D. R. Carlson (Kalamazoo, 2003); *The Westminster Chronicle 1381–1394*, ed. L. C. Hector and B. F. Harvey (Oxford, 1982); *The Chronicle of Bury St. Edmunds 1212–1301*, ed. A. Gransden (London, 1964); *The Anonimalle Chronicle*, ed. V. H. Galbraith (Manchester, 1927); *Froissart: Chronicles*, ed. G. Brereton (Harmondsworth, 1978). See below, Part II, for discussion of these general pardons.

28 *The Complete Works of John Gower*, ed. G. C. Macaulay (Oxford, 1901); *Robin Hood and Other Outlaw Tales*, ed. S. Knight and T. Ohlgren (Kalamazoo, 1997); *The Vision of Piers Plowman*, ed. A. V. C. Schmitt (London, 1995); *The Wakefield Pageants in the Towneley Cycle*, ed. A. C. Cawley (Manchester, 1958); *The Book of Vices and Virtues*, ed. W. N. Francis, EETS OS 217 (London, 1942); *The Pricke of Conscience*, ed. R. Morris, *Philological Society* 6 (Berlin, 1863); *The Mirour of the Blessed Lyf of Jesu Christ*,

petitioners themselves expressed perceptions of the royal pardon, perceptions often mediated through the pens of county lawyers, when they drafted written petitions for mercy and sent them to Parliament for consideration.

Discretionary Judgment

It is important to emphasise at the outset of this book that the royal pardon operated in a wider context of discretionary mitigation of the law: prosecution decisions, jury verdicts, judicial sentences and royal pardons all represented opportunities to modify or adapt the legal process.[29] The worst offenders might be singled out for exemplary punishment but jurors, justices and monarchs had the means to mitigate the severity of the law.[30]

The king's pardon was unique in the sense that it could be obtained on the recommendation of the justices after the case had been heard in court, or alternatively requested by individuals who by-passed the judicial process altogether. All other methods of mitigation can be roughly divided between those that arose out of trial proceedings, and those that circumvented the king's courts entirely. The former category comprised challenges to the validity of a charge, often on the basis of a technical flaw identified with some point of law.[31] Thomas Green has demonstrated that juries might play a crucial part in this process, determining why particular accusations had to be dropped because they failed to conform to the standards of written charges. Green argued that trial jurors worked around the strict rules of common law procedure so as to find reasons to pardon those people they thought to be deserving of mercy, but for whom the only penalty at law was forfeiture and death (Green terms this 'jury nullification'). The fact of their arrest, and the time they spent in prison before the arrival of the justices, satisfied the

---

ed. L. R. Powell (Oxford, 1908); *Ludus Coventriae or the Plaie Called Corpus Christi*, ed. K. S. Block, EETS OS 120 (Oxford, 1922); *Cursor Mundi*, ed. R. Morris, EETS OS 57, 59, 62, 66, 68, 69, 101 (London, 1874–93); *The Early English Versions of the Gesta Romanorum*, ed. S. J. H. Herrtage, EETS ES 33 (London, 1879); *The Macro Plays: The Castle of Perseverance; Wisdom; Mankind*, ed. M. Eccles, EETS OS 262 (London, 1969).

[29] Powell, 'Administration', *passim*; T. A. Green, 'A Retrospective on the Criminal Trial Jury, 1200–1800', in *Twelve Good Men and True: The Criminal Trial Jury in England, 1200–1800*, ed. J. S. Cockburn and T. A. Green (Princeton, 1988), *passim*.

[30] Green, 'A Retrospective', p. 386.

[31] An increasing number of challenges were based on technical flaws identified in the prosecution case. Refusal to plea could also be maintained if the principal in an alleged felony had died not yet convicted. C. J. Neville demonstrates that a broad cross-section of society was equipped with the legal knowledge to put forward challenges based on technical points of law: C. J. Neville, 'Common Knowledge of the Common Law in Later Medieval England', *Canadian Journal of History* 29 (1994), 461–78.

concerns of communal opinion and represented punishment for antisocial behaviour.[32]

In contrast, the latter category of mitigation by-passed the king's courts entirely, through an appeal to the ecclesiastical privileges of mercy. This could be granted to a layman who sought sanctuary, or to a cleric who pursued his right to 'benefit of clergy'.[33] For the layman, sanctuary and abjuration provided a potential means of avoiding a criminal trial altogether, while the claim of 'benefit of clergy' gave a cleric the chance to be sentenced, if not actually tried, by an ecclesiastical tribunal (and therefore avoid the death sentence). Abjuration was a familiar method of avoiding trial in the later Middle Ages, but the consequences of abjuration – the perpetual banishment of the abjurer on pain of execution – meant that few suspects actually chose to avoid prosecution in this manner. After a flight to a parish church or other consecrated ground, the offender confessed his or her crime to the king's coroner, and was accompanied to the coast to find passage out of the country after promising never to return.[34] Some did so, and then succeeded in having

---

32 Evidence of spoiled indictments perhaps testifies to an expression of communal sentiment: the poor quality of some written charges is so marked as to suggest there was never any intention that the suspects they named be subjected to a full trial (the law did not allow a suspect to be tried more than once on a single charge). See T. A. Green, *Verdict According to Conscience: Perspectives on the English Criminal Trial Jury, 1200–1800* (Chicago, 1985), *passim*. See also B. W. McLane, 'Juror Attitudes toward Local Disorder: The Evidence of the 1328 Trailbaston Proceedings', in *Twelve Good Men*, ed. Cockburn and Green, pp. 51–2; E. Powell, 'Jury Trial at Gaol Delivery in the Late Middle Ages: The Midland Circuit, 1400–1429', in *Twelve Good Men*, ed. Cockburn and Green, pp. 78–116 (p. 112); P. C. Maddern, *Violence and Social Order: East Anglia 1422–1442* (Oxford, 1992), pp. 33–63; B. A. Hanawalt, *Crime and Conflict in English Communities 1300–1348* (Cambridge MA, 1979), pp. 53–63.

33 Records of the numbers of sanctuary seekers only exist for the later fifteenth and early sixteenth centuries: the registers of the Durham sanctuary recorded the arrival of 332 individuals between 1464 and 1524; the Beverley sanctuary admitted some 493 sanctuary-seekers in the years between 1478 and 1531. A census of June 1533 from the Westminster sanctuary noted 95 residents. See *Sanctuarium Dunelmense et Sanctuarium Beverlacensis*, ed. J. Raine, Surtees Society 5 (Durham, 1837); *Letters and Papers, Foreign and Domestic, Henry VIII*, ed. J. S. Brewer, J. Gairdner and R. H. Brodie, 21 vols. (London, 1862–1932), I, no. 848. See also London, British Library [BL], MS Harleian 4292, for a Yorkshire register. While figures for the earlier period can only be conjectural, the pardon seems to have remained a far more popular method of mitigation, from the point of view of the defendant. See J. Bellamy, 'Benefit of Clergy in the Fifteenth and Sixteenth Centuries', in *Criminal Law and Society in Late Medieval and Tudor England*, ed. J. Bellamy (Gloucester, 1984), pp. 115–72; L. C. Gabel, *Benefit of Clergy in England in the Later Middle Ages* (Northampton MA, 1928–9); J. C. Cox, *The Sanctuaries and Sanctuary Seekers of Medieval England* (London, 1911).

34 J. Freeman, "'And he abjured the realm of England, never to return"', in *Freedom of Movement in the Middle Ages: Proceedings of the 2003 Harlaxton Symposium*, ed. P. Horden (Donington, 2007), pp. 287–304; Cox, *Sanctuaries*, pp. 1–20. See also R. F.

their abjuration adjudged null and void by demonstrating that the process had been unlawfully performed or imposed. These sanctuaries attained their status by custom and papal or royal grant and afforded protection to anyone who fled there for forty days.[35] During this time, they could be supplied with food by clergy or friends, and those who tried to intervene would be excommunicated. After that, the person either had to surrender for trial, or abjure the realm and leave by the nearest port. If neither action was taken, they could be seized for trial.[36] A few places had rights of permanent sanctuary. Although this was a secular jurisdictional privilege, such sanctuaries were theoretically independent of royal justice.[37]

The procedure that became known as 'benefit of clergy' allowed clerics to avoid trial in the king's courts. The privilege had been articulated in the conflict between Henry II and Archbishop Becket.[38] Clerks brought before the royal justices were to be handed over to the ecclesiastical courts. Originally the benefit provided the means for clerics to evade the penalties of the secular

---

Hunnisett, *The Medieval Coroner* (Cambridge, 1961), pp. 37–54; J. G. Bellamy, *Crime and Public Order in England in the Later Middle Ages* (London, 1973), pp. 106–12; R. F. Hunnisett, 'The Late Sussex Abjurations', *Sussex Archaeological Collections* 102 (1964), 39–51, and Kesselring, 'Abjuration', pp. 345–58. Records in TNA KB 9 show that at least 212 individuals did so between 1485 and 1545. This is the minimum number, as coroners did not have to submit records of abjuration.

[35] I. D. Thornley, 'The Destruction of Sanctuary', in *Tudor Studies Presented to Albert Frederick Pollard*, ed. R. W. Seton-Watson (London, 1924), pp. 182–207; I. D. Thornley, 'Sanctuary in Medieval London', *Journal of the British Archaeological Association*, 2nd ser. 38 (1932), 293–315; I. D. Thornley, 'The Sanctuary Register of Beverley', *EHR* 34 (1919), 393–7; Kesselring, *Mercy and Authority*, pp. 45–6.

[36] *Sanctuarium Dunelmense*, ed. Raine; *Letters and Papers, Foreign and Domestic, Henry VIII*, I, no. 848.

[37] The main chartered sanctuaries were Beverley and Durham in the north and Westminster, St Martin's le Grand and Beaulieu in the south. However, Cox demonstrates that several other churches received such charters. These comprised: York, Southwell, the Priory of Hexham, the Collegiate Church of Ripon, the priories of Tynemouth, Wetherhal and Armathwaite, and the church of Norham. All Cistercian abbeys also claimed the right of permanent sanctuary, through papal sanction. In addition, the abbeys of Battle, Colchester, Ramsey, Croyland, Glastonbury and Bury St Edmunds, the Liberty of Cuxham, the church of Abbots Kerswell, the priory of Leominster and the cathedral church of Lincoln all had claims to chartered sanctuaries. Cox also notes that William the Conqueror conferred on the abbot of Battle Abbey the right to pardon any condemned criminal in any part of his realm. The Battle Abbey Chronicle records one instance of an abbot claiming this privilege outside his own jurisdiction – in 1364 Abbot Robert de Bello apparently met a condemned felon on his way to the gallows in the king's Marshalsea, and pardoned him. Interestingly, the chronicle notes that the king and other magnates took much offence at the act, yet upon plea he had his charter confirmed. Cox, *Sanctuaries*, p. 197.

[38] Bellamy, 'Benefit of Clergy', pp. 115–72; A. J. Duggan, ed., *The Correspondence of Thomas Becket, Archbishop of Canterbury, 1162–1170* (Oxford, 2000), I, 78–9; A. J. Duggan, *Thomas Becket* (London, 2004), pp. 39–45.

law. Clerics claimed the privilege and were handed over to a church official to undergo a trial under canon law. Since this generally involved a period of confinement in the bishop's prison and forfeiture of goods, the privilege did not allow a complete evasion of punishment. By the mid-fourteenth century, however, a procedure seems to have been established whereby offenders were usually tried first in the king's courts; if they were found guilty, their goods would be seized into the king's hands until sentence had been passed by an ecclesiastical tribunal. The second half of the fourteenth century also saw the increasing use of the reading test as proof of clerical status. Inevitably, literate laymen began to claim the benefit successfully, and their ability to do so was acknowledged in a statute of 1489. It could be claimed only once for homicide, rape or robbery and offenders were to be branded M or T on their first conviction, which was sometimes followed by a term in prison. Further restrictions were added in the early sixteenth century, before an act of 1576 gave lay authorities complete control.[39]

It would be misleading, however, to assume that until this time, medieval royal government had been reluctantly conceding authority over mitigation of the law to judges, trial juries and local communities, or to the Church. Scholars of the early modern judicial system have tended to regard traditional methods of circumventing the law as signs of the powerlessness of medieval central government to assert its authority. Accordingly they contrast the situation in the late Middle Ages with the Tudor initiatives to curtail the various forms of mitigation, and to centralise those powers that continued to exist in the hands of royal government.[40] To continue to see the Church and the holders of the great palatinates of Durham and Chester bestowing mercy as a prerogative power, they argue, was an infringement on the royal power that Henry VII and his successors would not tolerate. However, it would be a mistake to assume that later medieval monarchs were powerless to rein in these privileges, or allowed them to be exercised with no guiding influence. The right to exercise privileges of mercy should be seen rather as a power ultimately held by the king, but devolved to certain of his subjects after careful negotiation between the Crown and the representatives of the clergy and the commonalty. Edward III's increasingly frequent requests for parliamentary sanction of direct taxation gave the Commons the opportunity to secure redress of grievances and grants of grace from the Crown. On several occasions, the Commons sought a grant of royal mercy, often in the form of a general pardon. The same was true of the clergy, who often met a proposed subsidy with a list of *gravamina*, usually including a request

---

[39] Restrictions were imposed in 1497, 1512, 1533 and 1536. See Kesselring, 'Pardon', p. 70, n. 84.

[40] Kesselring, *Mercy and Authority*, pp. 1–21; McCune, 'Ideology of Mercy', pp. 1–9. Kesselring asserts that, despite the increased severity of the law, mercy did remain an essential complement to justice.

for royal protection of Church privileges, including sanctuary and benefit of clergy.[41] The clergy, and subsequently the Commons, learned the wisdom of timing their petitions to coincide with meetings of Parliament where both finance and politics might favour their acceptance. Consent to grants of taxation contingent on pardons or agreements to protect clerical privileges of mercy followed a similar pattern. In 1311 and 1341 the prelates and the Commons both secured grants at times of political crisis; in 1327 they looked to capitalise on the change of regime, while in 1377 and 1399 they sought to mark a royal coronation with a gift of mercy. Rather than attack the privileges of the Church, Edward III and his government sought to ensure the co-operation of his prelates by establishing a working relationship based on a *quid pro quo* arrangement. In time it adopted the same arrangement with the parliamentary Commons. In both cases, an important element of the concessions sought from the Crown was guarantees over grants of mercy, whether in the form of a direct grant of royal grace or a promise that the Church could continue to exercise its own privileges concerning mercy.

Ecclesiastical and royal conceptions of mercy were closely related. The Church, of course, also had its own form of pardon in the shape of indulgences that granted forgiveness of temporal penalty for sin.[42] The origins and use of these dispensations were discussed in texts produced by the theologians and canonists of the mid-thirteenth century. Treatises by commentators such as Peter Cantor and William of Auxerre argued that penitents could

---

[41] W. R. Jones, 'Bishops, Politics, and the Two Laws: The *Gravamina* of the English Clergy 1287–1399', *Speculum* 41 (1966), 209–45; W. M. Ormrod, *The Reign of Edward III* (Stroud, 2000), pp. 122–36.

[42] The extensive scholarship on the subject includes several works of use in the study of royal pardons: see in particular H. C. Lea, *A History of Auricular Confession and Indulgences in the Latin Church* (New York, 1968), III, 1–293; N. Paulus, *Indulgences as a Social Factor in the Middle Ages* (New York, 1922); A. J. Minnis and P. Biller, eds., *Handling Sin: Confession in the Middle Ages* (York, 1998); D. Wood, *Clement VI: The Pontificate and Ideas of an Avignon Pope* (Cambridge, 2003); R. N. Swanson, *Religion and Devotion in Europe, c. 1215–c.1515* (Cambridge, 1995), pp. 217–25; E. Duffy, *The Stripping of the Altars: Traditional Religion in England c.1400–c.1580* (London, 1992), pp. 287–98; R. W. Shaffern, 'Learned Discussions of Indulgences for the Dead in the Middle Ages', *Church History* 61 (1992), 367–81. Recent work on the subject includes: R. N. Swanson, 'Indulgences at Norwich Cathedral Priory in the Later Middle Ages: Popular Piety in the Balance Sheet', *Historical Research* 76 (2003), 18–29; R. N. Swanson, 'Indulgences for Prayers for the Dead in the Diocese of Lincoln in the Early Fourteenth Century', *Journal of Ecclesiastical History* 52 (2001), 197–219; R. M. T. Hill, 'Fund-Raising in a Fourteenth-Century Province', in *Life and Thought in the Northern Church, c.1100–c.1700: Essays in Honour of Claire Cross*, Studies in Church History, Subsidia 12, ed. D. Wood (Woodbridge, 1999), pp. 31–6; P. N. R. Zutshi, 'Collective Indulgences from Rome and Avignon in English Collections', in *Medieval Ecclesiastical Studies in Honour of Dorothy M. Owen*, Studies in the History of Medieval Religion 7, ed. M. J. Franklin and C. Harper-Bill (Woodbridge, 1995), pp. 281–97.

seek forgiveness for the penalties that they had incurred through sin, and that indulgences could reduce time spent in purgatory.[43] Crucially, though, the recipient must be in a state of grace for the indulgence to have any validity. Indulgences were also required to prescribe a good work to be carried out by the recipient as penance for his or her sins, unless the indulgence specified that the desire to perform a good work was adequate. These dispensations could only be granted by episcopal authority or by a specially appointed agent. Legal tracts such as *Bracton* and *Fleta* were also attempting to make comparable stipulations with regard to royal pardons in the latter half of the thirteenth century.[44] The abuse of indulgences and the profits accrued from their sale also attracted much of the same type of hostile commentary directed at royal pardons.[45] While the scope of this book does not permit a thorough examination of these religious pardons, it is important to note that the processes and use of the king's pardon was closely aligned with ecclesiastical and sacramental structures. The use of religious language and allusion in public pronouncements by the king on the subject of pardon certainly bears this out, and is discussed in more detail in Part II of this book.

The royal pardon was one of several methods used to circumvent the law; some were used by the Crown, others by the bench, juries and other administrators of the law. Such measures spanned a whole spectrum of mitigation, from outright pardon of capital crime to ensuring that a lesser sanction was imposed than the one called for by the law. The purpose of this book is to examine how the royal pardon was used in the fourteenth century, and to elucidate medieval perceptions of pardoning. It is hoped that this will contribute to our understanding of fourteenth-century discourses of mercy.

---

43 Peter Cantor, *Summa de sacramentis et animae consilis*, 11, 110, in *Analecta mediaevalia Namurcensia* (Louvain, 1957–67), VII, 190–5; William of Auxerre, *Summa aurea omnia* (Paris, 1980–5), IV, 349–60. See Shaffern, 'Learned Discussions of Indulgences', p. 368, n. 4.

44 See below, Chapter 2, pp. 22–4.

45 For an account of the perversion of the system of indulgences by professional pardoners, see A. L. Kellogg and L. A. Haselmayer, 'Chaucer's Satire of the Pardoner', *Publications of the Modern Language Association* 66 (1951), 251–77; L. W. Patterson, 'Chaucerian Confession: Penitential Literature and the Pardoner', *Medievalia et Humanistica*, n.s. 7 (1976), 153–73; D. Pearsall, 'Chaucer's Pardoner: Death of a Salesman', *Chaucer Review* 17 (1983), 358–64. See also N. Vincent, 'Some Pardoners' Tales: The Earliest English Indulgences', *TRHS* 6th series 12 (2002), 23–58; W. E. Lunt, *Financial Relations of the Papacy with England, 1327–1534*, Studies in Anglo-Papal Relations during the Middle Ages 2 (Cambridge MA, 1962).

Part I
Individual Pardons

CHAPTER TWO

Procedures

By the beginning of the fourteenth century the production of a royal pardon was a familiar method of claiming immunity from common law procedures.[1] Suspects who could present a charter of pardon to the justices at the time of their arraignment were not required to answer formal charges, while those who secured one subsequently could seek acquittal, or even remission of a conviction.[2] Similarly those in danger of infringing the feudal and proprietary rights of the Crown, by purchasing land without royal licence, for example, could purchase a pardon and thus circumvent cumbersome legal procedures. For anyone who stood in need of such a letter, one form of pardon was theoretically available to all of the king's subjects at any time. This was the 'individual pardon', so called because it only ever covered the offences with which one person might be accused.[3] Those who sought an individual pardon would submit a petition, or have one submitted on their behalf, and each case was judged according to the particular circumstances that attended it. In routine cases the royal justices themselves could set the procedure of

---

[1] The other widely known methods for avoiding trial in the king's courts were to claim benefit of clergy, to abjure the realm, or, if indicted as an accessory, to establish that the principal had either died before conviction or had been acquitted: see Neville, 'Common Knowledge', pp. 465–7. See also above, Chapter 1, pp. 11–16.

[2] Contemporary texts refer to 'charters' of pardon, although the term was being used in a generic sense to cover all official government documents. Pardons were actually issued from Chancery as letters patent: see H. C. Maxwell-Lyte, *Historical Notes on the use of the Great Seal of England* (London, 1926), p. 332; B. Wilkinson, *The Chancery under Edward III* (Manchester, 1929), pp. 59–64; A. L. Brown, 'Authorisation of Letters under the Great Seal', *BIHR* 37 (1964), 125–55. The ability to obtain pardon before arraignment was somewhat controversial, and was finally outlawed in the Tudor period: see J. G. Bellamy, *The Criminal Trial in Later Medieval England* (Stroud, 1998), pp. 137–8; Hurnard, *Homicide*, pp. 31–67.

[3] It was normally accepted that fines would be charged for these individual pardons, but poverty did not, theoretically, exclude subjects from access to a pardon as the fee could be remitted. On such occasions the engrossments on the chancery rolls note that they were given 'for God', as an act of charity: see, for example, *CPR, 1327–30*, p. 308; *CPR, 1343–5*, p. 571. For further discussion, see Wilkinson, *Chancery*, p. 60; J. C. Davies, 'Common Law Writs and Returns, Richard I to Richard II', *BIHR* 26 (1953), 140–1; J. H. Baker, *An Introduction to English Legal History* (London, 1990), pp. 63–110; Musson and Ormrod, *Evolution*, pp. 14–15.

pardoning in motion, by exercising their power to recommend mercy.[4] The criteria on which cases were judged remained largely consistent, and most routine requests appear to have been approved as a matter of course on the authority of the chancellor, who was empowered to act in the king's name (these are referred to as pardons *de cursu*). Alternatively, if the circumstances of the case were unusual, the decision might be referred to the king and council (pardons *de gracia*). Accordingly, the issue of individual pardons continued steadily throughout the century.[5]

Regardless of the circumstances under which a royal pardon was issued, it must be remembered that it only ever provided indemnity from prosecution at the king's suit. After an individual had received a letter of pardon he or she was obliged to have it 'proved' in court, at which time it was declared that any appellant wishing to bring a suit against the recipient of pardon should come forward. Only after the pardon had been proved in this way would final peace be proclaimed. In one case from Edward II's reign it was noted that final peace was proclaimed by the marshal, who received 2s. for carrying out the service.[6] It was therefore a contract made specifically between the Crown and one of its subjects, offering mercy to those seeking readmission into the king's peace. Whether or not one of the king's subjects would ever need a pardon, the knowledge that this process existed played an influential role in shaping relations between the king and his people.

Procuring a Pardon: Recommendation of the Justices

Since the power to pardon was a matter of royal grace, no single procedure for obtaining a pardon was ever exclusively enforced. However, it is not true to say that there was no provision at law for recognising individuals who deserved pardon. The mitigating circumstances surrounding a particular case could be brought to the attention of the justices by the defendant, who would plead not guilty, and then hope to persuade the jury that the act was not felonious. Alternatively, the jury of presentment might refer to the circumstances of the case or the trial jury might recognise such factors in their verdict. Coroners' reports might also bring such details to the attention of the court.[7] If the presiding royal justices were persuaded of the need for mercy, they could

---

4 Theoretically, the king himself could also take the initiative in pardoning individual cases, although it would be rare for him to intervene, without it having first been brought to his attention by the defendant or by the justices. See Chapter 5, pp. 59–60.
5 See Appendix 1.
6 *The Eyre of Kent: 6 & 7 Edward II, A.D. 1313–1314*, ed. and trans. W. C. Bolland, Selden Society 24 (London, 1909), p. 139. See Hurnard, *Homicide*, p. 65.
7 See Hurnard, *Homicide*, p. 44.

then recommend pardon. By the fourteenth century a procedure appears to have been established in routine cases, whereby the justices presiding over the case would recommend mercy and would then forward their decision to the chancellor, who was empowered to act in the king's name, and who would approve a pardon as a matter of course, on payment of the requisite fee.[8] A 1329 Year Book statement describes this procedure:

> Note that when a man is acquitted before the justices errant for the death of a man in self-defence, the process is such that he shall have the writ of the Chief Justice, within which writ shall be contained the record of his acquittal to the Chancellor, who shall make him his writ of pardon without speaking to the king by course of law.[9]

A Year Book entry of 1330 also noted that Chief Justice Scrope had ordered this course of action to be taken: 'Scrope, C.J., and the other justices ordered the prisoner to remove the record into the Chancery; and the chancellor made him a charter in such a case without speaking to the king.'[10] Alternatively, the justices in eyre or Gaol Delivery would remand the prisoner in custody in order to let him petition for pardon, with the implication that they recommended mercy, but without taking on the task of sending a report to Chancery themselves.[11] The chancellor would then issue a writ of *certiorari* to the justices who would send him the record of the trial and their recommendation for mercy.[12]

Therefore it seems that the chancellor had, by this period, assumed

---

[8] Some pardons drawn up in Chancery were never handed over, presumably either because the fee was not paid, or, in the case of military service pardons, because the intended recipient had since died in the king's wars. Fifty letters patent of pardon remain in TNA C 266. See also *Year Books of the Reign of King Edward the Third*, ed. Horwood and Pike, p. 514.

[9] 'Nota que quant home est acquite devant justices errants de mort de homine soy defendendo le pl. est tiel que il aura breve de la chiefe justice deins quil breve serra continu tout le rec[ord] de sa acquite al chauncellor le quil luy fra sa chartre de pardon sans parler al roy per cours de ley.' *La graunde abridgement collect par le iudge tresreuerend Monsieur Anthony Fitzherbert* (London, 1565), 'Corone et plees del corone', fol. 257v (361).

[10] 'Scrope et justices commaund le prisoner de faier venir le record en le chauncellor et le chanceler ferrait a luy un charter en tiel cas sans parler al roy.' *La graunde abridgement*, 'Corone et plees del corone', fol. 256 (297). Cf. The Commons' petition to the king and the latter's reply in the Parliament of April 1309: PROME, 'Parliament of April 1309', introduction; *CCR, 1307–13*, p. 175; TNA SC 8/294/14698. The power was exercised by the king or his chancellor alone, except in the great franchises of Durham, Chester and Lancaster: see R. L. Storey, *The End of the House of Lancaster* (London, 1966), p. 210; H. M. Cam, 'The Evolution of the Mediaeval English Franchise', *Speculum* 32 (1957), 427–42.

[11] See, for example, TNA JUST 3/74, II, m. 11v; Hurnard, *Homicide*, p. 46.

[12] See, for example, TNA JUST 1/676, m. 2; the pardon is recorded in *CPR, 1301–7*, p. 421. See also TNA C 47/22/6–7.

primary responsibility for authorising royal pardons. While certain cases would still be forwarded for royal authorisation before being sent to Chancery under a warrant of the privy seal, the majority were processed by the chancellor under the executive authority of his office.[13] The same procedure was described in a statute of 1390, and continued to be used throughout the later Middle Ages.[14] The process was designed so that an individual pardon would be issued only after the defendant had submitted for trial and the verdict had recorded that there were sufficient mitigating circumstances to warrant mercy.[15] The definition of what constituted truly mitigating circumstances, however, was the subject of considerable debate.

Justification: Self-defence or Mischance

Strictly speaking, a pardon for felony could only be justified on grounds of diminished responsibility for the act, either through mischance or self-defence. However, an exact definition of mitigating circumstances, particularly those attending homicide cases, had not been formulated. Throughout the century it continued to be the subject of discussion among legal theorists, and a subject of government legislation.[16] In 1278 the Statute of Gloucester had identified self-defence or misfortune in homicide cases as justifying

---

13 This process is described in the 1278 Statute of Gloucester. It stated that if, after trial, it was concluded that the act had indeed been committed in self-defence or by misfortune, the justices were to submit a report to the king, who, if in agreement, would then grant pardon: *SR*, I, 49. Writs of the privy seal warranting the issue of pardons can be found in TNA C 81: see, for example, C 81/579/12649; C 81/570/11739; C 81/571/11819; C 81/581/12839; C 81/570/11745; C 81/573/12038; C 81/579/12693. Hurnard suggests that on occasion the king would approve bail rather than pardon, although this might still be obtained later. She concludes that on the whole the king may be supposed to have recognised a moral obligation to accept judicial recommendations to mercy, only rarely asserting his discretion in an attempt to define culpability more strictly. Hurnard, *Homicide*, pp. 50–1.

14 It stipulated that 'no charter of pardon … pass the Chancery without warrant of the privy seal, but in case where the chancellor may grant it of his office, without speaking thereof to the king', *SR*, II, 69. See below for discussion of the statute. See also Storey, *House of Lancaster*, p. 210, for discussion of the procedure in the reign of Henry VI.

15 For one example, see TNA KB 27/465, m. 12v. On 8 May 1377 the king ordered John de Cavendish and Thomas de Ingelby to make inquisition into the death of Thomas Chappe of Snetesham, Norfolk, as it was alleged by Margaret his wife that he had been killed by Thomas Panton, John Panton, Ralph Panton and Thomas Heygreve. The pardon of John Panton was enrolled on 17 October 1377 on the advice of the two justices that the act had been committed in self-defence: *CPR*, *1377–81*, p. 28.

16 Hurnard discusses the situation surrounding excusable homicide as it existed before 1307: Hurnard, *Homicide*, pp. 68–170.

pardon, but also referred to any other manner of killing committed 'without felony'.[17] This third category lacked further definition, and seemed to suggest some uncertainty as to how widely the concept of excusable homicide could be applied. Throughout the fourteenth century statutes were promulgated stating that the granting of pardons would be restricted to cases in which the king could give it according to his oath. This reference to the king's coronation oath concerned his obligation to recognise mitigating circumstances, and to pardon those involved accordingly.[18] The well-known Ordinances issued in October 1311 stated that no pardon would be granted unless in a case where the king could give grace according to his oath, by process of law and custom of the realm. Similarly, the 1328 Statute of Northampton stipulated that pardon would only be granted where the king 'may do it by his oath, that is to say, where a man slays another in his own defence, or by misfortune'. Again in April 1340 the king issued a promise not to pardon felony if it was inconsistent with his oath.[19]

The repetition of this formula in several statutes suggests that inconsistencies of interpretation were thought to persist, to the detriment of the king's peace. Certainly the legal theorists of the thirteenth century had struggled to fit the concept into their codification of common law. *Bracton* distinguished between justifiable homicide that was not felonious and did not even require pardon, on the one hand, and homicide that was not felonious but did require pardon, on the other. The former included slaying by infants and the insane, while the latter applied to killing in self-defence or by mischance.[20] Since pardon was a matter of royal grace, however, it was difficult to apply a precise classification. The king was supposedly guided by principles of equity that followed natural law, as laid down in the works of Justinian and the canonists.[21] However such concepts did not merge easily with the common law of the English legal system. Civil law absolved the perpetrator

---

[17] *SR*, I, 49.

[18] Musson states that these were vague assertions designed to placate concerns rather than commit to restrictions of the royal prerogative. While at times this seems to have been the chief motivation, the Statute of Northampton links the coronation oath to mitigating circumstances: *SR*, I, 257; A. Musson, 'Second "English Justinian" or Pragmatic Opportunist? A Re-Examination of the Legal Legislation of Edward III's Reign', in *The Age of Edward III*, ed. J. Bothwell (York, 2001), pp. 85–6, n. 83.

[19] *SR*, I, 164, 257, 286. A statute of 3 February 1331 confirms the Statute of Northampton in all points, but says that the statute stipulated that pardons could only be granted in Parliament, although there is not, in fact, any such clause in the original statute: *SR*, I, 264.

[20] *Bracton*, ed. Thorne, II, 375, 388; St Raymond of Peñafort, *Summa de Poenitentia* (Farnborough, 1967), II, 1; F. Schulz, 'Bracton and Raymond de Peñafort', *Law Quarterly Review* 61 (1945), 286–92; Hurnard, *Homicide*, pp. 68–170; H. G. Richardson, 'Tancred, Raymond, and Bracton', *EHR* 59 (1944), 376–84.

[21] Hurnard, *Homicide*, p. 68. See below, Chapter 5, pp. 73–81, for further discussion.

from guilt in most cases of homicide by accident or in self-defence, whereas canon law set a high standard of penance for divine forgiveness.

In cases of self-defence, the justices generally required a statement from the jurors that the killing had not been felonious or committed with malice aforethought and that the killer could not have escaped with his life. It was preferable for the jury to show that it had not been premeditated: that the defendant had not started the fight, for example, or that weapons had not been used. It was often asserted that the victim had been the aggressor, and that the defendant had taken every possible evasive action.[22] To claim self-defence it was necessary, as *Bracton* prescribed, to establish that no more force than necessary had been used to save one's life. However, in some cases a measure of leniency was allowed; if a man was killed in a brawl, only those who had mortally wounded him were adjudged guilty, while others were only guilty of breach of the peace. Alternatively, a case could be presented as mischance by contending that the assailant caused not only the attack but also the accident itself. The ability to define procedure was further hampered by those who sought pardon before trial, as the Crown was likely to grant mercy in such cases, rather than state that it was not necessary at all.

Alternative Justification

In addition to cases of slaying in self-defence or by mischance, there are some instances of other mitigating claims being proffered and accepted. The killing of fugitives resisting arrest, for example, while theoretically lawful, was often in practice excused with a pardon. Flaws in the legal process such as a malicious accusation or biased evidence were again often taken as justifiable grounds for pardon. Justices were expected to recommend mercy when they believed a person had been wrongly convicted by the jury. Defendants on occasion also challenged the validity of the indictment.[23] Alternatively, if the offence was a contravention of the royal feudal rights, defendants could receive pardon on payment of a fine. If, for example, they had acquired land held in-chief of the king without his consent, they could pay a fine, which was often set at the amount the original licence would have cost.

On occasion the justification for pardon was of a less strictly judicial nature, but instead stemmed from the king's moral obligation to protect his subjects. It seems that while in practice cases deserving pardon were routinely recommended for mercy, no clear definition of pardonable crime prevailed. This

---

22 The victim was sometimes said to have been impaled on his own knife when the defendant resisted the attack: *CPR, 1367–70*, p. 254. See below Chapter 3, pp. 37–8.

23 *State Trials: Or, A Collection of the Most Interesting Trials, Prior to the Revolution of 1688*, ed. S. M. Phillipps (London, 1826), I, 1298–9, 1301–5; R. C. Palmer 'The Origins of the Legal Profession in England', *Irish Jurist* n.s. 11 (1976), 126, 130–1.

clearly led some individuals who had been unjustly indicted to fear whether the trial justices would recognise the mitigating circumstances of their case. For them there was only one other way to circumvent the legal process, and that was to find a patron willing to present a petition directly to the Crown.

Proving a Pardon

After receiving a pardon, it was important, especially for the outlaw, to have the charter proclaimed in court, since most pardons were conditional on 'standing to right' in court to give appellants the opportunity to come forward. The sheriff would usually proclaim them in the county court with an invitation to anyone now wishing to prosecute, to come forward. Royal justices were required to make sure everything had been done correctly, and to proclaim that peace had been given, usually at a session of Oyer and Terminer or Gaol Delivery.[24] Peace could also be given in King's Bench.[25] Finally, because the pardon did not always provide for release of a felon from prison, he would sometimes have to pay his own prison charges before being released.

Theoretical procedures of pardoning, however, did not always fit with the reality experienced by people who had need to engage with the process. The three chapters that follow examine the role of individuals within the pardoning process, grouped into the 'supplicants', those who sought royal mercy; 'intercessors', those who acted as patrons or middle-men in the pardoning process; and finally the monarch himself. These chapters bring together a range of texts, from the petitions for pardon themselves to parliament rolls, outlaw ballads and advice literature.

---

[24] Proclamation was also required when a king pardoned a prisoner before trial: see TNA JUST 1/204, m. 50v. Early registers of writs contain these instructions to the sheriff, suggesting that the procedure was normal: see, for example, BL MS Harleian, 4351, fol. 48; MS Harleian, 1608, fol. 62.

[25] The relationship between the language of proclamation and the language of record has been the subject of considerable debate: see W. M Ormrod, 'The Use of English: Language, Law, and Political Culture in Fourteenth-Century England', *Speculum* 78 (2003), 750–87; W. M. Ormrod, 'The Language of Complaint: Multilingualism and Petitioning in Later Medieval England', in *Language and Culture in Medieval Britain: The French of England c.1100–c.1500*, ed. J. Wogan-Browne, with C. Collette, M. Kowaleski, L. Mooney, A. Putter and D. Trotter (York, 2009). See also below, Chapter 4, n. 32.

CHAPTER THREE

Supplicant

People petitioned for the king's grace in a variety of different circumstances. Sometimes they offered a reason for the king to pardon them; on other occasions they admitted guilt, but appealed to him to show mercy. In certain situations, supplicants were unable to get their own petition drawn up; they might be in prison awaiting trial, or, having already been outlawed, they might fear any face-to-face meeting with officers of the Crown. In such circumstances, they would seek a patron to have a petition written on their behalf. (The people who acted as 'intercessors' are discussed in the following chapter.) Others, however, were free to get their own petition written up – they might do so if they feared arrest, or if they were indignant at a rumour of a 'malicious accusation' against them, and sought to clear their name. Essentially, though, these were all people who wanted to take the initiative themselves (and had the means to do so), rather than come before the courts and trust that the trial judge would find in their favour and recommend pardon.

It is not always possible to tell how a particular person obtained their pardon. The text of the pardon itself survives in the government enrolments of all letters patent that were issued from Chancery. These entries record the terms of the letter of pardon as it was written up by the clerk. The salient facts of the pardon are recorded: the name of the recipient, the offence that is to be pardoned, and, on occasion, a reason for the pardon, most commonly self-defence or mischance, is also noted. What they do not reveal, however, is the way the original petition was worded, or if, indeed, it was ever actually presented in written form at all; it is clear that many petitions would have been made orally in this period. To ascertain whether a particular pardon was issued as a result of the recommendation of a trial judge, or a written petition from an individual, they have to be matched against the record of a court case, or, if it survives, against the original petition put forward to the Crown. The original petitions that do still exist have largely been overlooked by scholars, presumably because they are scattered among The National Archives class of 'Ancient Petitions'.[1] There is certainly

---

[1] TNA SC 8. The 'special collections' contain petitions, both originals and duplicates, with some enrolments, that have been brought together from various sources. They include petitions to the king, to the king and council, to Parliament, and to the chancellor and other officers of state. A few petitions can also be found among the

no comparative central archive of detailed petitions for pardon to the French collection of 'letters of remission', used to great effect in the work of Claude Gauvard and Natalie Zemon Davis.[2] Those English petitions for pardon that do survive thus constitute an important source for the study of supplications for royal grace. Seeking a pardon through this direct means of appeal to the king was somewhat controversial, in that it allowed individuals to by-pass the law courts altogether, and to exploit networks of influence and patronage to secure pardon. Why, then, did this method of appeal survive into the four-teenth century and beyond? To begin to answer this question, it is necessary to examine the extant petitions for pardon that were presented to the Crown, usually in the forum of Parliament or a council meeting. These records allow us to examine why, in certain cases, the individual felt that he or she deserved pardon, and why, in turn, the Crown granted them an audience.

Petitions for Pardon

The majority of people who received pardons did not themselves petition for one directly; in most instances it was the trial judge who recommended mercy on their behalf once their case had come to court. Those who did go to the trouble of writing their own petitions (or more probably commissioning professional county lawyers to draft it for them) were either awaiting trial, or presumably feared that an accusation might be made against them. Approxi-mately 500 of these petitions for pardon survive from the fourteenth century, in addition to which are several other petitions relating to pardons already

records of Chancery: TNA C 1, C 47, C 49, C 81. While researching the petitions for pardon in the SC 8 series, I have benefited greatly from the recent project, directed by Gwilym Dodd and Mark Ormrod, which catalogued the contents of the peti-tions and made the information accessible in the online Catalogue of TNA. For further details on this project, see Dodd, *Justice and Grace*, p. 13; W. M. Ormrod, G. Dodd and A. Musson, eds., *Medieval Petitions: Grace and Grievance* (York, 2009).

2   Gauvard, *'De grace especiall'*; Davis, *Fiction*. A major collection of *lettres de remission* is in the Tresor des Chartres (Paris, Archives Nationales, AN, series JJ), a register of royal letters issued by Chancery officers from 1300 to 1568. JJ is by no means a complete record – supplicants chose to have their letters of remission copied here at an extra cost. See also M. Francois, 'Note sur les lettres de remission trans-crites dans les registres du tresor des charters', *Bibliotheque de l'Ecole des Chartres* 103 (1942), 317–24; H. Michaud, *La Grande Chancellerie et les ecritures royals au seizieme siecle (1515–1589)* (Paris, 1967), pp. 359–68. Letters of remission can also be found scattered throughout the criminal registers of the Parlement of Paris (AN, X 2a), as they were ratified by that court for persons in their jurisdiction. English petitions from the early modern period and beyond can be found in TNA SP 36, 37 and 44, after 1782 in HO 47. For further discussion, see Beattie, *Crime and the Courts*; P. King, 'Decision Makers and Decision-Making in the English Criminal Law, 1750–1800', *Historical Journal* 27 (1984), 25–58; Hay, 'Criminal Law'.

granted.[3] These petitions are a valuable window on to medieval notions of pardon and mercy. At a basic level it is possible to observe patterns relating to the gender and social class of the petitioners, the types of offence being pardoned, the claims of mitigating circumstances and the actions taken by the Crown. Moreover, they also allow us to examine the way petitioners presented themselves, or at least their stories, in the petitions. Finally, we can ask how these records relate to constructions of pardon and mercy in other kinds of texts.

Petitioners

Twenty-nine of the 500 fourteenth-century petitions for pardon were submitted by women. Seven of these women were petitioning jointly with their husbands, and fourteen were referred to as widows.[4] Interestingly, these women were proportionally much more successful in securing pardon than the rest of the petitioners. Only one woman, petitioning on behalf of her husband, who stood accused of murder, was denied a pardon outright.[5] Fifteen of the women received pardon immediately. The other cases were either endorsed with a note for further information to be gathered, or were left blank. This success rate probably reflects the nature of the offences in question, rather than a gender bias. Seventeen of the petitions related to land transactions or debts owed to the Crown, and these are concentrated in the late 1320s and early 1330s, a period when the dominance of the Despenser family at court had come to an end, and the extent of their illegal and heavy-handed land dealings began to unravel. The lands and debts referred to in these petitions suggest that the women were of relatively high social standing. Only two supplicants claimed 'impoverishment' as a mitigating factor.[6] In a few cases these women identified themselves as members of the titled nobility; the wife of the lord of Powys, for example, or the countess of Pembroke. One of the petitions, dating from the early years of Richard II's reign, was

---

3   Several petitions for pardon contained the names of more than one petitioner, so one petition might generate the issue of several pardons.
4   TNA SC 8/305/15227; SC 8/141/7001; SC 8/56/2783; SC 8/103/5104; SC 8/332/15787; SC 8/224/11156; SC 8/189/9429; SC 8/66/3266; SC 8/72/3589; SC 8/128/6359; SC 8/252/12600; SC 8/146/7265; SC 8/247/12327; SC 8/63/3108; SC 8/218/10879; SC 8/62/3099; SC 8/141/7036; SC 8/278/13872; SC 8/307/15308; SC 8/46/2276; SC 8/90/4463; SC 8/35/1726; SC 8/92/4554; SC 8/233/11602; SC 8/52/2586; SC 8/130/6489; SC 8/99/4922; SC 8/40/1959; SC 8/129/6432.
5   TNA SC 8/52/2586.
6   TNA SC 8/129/6432; SC 8/128/6359. In the latter case, the couple claim to have been ruined by the payments they have already made to the Crown, which apparently totalled around 500 marks. This huge sum would have been beyond the means of anyone from the lower social orders.

made by William and Alice Windsor. Alice was more commonly known as Alice Perrers, the former mistress of Edward III. The petition requests pardon for William and protection against 'all other things which could harm him through Alice'. It also notes that the judgment that had been made against Alice in the first of Richard II's Parliaments was made against her as a single woman, but that she was in fact William's wife at that time. The petition therefore alludes to the clandestine marriage that historians suppose to have been contracted between Alice and William sometime between 1373 and 1376; either when William temporarily returned to England from Ireland, where he had been serving as the king's lieutenant, or after Alice had been exiled from court in 1376.[7] Alice's banishment had been overturned in 1379, and this petition represents one of the couple's attempts to regain their lost land and income.

Indeed, several petitions for pardon touched on contemporary political concerns. In 1377, for instance, John Pecche requested 'full pardon of the prosecution brought in Parliament by the accusation of de la Mare and others concerning the sale of sweet wine'. Pecche, a London merchant, had been convicted of exploiting the monopoly on sweet wine for his own profit in the notorious 'Good Parliament' of 1376.[8] This assembly was exceptional for the open attack that the Commons, led by their speaker, Sir Peter de la Mare, launched against corruption within government. Pecche, along with Richard Lyons and Adam Bury, had been singled out for their perceived profiteering at the expense of the public purse. Less than a year later, however, Pecche had petitioned for pardon, and received it on 10 April 1377. This was only one of several acts of the Good Parliament that were reversed in the months after its dissolution. However, Pecche never regained his position of power among the London merchants, and the parliamentary Commons had, for the first time, demonstrated that they were capable of unified and forthright opposition to governmental mismanagement.[9] Another of these petitions for pardon was presented by 'John Creyk, alias John Bettes of Wymondham', in 1383. Bettes had been one of the more notorious leaders of revolt in Norfolk during the Peasants' Rising of 1381, and his name had been entered on the list of those to be excluded from the general pardon.[10] In this petition for pardon, Bettes stated that he had been maliciously indicted of involvement in the rebellion by his enemies, and that he had been acquitted by several inquests. However, he said that because his name was on the list of those to be excluded from the pardon, the justices would not release him without the

---

7   TNA SC 8/146/7265. See W. M. Ormrod, 'Who Was Alice Perrers?', *The Chaucer Review* 40 (2006), 219–29 (p. 222); W. M. Ormrod, 'The Trials of Alice Perrers', *Speculum* 83 (2008), 366–96.
8   *PROME*, 'Parliament of 1376', item 33.
9   TNA SC 8/254/12658–9; *CPR, 1374–7*, pp. 448–9, 457.
10 TNA SC 8/262/13099; *PROME*, 'Parliament of 1381', item 63.

direct command of the king. Bettes was ultimately successful in his appeal; he was acquitted of all charges by royal mandate in May 1383.[11] This petition was unusual; none of the other suspected rebels appears to have put forward their own petition for pardon in this way. Bettes clearly had the knowledge and funds to have a petition drawn up for himself, rather than merely hoping that Parliament would extend the general pardon.

Two other petitions for pardon related to Richard II's famous 'revenge' Parliament of September 1397.[12] This was the venue for the show trials of the Lords Appellant, who had challenged the Crown and effectively taken over the running of government in the late 1380s. The king clearly wanted to intimidate his opponents, and ordered a large military gathering to surround the building near to Westminster Palace where the Parliament would be held. One petition for pardon gives further details of these preparations; the document was submitted by the dukes of Lancaster and York and the earl of Derby, ostensibly to ask pardon for mustering armed military retinues, which would ordinarily be illegal in peacetime.[13] However, the endorsement on the petition suggests that Lancaster, York and Derby had in fact been acting on Richard's orders; they had brought troops to Parliament in support of the king (they had also been told that they could levy money from 'the people' in order to perform this order). According to the petition, the duke of Lancaster had been told to bring 300 men-at-arms and 600 archers, the duke of York 100 men-at-arms and 200 archers, and the earl of Derby 200 men-at-arms and 400 archers. This sizeable military presence in Westminster would presumably have been hard to keep under control. Indeed, another petition for pardon indicates that, while they were in London, some of these soldiers pursued a private vendetta of their own, which ended in murder. The petition of John de Haukeston, one of Richard II's notorious Cheshire archers, asked pardon for the murder of William de Laken, an MP in London to attend Parliament. According to the petition, Laken had tried on several occasions to bring Haukeston and another man before the courts to answer certain grievances he had against them, but they had repeatedly failed to appear. Then, when Haukeston came to London for the September Parliament as part of Richard's personal retinue, he gathered a large group of accomplices and laid in wait for Laken on the Thames and on the high roads between London and Westminster, before finally ambushing him on Fleet Street and killing him.[14]

---

11 TNA KB 27/488, m. 25; A. Prescott, ' "The hand of God": The Suppression of the Peasants' Revolt of 1381', in *Prophecy, Apocalypse and the Day of Doom: Proceedings of the 2000 Harlaxton Symposium*, ed. N. Morgan (Donnington, 2004), pp. 317–41 (p.319, n. 6). See Chapter 9, pp. 157–8, for further discussion.
12 See Chapter 10, pp. 162–9.
13 TNA SC 8/221/11038.
14 TNA SC 8/249/12437; *CPR, 1396–9*, p. 427. See G. Dodd, 'Getting Away with Murder: Sir John Haukeston and Richard II's Cheshire Archers', *Nottingham Mediaeval Studies* 46 (2002), 102–17.

The power to pardon was clearly a powerful tool at Richard's disposal, and one that he put to use against his enemies, a subject that will be discussed in more detail in Chapter 10.

Petitions for pardon were also quite likely to come from groups rather than individuals. Merchants such as the 'weavers of the city of York', or the 'merchants of the Bardi' might request pardon for debts owed to the Crown in unpaid customs.[15] Groups of soldiers or sailors might also request pardon in recognition of their military service to the Crown.[16] Religious orders sometimes petitioned for pardon in the name of the abbot and convent, usually for debts owed to the Crown.[17] Several petitions were also put forward in the name of 'the people', 'the tenants', 'the citizens' or 'the commons' of a particular area. Again, these usually concerned communal debts owed to the Crown that could not be paid, perhaps because a poor harvest or a Scottish raid had impoverished the community.[18] In one instance, the chancellor and scholars of Cambridge University requested pardons for a group of scholars who had been 'maliciously and falsely' accused of various crimes.[19]

Most of the fourteenth-century petitions for pardon were endorsed with a note, either for pardon to be granted outright (in 168 cases) or for further action to be taken (in 129 cases). Only fifteen petitioners were refused pardon straight away.[20] The main reason for the Crown's refusal to grant pardon appears to have been money; ten of these unsuccessful petitioners were requesting pardon of debts owed to the Crown. The response in these cases was that the debt could be paid in instalments, but not waived altogether.

---

[15] Weavers of city of York: TNA SC 8/108/5371; Merchants of the Bardi: SC 8/193/9643.

[16] Mariners of Hythe: TNA SC 8/260/12997. See below, Chapter 7, pp. 100–6, for further discussion of military pardons.

[17] TNA SC 8/131/6522; SC 8/186/9287; SC 8/225/11245; SC 8/150/7483; SC 8/255/12734; SC 8/34/1683; SC 8/264/13192; SC 8/52/2588; SC 8/20/994; SC 8/233/11621; SC 8/71/3530; SC 8/239/11914; SC 8/278/13889; SC 8/160/7959; SC 8/253/12627; SC 8/38/1899; SC 8/17/821A; SC 8/36/1798A; SC 8/243/12146; SC 8/243/12145; SC 8/44/2156; SC 8/44/2159; SC 8/183/9143; SC 8/115/5749; SC 8/263/13123; SC 8/84/4170; SC 8/45/2230.

[18] TNA SC 8/65/3218; SC 8/63/3133; SC 8/337/15941; SC 8/64/3199; SC 8/95/4725; SC 8/32/1565; SC 8/32/1563; SC 8/32/1566; SC 8/54/2685; SC 8/54/2686; SC 8/165/8209; SC 8/129/6436; SC 8/11/506; SC 8/141/7046; SC 8/99/4927; SC 8/171/8520; SC 8/41/2036; SC 8/82/4086; SC 8/12/594; SC 8/78/3856; SC 8/162/8087; SC 8/130/6490; SC 8/155/7717; SC 8/112/5581; SC 8/74/3681; SC 8/86/4296; SC 8/107/5311; SC 8/106/5283; SC 8/212/10585; SC 8/125/6206; SC 8/274/13655; SC 8/341/16100; SC 8/58/2866; SC 8/229/11407; SC 8/86/4263; SC 8/156/7796; SC 8/103/5109; SC 8/342/16132; SC 8/147/7342; SC 8/261/13003; SC 8/64/3189; SC 8/257/12809; SC 8/18/855; SC 8/53/2626.

[19] TNA SC 8/183/9101.

[20] TNA SC 8/67/3337; SC 8/82/4085; SC 8/42/2064; SC 8/138/6896; SC 8/179/8919; SC 8/15/702; SC 8/264/13164; SC 8/52/2586; SC 8/12/573; SC 8/346/E1382; SC 8/106/5283; SC 8/16/772; SC 8/52/2595; SC 8/61/3005; SC 8/112/5570.

Two other petitions for pardon of felony and trespass were also refused, and two for murder. The grounds for refusal here were not given explicitly, other than to say that the request 'seems unreasonable'. However, it can perhaps be inferred that one of the petitions was seen to be somewhat irregular, in that it came from the wife of a man 'maliciously indicted' for murder, rather than the man himself. Another petitioner requested pardon in return for military service in Scotland, but admitted that he did not perform this service himself, instead sending another man to fight on his behalf. His petition was initially rejected, but in fact a later pardon appears on patent rolls. On rare occasions, it seems, the Crown would consider granting pardon to petitioners who had initially been refused grace. Presumably this change of heart was brought about by further supplication or the receipt of new information, although the evidence for this is lacking.[21] It seems, then, that an individual submitting a petition for pardon could expect either a favourable answer or at least further action to be taken. The chances of an outright rejection were slim enough not to act as a significant deterrent. The requests that the Crown made for more information also suggest that the contents of the petitions were carefully scrutinised. These documents had to conform to established expectations surrounding pardonable offences, and were written in a uniform format. It is therefore likely that the majority were drawn up by professional county lawyers (as Gwilym Dodd and Tim Haskett have both asserted) and most petitioners were therefore of high enough social standing to pay for their services.[22] The recognisable vocabulary of pardon that these lawyers deployed had several characteristic themes, which warrant further discussion.

Victimisation

Complaints of victimisation were a feature of several petitions for pardon. Like the classic equity cases identified by Tim Haskett and others in the Court of Chancery, the petitioners often presented themselves as victims of a powerful faction, who exerted influence over the local law courts, to the extent that they had been prevented from receiving a fair trial.[23] For instance,

---

21 *CPR, 1327–30*, p. 528.
22 Dodd, *Justice and Grace*, p. 306; T. S. Haskett, 'County Lawyers? The Composers of English Chancery Bills', in *The Life of the Law: Proceedings of the Tenth British Legal History Conference, Oxford 1991*, ed. P. Birks (London, 1993), pp. 9–23.
23 T. S. Haskett, 'Conscience, Justice and Authority in the Late-Medieval English Court of Chancery', in *Expectations of the Law in the Middle Ages*, ed. A. Musson (Woodbridge, 2001), pp. 151–63; T. S. Haskett, 'The Medieval English Court of Chancery', *Law and History Review* 14 (1996), 245–313. See also C. Beattie, 'Single Women, Work and Family: The Chancery Dispute of Jane Wynde and Margaret Clerk', in *Voices from the Bench: The Narratives of Lesser Folk in Medieval Trials*, ed.

in the petition of Robert Martin of Yeovilton, presented to the Crown in 1338, the supplicant sought a pardon because, through the corruption of local office holders, he and his men had been maliciously indicted.[24] Martin claimed that his wife, Margaret, had been ravished by one John de Croucheston. The offender had been arrested by the king's officer, Thomas Galeberd, and was then indicted of felony and outlawed by 'many writs of the king'. Galeberd was ordered to move the accused to Winchester to stand trial, but instead of doing so, he allowed him to go free. Moreover, Galeberd then conspired with the sub-sheriff and the receiver of Wiltshire to have Martin himself indicted. As a result, at the time of the petition Martin and his men were in danger of being outlawed.

In similar cases, the petitioners portrayed themselves as the victims of malicious indictments, again implying corruption in the local law courts. In one example from 1331, the petitioner, Richard de Beverley, stated that he had been maliciously indicted for involvement in the plot to abduct the abbot of Bury St Edmunds.[25] The episode he alluded to concerned the abduction of Abbot Draughton of Bury St Edmunds, following the 'great revolt' of 1327. In October 1328, the notorious outlaw gang of Thomas Thornham came to the town and joined the leaders of the insurgency. A group of them managed to kidnap the Abbot and smuggle him to London, where they moved him from house to house. He was later taken to Dover and from there to Brabant. By 1329 the archbishop of Canterbury had excommunicated Draughton's abductors and the king had appointed four justices to investigate the kidnapping.[26] Richard de Beverley's petition stated that he owned a hostelry in London, and at the time of the enquiry he had been maliciously indicted of involvement in the abduction and was subsequently outlawed. The king, in this case,

---

M. Goodich (New York, 2006), pp. 177–202. Recent work on the Court of Chancery suggests that procedures for accessing judgments based on equity rather than on common law principles were in fact more likely to be favoured by the underdog: the powerless victim who could not find redress at common law.

[24] TNA SC 8/60/2979A. In this case the king ordered the justices of trailbaston to review the record and process of the indictment. The man accused of ravishing Robert Martin's wife was later pardoned and a commission of *oyer et terminer* was sent to investigate Martin's actions in the matter: *CPR, 1338–40*, pp. 58, 352–3.

[25] TNA SC 8/33/1635.

[26] Abbot Draughton remained in captivity in Brabant until he was discovered in April 1329. Draughton returned to Bury St Edmunds late in 1329 and remained as abbot until his death in 1334. The fate of the kidnappers Berton and Barbour is unknown, but there has been a suggestion that Berton was caught and died in Bury St Edmunds gaol. See D. M. Smith and V. C. M. London, ed., *The Heads of Religious Houses: England and Wales* (Cambridge, 2001), II, 27. For letters concerning his abduction, dated to 31 October 1328, see *The Registers of Roger Martival, Bishop of Salisbury, 1315–30*, ed. C. R. Elrington, Canterbury and York Society 58 (1972), II, 579–81.

recognised that Beverley's accusers were concocting the case against him for their own benefit, and so granted him a pardon.[27]

Another interesting sub-set of these petitions concerning victimisation were those in which individuals attempted to pre-empt a claim for pardon from someone who had wronged them to ensure they did not receive the king's mercy. In one petition of the late 1330s, Isabel de Cleterne claimed that she was abducted from her manor by Adam de Culwen and others and held at Aykhurst castle until she was rescued by the power and aid of Sir Anthony de Lucy.[28] Isabel, on hearing that the malefactors, by their proctors, were seeking charters of pardon, requested that for 'the honour of women' this peace be denied them. In 1308 Margery de Treverbin entered a similar claim. According to her petition, one Thomas de Gevely had, with two friends, broken into her lodgings in London. He had then raped her daughter and robbed her of her possessions. Margery had brought a case against him, and had succeeded in having him attached to come before the marshals, but because he appeared in the company of Henry de Beaumont no-one dared to accuse him, and he was freed.[29] In these cases, the petitioners were of relatively high social standing. However, in several extant petitions there are references to the humble status of the supplicant. In 1325, for example, William Crok pleaded for pardon of a false inquisition that had been passed against him – he claimed that the case had dragged on for seventeen years and as a result his wife and children were reduced to begging and he himself was threatened with imprisonment.[30] It would seem, then, that at least some of the petitions for pardon are what we might term 'classic equity cases', in which the victims of a powerful local individual seek the impartial justice of the king that they could not find in the local courts.

However, it would be wrong to over-emphasise these cases, or to claim that the extant petitions for pardon mirror the kinds of cases that were later to be presented to the Court of Chancery. The largest percentage of petitions for pardon concern arrears on debts owed to the Crown, usually for rents payable on Crown lands. A significant proportion are concerned with the purchase or inheritance of lands without a royal licence – in such cases the petitioners seek pardon and restitution of lands that had been seized by the Crown. The early years of Edward III's reign, in particular, saw a concentration of petitions concerning the Despenser lands, which had been accrued by the family through dubious means in the latter years of Edward II's reign, while they enjoyed royal favour. Petitioners in such cases are overwhelmingly of gentle or noble status. It is perhaps true to say, then, that the status of the petitioner could be a positive influence in bringing the case to the atten-

---

[27] Letters of pardon were issued on 6 November 1331: *CPR, 1330–4*, p. 216.
[28] TNA SC 8/39/1937.
[29] TNA SC 8/76/3756.
[30] TNA SC 8/41/2026.

30th ANNIVERSARY CELEBRATION GAME!

ARE YOU HOLDING THE £1 MILLION SCRATCHCARD?

THREE MATCHING SYMBOLS=
ONE IN THREE CHANCE OF A **LEVEL 1** PRIZE

LEVEL 1 PRIZES

- £1MILLION • £100,000 • £10,000 • £75
- **AFTERNOON TEA FOR 2 AT THE SHARD**
- £12,000 TO SPEND ON A **CUNARD CRUISE**
- £5,000 TO SPEND ON ANYTHING FROM **ASOS**
- **WEEK FOR 4 AT BEACH RESORT IN PORTUGAL**
- **PS4 WITH ANY 5 TOP CHART GAMES**
- **TED BAKER LEATHER WEEKEND BAG**
- **£400 MARKS & SPENCER GIFTCARD**
- **NEW KÄRCHER STEAM STICK CLEANER**

TWO MATCHING SYMBOLS=
ONE IN THREE CHANCE OF A **LEVEL 2** PRIZE

LEVEL 2 PRIZES

- £5,000 • £2,500 • £1,000 • £500 • £250
- **FINE DINING DAY TRIP FOR 2 ABOARD THE BELMOND BRITISH PULLMAN**
- **NEW APPLE WATCH** (SPORT EDITION)
- **HIS OR HER PAUL SMITH FRAGRANCE**
- **VIRGIN SUNRISE BALLOON FLIGHT** FOR 2
- **RUSSELL HOBBS 3.5L SLOW COOKER**
- **NUTRIBULLET GRAPHITE JUICER** • £20

3,2 & 0 MATCHING SYMBOLS ON EVERY CARD

To celebrate
30 YEARS
of scratchcard fun,
EVERYONE who takes part
in this unique
anniversary game is
GUARANTEED a special

FREE BONUS GIFT
worth **£49.95**
as well as any prize claimed!

This is one game you really don't want to miss!

Scratch off the panels below

CROWN • ORANGE • ORANGE

2 MATCHING SYMBOLS
Have you won a prize of up to £5,000?
To find out and obtain a claim number you c...
Call **0906 158 2914**
Calls cost £1.53 per min...
from other networ...
6 minute...

Scratch off the panels below

Scratch off the panels below

TO CLAIM: 1. Complete form below – see over for how to get your claim numbers. 2. Send **WHOLE** card to:
FREEPOST RTLA-GTHS-TYTG £1MSC, Purely Creative, 1 Mannin Way, Caton Road, Lancaster LA1 3SU

Title:	First Name:		Surname:

Address:

Postcode:

(You must be 18+ to enter)

Tel: Date of Birth:

E-mail:

I have won a '3 matching symbols' prize [ ] Tick if applicable.	I have won a '2 matching symbols' prize [ ] Tick if applicable.
My prize is:	My prize is:
Claim number:	Claim number:
Date:	Date:

Any cards submitted without a valid claim number will be void. Claim number valid for single use only.

tion of the monarch, particularly if the petition was brought to Parliament.[31] Certainly, the pressure on parliamentary time and the prestige of the forum were combining to make Parliament a place where increasingly only the elite could seek redress of grievances. However, there *were* some exceptions, and these were often petitions for pardon.

Charity

The system of pardoning was not exclusively the preserve of the elite orders of society. Some petitioners convinced the Crown that an illegal act had been committed out of desperation, in circumstances of extreme poverty. In one example from 1302, a woman called Alice Chapele was pardoned for stealing corn on the grounds that the deed had been committed out of poverty, and in order to support a famished infant.[32] In these circumstances petitions for grace appealed to the moral obligation of the monarch to protect his subjects and provide effective justice. Christian notions of forgiveness were sometimes overtly expressed: the monarch occasionally granted pardons because of a religious festival, for instance, and there are several examples of pardons given in recognition of Good Friday.[33] In exceptional cases criminals who survived the attempt to execute them were also pardoned, on the basis that their survival constituted a miracle.[34] In cases that appealed to the king's conscience and moral duty, the contrition of the supplicant was a key factor. The defendant might even admit his guilt, but claim to be truly contrite and beg forgiveness. This was clearly an appeal for the king to recognise the canon law dictates of penance and forgiveness, according to which a king or judge should respond with mercy to humility and repentance in the malefactor. If the criminal was ashamed of his sin and acknowledged it, he would be worthy of mercy.[35] However he might, in some instances, be required to

---

[31] Dodd discusses private petitioning in Parliament: Dodd, *Justice and Grace*, pp. 200–5.

[32] *PROME*, 'Edward I: petition 2', item 1. A further twenty-three petitions from the fourteenth century claimed 'impoverishment' as a mitigating factor: TNA SC 8/168/8372; SC 8/31/1537; SC 8/129/6432; SC 8/17/821A; SC 8/15/702; SC 8/129/6436; SC 8/18/855; SC 8/102/5079; SC 8/183/9143; SC 8/226/11266; SC 8/212/10585; SC 8/271/13531; SC 8/108/5371; SC 8/268/13388; SC 8/47/2348; SC 8/195/9706; SC 8/80/3978; SC 8/128/6359; SC 8/40/1954; SC 8/78/3856; SC 8/201/10009; SC 8/65/3246; SC 8/41/2026.

[33] *CPR, 1385–9*, pp. 134, 136, 137, 140, 145, 151, 159, 164, 191, 194, 288, 291, 297–8, 304, 309, 313, 332, 337, 346, 426–7, 429, 430, 435, 437, 441, 443, 452, 455, 457, 459, 461, 521; *CPR, 1388–92*, pp. 26–7, 29, 31–2, 36, 37–9, 41–2, 74, 170, 245, 391–2, 394, 398, 404.

[34] See Chapter 5, pp. 69–70.

[35] One petition dated to 1333 seems unusual, in that it plainly states that the petitioner robbed and killed a man, without offering any mitigating circumstances, or claims of false accusation: TNA SC 8/243/12106.

perform some act of penance in return. Edward I issued a pardon to William de Dun in 1285 for harbouring his son while he was a fugitive from the law. William was held in prison for refusing to submit to trial, but the king pardoned him on condition that he went to the Holy Land and remained there until given a special licence to return.[36] Admitting to wrongdoing and appealing to the king's discretionary powers was not, however, guaranteed success, and the extant pardons show that it was infrequently attempted.

Language and Structure of Petitions

The authors of these petitions, then, needed to convince the Crown of the extenuating circumstances surrounding their case, or of their sincere contrition, in order to elicit a favourable response. The petitions allow us an insight into the way the protagonists wanted to present themselves or alternately how they were represented by their adversaries. The main point – that people regularly drew upon established stereotypes – is unsurprising. Female petitioners, for example, were often presented as victims of force and intimidation, as Natalie Zemon Davis noted from her examination of the French letters of remission.[37] Interestingly, however, they may also be constructed as strong-willed where their course of action could be deemed virtuous. Lettice Kiriell, for example, presented a petition to the king in order to deny Sir John de Cornwaille any pardon for his 'detestable wickedness' towards her. Her petition stated that Cornwaille had entered her manor in the habit of a friar and stripped her servants of their clothes and then allowed into the castle forty armed men who held her in torment for four hours until she paid him. He had since returned on a number of occasions for the previous four years, and had assaulted her. Finally, he came to the castle to reduce it with armed men and scaling ladders and pursued Lettice into a river where she remained in fear for four hours until she was 'as good as dead'. Believing she was dead, Cornwaille took her horses and other goods and chattels worth £1,000. Despite the fear and intimidation he exerted over her, she had initiated various suits against him, and now petitioned the king to prevent Cornwaille from receiving pardon.[38] The petition repeats several times the extent of Lettice's despair and the severity of Cornwaille's attacks on her. But the very existence of the petition itself also demonstrates that Lettice was suffi-

---

[36] *CPR, 1281–92*, p. 194. In 1286 a man who had been placed in exigent after an accusation of trespass had been levelled against him was also pardoned on condition that he travelled to the Holy Land: *CPR, 1281–92*, p. 247. In another instance, a man outlawed for felony and trespass was pardoned when it was found that he had been abroad on pilgrimage at the time of his summons to court: *CPR, 1350–4*, p. 1.

[37] Davis, *Fiction*, p. 79.

[38] TNA SC 8/55/2713.

ciently assertive to petition the king in order to see that her assailant was not pardoned.

Several cases recorded in these petitions involve standard reasons for pardon such as killing in self-defence. In such instances petitioners should have been confident that a trial judge would recommend pardon. It might be supposed, therefore, that they simply wanted to avoid the lengthy and sometimes costly procedures of the courts or that their connection to an influential patron was the determining factor. However, of the eight self-defence cases identified from the fourteenth century, none of the petitioners were from an aristocratic background, and none cited a patron.[39] Instead, the common factor seems to be that the circumstances of the case were in fact unusual in some way, and might not have been easily dealt with by a trial judge. In one case the petitioner seems to imply that he had been outlawed, since he stated that if he received a pardon he would surrender to prison and stand to right.[40] In two cases the petitioner had abjured the realm, one then claiming that an *ex officio* inquisition by the coroner found that he had killed in self-defence.[41] Outlaws and those who had abjured the realm needed a pardon for the outlawry or the abjuration before they could safely return to their home and submit themselves for trial.[42] In another case the petitioner, a woman, asked pardon on behalf of her husband who had killed in self-defence.[43] One other case was unusual in that the petitioner, a woman called Benedicta Choffyn of Guernsey, claimed to have killed her husband in self-defence when he beat her. She had then fled to Normandy. In this case, the petition, addressed to the king, was endorsed twice; firstly with the statement that 'it is unworthy to grant grace in this case', but then with a warrant for further action: 'the king agrees that the bailiff should certify him of the matter at the Parliament to be held at Michaelmas next'. A pardon was then issued to the woman soon after the relevant parliament.[44] Therefore although a self-defence claim would usually be easily dealt with by a trial judge, in these particular cases, the circumstances were more complicated. The petitions were again formulated so as to provide details necessary for a pardon to be granted. Supplicants needed to prove that the attack on them had been unprovoked, and that they were genuinely in fear of their lives. They also

---

[39] TNA SC 8/90/4500; SC 8/55/2742; SC 8/99/4922; SC 8/226/11293; SC 8/255/12746; SC 8/253/12605; SC 8/319/E405; SC 8/278/13872.

[40] TNA SC 8/319/E405.

[41] TNA SC 8/90/4500; SC 8/226/11293.

[42] Hurnard states that pardons for outlawry or abjuration would often pardon the original crime as well. However, there are many fourteenth-century pardons that forgive only the outlawry or abjuration, and require the petitioner to surrender to prison and await trial: Hurnard, *Homicide*, p. 32.

[43] TNA SC 8/99/4922.

[44] TNA SC 8/278/13872; *CPR, 1301–7*, p. 69.

needed to suggest that they had taken every possible opportunity to escape, rather than to slay their assailant.

The type of weapon used was also often important. One common definition borrowed from Justinian asserted that the type of weapon used gave some guidance as to the intent of the assailant: 'If the aggressor drew a sword and struck him with it, there is no doubt of his having done this with the intention of killing him. Where, however, during a quarrel, he struck him with a spike ... the attack was not made with the intention of killing him.'[45] Such principles are discernible in the petition of Hugh Kynson of Boxworth, for example, who sought pardon in 1320 for killing Richard Musters in self-defence. Hugh had been travelling by horseback on the highway from the market at Cambridge when he was attacked by Musters with a drawn sword and pursued to a ditch. He claimed that he could not have escaped with his life, and that defending himself against his assailant was the only possible course of action.[46] The standardised construction of some of these pardons clearly demonstrates that those who wrote them had some understanding of the grounds on which pardon would be granted, even if no formal criteria had actually ever been set down. Extant evidence would suggest, then, that in several cases the procedure provided a means of access to pardon for those who, despite deserving one, could not get such a letter through formal legal channels. However, it is also apparent that the petitions for pardon could be a means for those of high social standing to air their grievances and seek redress in the prestigious forum of Parliament.

Pardon Scenes

So far the texts discussed in this chapter have been predominantly 'governmental' in the sense that they were written with bureaucratic processes in mind. However, descriptions of 'pardon scenes' can be found in several other genres: chroniclers might describe prominent political figures petitioning the king for mercy, while outlaw tales and other vernacular texts invoked the idea of the royal pardon in a way that might have been expected to resonate with their audiences.

While few petitioners would actually have come before the monarch themselves to present their petition, the face-to-face scene of supplication was more popular in literary descriptions, presumably because of the immediacy and drama that could then be conveyed, rather than the more mundane reality of the bureaucratic procedures of Chancery. In such descriptions, the physical appearance of the supplicant was particularly important. In cases involving a

---

45 Hurnard, *Homicide*, p. 75; Davis, *Fiction*, p. 36.
46 TNA SC 8/55/2742.

murder the culprit would often be described as wearing clothes that symbolised their mourning for the deceased, and would perform physical actions to convey their remorse: throwing themselves to the floor, crying and wailing with regret. The presence of patrons willing to intercede on behalf of the supplicant was also important; women or churchmen might be favoured for this role. In some cases, the injured party (a relative of the victim in a homicide case, for example) would be persuaded to publicly forgive the felon, in the king's presence. The audience who witnessed this scene of supplication were also important; the earnest entreaty of the supplicant would move them to pity, even to tears themselves, according to some writers.

In one high-profile case from 1386 the Westminster chronicler described Sir John Holland's supplication for pardon, before his half-brother, Richard II.[47] Holland had killed Ralph Stafford the previous summer, in revenge for the death of one of his own esquires. The Westminster Chronicler notes that when the king first heard of the murder, he declared upon oath that Holland would be subject to the full force of the law as a vulgar homicide, despite his bond of kinship with his brother. Yet, by February 1386, Holland felt it safe to appear before the king to beg mercy. The chronicler describes him as 'attired in mourning'. In other examples the petitioners are described as appearing with bare head and feet. John Holland also brought with him two prominent churchmen to intercede on his behalf; the chronicler describes how he approached the king supported on the arms of the archbishop of Canterbury and the bishop of London. Ralph Stafford's father, the earl, was persuaded to forgive Holland, after the latter agreed to found a chantry of three chaplains to pray for the soul of his son.[48]

In some instances the wronged party was even persuaded to express their forgiveness and endorse the request for the king's pardon. This brings to mind older, Anglo-Saxon notions of private settlement with the injured parties, or relatives of the deceased, which still found a place in pardons of the later period.[49] In one case reported in the York Memorandum Book for 1390, the son of a man who had been murdered was persuaded to endorse a pardon for the murderer. The entry describes how a man called Robert Ellerbek, a mercer of York, had gained an audience before the mayor and civic dignitaries at the city chambers. Ellerbek proceeded to beg mercy from one of the men present, a man called Ranulph del See, for killing his father. According to the record, Ellerbek entered the chamber with bare head and feet, and prostrated himself before the feet of Ranulph. He then proceeded

---

[47] *Westminster Chronicle*, ed. Hector and Harvey, pp. 122, 159–61.

[48] *CPR, 1385–9*, pp. 114, 368; *Knighton's Chronicle*, ed. Martin, p. 339.

[49] TNA SC 8/141/7004; SC 8/247/12324. Almost all late medieval pardons contained the clause that the petitioner should 'stand to right' in court, so that an appeal could be brought by an aggrieved party: 'Ita tamen quod stet recto in curia nostra si quis versus eum loqui voluerit de felonia supradicta.'

to beg pardon for killing his father, asking for it in the name of 'God and his son Jesus Christ, who gave his precious blood on the Cross to redeem all mankind.' Moved by his entreaty, the mayor and the dignitaries present added their voice to the call for mercy. Ranulph agreed to endorse his request for a royal pardon, in honour of the soul of his father.[50] It was clear, though, that forgiveness had to be sincerely given. Pardons could be nullified if it was later proved that forgiveness had been extorted under duress, and in some instances the supplicant would be required to perform an act of penance in return for pardon.[51]

Outlaw heroes in ballads such as *Gamelyn* and *Adam Bell* were also portrayed as supplicants for royal mercy. Most of the ballads in the Robin Hood tradition only survive in fifteenth-century manuscripts, although they are first mentioned in the 1377 B-text of *Piers Plowman*.[52] The pardon scenes they describe are therefore conceived by mid-fifteenth-century writers, but underlying them is an idealised vision of royal justice that had a far older provenance. In *Adam Bell*, the outlaws try to petition for pardon before the king discovers the true extent of their crimes, knowing that a pardon framed in general terms will cover any other offences they may have committed.[53] The protagonists evade capture for the crimes they commit in rescuing one of their number from the gallows, and seek a pardon from the king. However, they neglect to mention their most recent offences, and merely ask forgiveness for poaching in the king's forest:

---

[50] *York Memorandum Book II*, ed. M. Sellers, Surtees Society 125 (1914), pp. 30–1.

[51] TNA SC 8/214/10683. See above, n. 36.

[52] *Robin Hood and the Monk* is an early example – the oldest surviving manuscript dates from some time after 1450, but Knight and Ohlgren suggest it can be related to Langland's reference to the tales of Robin Hood, made c. 1377. For further discussion, see *Rymes of Robyn Hood: An Introduction to the English Outlaw*, ed. R. B. Dobson and J. Taylor (London, 1976), pp. 109, 122, 71–9, 113–15; *English and Scottish Popular Ballads*, ed. F. J. Child (New York, 1965), III, 94–6; A. J. Pollard, *Imagining Robin Hood: The Late-Medieval Stories in Historical Context* (Abingdon, 2004); Musson and Ormrod, *Evolution*, p. 169.

[53] For the text, see *Robin Hood*, ed. Knight and Ohlgren, pp. 235–67. The earliest full version survives in Copeland's text of the mid-sixteenth century, although two earlier fragments also exist, one from 1536 and one from slightly earlier. However, references to the names of the outlaw protagonists were made in a parliament roll of 1432, suggesting that the tale was well known at this time (see *Robin Hood*, ed. Knight and Ohlgren, p. 235). Dobson and Taylor suggest *Adam Bell* emerged at the same time as the earliest extant Robin Hood tales (see *Rymes of Robyn Hood*, ed. Dobson and Taylor, p. 259). For further discussion, see *Popular Ballads*, ed. Child, III, 14–22; D. Gray, 'The Robin Hood Ballads', *Poetica* 18 (1984), 1–39; E. J. Hobsbawm, *Bandits*, 2nd edn (London, 1985); J. C. Holt, *Robin Hood*, 2nd edn (London, 1989); T. Wright, 'On the Popular Cycle of the Robin Hood Ballads', in *Essays on Subjects Connected with the Literature, Popular Superstition, and History of England in the Middle Ages*, ed. T. Wright (London, 1846), pp. 164–211.

> And whan they came before our kynge,
> As it was the lawe of the lande,
> They kneled downe without lettynge,
> And eche helde up his hande.
> They sayd, 'Lord, we beseche you here,
> That ye wyll graunte us grace;
> For we have slayne your fatte falowe dere,
> In many a sondry place.'   (Fitt. III, lines 464–71)

The outlaws are shown to be aware of the procedure for pardoning and demonstrate knowledge of the transmission of royal orders when they used forged letters with the king's seal attached.[54] Despite certain misgivings, the king is swayed by the entreaty of the queen to accede to their request (Fitt. III, lines 496–9).[55] However, when messengers arrive from the north to inform the king that the outlaws are responsible for atrocities recently committed in the city of Carlisle, the king realises that he has been duped into pardoning them, and is furious at being deceived.[56] The king summons his archers to arrest the wanted men, but before they are able to do so the outlaw hero, William of Cloudesley, appears and dazzles them all with a display of his archery skills.[57] The king is won over by this feat and the tale ends in tradi-

---

[54] The extent to which legal knowledge permeated all classes has been examined in several studies: Neville, 'Common Knowledge'; A. Musson, 'Social Exclusivity or Justice for All? Access to Justice in Fourteenth-Century England', in *Pragmatic Utopias: Ideals and Communities, 1200–1630*, ed. R. Horrox and S. Rees-Jones (Cambridge, 2001), pp. 136–55; P. Hyams, 'What did Edwardian Villagers understand by the Law?', in *Medieval Society and the Manor Court*, ed. Z. Razi and R. M. Smith (Oxford, 1996), pp. 69–102 (pp. 78–9).

[55] It is interesting that in this instance the queen intercedes on behalf of the outlaws without any apparent appeal from them. In a parallel scene from Chaucer's *Tale of Melibee*, for instance, the criminals seek an audience with Dame Prudence, and impress upon her their contrition, in order to persuade her to act for them: *Tale of Melibee*, lines 1773–5. [All references to the *Tale of Melibee* are to *The Riverside Chaucer*, ed. L. D. Benson, 3rd edn (Oxford, 1987), unless otherwise stated.] Here, the queen seems to be acting purely in the interests of mercy, without regard for the circumstances of the crime or the contrition of the criminals. For further discussion of queens as intercessors for mercy, see Chapter 4, pp. 45–7.

[56] The king is also beguiled into granting pardon in *Robin Hood and the Monk*. At first he is angered at being tricked by Little John, but this time he quickly relents and renews his pardon to John and to Robin, praising John's loyal service to his master and highlighting the debt Robin now owes John: 'I gaf theym grith [pardon],' then seid oure Kyng;/ 'I say, so mot I the/ Fforsothe soch a yeman as he is on/ In all Inglond ar not thre./ … 'Robyn Hode is ever bond to hym,/ Bothe in strete and stalle/ Speke no more of this mater,' seid oure Kyng,/ 'But John has begyled us alle.' lines 343–6, 351–4. See also Holt, *Robin Hood*, pp. 28–30.

[57] See *Popular Ballads*, ed. Child, III, 16–21. Dobson and Taylor suggest that the compiler of *Adam Bell* was merely adapting to his own purposes the William Tell ballad, one of the most popular stories of north European literature (*Rymes of Robyn Hood*, ed. Dobson and Taylor, p. 260, n. 3).

tional fashion, with the monarch standing by his original grant of pardon and appointing William to high office, as happens in the *Tale of Gamelyn*, and the *Gest of Robyn Hode*, and is implicit in *Robin Hood and the Monk*.[58]

Seen from one perspective, the king's grant of pardon to guilty men on the basis of their physical prowess alone is itself clearly an abuse of his powers. However, none of the tales make this point; instead the pardon is justified on the grounds that the outlaws have been fighting injustice and display honour and loyalty within the outlaw band. From the opening lines of the *Adam Bell* ballad, the outlaws are portrayed sympathetically: the whole sequence of events is set in motion by William's desire to see his wife and three children, who live within the city walls, despite the dangerous position in which this would place him. After his presence is revealed to the justice and sheriff, he puts up a valiant fight, and ensures that his wife and children are safe, before finally being overpowered. The essentially moral and pious character of the men is also emphasised in their final resolve to go to Rome to be absolved of their sins, before returning to take up their offices and live out their lives in the service of the king.[59] The king implicitly recognises the essential justice of their cause. Their violence has been targeted against corrupt clerics or officers of the Crown who get no more than they deserve, and by pardoning the outlaws the king receives them back into his peace, quelling the threat that their violent deeds present to the maintenance of law and order, and emphasising the active role of the monarchy in bringing about reconciliation and guaranteeing the rights of its subjects.[60] This ending also provides an escapist notion of the idealised justice that only the monarch can bestow.[61]

These ballads go some way to demonstrating the extent to which the law

---

58 William is made chief ranger of the north, and the queen also grants him a wage and appoints him a gentleman. His fellow outlaws are appointed yeomen of the chamber, and his wife and son are granted places in the royal household. In the *Gest of Robyn Hode*, King Edward, disguised as a monk, infiltrates the outlaw camp, and witnesses a display of their archery skills. Seeing their prowess, he abandons his intention to arrest them and grants them pardon and high office. For the text of the *Gest*, see *Robin Hood*, ed. Knight and Ohlgren, Fitt. VII, lines 1645–64; for *Robin Hood and the Monk*, see *Robin Hood*, ed. Knight and Ohlgren, lines 339–42. Again in the *Tale of Gamelyn* it is the outlaw's physical strength and aptitude for violence that ultimately win the king's grace and appointment to high office. Knight and Ohlgren date the tale to c. 1350–70 (*Robin Hood*, ed. Knight and Ohlgren, pp. 184–226). See *The Tale of Gamelyn*, ed. W. W. Skeat (Oxford, 1884), p. 33, lines 887–94; R. W. Kaeuper; 'An Historian's Reading of The Tale of Gamelyn', *Medium Aevum* 52 (1983), 51–62; V. J. Scattergood, '*The Tale of Gamelyn*: The Noble Robber as Provincial Hero', in *Readings in Medieval English Romance*, ed. C. Meale (Cambridge, 1994), pp. 159–94 (pp. 167–8); E. F. Shannon, 'Medieval Law in *The Tale of Gamelyn*', *Speculum* 26 (1951), 458–64.

59 The pious character of Robin Hood is often emphasised, most notably in the *Gest*, Fitt. I, lines 29–40.

60 Ormrod and Musson, *Evolution*, p. 170.

61 See Chapter 5, pp. 68–9.

of the realm was regarded as personal to the king. As the supreme lawgiver, he played an active role at the head of the judicial system, and the king's subjects valued their right to appeal directly to him for judgment. The value of the genre of outlaw ballads for a study of royal mercy, then, lies in its ability to convey idealised concepts of the king's role in the judicial system. While the person of the monarch was, by the later fourteenth century, largely removed from the day-to-day procedures of the royal courts, the ballads serve as a reminder that certain sections of society, at least, still closely associated the monarch with the judicial system that operated in his name. In responding to requests for royal arbitration, in answering petitions for grace, and in actively seeking to intervene in particular cases, the monarch exercised some practical influence over the legal system.[62]

The extant evidence of royal arbitration and petitions for grace, as well as the outlaw ballads discussed above, suggest that the king's subjects still conceived of a particular brand of justice dispensed by the monarch himself. Moreover, this perception is echoed in texts from a diverse range of genres: the visionary–political discourse of *Piers Plowman* expresses a profound sense of disappointment in the inability of the late medieval English legal system to rectify the injustices of the times, but places its emphasis on the person of the monarch as the means to overcome the corruption inherent in the judicial process. So too, the satire of the Wakefield master, in the Towneley Corpus Christi play *The Killing of Abel*, demonstrates the dramatic potential of proclamations of royal pardon. These texts will be discussed in more detail in the chapters that follow.

---

[62] See, for example, *Year Books of the Reign of Edward the Third*, ed. Horwood and Pike, III, 196–7; TNA KB 145/1/18; JUST 1/425, fols. 12v, 13, 21v, 22; SC 1/39/27; SC 1/55/86; *Calendar of Letter Books of the City of London*, G, II, 23. For royal arbitration, see Powell, 'Arbitration', pp. 49–67; Powell, 'Settlement of Disputes by Arbitration', pp. 21–43; Rawcliffe, 'English Noblemen and their Advisers', pp. 157–77; Rawcliffe, 'Parliament and the Settlement of Disputes', pp. 316–42.

CHAPTER FOUR

Intercessor

Those who sought pardon in the later Middle Ages often looked to a patron to intervene on their behalf. Members of the royal family or servants of the Crown might be able to use their influence at court to help to secure a grant of mercy, or at least ensure that the case received attention. For those who were in prison awaiting trial, or for those who had already been outlawed, finding someone to act on their behalf was the only route to pardon.[1] A significant percentage of fourteenth-century pardons issued from Chancery record the name of a person who intervened on behalf of the supplicant. The usual formula was to note that the pardon had been issued 'at the request of' a named patron. When lists of these intercessors are compiled (see Appendix 4) it is possible to identify those members of the royal family and extended household who were particularly active in securing grants of mercy. This chapter discusses these prominent patrons, but also examines the role of other 'middle-men' involved in the pardoning process. Those individuals who stood surety as 'mainpernors' for recipients of pardon, for example, guaranteed their future good conduct and were liable to be fined themselves if the pardoned individual subsequently reoffended. Other people sometimes played a more clandestine role in securing pardons, by bribing intermediaries or even providing forged documents, at the right price.

These less than legitimate practices did not go unnoticed, and the rolls of parliament record discussion on the subject of pardons procured through deceitful means. However, despite the discontent at the potential for corruption, the legislation enacted to address the matter sought to regularise the role of the intercessor for pardon, rather than to outlaw the practice altogether.[2] The role of the intercessor was therefore a somewhat controversial, but widely recognised, part of the process. This chapter examines the ways

---

[1] One petition dated to 1385 explicitly stated that John de Felsted, usher of the royal exchequer, petitioned for pardon through another man, one Adam Ramsey, esquire, because John had been imprisoned in the Fleet prison by the chief baron of the exchequer. The petition asked for pardon on the grounds of self-defence; John had been instructed to guard the door of the exchequer against a certain chaplain who had gone mad and was wandering around Westminster Hall. On being denied entry, the chaplain beat John severely with a staff, and in self-defence John struck him with a dagger. Pardon was duly granted in this case: TNA SC 8/255/12746.

[2] See the statute of 1353, for example, which stipulated that all letters requesting

in which people acted as intermediaries (legitimate or otherwise) in the pardoning process, and their depictions in a variety of different texts.

Patrons

When a pardon was issued from Chancery the clerks tended to note the intercession of a prominent patron if he or she had been instrumental in securing the grant. In 1353 this was made a legal requirement; the name of the patron was to be stated, when relevant, on the letter of pardon itself.[3] However, the percentage of individual pardons mentioning a patron remained relatively low (approximately 12 per cent of all individual pardons in each of the reigns of Edward II, Edward III and Richard II). The list of intercessors in Appendix 4 shows that the most active patrons were, fairly predictably, members of the royal family (queens in particular) and close royal advisers, who might sometimes be acting in their capacity as military commanders.

In the reigns of Edward II and Richard II, their respective queens were among the most frequent intercessors for mercy. Queen Isabella secured pardons in most years after her arrival in England and marriage to Edward in 1308, until 1320, when the rise of the Despensers at court and the estrangement of the royal couple limited her power as an intercessor. Similarly Queen Anne secured a steady stream of pardons throughout the 1380s, and continued until the year of her death in 1394. Edward III's queen, Philippa, secured more pardons than either Isabella or Anne, unsurprisingly given that her forty-year marriage was at least twice as long as either of theirs, but this did not make her the most prolific of patrons during Edward's reign. Her posthumous reputation as an intercessor was nonetheless secured by Froissart's famous description of her pleading with Edward for mercy on behalf of the defeated burghers of Calais after the siege of the town in 1347.[4] The other fourteenth-century queens were less prolific, but all were responsible for endorsing at least a few petitions for pardon. Queen Margaret, Edward I's second wife, promoted several petitions in the early 1300s (Edward I's first wife, Eleanor of Castile, and his mother, Eleanor of Provence, had also acted as patrons in the latter years of the thirteenth century). At the end of the fourteenth century, Richard II's second wife, Isabella, also acted as a patron, at least in name, although she was only seven years old at the time of their

---

pardon for felony should record the name of the intercessor: *SR*, I, 330. See Appendix 4.

3   *SR*, I, 330.
4   Philippa's role as intercessor was promoted by Froissart in his well-known description of the surrender of the burghers of Calais in 1347. For further discussion, see Strohm, *Hochon's Arrow*, pp. 95–119; J. C. Parsons and B. Wheeler, ed., *Medieval Mothering* (London, 1996), pp. 40–2.

marriage. Despite her youth, she was named in several pardons of the late 1390s, with the note: 'pardon at the supplication of the queen consort'.[5] Obviously as a child Isabella was not actually championing these causes herself, but the evocation of her name was clearly thought to be useful; possibly it suggests that supplicants for pardon were able to approach the servants and officials surrounding the young queen in order to secure her theoretical backing. Maintaining the fiction that Isabella was able to intercede for mercy also perhaps indicates that there were certain virtues of queenship that contemporaries sought to uphold, regardless of the practical limitations imposed by a seven-year-old queen-consort.[6] Dowager queens also continued to secure grants of mercy; Edward III's mother, Queen Isabella, sought more pardons in the reign of her son than she had as queen to Edward II. Joan of Kent also acted as an intercessor during the reign of her son, Richard II, right up until the year of her death in 1385.[7] In the months before her death she was also involved in attempts to promote reconciliation between the king and his uncle John of Gaunt and pleaded with Richard to show mercy to her second son, John Holland, earl of Huntingdon, who had murdered Ralph Stafford. Indeed, it was Richard's recalcitrance in the face of her entreaty which, according to Walsingham at least, hastened her demise.[8]

This data on queens acting as intercessors for pardon therefore accords with the substantial body of medieval literature representing the ideology of mercy and medieval queenship.[9] Recent scholarship has done much to eluci-

---

[5] See Appendix 4.
[6] See Chapter 10 for discussion of pardons issued during Richard II's minority.
[7] J. C. Parsons, 'The Intercessionary Patronage of Queens Margaret and Isabella of France', in *Thirteenth Century England VI*, ed. M. Prestwich, R. H. Britnell and R. Frame (Woodbridge, 1997), pp. 145–56; C. P. Collette, 'Joan of Kent and Noble Women's Roles in Chaucer's World', *Chaucer Review* 33 (1999), 350–62; W. M. Ormrod, 'In Bed with Joan of Kent: The King's Mother and the Peasants' Revolt', in *Medieval Women: Texts and Contexts in Late Medieval Britain. Essays for Felicity Riddy*, ed. J. Wogan-Browne, F. Riddy and A. Diamond (Turnhout, 2000), pp. 277–92.
[8] *The St. Albans Chronicle: The Chronica maiora of Thomas Walsingham, vol. 1, 1376–1394*, ed. J. Taylor, W. R. Childs and L. Watkiss (Oxford, 2003), p. 759. See above, Chapter 3, p. 39, for discussion of Holland's plea for mercy.
[9] See, for example, the intercessory role of Dame Prudence in Chaucer's *Tale of Melibee: Melibee*, lines 1773–5. See also D. Wallace, *Chaucerian Polity, Absolutist Lineages and Associational Forms in England and Italy* (Stanford, 1997), pp. 215–16; D. Pearsall, *The Canterbury Tales* (London, 1985), pp. 285–8; J. Dillon, *Geoffrey Chaucer* (London, 1993), pp. 57–9. The 'Four Daughters of God' allegory (based on an interpretation of Psalms 83. 11) also circulated in a number of late medieval texts: *Piers Plowman*, ed Schmidt, B-text, XVIII, lines 112–228; *Mirour of the Blessed Lyf*, ed. Powell, pp. 14–19; *Vices and Virtues: A Soul's Confession of its Sins with the Reason's Description of the Virtues*, ed. F. Holthausen, EETS OS 89, 159 (London, 1888, 1921), pp. 111–21; *The Life of Christ and the Virgin Mary*, in 'The Four Daughters of God: A New Version', ed. R. A. Klinefelter, *Journal of English and German Philology* 52 (1953), 90–5; *Charter of the Abbey of the Holy Ghost, Yorkshire Writers*, ed. C. Horstman (London, 1895), I,

date this area; John Carmi Parsons, for example, discussed the evocation of Marian intercession and its association with earthly queenship in thirteenth-century texts. Importantly, Joanna Laynesmith has argued that this role was fading in importance by the fifteenth century, and that intercession was not one of the defining characteristics of late medieval queenship. However, queens continued to emphasise the human qualities of kings, particularly by providing a voice of mercy and domesticity.[10]

Aside from queens, certain other nobles with the ear of the king were prolific intercessors for mercy. In Edward II's reign Aymer de Valence, earl of Pembroke stood out as a patron in this respect, particularly in 1318 and 1319; years when he was acting as a member of royal council formed at the York Parliament. In succeeding generations, men such as John of Gaunt, duke of Lancaster and Henry Percy, earl of Northumberland played a similar role, mediating with the king and securing at least one or two pardons every year.[11] In terms of sheer numbers of pardons secured, however, Edward III's military commanders stand out from the other patrons.[12] Their patronage was of a different kind; they secured high numbers of pardons for lists of retainers in preparation for a forthcoming military campaign, or to reward them for recent service. Henry de Grosmont, earl of Derby (and first duke of Lancaster from 1351 onwards) secured close to 300 pardons for others in the middle decades of Edward III's reign, most as part of large grants to his military retinues. In 1345, for instance, he sought pardons for soldiers in return for their service in the Gascon campaign. Similarly the Black Prince secured over 200 pardons, over one hundred of which were given in 1357 for service in Gascony over the previous three years. Lower down the social scale, men such as Robert Knolles were also able to secure pardons for others in this

---

337–62; *The Macro Plays,* ed. M. Eccles, lines 3129–3649. For kingdom allegories, see *Gesta Romanorum,* ed. Herrtage, pp. 132–5; *Court of Sapience,* ed. E. R. Harvey (Toronto, 1984), lines 176–903. John Lydgate, *Life of Our Lady,* ed. J. A. Lauritis, R. A. Klinefelter and V. F. Gallagher, Philological Series 2 (Pittsburgh, 1961), lines 185–91.

[10] J. C. Parsons, 'The Queen's Intercession in Thirteenth-Century England', in *The Power of the Weak: Studies on Medieval Women,* ed. J. Carpenter and S.-B. MacLean (Urbana, 1995), pp. 147–77; J. L. Laynesmith, *The Last Medieval Queens: English Queenship 1445–1503* (Oxford, 2005), pp. 34, 131–80, 220–61, 263; C. P. Collette, *Performing Polity: Women and Agency in the Anglo-French Tradition, 1385–1620* (Turnhout, 2006), pp. 99–121. See also L. L. Honeycutt, 'Intercession and the High-Medieval Queen: The Esther Topos', in *Power of the Weak,* ed. Carpenter and MacLean, pp. 126–46.

[11] See Appendix 4. It is interesting to compare these figures for intercessors with those compiled from the charter witness lists: J. S. Hamilton, 'Charter Witness Lists for the Reign of Edward II', in *Fourteenth Century England I,* ed. N. Saul (Woodbridge, 2000), pp. 1–20; C. Given-Wilson, 'Royal Charter Witness Lists, 1327–1399', *Medieval Prosopography* 12 (1991), 35–94.

[12] See Chapter 7, pp. 100–6, for further discussion of pardons given in return for military service.

way. In 1370 Knolles was the first military commander below the rank of earl to lead a campaign in France, and he was able to secure sixty-one pardons for his soldiers.

The role of these influential patrons in the pardoning process was somewhat controversial. In 1353 the parliamentary Commons sought to address the issue head on, and a statute was drafted, which declared that charters of pardon had in the past been issued 'upon feigned and untrue suggestions of divers people, whereof much evil hath chanced in times past'.[13] To counter this it introduced the requirement that every charter of pardon granted at the suggestion of an intercessor would record the name of the patron, and the reasons put forward to secure the pardon. The justices before whom such charters were presented were to enquire into these particulars, and if they found them to be untrue they were to reject the charter. This would also address the problem of desertion from the royal armies, for the Commons claimed that charters of pardon had often been granted to well-known thieves and common murderers on the understanding that they would remain overseas in the king's wars, when in fact they quickly returned home to continue their criminal activity without hindrance.[14] Again in 1390 further legislation attempted to introduce severe penalties for those who did not follow these procedures.[15] In the Parliament that opened at Westminster on 17 January 1390, the Commons requested that no pardons would in future be granted for felony at the instigation of powerful intercessors. Moreover, if anyone 'demanded' such a pardon of the king, he or she would be fined according to their social rank.[16] The king answered that although he would save his 'liberty and regality' as his progenitors had done before, he would consent to certain points in order to promote peace within his realm. The resultant statute stipulated that the names of any patrons who had interceded on behalf of a supplicant should be recorded on any writ of pardon subsequently issued. A sliding scale of fines would then be imposed for anyone found to have procured a pardon for another person through deceitful means.[17] An archbishop or duke was to pay one thousand marks; an abbot, prior, baron or banneret would pay five hundred marks, and a clerk, bachelor, or other

---

13 'per feintes et nient veritables suggestions de pluseurs gentz, dount pluseurs malx sont avenuz cea en arere'. *SR*, I, 330.

14 *PROME*, 'Parliament of 1353', item 41.

15 *SR*, II, 68–9.

16 *PROME*, 'Parliament of January 1390', item 36. See also Green, *Verdict According to Conscience*, p. 33.

17 The statute also sought to eradicate the use of all-inclusive pardons, which remitted a range of serious crimes. It was stated that in pardons of felony the crime should be specifically named in the charter. If a pardon for murder came before the justices without this record, they were to enquire, by inquest of the visne where the dead was slain, if he had been murdered by await, assault or malice prepensed. If this was found to be the case, the pardon was to be disallowed.

of less estate, 'of whatsoever condition that he be', was to pay two hundred marks and be imprisoned for one year. However, by 1393 it was recognised that these fines were proving unworkable – the threat of heavy penalties had intimidated those genuinely in need of pardons, and malicious indictments had been made in the knowledge that no man would risk suing out a pardon. Accordingly, this part of the statute was soon repealed.[18] However, in 1404 the remaining statute was extended, because of the complaints surrounding pardons procured for criminals who had turned king's evidence and become approvers.[19] According to the statute, those indicted of felony sometimes turned approver to safeguard their lives, and then sought to secure pardon through 'brokage, grants and gifts' to intermediaries. It was therefore enacted that any pardon granted to an approver must be endorsed with the name of the intercessor who procured it. This intermediary was then to be fined £100 if the recipient offended again.[20] There was clearly some unease at the idea that simony and corruption might infiltrate the networks of patronage, but the legislation looked to regularise, rather than outlaw the practice altogether.

Sureties

Aside from influential patrons, other people might act as 'middle-men' in the pardoning process. One way was to agree to stand surety for someone seeking a pardon and guarantee their future good conduct. It was a concept that found a place in the vernacular literature of the late fourteenth century: in *Piers Plowman*, for instance, mainprise is offered during the Trial of Wrong,

---

[18] *SR*, II, 86. Kesselring has pointed out that the wording of the statute caused some confusion. It does seem to imply that these sums were to be paid every time a pardon was sought, but, as she points out, the provision of one year's imprisonment suggests they were intended as penalties (Kesselring, *Mercy and Authority*, p. 22, n. 21). In fact, it would seem that the confusion arose from the wording of the original Commons petition presented in Parliament. The petition requested that no pardon would be granted for treason, murder or rape at the instance or request of anyone. If anyone did attempt to demand such a charter of the king they were to be fined on the same sliding scale that was included in the statute. Importantly the Commons' petition also asked that if anyone requested pardon for felony, and it was later proved to be treason or murder, they should incur the penalties prescribed. While the king had rejected the clause, he had kept the sliding scale of fines. However, without the explanatory clause of the Commons it is not clear from the statute that they are intended as punishment for a false petition.

[19] An approver was a prisoner who confessed to a felony and agreed to inform on his accomplices in order to delay or avoid altogether his own execution: see A. Musson, 'Turning King's Evidence: The Prosecution of Crime in Late Medieval England', *Oxford Journal of Legal Studies* 19 (1999), 467–79; F. C. Hamil, 'The King's Approvers', *Speculum* 11 (1936), 238–58.

[20] *SR*, II, 144.

and in Chaucer's *Tale of Melibee* the criminals take friends with them to court to stand as guarantors.[21] Indeed, an attempt was made in 1336 to make this a standard procedure: a statute stipulated that any person who had been pardoned should find sureties or their charters would be void. These individuals were to come before the sheriffs and coroners of the county between 1 April and 29 August and give the names of those men willing to vouch for them. The documents were then to be sealed and returned to Chancery by 12 September. Any recipients in the future would have three months to present such 'mainprise' to the coroner and sheriff, and a further three weeks to send it to Chancery.[22] News of the new statute caused one soldier, serving in Scotland in the summer of 1336, to petition the king for leniency; he was concerned that his pardon had lapsed because he had not been able to provide surety while he was away. The king and council ordered that the soldier's claim should be verified by his commander in Scotland, Edward de Kendale. He was then given until the following June to present the names of his sureties to Chancery.[23] The 1336 statute was not the first attempt to make the procedure of pardoning more stringently regulated, but it did signal something of a shift away from attempts to limit the numbers of pardons being granted, and instead focus on the administrative process.[24] However, the force of this statute weakened over time, and increasingly pardons were issued with clauses allowing the obligation to find sureties to be ignored.[25]

21 C-text, IV, lines 84–6, 90–3; *Melibee*, lines 1805–6.
22 *SR*, I, 275. See Bails on Special Pardons: TNA C 237, which record the names of six sureties put forward by those receiving pardons. Some are single membranes relating to the finding of sureties in Chancery; others are writs to the sheriff and coroner ordering them to see that such sureties were found in the county court, with their return either endorsed or more usually, attached.
23 TNA SC 8/48/2379.
24 Kesselring identifies the Parliaments of 1328, 1330 and 1336 as assemblies that sought to limit the king's ability to pardon, after which, she comments, medieval parliaments did not try to impose any restriction on the king's power to pardon, but instead sought to prevent abuses by recipients and petitioners (Kesselring, *Mercy and Authority*, p. 20). In fact, attempts to restrict the use of the prerogative of mercy surfaced before 1328, and three further attempts were made after 1336 – in 1337, 1340 and 1390. However, it is true to say that by the end of the 1330s the Commons were shifting their focus to the administrative process of pardoning, and away from limiting the scope of the king's power to pardon.
25 T. F. T. Plucknett, 'Parliament', in *The English Government at Work, 1327–1336. Vol. 1. Central and Prerogative Administration* (Mediaeval Academy of America Pubn, 37), ed. J. F. Willard and W. A. Morris (Cambridge MA, 1940), I, 119–20.

Illicit Intercession: Forgers

While patrons and guarantors had an official role to play in securing pardons, there were others who promised to secure documents of pardon through less official channels. The forging of pardons along with other royal charters, while not common, did at times come to light. In 1301 a man called Richard de Haumon was found to have purchased a false pardon for robbery from a forger of the king's seal. Interestingly, Richard had then managed to secure an authentic pardon for both offences (robbery, and obtaining forged letters), by serving with the royal army in Scotland.[26]

Another case involving a forged pardon came before the court of King's Bench in 1305.[27] William of Truro had been arrested and kept in prison in York for suing out a 'certain false charter of pardon', in the name of another man. William declared that the charter had been handed to him by the man named in the pardon, one Thomas Trewyder of Fowey, and by John Pervet of Lostwithiel. The two men were summoned to appear before the king, but the sheriff reported that Thomas had been outlawed for the death recorded in the pardon, and could not be found (it was later revealed that he had fled 'to parts overseas'). John, however, surrendered himself to prison. At the trial William said that the two men had handed him the charter so that he could carry it to the king's Chancery on their behalf, and once there he could obtain a writ of pardon. John's version of events was that Thomas (his uncle) had told him that he had obtained the lord king's peace, and asked John to present the charter in the county court, and have it proclaimed. John had duly taken the pardon to the county court, but had been told by the sheriff that he would not validate it without the king's writ. John and his uncle had then gone to William, who was about to set out for Westminster on his own business, and handed the charter to him so that he would obtain a writ for them. As a result of John's testimony, William was freed. At a further hearing John implicated another man, a certain Stephen, goldsmith of Winchelsea, who was present when the charter of pardon was sued out and made, and had lent Thomas 18s. for the purpose. Stephen was duly summoned, but testified that he had never seen the charter before and had nothing to do with the case. He claimed that he was merely a business associate of Thomas – they were partners in a certain ship. He had, he acknowledged, lent Thomas the money in order to accomplish certain business of his in the same ship, but not for the purpose of suing out any charter. Stephen surrendered for trial and was found innocent of any wrongdoing. Finally, in 1309 John himself was tried and released after the jurors found him innocent.

---

[26] *CPR, 1301–7*, p. 40; Hurnard, *Homicide*, p. 304.
[27] *SCCKB*, LVIII, 149–52; Hurnard, *Homicide*, p. 304.

While this seems to have been a particularly protracted and complex case, it is clear that the parties involved were aware that the forging of pardons was practised in some quarters, and knew that to be accused of such activity was a serious charge. The Crown, too, recognised the potential disruption such forgeries might cause. In 1345, Edward III's government took the step of appointing three commissioners to 'follow and take wherever found men, who, as is said, in large numbers stay in secret places in divers parts of the realm with counterfeits of the king's great and little seals and daily seal with the counterfeit great seal letters patent of pardon of felonies'.[28]

Views on the Role of Intercessor

The preceding discussion has shown that the intercessor for pardon continued to play an important role throughout the fourteenth century. Anxiety about the ease with which some powerful patrons appeared to secure pardons was explicitly expressed by the parliamentary Commons, and one petitioner even went as far as to comment, in her own petition for pardon, that: 'charters of pardon are so commonly granted by the procurement of those close to the king'.[29] In other quarters, medieval commentators expressed a range of views on the practice of interceding for pardon. Praise for the merciful role of medieval queens has already been noted, but not all commentators were so positive about the process of intercession.[30] One interesting text that refers to the procurement of 'false' pardons through a nefarious intercessor is the script written by the Wakefield master for the Towneley Corpus Christi play *The*

---

28   *CPR, 1343–5*, p. 589.
29   SC 8/39/1937.
30   See above, nn. 9–10. General themes of corruption and maintenance within the legal system were a common trope of many politically aware texts. Poems such as *The Simonie* and *Winner and Waster* attacked the venality of the courts, as did outlaw romances such as the *Tale of Gamelyn* and the Robin Hood ballads. More specific injustices were depicted in the *Outlaw's Song of Trailbaston*, while *Piers Plowman* provided a far-reaching denunciation of judicial corruption. For discussion of such texts, see J. R. Maddicott, 'Poems of Social Protest in Early Fourteenth Century England', in *England in the Fourteenth Century: Proceedings of the 1985 Harlaxton Symposium*, ed. W. M. Ormrod (Woodbridge, 1986), pp.130–44; *Thomas Wright's Political Songs*, ed. P. R. Coss (Cambridge, 1996), pp. 224–30, 323–45; *Political Poems and Songs*, ed. T. Wright, RS 14 (London, 1859–61); J. Coleman, *English Literature in History 1350–1400: Medieval Readers and Writers* (London, 1981), pp. 58–156; Green, *A Crisis of Truth*, pp. 198–205; Musson and Ormrod, *Evolution*, pp. 161–93; *Rymes of Robyn Hood*, ed. Dobson and Taylor; *Tale of Gamelyn*, ed. Skeat; Kaeuper, 'Tale of Gamelyn', pp. 51–62; Scattergood, 'Noble Robber', pp. 159–94; Shannon, 'Medieval Law', pp. 458–64; Baldwin, *Government*, *passim*; *Robin Hood*, ed. Knight and Ohlgren.

Killing of Abel.[31] The Towneley cycle survives in a single manuscript dated to c. 1475–1500, but Arthur Cawley, the modern editor, endorsed the consensus of opinion when he said that performance of the pageants would have predated the text by a significant period of time. The play's satirical comments on the abuse of judicial authority and attitudes to pardoning are worth a closer examination than they have hitherto received. In the second half of the play, after Cain has slain his brother Abel, the focus of the drama shifts to the punishment that awaits Cain, and his attempts to avoid the censure of divine and earthly law. The dialogue between Cain and his servant mocks the efficacy of the royal legal system. In an attempt to persuade his servant to help him dispose of Abel's body, Cain assures his servant that he has the authority to proclaim a pardon for them both:

> Cayn: A, syr, I cry you mercy! Seasse,
> And I shall make you a release.
> Garcio: what, wilt thou cry my peasse
> Throughout this land? (lines 406–9)

The idea of 'crying peace' would have been familiar to the medieval audience; according to *Glanvill*, 'criers' (*criatores*) were required to inform the parties involved in a judicial case openly and proclaim summonses to court in a public place. Writs were then sent to sheriffs ordering them to publicly proclaim a charter of pardon in a full county court.[32] For those watching the play, therefore, Cain's proclamation of pardon would have been a familiar

---

[31] *Wakefield Pageants*, ed. Cawley, pp. xiv–xvii. All references are to this edition unless otherwise stated. See B. A. Brockman, 'The Law of Man and the Peace of God: Judicial Process as Satiric Theme in the Wakefield Mactacio Abel', *Speculum* 49 (1974), 699–707, for discussion of the themes of sanctuary and the king's peace.

[32] The writs referred to here were written in Latin, as were the letters patent of pardon themselves, but they were most likely to have been proclaimed in English: for further discussion on this, see J. A. Doig, 'Political Propaganda and Royal Proclamations in Late Medieval England', *Historical Research* 71 (1998), 253–80 (p. 264); Ormrod, 'The Use of English', pp. 750–87. For early fourteenth-century writs, see *Early Registers of Writs*, ed. E. Haas and G. D. G. Hall, Selden Society 87 (London, 1970), 197. Brockman notes that justices of the peace may have assumed responsibility for proclaiming pardons by the early years of the fifteenth century (Brockman, 'Wakefield Mactacio Abel', p. 703). On royal messengers, see M. C. Hill, *The King's Messengers, 1199–1377: A Contribution to the History of the Royal Household* (London, 1961), pp. 14–26, 141–2; M. C. Hill, 'The King's Messengers in England, 1199–1377', *Medieval Prosopography* 17 (1996), 63–96; K. A. Fowler, 'News from the Front: Letters and Despatches of the Fourteenth Century', in *Guerre et société en France, en Angleterre et en Bourgogne, XIVe–XVe siècle*, ed. P. Contamine, C. Giry-Deloison and M. H. Keen (Lille, 1991), pp. 63–92; M. C. Hill, 'King's Messengers and Administrative Developments in the Thirteenth and Fourteenth centuries', *EHR* 61 (1946), 315–28. See also Musson, *Medieval Law*, p. 97; M. T. Clanchy, *From Memory to Written Record: England 1066–1307*, 2nd edn (Oxford, 1993), pp. 272–3.

scene, and one readily interpreted as an ironic mockery of the official royal procedure.

Cain's reading of the pardon itself attempts to invoke the idea of divine protection, making reference to God's earlier decree that no one should murder him in punishment for his crime. This injunction is interpreted as divine forgiveness, and then formulated into a royal proclamation of pardon. Cain declares it to be the king's will that he and his servant both remain safe, and that no man find 'fault or blame' with them:

> Caym: I commund you in the kyngys nayme,
> Garcio: And in my masteres, fals Cayme,
> Caym: That no man at thame fynd fawt ne blame,
> Garcio: Yey, cold rost is at my masteres hame.
> Caym: Nowther with hym nor with his knafe,
> Garcio: What! I hope my mastere rafe.
> Caym: for thay ar trew full manyfold.
> Garcio: My master suppys no coyle bot cold.
> Caym: the kyng wrytys you untill.
> Garcio: Yit ete I neuer half my fill.
> Caym: The kyng wills that they be safe.
> Garcio: Yey, a draght of drynke fayne wold I hayfe.
> Caym: At thare awne will let tham wafe.
> Garcio: My stomak is redy to receyfe.
> Caym: Loke no man say to them, on nor other-
> Garcio: This same is he that slo his brother.
> Caym: Byd euery man thaym luf and lowt.
> Garcio: Yey, ill-spon weft ay comes foule out.
> Caym: Long or thou get thi hoyse and thou go thus aboute!
>   Bid euery man theym pleasse to pay.   (lines 419–38)

Despite their scriptural context, Cain's words are clearly intended to invoke the idea of a secular royal pardon: he refers to commands in the 'kyngys nayme' and asserts that 'The kyng wills that they be safe' (lines 419, 429). However, the authority of Cain's speech is undermined by the mocking interruptions of his servant. Moreover, as Brockman has noted, the standard phrasing of a royal pardon is here condensed into an abrupt form, which would have amused the audience: rather than the standard formula 'know that we have pardoned … by our special grace the suit of our peace …' Cain's speech reduces this to 'The kyng wills that they be safe.'[33] The direct references to the king here are clearly included for dramatic purposes, in a bid to command the attention of the audience and mockingly instil in them a due sense of solemnity, as Cain battles against the constant interruptions of his servant.

---

[33] Brockman, 'Wakefield Mactacio Abel', p. 701.

This scene evokes the idea that royal pardons could be abused, and might well be given to notorious criminals. The corrupt nature of royal mercy on earth is directly contrasted with the equity of God's grace, which cannot be manipulated or abused. Earlier in the play, Cain has been put out of God's grace for the murder of his brother (lines 356–69).[34] Like the medieval outlaw, Cain is at risk of being killed by officers of the Crown, but God will not let this happen, putting a mark on Cain to serve as a warning that if he is killed, seven lives will be taken in revenge. While Cain can convince his audience that the king's judicial system is pliant enough to pardon him despite the seriousness of his offence, this merely serves to reinforce divergence between standards of earthly justice and the model of divine law. The scene also emphasises the power of the charter of pardon and the importance of the physical document: it seems likely, for instance, that the actor playing Cain would produce a mock charter as a prop from which to read. The audience were clearly aware of the real power a charter of pardon had to avert the immediate threat of prosecution. However, the overriding effect is that the play makes a satirical comment on the abuse of authority. The play's use of the figure of Cain as an intercessor for pardon reflects the sense of unease felt in some quarters over the potential for corruption in the process. The closing lines of the play remind the audience that Cain is eternally damned for the murder of his brother: 'And to the dwill be thrall, warld withoutten end/ Ordand ther is my stall, with Sathanas the feynd' (lines 464–5). This proclamation scene was surely intended to invoke widely held feelings of contempt for the injustice the audience associated with pardoning, and to appeal to popular sentiment by mocking it. This view is consonant with the awareness of injustice and corruption elsewhere in the Towneley plays.[35]

A similar sentiment also found expression in other politically conscious vernacular texts of the period. In *Piers Plowman*, for example, Langland casts Lady Meed as an intercessor for mercy on behalf of Wrong. The names of the characters alone leave the reader in no doubt of Langland's condemnation of

---

34 Genesis 4. 8–16.
35 See, for example, Mak's assumption of bogus royal authority in 'The Second Shepherd's Play'. Mak pretends to the shepherds that he is a 'yeoman of the Crown', by imitating a southern English accent, in order to deceive them and steal one of their sheep; *Wakefield Pageants*, ed. Cawley, lines 190–220. Again in 'The Conspiracy', the Wakefield author emphasises the corruption of the High Priests; *Wakefield Pageants*, ed. Cawley, lines 46–450. Cawley comments that it is likely that this characterisation of Annas and Caiaphas was influenced by the Wakefield author's dislike of the corrupt ecclesiastical lawyers of his own day (*Wakefield Pageants*, ed. Cawley, p. 119). See also G. R. Owst, *Literature and Pulpit in Medieval England: A Neglected Chapter in the History of English Letters and of the English People*, 2nd edn (Oxford, 1961), p. 496.

such practices.[36] In the fourth passus of the B-text, there is a scene in which Meed colludes with Wisdom and Wit (who appear to be Wrong's lawyers) in an attempt to extract a pardon from the king through persuasion and bribery, echoing familiar concerns that the system of pardoning was open to abuse by those with access to powerful patrons or to officials with some knowledge of the workings of the law.

The scene is set in the royal court, with Peace arriving to present a petition to the king concerning the crimes of Wrong, a royal purveyor (an official tasked with requisitioning supplies for the king's armies and thus a figure often accused of corruption). Langland also places the characters Reason and Conscience in attendance at this hearing, as a reminder of the ideal principles with which royal mercy should be dispensed. The charges with which Wrong is accused amount to a list of those crimes classed as felony under the criminal law, including larceny, rape, murder and riding armed, as well as forcible entry, ravishment, forestalling and maintenance. Although Peace in fact drops his suit later in the passage (after being bribed) the king takes up the case, seeing the essential justice of Peace's cause.[37]

At this point, the issue of intercession and bribery comes to the fore: Wrong seeks the help of a powerful patron to intervene on his behalf and secure a pardon for him. He procures the assistance of Worldly Wisdom, offering him a bribe to intercede for him and win the king's favour. Wisdom and Wit (the other lawyer) at first admonish Wrong, saying that people who act on impulse often provoke trouble. However, the pair are still ultimately willing to accept Wrong's request for help. They depart from him with the warning that his life and lands will hang in the balance if Meed cannot prevail upon the king to be lenient: 'But if Mede it make, thi meschief is uppe;/ For bothe thi lif and thy lond lyth in his grace' (B-text, IV, lines 72–3). The essence of their case is that pragmatism should win out: the king should accept the financial benefits of granting bail in return for a payment of compensation. If Wrong can find someone willing to stand surety on his behalf and pay out a ransom for him, the whole affair can be settled to the benefit of all concerned.[38]

This bargaining position would have resonated with a contemporary audience familiar with large sums of money being charged for pardon in some cases, and with the idea of finding surety for future good behaviour. It

---

36 B-text, IV, lines 76–7. See G. Dodd, 'A Parliament Full of Rats? *Piers Plowman* and the Good Parliament of 1376', *Historical Research* 77 (2004), 1–29. See Appendix 4 below.

37 B-text, IV, lines 48–62; C-text, IV, lines 46–8, 52–4, 58–9, 63. Peace drops his suit in B-text, IV, lines 104–5. Peace is a pliable figure, ready to compromise rather than uphold strict justice, as later in B-text, XX, line 335, when he agrees to admit Flatterer into Unity. See Schmidt's note on this in *Piers Plowman*, ed. Schmitt, p. 422. However, he does try to resist when the friar is revealed as *Penetrans-domos* (lines 340–8), but Hende-Speche intervenes and lets him in (lines 349–50).

38 B-text, IV, lines 87–93.

would also have brought to mind the 'pragmatic' policy of pardoning those men willing to serve in the royal army.[39] Financial or other practical benefits were therefore seen at times to override the principles of equitable justice. Langland is clear that while the king might benefit financially from making such pardons freely available, in doing so he would compromise the standards of justice he had sworn to uphold.

Ultimately, Langland's monarch is resistant to Meed's plan to bribe him, and instead rules that Wrong will not be released unless Reason takes pity on him, or Humility stands bail.[40] This scene is followed by Reason's impassioned speech, in which he attacks the abuse and corruption he sees among the clergy and king's courtiers. He concludes with the advice that if he were a king with a realm to protect, he would leave no wrong unpunished, nor would he let anyone win favour through gifts, or gain mercy through Meed. Only their meekness would sway him:

> ... I seye it by myself,' quod he, 'and it so were
> That I were a kyng with coroune to kepen a reaume,
> Sholde nevere Wrong in this world that I wite myghte
> Ben unpunysshed in my power, for peril of my soule,
> Ne gete my grace thorugh giftes, so me God save!
> Ne for no mede have mercy, but meeknesse it made;
> For '*Nullum malum* the man mette with *inpunitum*
> And bad *Nullum bonum* be *irremuneratum*.'
>
> (B-text, Passus IV, lines 137–44)

His final words quote Innocent III's definition of a just judge, who leaves no evil man unpunished and no just man unrewarded, and advises the king that if he follows this principle, the law will serve the interests of justice and love shall rule the land. All the just men agree with him and even Wit praises Reason's speech. The king gives his verdict in favour of Reason and swears that he will be counselled by Conscience and Reason in all things. Reason extols the uncompromising principle of retributive justice, although Conscience recognises this as an ideal rather than a workable reality:

> Quod Conscience to the Kyng, 'But the commune wole assente,
> It is ful hard, by myn heed, herto to brynge it,
> [And] alle youre liege leodes to lede thus evene.
>
> (B-text, Passus IV, lines 182–4)

Despite his scepticism regarding the role of influential patrons, Langland sets his denunciation in the context of a more general condemnation of the

---

[39] See Chapter 7, pp. 100–6, for further discussion.
[40] The king listens to the voice of natural reason and rejects false counsel: C-text, IV, lines 131–2, 136–7.

corruptible processes of the law (B-text, IV, lines 27–41). His solution in this instance is for the king himself to pass judgment, albeit with the counsel of Reason and Conscience, rather than leaving the case to be heard in the royal courts.[41] While the king's personal role in the pardoning process was, in reality, limited to a small percentage of cases, it was the immediacy of the king's role in the pardoning process that prompted comment in Corpus Christi plays and in politically aware vernacular literature.

The initiative for seeking pardon therefore lay with the supplicant, but, as this chapter has shown, several other people were often involved in the process, and the final letter of pardon reflected the input of patrons, sureties and professional county lawyers. The process was satirised in some quarters, and expressions of concern about the influence of powerful patrons were made in Parliament. Above all, it seems, the Commons in Parliament were calling for the system to be standardised, rather than prohibited altogether. In its response to such grievances, the Crown did seek to formulate a recognisable procedure for pardoning, and issued statutes to this effect. However, kings ultimately protected their power to make discretionary judgments on grants of mercy, and it is this personal role of the monarch that will be explored in the following chapter.

---

[41] B-text, IV, lines 188–95; Baldwin, *Government*, pp. 45–50.

CHAPTER FIVE

Monarch

Fourteenth-century monarchs did not usually intervene in the day-to-day business of the law courts, but they did still occasionally involve themselves in the business of granting pardon. Particularly complex or unusual cases might be referred to the king for a decision 'of grace' (rather than the routine matters 'of course', which could be dealt with by the chancellor).[1] However the surviving documentary evidence does not always help to shed light on the nature of the monarch's role in the process. It is likely that in some cases the king's decision was conveyed orally to his chancellor, and the only archival record that exists is the note that a pardon was issued. In other cases, a written petition for pardon was submitted.[2] These petitions were often endorsed by the 'receivers' (men assigned to collect petitions in Parliament) with a note stipulating the course of action to be taken, and sometimes this meant they were earmarked for royal attention.[3] Some of these petitions also record the decision made by the king in Parliament, or at a meeting of the council. Cases might also be referred to the king from his justices in the royal courts, perhaps with a recommendation for mercy. If the justices found something suspicious about a charter of pardon it was possible for them to postpone the proclamation and in the meantime consult the king. In one instance, the justices of gaol delivery at Northampton referred William Frere's case to the king when he produced two pardons, given on different dates for different offences. The king's solution in this instance was to grant a third pardon.[4] Alternatively, the monarch himself sometimes initiated a grant of mercy; to mark a royal anniversary or a religious festival, or to reward a group of people for their service to the Crown. On such occasions the public, performative aspects of the act were of utmost importance. One such episode occurred in 1392, when Richard II famously processed through the streets of London as part of a public display of reconciliation with the civic authorities,

---

[1] B. Wilkinson, 'The Authorisation of Chancery Writs under Edward III', *Bulletin of the John Rylands Library* 8 (1924), 107–39.

[2] TNA SC 8. See G. Dodd, *Justice and Grace, passim*. A few documents relating to pardons, and one petition, are filed in C 49, the records relating to the king's remembrancer: TNA C 49/34/25; C 49/8/4; C 49/7/17; C 49/9/2.

[3] Dodd, *Justice and Grace*, pp. 51–2.

[4] TNA C 47/124/1/1; *CPR, 1301–7*, pp. 171, 527; *CPR, 1307–13*, pp. 155–6.

who had recently refused to loan the Crown a substantial sum of money. As the king passed through Southwark he stopped to pardon a criminal in what was no doubt a carefully orchestrated display of mercy.[5]

Contemporary attitudes towards the king's personal involvement in the pardoning process were expressed in a variety of medieval texts. Properly administered, pardons were seen as a valuable safeguard, and might even be portrayed as part of the king's moral duty – the practical application of the promise sworn in the coronation oath to uphold justice in his realm.[6] However, one point in particular proved controversial; the theoretical power of the king to intervene in the legal process, and grant pardon to one of his subjects at his own discretion, whether or not the recipient could give any valid excuse for their actions and before a trial jury had reached a verdict. The prominent legal theorists of the thirteenth century had already sought to restrict this power; for *Bracton* it was legitimate for the king to grant pardon only in cases where a jury had confirmed the existence of extenuating circumstances; homicide in self-defence, for example, or death by misadventure.[7] The author of *Fleta* had gone even further, claiming that where there were clear extenuating circumstances, pardon was a matter of right rather than royal grace.[8] By the fourteenth century most of the concern expressed about pardons in Parliament and in resultant legislation followed *Bracton*'s line in focusing on the instances in which the king intervened before a trial jury had been given the chance to reach a verdict. There were other texts, however, which presented an idealised picture of the discretionary aspect of royal mercy. In the outlaw ballad tradition of *Gamelyn* and *Robin Hood*, for example, it was the monarch's ability to act outside the confines of the legal system and give judgments based on principles of equity that ultimately saw justice prevail for the wronged outlaw. Unsurprisingly, then, it was the role of the monarch in the pardoning process that caught the attention of contemporary writers, even though only a few of the several hundred pardons issued every year were personally overseen by the king himself. The three sections of this chapter discuss the different ways in which the monarch was still personally responsible for the dispensation of mercy and the comment his involvement attracted from contemporary chroniclers, legal theorists and members of Parliament.

---

5   A. G. Rigg, *History of Anglo-Latin Literature, 1066–1422* (Cambridge, 1992), pp. 285–6. See below, p. 73.
6   See Chapter 2, pp. 22–4.
7   *Bracton*, ed. Thorne, II, 388.
8   'Tenetur rex de iure quod suum fuerit perdonare.' *Fleta*, ed. Richardson and Sayles, II, 75. See Hurnard, *Homicide*, p. 275, n. 3.

Petitioning

It is clear that at least some of the 500 or so fourteenth-century petitions for pardon came before the monarch himself, rather than being dealt with by the chancellor. However, the logic that governed their selection for royal attention is not always obvious, and the basis on which the king made his decision is sometimes unclear; some simply state that they have been granted 'by the grace of the king' or that they are 'pardons of grace'. The use of such terms might suggest that kings took a vague, undefined approach to symbolic acts of pardon, concerned only to promote a general sense of munificent royal mercy allied with divine grace and forgiveness (particularly in high-profile cases, when the benevolent grant of a pardon would cast the monarch in a favourable light). However, in some cases a greater level of detail was recorded, which allows for a more nuanced examination of the reasons for granting, or denying, these petitions for grace.

The majority of the fourteenth-century petitions for pardon were addressed to the king himself: 312 simply addressed the monarch, a further 150 addressed the king in council, and seven addressed the king in Parliament. The rest were addressed solely to the council, to the chancellor, or, in rare instances, a person close to the king, such as Edward II's favourite Hugh Despenser, Queen Philippa, or John of Gaunt.[9] It is not, of course, definite that a petition addressed to the king would actually be seen by him, but over one hundred of these documents are also endorsed with a note about further action to be taken, which purports to express the will of the king: 'the king wishes that' or 'it pleases the king' or 'the king is not minded to grant'.[10] In other cases the privy seal was attached to the petition to signify

---

[9]   Four petitions for pardon were addressed solely to the council, over the period 1331–81. No more appear later in the century. Six were addressed to the chancellor, from 1333 to 1399, and they continued to be addressed to him into the fifteenth century. One petition for pardon was addressed to Hugh Despenser in 1324 (TNA SC 8/138/6896); one to the queen in 1333 (SC 8/307/15308); one to the Black Prince in 1375/6 (SC 8/333/E1026), and one to the duke of Lancaster in 1378/9 (SC 8/102/5085). Of these, the one addressed to Hugh Despenser was endorsed with the decision of the king, and the one to the duke of Lancaster asked him to 'pray to the king for his pardon'. Neither the petition to the queen nor to the Black Prince were endorsed with a decision. The petition addressed to Despenser attests to his influence over Edward II in the later years of his reign (already noted by Jeffrey Hamilton in his study of the royal charter witness lists: Hamilton, 'Charter Witness Lists', pp. 1–20). There were also several petitions asking for pardon and restitution of lands taken by the Despensers in the early years of Edward III's reign.

[10] TNA SC 8/67/3337; SC 8/179/8919; SC 8/42/2064; SC 8/243/12146; SC 8/243/12145; SC 8/270/13486; SC 8/141/7046; SC 8/305/15227; SC 8/138/6896; SC 8/66/3266; SC 8/42/2064; SC 8/106/5283; SC 8/141/7001; SC 8/66/3266; SC 8/10/497; SC 8/148/7373; SC 8/186/9265; SC 8/31/1547; SC 8/10/490; SC 8/106/5283; SC

royal consent, and on one occasion the sign manual was used for the same purpose.[11] These decisions might be taken by the king while he presided over Parliament, or at a meeting of the council. When, on occasion, the council met without the monarch in attendance, it usually endorsed the petition with its opinion, but sent it for final royal approval; so, for instance, one petition addressed to Edward III in the early 1330s was endorsed with an initial decision, but then handed to Richard de Bury, who was instructed to seek out Edward's decision on the matter. Bury was a close adviser to the king at the beginning of his reign, and this note suggests that he might well have been counselling him on the use of the royal prerogative of pardon. Indeed, as Mark Ormrod has demonstrated, Bury's close proximity to Edward made him the main conduit for grants of royal grace in this period.[12] By the end of

8/251/12537; SC 8/189/9429; SC 8/254/12679; SC 8/176/8753; SC 8/270/13486; SC 8/99/4927; SC 8/227/11338; SC 8/140/6964; SC 8/127/6329; SC 8/180/8960; SC 8/218/10879; SC 8/252/12559; SC 8/111/5532; SC 8/196/9800; SC 8/227/11320; SC 8/332/15786; SC 8/150/7483; SC 8/274/13655; SC 8/222/11093; SC 8/224/11161; SC 8/67/3337; SC 8/148/7397; SC 8/66/3277; SC 8/179/8919; SC 8/145/7220; SC 8/130/6490; SC 8/80/3966; SC 8/272/13566; SC 8/286/14261; SC 8/221/11038; SC 8/80/3978; SC 8/229/11407; SC 8/247/12302; SC 8/57/2829; SC 8/195/9706; SC 8/82/4086; SC 8/268/13391; SC 8/227/11301; SC 8/295/14749; SC 8/226/11300; SC 8/251/12547; SC 8/252/12558; SC 8/254/12658; SC 8/11/533; SC 8/253/12645; SC 8/254/12656; SC 8/253/12608; SC 8/253/12627; SC 8/254/12699; SC 8/252/12591; SC 8/253/12615; SC 8/253/12605; SC 8/253/12601; SC 8/253/12609; SC 8/253/12610; SC 8/252/12600; SC 8/253/12618; SC 8/253/12622; SC 8/252/12568; SC 8/252/12575; SC 8/252/12572; SC 8/252/12587; SC 8/252/12555; SC 8/68/3351; SC 8/255/12745; SC 8/255/12746; SC 8/255/12750; SC 8/255/12734; SC 8/252/12574; SC 8/227/11331; SC 8/253/12650; SC 8/252/12567; SC 8/252/12580; SC 8/1/15; SC 8/62/3053; SC 8/74/3681; SC 8/171/8520; SC 8/258/12886; SC 8/95/4725; SC 8/100/4953; SC 8/155/7717; SC 8/112/5566; SC 8/265/13246; SC 8/266/13271; SC 8/208/10351; SC 8/201/10009; SC 8/20/984; SC 8/128/6359; SC 8/341/16079; SC 8/107/5311; SC 8/271/13531.

11 TNA SC 8/93/4616; SC 8/228/11380; SC 8/228/11384; SC 8/228/11378; SC 8/228/11383; SC 8/228/11382; SC 8/228/11386; SC 8/228/11381; SC 8/228/11372; SC 8/228/11373; SC 8/228/11376. The petitions endorsed with the privy seal date solely from the year 1352. The one petition endorsed with the sign manual is dated to 1399. The remainder do no more than note the initial filtering process in operation, whereby the receiver of petitions would decide to whom the petition should be sent. Twenty-seven petitions from this period bear notes that they were to be sent on to the king in council. They are often endorsed with the phrase 'coram rege': SC 8/272/13551; SC 8/319/E366; SC 8/6/269B; SC 8/12/594; SC 8/319/E370; SC 8/133/6623; SC 8/68/3352; SC 8/52/2588; SC 8/319/E405; SC 8/72/3588; SC 8/62/3082; SC; 8/127/6317; SC 8/86/4296; SC 8/66/3266; SC 8/141/7001; SC 8/52/2595; SC 8/76/3753; SC 8/10/497; SC 8/148/7373; SC 8/186/9265; SC 8/31/1547; SC 8/10/490; SC 8/106/5283; SC 8/221/11001; SC 8/15/702; SC 8/266/13290; SC 8/56/2783.

12 TNA SC 8/268/13388; W. M. Ormrod, 'The King's Secrets: Richard de Bury and the Monarchy of Edward III', in *War, Government and Aristocracy in the British Isles c. 1150–1500: Essays in Honour of Michael Prestwich*, ed. C. Given-Wilson, A. Kettle

Edward III's reign, the old king was too frail to move from the royal palace at Havering-atte-Bower, but was still handing authorisations for pardons to his chancellor, John Knyvet, in the presence of his advisers and clerks of Chancery. One such pardon was granted on 8 October 1376, the same day that the king's dire state of health had forced him to make his will and appoint trustees of his personal estates.[13] Alternatively, the king might send a warrant to Chancery, authorising the issue of a pardon.[14] The overall impression must be that these were not decisions made by the king alone, but were for the most part authorised by the monarch or his representative after consultation with the council or Parliament. One petition, for example, was addressed to the king, and it was noted that it had come into his presence, but it was endorsed with the statement that 'the council of parliament does not assent'.[15] It was also usual for the king and council to ask for further documentation (often

and L. Scales (Woodbridge, 2008), pp. 163–78 (pp. 169–72). Another, from the reign of Edward I, is endorsed with the note that the treasurer 'took this business in mind to show the king' (SC 8/182/9072). For other examples, see SC 8/41/2036; SC 8/105/5230; SC 8/44/2159; SC 8/54/2685; SC 8/119/5946; SC 8/272/13551; SC 8/219/10921; SC 8/76/3778; SC 8/112/5570; SC 8/115/5749; SC 8/34/1683; SC 8/175/8723; SC 8/105/5230; SC 8/35/1726; SC 8/265/13236; SC 8/64/3199; SC 8/36/1798A; SC 8/63/3133; SC 8/45/2230. One case that came before Chancery was endorsed with the note that, since the petitioner sought the king's pardon, it could only be dealt with by the monarch himself (SC 8/272/13556). There are a few cases where a decision appears to have been taken by the council, with no mention of the king's assent, although the monarch might well have been present: SC 8/112/5570; SC 8/215/10746; SC 8/160/7959; SC 8/178/8855; SC 8/134/6653; SC 8/224/11163; SC 8/171/8510; SC 8/11/506; SC 8/153/7648; SC 8/162/8087; SC 8/172/8561. One petition states that it was delivered to the chancellor, who granted pardon, seemingly without consulting with the king (SC 8/243/12108). One petition addressed to the king in Parliament was sent to the council, which was instructed to 'provide a remedy at their discretion' (SC 8/84/4190). A petition might also be sent on to a particular royal official because of their professional expertise in the matter: SC 8/86/4296; SC 8/179/8946; SC 8/176/8790; SC 8/46/2276; SC 8/201/10031; SC 8/75/3711.

13 TNA SC 8/180/8960. Another petition sent to the king was attached to a letter commanding that 'the enclosed petition of Cornwall given to the king is viewed, and if it is not against the law then they are to make him such letters [of pardon]'. (SC 8/244/12187.)

14 Writs of Privy Seal: TNA C 81/1– 582. In some instances, a warrant for pardon exists but the document itself does not seem to have been issued (or at least was never recorded as being issued on the patent rolls): for examples, see H. C. Maxwell Lyte, *Calendar of Chancery Warrants Preserved in the Public Record Office, A. D. 1244–1326* (London, 1927). One warrant also survives in the ancient petitions: SC 8/246/12292. The pardon was subsequently issued on 1 September 1354 (*CPR, 1354–8*, p. 101). It is not usually possible to tell how long this process took, although in one case, the petition is endorsed with the day on which the king made the decision to pardon – 12 October 1398 (SC 8/252/12559). The patent rolls record that the pardon itself was issued on the same day (*CPR, 1396–9*, p. 417).

15 TNA SC 8/52/2595.

trial records) before passing judgment on a particular case.[16] Once a decision had been reached more writs would be sent out to relevant departments of government, notably the exchequer, to advise them of the action they should take now pardon had been granted.[17]

Some of the possible reasons why these individuals petitioned for pardon directly have already been explored in Chapter 3, but it is worth noting here that one justification given for pardon was a personal link with the monarch, or at least with the royal household. In several instances a supplicant would admit to wrongdoing, but ask for pardon on the grounds of long and loyal service to the Crown (usually as a soldier or as a servant in the household of the king or queen). So in 1302, for example, Maurice Russel requested the king's charter of pardon for himself and for his valet, explicitly as a reward for their military service in Scotland. In the same year a man called Adam Moy asked pardon for murder, on account of his service to the king's justiciar in Ireland.[18] In all, 16 per cent of the fourteenth-century petitions for pardon mention royal service, most of them in the king's armies.[19]

Allowing such claims as admissible grounds for pardon clearly left the way open for some corruption of the system. In one interesting case from the 1340s the petitioner, a man called John Legat, said that he had been robbed, but that he could not obtain justice because the culprit claimed immunity as a member of the king's chamber. Legat's petition describes how a large number of armed men had broken into his house and seized his servants, restraining them to prevent them from making a noise. The intruders had apparently then turned on Legat himself, attacking him and threatening him with violence if he did not hand over money and valuable possessions. The leader of the criminal band, a man called Edmund Odsey, was apparently well known in the local area; in the past he had assembled crowds of criminals at fairs and markets, encouraging them to threaten the local people, and to commit a range of crimes, including homicide, robbery and trespass in the royal parks. Legat described the situation as so dire that it was 'as if the country was at war'. However, Legat added that everyone was afraid of Edmund Odsey because he had been claiming that, as a member of the king's chamber, he would be granted a pardon for 'all manner of felonies and tres-

---

16 In one such case the petition and the relevant document sent for by the king and council were filed together in the ancient petitions (TNA SC 8/133/6623; SC 8/133/6624).

17 TNA SC 8/337/15913, for example, is a copy of a writ sent by Edward III to the exchequer, reciting a pardon to Alexander, archbishop of Dublin for falsifying his accounts as treasurer of Ireland, and ordering the restoration of his temporalities.

18 TNA SC 8/69/3426; SC 8/127/6317.

19 Three petitions list the names of several soldiers requesting pardon in recognition of their military service: TNA SC 8/185/9212; SC 8/185/9213; SC 8/246/12251. See below, Chapter 7, pp. 100–6, for further discussion of pardons for military service.

passes' whenever he wanted.[20] Whether or not this man was overestimating his ability to influence the king, it is clear that his claims were an attempt to intimidate the local people, and Legat thought them important enough to mention in his petition. While such complaints were uncommon, it is true to say that some royal servants did attempt to use their service to the monarch as grounds for requesting pardon.

The Crown's willingness to receive petitions for pardon was in itself a symbolic act, and might have political overtones, if, for instance, the petitioners were inhabitants of the king's territorial possessions overseas. During Edward III's reign, petitions from some of the contested French provinces were submitted to him, in an attempt to appeal a decision passed by the French courts. The king's ability to pardon these subjects of course rested on his claim to be their lord.[21] In two cases petitioners asked pardon for having been in the obedience of Edward's enemy, the king of France. They subsequently returned to their 'true obedience' and asked Edward's pardon for having offended him.[22] One petition, dating from the first half of Edward III's reign, includes detailed advice relating to the dispensation of pardons. The unidentified petitioner suggests that the king and council might send this advice to the King of France. The petition purportedly followed three earlier letters sent to the French monarch in the hands of English royal messengers, concerning 'pardons and release of penalties for excesses and disobediences made by the king, his ministers and subjects'. The tenor of the message is that the King of France should not arrest English subjects for certain acts listed in the petition. The messengers sent to convey the petition to the French court were instructed to stay until they had been given a reply.[23] In this instance the reference to pardon was designed to invoke the wider issue of the jurisdictional privileges exercised by the two kings.

This was not just a national concern either; within England the privileges granted to the inhabitants of the great palatinates of Durham, Chester and Lancaster, made the granting of pardons in these areas a complex issue. In one case the 'people of the liberty of Durham and Norhamshire' petitioned the king and council requesting a copy of the pardon granted to the people of Northumberland for debts, 'as the liberties are within the county'. The

---

20 TNA SC 8/238/11898.
21 TNA SC 8/176/8790; SC 8/177/8804; SC 8/193/9620; SC 8/194/9688; SC 8/215/10732; SC 8/215/10742; SC 8/216/10752; SC 8/281/14009; SC 8/293/14609 (the pardon relating to this case is enrolled on the Gascon rolls: C 61/43, m. 10); SC 8/67/3337; SC 8/254/12679; SC 8/286/14261; SC 8/274/13655; SC 8/229/11407; SC 8/292/14589 (the pardon relating to this case is enrolled on the Gascon rolls: C 61/43, m. 10); SC 8/325/E672; SC 8/175/8741 (the pardon is enrolled at *CPR, 1307–13*, p. 58); SC 8/172/8588; SC 8/262/13093 (the pardon is enrolled at C 61/54, m. 28); SC 8/215/10749; SC 8/215/10732.
22 TNA SC 8/215/10742; SC 8/216/10752.
23 TNA SC 8/266/13283.

council did not feel competent to pass judgment on the matter, commenting that 'because this grace was made to the people of that county, the council does not dare to extend it to the people of the bishop [of Durham] without advising the king'. The king did subsequently pardon them, but was careful to make the grant separate from that given to the county of Northumberland.[24]

Written petitions for pardon would, on the whole, have been submitted to Parliament and sorted by the receivers of petitions, before being sent to the king or an officer of the Crown for further consideration. However, there were rare instances in which a petitioner was able to gain direct access to the monarch to put their case forward in person. In one early fifteenth-century petition, for example, the female supplicant claimed that Henry IV had personally promised her grace on his last visit to York and requested a written pardon to guarantee this promise.[25] On another occasion, a written petition was submitted asking for the chance to appeal to the king in person. The petitioner asked for orders to be issued to the royal porters, to allow her free entry to the court.[26] What happened once the supplicant made it into the royal presence is less clear, although in some high-profile cases these 'pardon scenes' might be described in chronicles, court rolls and vernacular literature of the period. Whether these scenes reflected or informed practice is of course impossible to tell, but their existence attests to some shared assumptions about how individuals might petition for mercy.[27]

The pardon scenes depicted in late medieval chronicles sometimes left the monarch as an unseen presence in proceedings; while he was the focus of supplicants' exhortations, the petitioner, their patrons and the other people who witnessed the proceedings took centre stage. The writer might note, as the Westminster Chronicler did when describing Sir John Holland's plea for a pardon, that the king was 'stirred by compassion', but other than actually bestowing mercy his actions are not always given prominence.[28] The language used to describe the moment at which the monarch granted pardon did become more formal and legal in tone throughout the course of the four-

---

[24] TNA SC 8/44/2169. For the pardon, see *CPR, 1330–4*, p. 528. In another petition from the 1330s, the bishop of Durham asked pardon of a debt, on the basis that the king had pardoned 'all manner of debts to the men of Northumberland'. Again, the council was careful to refer the case to the king 'because this grace is made to the people of Northumberland the council cannot extend the same to the bishopric of Durham or the people of the bishop's franchise without the king's advice' (SC 8/105/5230). The two petitions might indeed be related, the pardon then covering both debts.

[25] TNA SC 8/184/9174. The pardon was granted on 4 August 1404 (*CPR, 1401–5*, p. 412).

[26] TNA SC 8/255/12707.

[27] See Chapter 3, pp. 38–43.

[28] *Westminster Chronicle*, ed. Hector and Harvey, pp. 159–61.

teenth century; the use of the verb 'to pardon' in legal texts and chronicles gained currency by the end of the thirteenth century. The written document of pardon was also given specific mention. When Knighton, writing from the late 1370s to the 1390s, described the reconciliation between Edward I and Llywelyn, the word he used was *pardonavit*.[29] The Westminster Chronicle similarly referred to John Holland receiving a charter of pardon in 1386, after Richard II had granted mercy, 'et acceptis cartis perdonacionis'.[30] This formal, legal language might have signalled a change from the more emotive words such as 'forgiveness' or 'peace' sometimes used by earlier writers. There was, however, an emphasis on the personal opinion of the monarch that remained constant.[31] The idea that the monarch might seek vengeance on his opponents was particularly potent, and seemingly as relevant to the Lords Appellant in their quarrel with Richard II at the end of the fourteenth century, as it had been to the earls who opposed Edward I in 1297. The amnesty Edward I issued to his marshal and constable released the earls and their followers from 'all manner of rancour and indignation which we [Edward] had conceived against them'.[32] In 1388, Richard II was persuaded to issue the Lords with a pardon for 'all acts done against the appellees'.[33] However much the Lords Appellant might have wanted to reduce Richard's role to a formality by emphasising his youth and the evil counsel that had led him astray, they still saw the value of obtaining a pardon, and implicitly recog-

---

[29] *Chronicon Henrici Knighton*, ed. J. R. Lumby, RS 92, 2 vols. (London, 1889–95), I, 272.
[30] *Westminster Chronicle*, ed. Hector and Harvey, p. 160.
[31] Phrases such as 'remissimus et condonavimus' were used in the penultimate clause of Magna Carta, for example; see *Magna Carta*, ed. J. C. Holt (Cambridge, 1965), p. 336.
[32] *SR*, I, 124; *Bury St Edmunds*, ed. Gransden, p. 141. See also M. C. Prestwich, *Documents Illustrating the Crisis of 1297–8 in England*, Camden Society, 4th series 24 (1980). The document *De Tallagio non concedendo*, which is assumed to contain the demands made of the government by the barons in the Parliament of 30 September 1297, contains a pardon clause (*SR*, I, 125). At the Parliament that opened on 8 July 1297, the king received the archbishop of Canterbury into his grace (Walsingham, *HA*, I, 66). In 1215 the Magna Carta amnesty remitted and pardoned any ill-will, grudge and rancour that had arisen between the parties since the time of the quarrel, and the Dictum of Kenilworth promised that the king would not take vengeance on the offenders or punish them for past wrongs or offences: *Magna Carta*, Clause 62, 'Et omnes malas voluntates, indignaciones, et rancores, ortos inter nos et homines nostros, clericos et laicos, a tempore discordie, plene omnibus remisimus et condonavimus,' in *Magna Carta*, ed. Holt, p. 337; *Dictum*: 'Ita quod nullo modo nullaque causa vel occasione, propter hujusmodi preteritas injurias vel offensas, in eosdem nullam exercet ulcionem; aut ipsius penam vite, membri, carceris, vel exilii, aut pecunie inferat, vel vindicatum,' *SR*, I, 13.
[33] *PROME*, 'Parliament of February 1388', items 35, 37, 38–9; *Westminster Chronicle*, ed. Hector and Harvey, pp. 314–32; *Knighton's Chronicle*, ed. Martin, pp. 442–50.

nised his power to grant mercy. Ultimately, of course, they were right to fear that Richard would seek vengeance against them.[34]

Scenes of supplication for royal mercy were also depicted in vernacular literature, where an idealised vision of equitable royal justice tended to dominate. In the outlaw romances, for example, the heroes tend to go directly to the king and place themselves at his mercy. In the tales of *Fouke le Fitz Waryn*, which were circulating in the early fourteenth century, the king pardons Fouke and his companions the ill-will he harboured against them, and restores them to their inheritance. This is also the case in the fourteenth-century *Tale of Gamelyn*, which concludes with the king acknowledging the essential justice of the outlaws' case and pardoning them the crimes they were forced, by circumstances beyond their control, to commit.[35] These themes, perpetuated in the ballads of the Robin Hood tradition, were mentioned for the first time in the 1377 B-text of *Piers Plowman*, but survive in fifteenth-century manuscripts.[36] In the *Gest of Robin Hood*, the pardon scene takes place in a moment of royal vulnerability, immediately after the king's disguise falls away and he is recognised by Robin and his men, so that the resulting plea for mercy is reciprocal, the king asking first, and Robin seizing his moment:

> 'Mercy then, Robyn,' sayd our kynge,
> 'Under your trystyll-tre,
> Of thy goodnesse and thy grace,
> For my men and me!'

> 'Yes, for God,' sayde Robyn,
> 'And also God me save,
> I aske mercy, my lorde the kynge,
> And for my men I crave.'

> 'Yes, for God,' then sayd our kynge,
> 'And therto sent I me,
> With that thou leve the grene wode,
> And all thy company,

---

[34] *SR*, II, 47–8; *Knighton's Chronicle*, ed. Martin, pp. 504–5; *Westminster Chronicle*, ed. Hector and Harvey, pp. 296–306; *Adam Usk*, ed. Given-Wilson, pp. 9–10.

[35] *Robin Hood*, ed. Knight and Ohlgren, lines 883–98. Knight and Ohlgren date *Gamelyn* to c. 1350–70 (*Robin Hood*, ed. Knight and Ohlgren, pp. 184–226). See also *The Tale of Gamelyn*, ed. Skeat, p. 33, lines 887–94; Kaeuper; 'Tale of Gamelyn', pp. 51–62; Scattergood, 'Noble Robber', pp. 167–8; Shannon, 'Medieval Law', pp. 458–64. The extent of the similarity between the earlier, French tradition of *Fouke le Fitz Waryn* and the later, English *Tale of Gamelyn* and *Gest of Robin Hood* is the subject of debate. It can at least be said that the king's pardon is a feature of both: see E. J. Hathaway, P. T. Ricketts, C. A. Robson, and A. D. Wilshere, ed., *Fouke Le Fitz Waryn*, Anglo-Norman Text Society (Oxford, 1975); G. S. Burgess, trans., *Two Medieval Outlaws: Eustace the Monk and Fouke Fitz Waryn* (Cambridge, 1997).

[36] See Chapter 3, pp. 40–3.

'And come home, syr, to my courte,
And there dwell with me.'   (*Gest of Robyn Hode*, lines 1645–58)

This fifteenth-century version of the ballad drew on ideas of immediate and equitable royal justice that had a far older provenance.

Royal Initiative

In certain other exceptional circumstances it had become custom for the king to intervene after conviction, and allow the prisoner a reprieve, or at least a temporary stay of execution. Those who had already been sentenced could not have their case moved by appeal to a superior court, but they could still theoretically present a pardon or continue to petition for one. Examples of people doing so at this late stage are rare as there was not usually a long delay between the verdict being passed and the death sentence being carried out. However, in exceptional circumstances a postponement would be ordered by the justices. If the convict was a pregnant woman, for example, execution would not be carried out until after the birth of the child. In such cases the mother might be pardoned altogether after the birth. Sixteen such cases can be identified over the period 1307–99, ten of which involved charges of theft or burglary, with some implication that the crime had been committed out of poverty.[37] There are also rare examples of pardon being granted in cases where the execution had been attempted, but the felon had survived, either because the rope had given way, or because they had been cut down too soon after hanging and had revived on the way for burial.[38] One extreme example of this occurred in 1264, when Juetta de Balsham, previously convicted of receiving thieves, was hanged 'from the ninth hour of Monday until sunrise

---

[37] In two cases from Edward II's reign, pregnant women were convicted at Gaol Delivery, but their cases were postponed and later pardoned, *CPR, 1307–13*, p. 349; *CPR, 1313–17*, p. 20; Edward III: *CPR, 1327–30*, pp. 357, 372; *CPR, 1350–4*, pp. 366, 535; *CPR, 1354–8*, p. 100; *CPR, 1367–70*, pp. 274, 285. Richard II: *CPR, 1377–81*, p. 86; *CPR, 1381–5*, pp. 243, 302; *CPR, 1392–6*, pp. 8, 28; *CPR, 1396–9*, pp. 5, 515. Of these sixteen cases, ten involved charges of theft or burglary. A pardon of 1302 recorded that a woman had stolen corn as an act of poverty, to support a famished infant: *PROME*, 'Edward I: petition 2', item 1.

[38] Six men were pardoned in this way in Edward I's reign. In one case the rope was said to have broken, and the convict then fled the realm: *CPR, 1272–81*, p. 327. In two others the felon was found to be alive when taken down from the gallows: *CPR, 1272–81*, p. 396; *CPR, 1281–92*, p. 155. Three others were recorded as having survived hanging: *CPR, 1281–92*, pp. 113, 155; *CPR, 1292–1301*, p. 147. Two such pardons were granted in the reign of Edward III. In one case the convict revived after hanging, and was subsequently found to be innocent: *CPR, 1348–50*, p. 96. In the other, the felon revived, and was then pardoned by the king who was in the area at the time: *CPR, 1364–7*, pp. 60–1.

of the Tuesday following'. Despite this she revived after being cut down and on 16 August she was given a pardon as a result of 'imperfect hanging'.[39]

On rare occasions, later medieval monarchs took more direct action in granting mercy to one of their subjects. In such instances it seems that they were seeking to uphold what was perceived to be 'ancient' custom; for example, there are several fourteenth-century references to a somewhat unusual tradition that held that the king would pardon anyone about to be executed, if he happened to be passing by in the moments before the sentence was carried out and 'look upon' the condemned man. One instance of this happening is recorded on the King's Bench rolls. A man called William Walshman had been caught in possession of a stolen silver pendant, and had then been appealed by Richard Durville for the felony on 13 February 1397. William was found guilty and sentenced to death. The execution was about to take place when the king, happening to pass by, ordered that William be released and taken into safe custody.[40] William later received a charter of pardon, dated 18 April, and presented it at King's Bench on 4 June.[41]

Another similar case is recorded by the chronicler Henry Knighton, during Edward III's visit to Leicester in November 1363. According to the chronicle a man called Walter Poynant of Hambledon had been convicted of robbing a merchant and had been hanged at the town gallows. His body had been placed in a cart and was being taken for burial in the churchyard of St James, when he revived.[42] It was decided that he should be taken to the church, and

---

[39] *CPR, 1258–66*, p. 342. This pardon was recorded in the Luffield priory register of writs: *Early Registers of Writs*, ed. Haas and Hall, p. 101. The register is a small part of a volume written for use of the Benedictine priory of Luffield, on the borders of Buckinghamshire and Northamptonshire, in the late thirteenth century. The pardon was perhaps included because Juetta de Balsham resided locally, or because her case was heard by the court of the priory.

[40] 'dominus rex superveniens per viam precepit prefato Ricardo locum tenenti predicti marescalli, oretenus quod expectaret de execucione predicta facienda et quod ipsum Willelmum salvo custodiret'. (*SCCKB*, VII, 90–1.) Alford refers to this case: J. A. Alford, *Piers Plowman, A Glossary of Legal Diction* (Cambridge, 1988), p. 67.

[41] *CPR, 1396–9*, p. 146. Hurnard also points to another example from the reign of Henry III. In 1226, when the king was only just coming of age, and was perhaps eager to use his prerogative of mercy, John de Herlisun was convicted at the Tower for the death of Lambert de Legis. The king granted him life and limb at the prayer of the women of the city, and he became a Hospitaller: see Hurnard, *Homicide*, p. 43.

[42] Skeat asserts that this case 'can hardly be other than the very one of which William [Langland] was thinking' (*The Vision of Piers Plowman by William Langland*, ed. W. W. Skeat, EETS OS 67, part IV, section I (London, 1877), 423–4). Pearsall endorses this proposition in his notes on the C-text (*Piers Plowman*, ed. D. Pearsall, p. 338). However, Alford says that Skeat claims too much in linking this specific incident with the passage in *Piers Plowman*. As Alford asserts, the principle was well established (Alford, *Glossary*, p. 67).

once there the clergy carefully guarded him, to protect him from being seized and hanged again. At this point the king, who was visiting Leicester Abbey, was notified of events. In response, the chronicler has the king saying to Walter: 'God gave you life, and we shall give you a charter.'[43] Walter was then immediately issued with letters of protection, which the king authorised by word of mouth. His pardon appears on the patent roll a year later, covering indictments against him dating back to 1352.

The origins of this custom are obscure, although when William Langland referred to it in the 'Harrowing of Hell' scene in *Piers Plowman* (Passus XVIII of the B-text) he emphasised the theological justification for such a tradition. Langland frames this scene as an argument between Christ and the devil over the legality of saving the souls held captive in hell since the beginning of the world. The devil argues that these souls were condemned to hell according to God's own law, when Adam first disobeyed God's command. Christ refutes this by arguing that the devil won these souls through deceit 'falsely and feloniously', by appearing as a serpent in paradise to entice Adam into disobedience, and that he has redeemed these souls with the sacrifice of his own life. Christ says that he will not damn the souls already in hell to death without end. He equates this to an 'earthly custom', which decrees that a felon cannot be hanged a second time if the first attempt fails. Equally the souls in hell have already suffered death, and should not be condemned to eternal damnation. Moreover, Langland says that a king is obliged, under the law, to show mercy, if he 'looks upon' a condemned man:

> And if the kyng of that kyngdom come in that tyme
> There the feloun thole sholde deeth or oother juwise
> Lawe wolde he yeve hym lif, and he loked on hym.[44]

This custom seems to be one aspect of a more general notion that the person of the king was a focal point for justice. The court of the king's household

---

43 'Deus tibi dedit vitam, et nos dabimus tibi cartam.' (*Knighton's Chronicle*, ed. Martin, pp. 189–90.) Knighton says that Edward pardoned Walter 'and gave him a charter'. This refers to the letters of protection the king authorised immediately, by an oral warranty (dated 10 November 1363): *CPR, 1361–4*, p. 422. His pardon was subsequently enrolled on 15 January 1365, covering indictments against him dating back to 1352: *CPR, 1364–7*, pp. 60–1.

44 B-text, XVIII, lines 380–4; C-text, XX, lines 421–5. 'When on earth a criminal is put to death, it is not the custom to hang the man again if the first hanging fails, even though he may be a traitor. And if the king of the country comes to the place of execution at the moment when the man is about to die, the law says that the king can grant him his life, if he but looks at the condemned man. So I, the King of kings, shall come at the moment when all the wicked are under sentence of death; and if the Law lets me look upon them, then it rests with my mercy whether they die or not, no matter what crimes they may have committed' (*Piers the Plowman*, *William Langland*, trans. J. F. Goodridge (London, 1966), p. 228).

(known as the Court of the Verge or Marshalsea Court) dealt with breaches of the peace occurring within the verge, an area defined as extending twelve miles from the king's person. While the king himself did not always sit in session, the court's proximity to the monarch at any one time again reinforced the idea that he was a focal point for justice.

On other occasions, the grant of mercy was more carefully orchestrated by the Crown as a public demonstration of princely clemency. We know from the financial records of government that the king often marked important moments in the Church calendar with the distribution of alms to paupers. The king also sometimes exercised his healing powers at these occasions: the phenomenon known as the 'royal touch', which Marc Bloch elucidated in his book on the subject.[45] On Good Friday, for example, it was the custom to place money before the Neith Cross to be melted down and made into cramp rings for the relief of epilepsy. In this context, it seems significant that royal pardons also began to be distributed to mark Good Friday, at least from the beginning of Richard II's reign. Good Friday was a day particularly associated with ideas of mercy, because of Christ's pardon of the 'good thief' crucified beside him, and there are a significant number of pardons, dating from 1380 onwards, which state that the recipient is being pardoned in recognition of Good Friday, and for no other reason.[46] A rough average of seven pardons were given each year to mark this day, although the number fluctuated; in 1394, twenty-two such pardons were issued. It is difficult to reconstruct the details of these court ceremonies, and Bloch draws predominantly on the financial records for his evidence. But it does seem conceivable to suggest that these pardons add something to the picture Bloch gives of ritual healings. The practice was certainly continued by Henry IV, and there are peti-

---

45 M. Bloch, *The Royal Touch: Sacred Monarchy and Scrofula in England and France*, trans. J. E. Anderson (London, 1973), pp. 56–67; W. M. Ormrod, 'The Personal Religion of Edward III', *Speculum* 64 (1989), 849–77.

46 According to the gospel of Luke, two criminals were crucificed next to Christ. One of them told Christ to prove that he was the son of God by saving himself and them. However, the other criminal rebuked him for these words, saying that they were both receiving just punishment for their sins, whereas Christ had done nothing wrong. He then asked Christ to remember him when he came into the kingdom of heaven. Christ promised the latter criminal that he would join him in paradise the same day (Luke 23. 39–43). *CPR, 1377–81*, pp. 453, 454, 456; *CPR, 1381–5*, pp. 389, 390, 391, 392, 398, 400, 416, 533, 546, 547, 548, 551, 552, 554, 555, 564, 569; *CPR, 1385–9*, pp. 134, 136, 137, 140, 145, 151, 159, 164, 191, 194, 288, 291, 297–8, 304, 309, 313, 332, 337, 346, 426–7, 429, 430, 435, 437, 441, 443, 452, 455, 457, 459, 461, 521; *CPR, 1388–92*, pp. 26–7, 29, 31–2, 36, 37–9, 41–2, 74, 170, 245, 391–2, 394, 398, 404; *CPR, 1391–6*, pp. 19, 194, 300, 325, 405, 406, 408, 409, 410, 411, 414, 415, 416, 421, 422, 426, 428, 567, 571, 573, 580, 605, 687, 709, 710, 718; *CPR, 1396–9*, pp. 41, 115, 118, 119, 124, 524, 532, 543, 560; TNA SC 8/255/12728.

tions for pardon that are endorsed on Good Friday, 'out of reverence for God and the day'.[47]

Public pardons were sometimes incorporated into royal pageants in order to emphasise the benevolence of the sovereign and the duties of the subject. Intended as instructional and didactic, these spectacles also comprised a form of social and political interaction. Richard of Maidstone's *Concordia*, for example, describes the pageantry and display of mercy that heralded Richard II's reconciliation with the city of London in August 1392.[48] As part of the procession, the king accepted the keys and sword of the city together with its surrender. The entourage then passed through Southwark, and the king stopped to pardon a criminal. Further on, the king and queen were presented with gold tablets representing the crucifixion, to promote the divine quality of mercy. At Westminster, the queen fulfilled an earlier promise to intercede with the king on behalf of the citizens of London. King Richard then warned the Londoners of the dangers of pride in their wealth, but pardoned them, restoring their keys and ancient privileges, to which the crowd, in response, cried 'Long live the king'. The Crown clearly recognised the value of promoting generalised concepts of mercy in public displays of pardon and reconciliation.[49]

Contemporary Opinion

The power of the monarch to intervene in the legal process and pardon one of his subjects had generated debate among legal theorists and parliamentary representatives at least since the late thirteenth century. Modern scholars have seized on the anxiety surrounding the king's use of military pardons, expressed in the Parliaments of the 1340s and 1350s, and located this within a broader debate on late medieval public order.[50] However, there was already a precedent for questioning the monarch's ability to issue a pardon before a trial had been held. This was not part of a public order debate, but instead

---

[47] TNA SC 8/255/12728.
[48] Richard Maidstone, *Concordia: The Reconciliation of Richard II with London*, ed. A. G. Rigg and D. R. Carlson (Kalamazoo, 2003); lines 185–90; Rigg, *Anglo-Latin Literature*, pp. 285–6.
[49] C. M. Barron, 'Chivalry, Pageantry and Merchant Culture in Medieval London', in *Heraldry, Pageantry, and Social Display in Medieval England*, ed. P. R. Coss and M. H. Keen (Woodbridge, 2002), pp. 219–41; B. A. Hanawalt and K. L. Reyerson, ed., *City and Spectacle in Medieval Europe* (Minneapolis, 1994); G. Kipling, *Enter the King: Theatre, Liturgy, and Ritual in the Medieval Civic Triumph* (Oxford, 1998); G. Kipling, 'Richard II's Sumptuous Pageants and the Idea of the Civic Triumph', in *Pageantry in the Shakespearian Theatre*, ed. D. M. Bergeron (Athens GA, 1985), pp. 83–103.
[50] See Chapter 7, pp. 100–6.

concerned the extent of the king's discretionary powers within the bounds of the legal system that operated in his name.

In the second half of the thirteenth century the need to reconcile the prerogative of pardon with the dictates of the common law was an issue discussed in *Bracton* and *Fleta*, and acknowledged in statute law. While the king's *right* to pardon was largely unchallenged, the *way* in which the prerogative was to be used certainly became the focus of extensive debate. Several scholars have read into this debate an early awareness of the obstacle presented by the discretionary pardon to the development of the common law.[51] However, this reading of the debate surely projects modern notions of the law on to medieval commentators, whose concern was focused on the way in which the king could grant pardon before trial and thus override the legal process, rather than on the existence of the prerogative itself. The need for the king to retain discretionary powers went unquestioned, and it was recognised that the prerogative could play a legitimate role in moderating the severity of the law in certain cases. The author of *Fleta*, writing in the 1290s, went as far as to claim that, in cases of death by misadventure or in self-defence, 'The king is bound, as of right, to pardon what belonged to him.'[52]

It was the instances in which a king intervened before trial, or went against the decision of a court, that caused concern. By the second half of the thirteenth century, *Bracton* was openly questioning the extent of the discretionary powers of pardon:

> But if he has slain another in felony and premeditated assault he ought never to be restored, of right or of grace, because to such no grace is to be done lest it furnish others the temerity to perpetrate similar deeds, because the ease of pardon etc. Yet the king sometimes does grace to such persons, in contravention of justice, when they have been outlawed at his suit, but only on condition that they answer all charges against them.[53]

---

51 Pollock and Maitland, *English Law*, II, 483–4; Stephen, *Criminal Law*, III, 42–4. This view was later taken up by Hurnard, who condemns medieval pardons for nullifying the deterrent force of prospective punishment (Hurnard, *Homicide*, p. vii). Krista Kesselring has already taken issue with these views, commenting that modern eyes often have difficulty seeing pardons as anything but corrupt and counterproductive, influenced as they are by post-Enlightenment assumptions about the nature and uses of punishment. She notes that Hurnard obscured the role of pardons in medieval law and society by imposing twentieth-century views of justice and punishment (Kesselring, *Mercy and* Authority, p. 17).

52 'Tenetur rex de iure quod suum fuerit perdonare' (*Fleta*, ed. Richardson and Sayles, II, 75). See also Hurnard, *Homicide*, p. 275, n. 3; *Britton*, ed. Nichols, book 1, ch. 24.

53 'Si quis autem per feloniam et in assultu præmeditato alium interfecerit, talis numquam de iure restitui deberet nec de gratia, quia cum talibus nulla gratia facienda, ne talis gratia aliis præbeat audaciam consimilia perpetrandi, quia facilitas veniæ etcetera. Facit tamen rex aliquando gratiam talibus sed contra iustitiam, cum ad sectam suam fuerint utlagati, sed tamen ut omnibus respondeant' (*Bracton*, ed. Thorne, II, 375).

Bracton's concerns were echoed in the 1278 Statute of Gloucester, which stipulated in one clause that for the first time all defendants were to put themselves 'upon the country' and stand trial before receiving pardon.[54] By insisting on the due process of the law, it seems that the intention behind the statute was to define the role of the king's pardon more precisely. The statute stipulated that grace should only be granted after the accused had been acquitted by the jury, a measure that would reconcile the use of the prerogative with the procedures of the judicial system.[55] In one sense this showed the Crown taking the lead in defining the process of pardoning more precisely, yet it also acknowledged the legitimate role of the prerogative of mercy in the legal system.[56]

The Statute of Gloucester proved to be something of a touchstone in the fourteenth century, and several attempts were made to revive its underlying principles.[57] In 1309 and 1311 concerns were raised about the number of

---

[54] It stated that no writ of enquiry into mitigating circumstances should be issued from Chancery before trial. Instead the defendant was to be held in prison until a trial could be held by the justices in eyre or Gaol Delivery. If they found that the defendant had killed accidentally or in self-defence the justices were to submit a report to the king, who would then take the defendant 'into his grace', if it pleased him to do so (*SR*, I, 49).

[55] Hurnard suggests that one aim of the statute was to halt the pardoning of those who were still fugitives. If they sought pardon they were obliged to surrender and stand trial. It seems that fugitives were perceived to be at an unfair advantage so long as friends could request a special inquisition which, if favourable, would lead to pardon, and if adverse would leave them in no worse position, whereas those who surrendered and stood trial risked their lives. The requirement that fugitives seeking pardon should appear in court would at least ensure that there was an opportunity for an appeal to be made (Hurnard, *Homicide*, pp. 281–2).

[56] F. M. Powicke, *The Thirteenth Century: 1216–1307*, 2nd edn (Oxford, 1991), pp. 371–80. Pardons were still occasionally granted on the verdict of a special inquisition after the passing of this statute, and the monarch did still pardon fugitives and outlaws who had not yet surrendered to custody, for example, *CPR, 1272–81*, pp. 282, 308. Some pardons issued after the statute covered only the outlawry of the recipient and not the felony itself, with the intention that the holder would then submit to trial for the crime, for example, TNA JUST 1/739, m. 47. In 1279 Edward also ordered Yorkshire justices to acquit those killed by accident: TNA JUST 1/1060, m. 13v; *CCR, 1272–9*, p. 213; TNA C 144/14, no. 41. It seems likely that while the king intended to by-pass the statute on certain occasions, it was thought that the proclamation of the statute would indicate that the procedure was to be tightened and thus discourage claims for pardon outside the judicial channels (Hurnard, *Homicide*, p. 285).

[57] For discussion of the efforts made by Chancery officials at stricter handling of evidence supplied as grounds for pardon, see Hurnard, *Homicide*, p. 292. *Fleta*, written c. 1290, echoed the principle of the Statute of Gloucester: 'Yet it is forbidden that a writ shall issue from the court to enquire whether a man slew another by mischance or while defending himself or in some way other than feloniously. But if such a one, lying in prison, submits to trial by jury for good or ill before the justices and it is found by the jury that he did the deed by mischance or while defending

felons who were able to secure royal pardons, and it was noted that their accusers were forced to flee to other districts in fear of reprisals from the pardoned men.[58] The Crown responded to the first of these, the so-called 'Stamford Articles' of 1309, by promising to issue pardons only in cases of excusable felony that had been recorded as such by his justices.[59] These complaints might have been given renewed impetus by the introduction of military pardons in 1294, but they followed a formula already propounded by commentators and members of the polity before the notorious military pardons had been introduced. The king's response confirmed this continuity by echoing the principles of trial before pardon. The persistence of such a sentiment was confirmed only two years later when the framers of the 1311 Ordinances again returned to the issue. They asserted that the people were aggrieved that the king, on evil advice, was giving his peace so lightly, 'against the form of the law', and therefore emboldening criminals to kill and rob others.[60] Instead they proposed that neither felon nor fugitive should be protected or defended from a charge of felony by the king's pardon, unless the case was one in which the king could give grace according to his oath, by process of law and the custom of the realm:

> no felon nor fugitive be from henceforth protected or defended from any manner of felony, by the king's charter of his peace granted to him, unless in a case where the king can give grace according to his oath, and that by process of law and custom of the realm.[61]

The reference to the coronation oath was intended to bring to mind the king's duty to pardon excusable felony.[62] A charter given for any other reason was

---

himself, then let him be sent back to gaol and, when the king is certified of the truth of the matter, he will deal graciously with him, saving the right of any other person.' 'Inhibetur tamen ne breue exeat a curia ad inquirendum si quis alium interfecit per infortunium vel se defendendo vel alio modo quam per feloniam, set si talis in prisona existens, coram iusticiariis se ponat in patriam de bono et malo, et conuincatur per patriam quod id fecit per infortunium vel se defendendo, tunc remittatur gaole et cum regi super facti veritate cercioretur, graciose dispensabit cum tali, saluo iure cuiuslibet' (*Fleta*, ed. Richardson and Sayles, p. 61).

58 *PROME*, 'Parliament of April 1309', introduction; TNA SC 8/294/14698; *SR*, I, 164, c. 28. The 1309 petition was the first to address a matter of law and order: see A. J. Verduyn, 'The Attitude of the Parliamentary Commons to Law and Order Under Edward III' (unpublished DPhil thesis, University of Oxford, 1991), p. 6.

59 'Si hom tue autre par mesaventure, ou soy defendant, ou en deverie, et ce soit trove par Record de Justices.' 'If a man kills another by misadventure, or in self-defence, or in delirium, and that be found by the record of the justices.'

60 *SR*, I, 164, c. 28.

61 'nul felon ne futif ne soit covert ne defendu desormes de nul maner de felonie, par la chartre le Roi de sa pees a luy grantes, nen autre maner si non en cas ou le Roi poet faire grace solom son serment, e ceo par proces de ley, e la custume de Realme.'

62 This interpretation was made clear in the 1328 Statute of Northampton, which

to be null and void. Again the statute sought to reconcile the use of the pardon with the process of the law and with past custom in order to curtail the unpredictable element of royal mercy.[63]

Early in Edward III's reign further legislation sought to regularise the procedure for pardoning, and to limit its use to felony attended by mitigating circumstances. Attempts were made in 1328, 1330, 1334 and 1336 to implement a clear legal procedure in such cases.[64] The 1330 statute also introduced the idea that the king had agreed to confine the issuing of pardons to sessions of Parliament. This seems to be based on a misinterpretation of the earlier Statute of Northampton, but was still present in a petition on the subject made four years later. Unsurprisingly, it was not adhered to by King Edward.[65] The 1336 statute stipulated that sureties were to be found or charters of pardon would be null and void. Such measures were concerned to enforce trial before pardon, and to bring pardoning within the scope of the judicial system. By the late 1330s, however, attention was diverted towards the particular problem of military pardons, and this dominated proposals for legislation for the next twenty years.[66] While the main aim was to curtail the use of military pardons, however, opponents continued to resort to a similar formula, requesting that henceforward pardons would only be issued in accordance with the coronation oath. The proposals for legislation made only limited headway, and by 1353 the parliamentary Commons seem to have decided on a new approach: from then on, rather than attempting to limit the use of the prerogative, efforts were focused on preventing abuses by recipients and petitioners.

Balancing Justice and Mercy

Concerns about the king's ability to balance the demands of justice and mercy were expressed in a variety of other texts. John Gower, for example,

---

repeated the stipulation that a pardon would not be granted unless the king could give it according to his oath, but went on to say that this was intended as a shorthand reference to the king's duty to pardon excusable felony: 'tiels chartres ne soient mes grantees fors qen cas ou le Roi le poet faire par son serment, cest assavoir en cas ou home tue autre soi defendant, ou par infortune'; 'that such charter shall not be granted, but only where the king may do it by his oath, that is to say, where a man slayeth another in his own defence, or by misfortune' (*SR*, I, 257).

[63] Its terms were subsequently confirmed in 1331 (*SR*, I, 264).

[64] *SR*, I, 257; *SR*, I, 264; *RPHI*, pp. 237 (18), 238 (19); *PROME*, 'Parliament of February 1334', item 3; *SR*, I, 275.

[65] The authors of the petition seem to have believed that the 1328 Statute of Northampton had already confined the granting of pardons to sessions of Parliament, but the statute in fact contains no such regulation (*SR*, I, 257, 264).

[66] See above Chapter 4, pp. 49–50.

warned that the excessive use of mercy posed a real danger to the proper execution of justice throughout the realm. In book 7 of *Confessio Amantis* he discussed the relationship between justice and mercy in the context of the virtues a king must have to rule properly. Justice is presented in terms of equity. Gower claimed that five principal points of policy for a king were truth (claimed to be most important, though treated briefly), largesse, justice, pity and chastity.[67] The confessor explains that the king must not go against the law either for love or for hate. However, throughout the discussion of pity, the real subject is the danger of excessive mercy. Gower insisted that the king is righteous if he slays in the cause of justice. Indeed, the king is obliged, in the interests of justice, to slay those who deserve it:

> Bot above alle in his noblesse
> Between the reddour and pite
> A king schal do such equite
> And sette the balance in evene.[68]

The fact that mercy must be joined to justice indicates that it is not the virtue that must take precedence in royal rule:

> And every governance is due
> To Pite: thus I mai argue
> That Pite is the foundement
> Of every kinges regiment,
> If it be medled with justice.
> Thei tuo remuen alle vice,
> And ben of vertu most vailable
> To make a kinges regne stable.[69]

It seems likely that Gower reflected the anger engendered by Richard II's continued misuse of the royal pardon and his failure to distribute the justice required of his office. The circumstances surrounding the use of the pardon in Richard's final, 'tyrannical' years certainly aroused the resentment of his political opponents: a resentment that they ultimately expressed in the

---

67 *Confessio*, book 7, lines 1782–4. [All references to *Confessio Amantis* are taken from: *Confessio Amantis*, ed. R. A. Peck, 2nd edn (Kalamazoo, 2006)]. Instead of the virtues of the Four Daughters, largesse as an aspect of mercy has displaced peace, and chastity is joined on.

68 *Confessio*, book 7, lines 3851–9; 3918–21. Gower does also make the link between the divine and royal mercy through the figure of the Virgin.

69 *Confessio*, book 7, lines 4195–4202. A similar joining of justice with equity occurs in Passus XIX of *Piers Plowman*. Here Spiritus Iusticie is the fourth seed that Grace gave Piers to sow, along with the other cardinal virtues. 'Spiritus Iusticie spareth noght to spille hem that ben gilty. ... He dide equyte to alle evenforth his power' (lines 299, 310).

charges presented against Richard at his deposition in 1399.[70] Mercy was valued and desirable, but not when it was used for selfish ends, or resulted in the failure to punish the wrongdoer. The king's use of his powers of mercy must be guided by more than a desire to demonstrate his majesty and power.

A more didactic representation of the king's dispensation of justice and mercy was evident in the Four Daughters of God allegory, which circulated in several versions throughout the Middle Ages.[71] The allegory attempted to explain that adhering to the absolute letter of the law was undesirable and that the ideal state resulted from a monarch who could balance the demands of truth and justice, mercy and peace. The arguments presented by the four daughters are easily recognisable as the age-old problem of whether it is better to adhere to the letter of law and accept the possibility of its divisiveness or whether to seek reconciliation and compromise in principle. Ultimately the debate presented in the allegories represents the question in terms of the demand for revenge versus the need for atonement. It extols the belief that allowing the transgressor to make satisfaction and be reintegrated into the community is more important than exacting the justice of the law.

One version of the Four Daughters allegory, known as *Rex et Famulus*, gives the 'kingdom' version of the parable, setting the events in an earthly kingdom where Mercy, Justice, Peace and Truth are the king's four daughters.[72] The allegory was popularised in English translations of the *Meditationes*

---

70 See Chapter 10, pp. 166–7.
71 The allegory is based on an interpretation of Psalms 83. 11. It has a long and complex lineage in Judeo-Christian literature, but its popularity in medieval literature resulted from the dissemination of the allegory in Bernard of Clairvaux's *Annuntiatione Beati Mariae, Sancti Bernardi Opera* [ed. J. Leclerc and H. Rochais, 8 vols. (Rome, 1957), V], and in the *Rex et Famulus* [printed in: Sister Mary Immaculate C. S. C, 'The Four Daughters of God in the Gesta Romanorum and the Court of Sapience', *Publications of the Modern Language Association* 57 (1942), 951–65]. Their influence was felt by means of two other works based on them: *Meditationes Vitae Christi* and *Chasteau d'Amour*. Both were translated into English, and served as sources for a number of works. [John of Caulibus, *Meditationes Vitae Christi*, ed. and trans. F. X. Taney, A. Miller and C. M. Stallings-Taney (Asheville NC, 2000); Robert Grosseteste, *Le Chateau d'Amour*, ed. and trans. J. Murray (Paris, 1918).] See also Sister Mary Immaculate, 'The Four Daughters of God', pp. 951–65; *The Middle English Translations of Robert Grosseteste's Chasteau d'Amour*, ed. K. Sajavaara, Memoires de la Société Néophilologique de Helsinki 32 (Helsinki, Société Néophilologique, 1967); H. Traver, 'The Four Daughters of God: A Mirror of Changing Doctrine', *Publications of the Modern Language Association* 40 (1925), 44–92; H. Traver, The *Four Daughters of God* (Philadelphia, 1907); T. J. Janecek, 'The Parliament of Heaven' (unpublished PhD thesis, University of Illinois, 1975); C. W. Marx, *The Devil's Rights and the Redemption in the Literature of Medieval England* (Cambridge, 1995), pp. 65–9, 100–13.
72 Bernard of Clairvaux's version of the Four Daughters allegory, in his sermon *In Festo Annuntiationis Beatae Virginis*, was replicated in later texts, referred to as the 'heaven' allegories (Bernard of Clairvaux, *Annuntiatione Beati Mariae*, p. 5). Sister

Vitae Christi and the *Chasteau d'Amour*.[73] The substance of the four daughters' pleas touches on matters of salvation, yet essentially they are concerned with who shall have dominance in the king's court, and the effect that their sister's requests would have on the kingdom as a whole. The subtext of the allegory rests in the need to secure peace in the realm and for the transgressor to achieve atonement so that the community may enjoy peace. The demands of Justice and Truth are not presented in the end as righteous, but destructive. The king realises that to protect peace he must show mercy and pardon the wrongdoer.

The version of the allegory presented by Langland infused the poem with the legal terminology of the fourteenth century. In *Piers Plowman*, Peace explains to Justice that she is going to welcome all those who are being released from Hell because:

> Love, that is my lemman, swiche lettres he me sente
> That Mercy, my suster, and I mankynde sholde save,
> And that God hath forgiven and graunted me, Pees, and Mercy
> To be mannes meynpernour for evermore after.[74]

She then shows the appropriate patent. The licence that Love has given to Peace to be man's mainpernor is represented as a formal legal document. This passage employs the specific legal terminology of the king's courts in its use of the word 'meynpernour' (meaning guarantor, literally 'hand taker'). It also emphasises the iconic significance of the written, sealed text.[75] The allegories seem to reflect a contemporary opinion that royal power would be weakened if it lacked the ability to be merciful and exercise the prerogative to pardon. Yet the fear still persisted that the king would eventually be seen as powerless if he did not rule consistently under the terms of the law. The rationalisation for the ultimate choice of mercy is given by Peace:

Mary Immaculate, 'The Four Daughters of God', pp. 955–6, analyses the differences between the *Rex et Famulus* and Bernard's version, and the possible influence of another version by Stephen of Tourney.

73 Sources of the heaven allegories are found in the following texts: *Piers Plowman*, B-text, XVIII, lines 112–228; *Blessed Lyf of Jesu Christ*, ed. Powell, pp. 14–19; *Vices and Virtues*, ed. Holthausen; pp. 111–21; *Life of Christ*, in 'The Four Daughters of God: A New Version', ed. Klinefelter, pp. 90–5; *Charter of the Abbey of the Holy Ghost*, ed. Horstman, I, 337–62; *Castle of Perseverence*, ed. Eccles, lines 3129–3649. For kingdom allegories, see *Gesta Romanorum*, ed. Herrtage, pp. 132–5; *Court of Sapience*, ed. Harvey, lines 176–903.

74 B-text, XVIII, lines 181–4.

75 The metaphorical references to such charters were echoed in other contexts. For example, they appear in the 'charters of Christ' theme, in which the New Covenant made by Christ at the Last Supper is etched as a sealed document onto his own crucified body: see C. W. Bynum, *The Resurrection of the Body in Western Christianity, 200–1336* (New York, 1995); J. A. Keen, *The Charters of Christ and* Piers Plowman: *Documenting Salvation* (Oxford, 2002).

Justice's most fundamental obligation is to ensure order in the realm. There-fore the demands of both sides are met when the king turns to pardon as a means for maintaining the integrity of society. Langland's adaptation of the Four Daughters allegory for a fourteenth-century audience still promoted the sense that royal mercy was a valuable safeguard, and one that should be used wisely by the monarch.

Discussion of the works of authors such as Gower and Langland will always prompt questions of readership and audience. Scholars have long accepted that these ideas disseminated among a public extending from elite courtly circles to the merchant and gentry classes, who were participating in the fourteenth-century political community in increasing numbers. More recently, several historians and literary critics have suggested that we need to expand this audience further, to include a much broader section of society.[76] Questions of audience and of the ways in which people received, adapted and appropriated ideas of justice and mercy can be explored through an examination of the fourteenth-century general pardons; these pardons are therefore the focus of the second section of this book.

---

[76] A. Middleton, 'The Idea of Public Poetry in the Reign of Richard II', *Speculum* 53 (1978), 94–114; Coleman, *English Literature*; J. Wogan-Browne, N. Watson, A. Taylor and R. Evans, ed., *The Idea of the Vernacular: An Anthology of Middle English Literary Theory* (Exeter, 1999); Watts, 'Pressure of the Public', p. 162.

Part II
General Pardons

CHAPTER SIX

Procedures

The individual pardons considered so far were obtained by the exercise of the king's grace in each separate case. The supplicant therefore relied on a royal justice or an influential patron to recommend a grant of mercy. In contrast, group pardons (political amnesties, military service pardons, and remissions of debts) and general pardons, were crucially different in that the initiative was taken by the Crown, usually with the advice of Parliament rather than an individual intercessor. The pardon was therefore issued in the form of a royal ordinance or statute, which informed the wider community of the range of offences that were to be pardoned, and the procedure they were to follow in order to obtain their own copy. These grants of mercy often had an immediate and important purpose for the recipients. Moreover they demonstrate that the royal pardon might occupy a central role in medieval political life.

By the outset of the fourteenth century the issuing of royal pardons had become a familiar process to members of the political community. The decision to bestow the king's mercy on an individual or particular group was often taken on the advice of Parliament, and, in certain cases, the act carried with it clear political significance. Throughout the century, the subject of pardon repeatedly found its way on to the parliamentary agenda in a variety of contexts. Clearly, not all of the pardons discussed in Parliament had a wider political significance. Standard legal cases from the lower courts were on occasion adjourned into Parliament, although the individuals involved were not necessarily members of the polity, or contesting matters of national importance.[1] The presence of such cases on the parliamentary agenda demonstrated the judicial nature of these assemblies, and reinforced the status of Parliament as the highest court of appeal.[2] Such pardons were often issued as a matter of course, the king simply endorsing a petition presented on behalf of the supplicant, whether it had been put before him in Parliament or in private audience, or simply forwarded by his royal justices. However, the

---

[1] See, for example, *PROME*, 'Edward I: petition 2', item 1.
[2] J. G. Edwards, '"Justice" in Early English Parliaments', in *Historical Studies of the English Parliament*, ed. E. B. Fryde and E. Millar (Cambridge, 1970), I, 280–97; R. G. Davies and J. H. Denton, ed., *The English Parliament in the Middle Ages* (Manchester, 1981), pp. 34–87.

wider import of such cases was usually limited, and as the status of Parliament evolved, the pressing business of the realm inevitably and increasingly sidelined them from the political agenda. Conversely, not all politically significant pardons were put forward to Parliament for consideration, although by at least the middle of the century most grants of mercy were being discussed by the Lords and shire representatives.[3]

One such group of politically significant pardons were those issued in response to acts of defiance committed by opponents of the king (referred to here as 'political amnesties'). Such pardons were usually issued at the initiative of the king in Parliament, and often concerned members of the political elite who had been involved in co-ordinating an opposition faction or instigating an act of rebellion.[4] By at least the 1320s, they had come to play a more central part in the process of political reconciliation than ever before. This represented something of an evolution away from the traditional process of reconciliation defined in feudal terms and centred on a re-enactment of homage and fealty. The reconciliation embodied in Magna Carta, for example, placed little emphasis on the notion of pardon, and the chroniclers of Coggeshall, Dunstable and Barnwell all agreed that the essential features of the peace were verbal, while the charter was simply confirmatory.[5] However, the political amnesties of the first half of the fourteenth century, discussed below, increasingly drew on common law concepts and evolved to occupy a prominent place in the act of reconciliation. Their role was then in turn assumed by the general pardon in the second half of the century.

Another reason for issuing a group pardon was to bolster the ranks of the royal army in anticipation of a military campaign. Edward I was the first

---

3   Before 1339 the parliament rolls are of limited use as an index of political debate, and so several of the politically important pardons issued by Edward I and Edward II, such as the pardon of the recalcitrant earls in 1297, or the revocation of the pardon granted to the opponents of the Despensers in 1322, do not appear in the record: see W. M. Ormrod, 'Agenda for Legislation, 1322–c. 1340', *EHR* 105 (1990), 1–33 (p. 3).

4   There were certain pardons issued to prominent individuals that were of a more routine nature, and these should perhaps be classed in a sub-category of their own. For instance, a case of entry on a manor without the king's licence was discussed in Parliament in 1302, and involved the bishop of Bath and Wells (*PROME*, 'Edward I: Petition 2', item 10). In 1315 the executors of the late major of London obtained a writ of pardon (*PROME*, 'Parliament of 1315', item 222). In 1384 the earl of Northumberland was pardoned for neglect of the castle of Berwick (Walsingham, *HA*, II, 118).

5   W. L. Warren, *King John* (New York, 1961), pp. 252–6; *Magna Carta*, ed. Holt, pp. 163–6; *Radulphi Abbatis de Coggeshal Opera quae supersunt curante Alf. Jhno. Dunkin, nunc primum edita* (Noviomago, 1856), p. 172; *Annales Monastici*, ed. H. R. Luard, RS 36 (London, 1864–9), III, 43. Holt stresses that the peace 'was reinforced not by bonds of parchment, but by the solemnity of an oath …' although he still views the document as an important legal record (*Magna Carta*, ed. Holt, pp. 166, 168).

king to use the pardon in such a way when, in 1294, he issued a proclamation that invited any man charged with felony, whether detained in prison or at large, to volunteer for paid service in the army bound for Gascony.[6] As time went on, the protracted warfare of the fourteenth century meant that these pardons could have been useful at almost any time, but in fact they were only ever used in preparation for a few specific campaigns.[7] At such times indicted men could obtain a conditional pardon in return for service in the retinue of military leaders such as the Black Prince or the earl of Lancaster. These pardons were conditional on completion of military service, and usually had to be 'proved' in court before being validated. Military service pardons were theoretically available as individual pardons, to any suppli-cant who could successfully petition the monarch, on condition that they were able to serve in his army. However, by far the majority were in practice granted under proclamations issued by the king as a method of recruitment for specific campaigns.

In the latter half of Edward II's reign a third category of pardons emerged in a primarily financial context to remit judicial and feudal fines (discussed below). The parliamentary Commons had begun to consistently oppose the imposition of such payments, and the levying of ancient feudal dues was becoming increasingly anachronistic. In 1316, the first remission of this type pardoned all outstanding fines imposed before 20 November 1291.[8] However, while the Crown issued remissions of these dues, they were given of the king's grace and his authority to enforce them remained unquestioned.[9] This type of financial remission was to become another important element of the general pardons that emerged in the later fourteenth century. Importantly, the negotiation of these remissions in Parliament also serves to demonstrate a fundamental point about the nature of relations between the Crown and the political community. While the royal government consistently granted these remissions when presented with a petition from the parliamentary Commons, it did so on each occasion as an act of grace – an act, therefore, that could be overturned by the authority of the Crown alone: it was not conceding to any permanent diminution of royal power.

The 'general pardon' emerged as a new and distinct form of royal mercy at

---

6   The standard letter patent of pardon issued under this grant was copied into the pardon roll, and dated 11 November 1294: *Rôles gascons*, nos. 3032–3, and *passim* (12 June); TNA C 67/26, 27, 28A. The letter of pardon referred to all indictments or appeals by approvers of homicides, robberies and other crimes, and a diverse list of transgressions against the king's peace, as well as offences of the forest: TNA C 67/26 mm. 4, 6, 7–8.
7   See Appendix 2.
8   *CPR, 1313–17*, p. 532. Such amnesties covered all the inhabitants of a named county or town. Accordingly, their issue did not significantly increase the overall number of pardons granted in the particular year.
9   Harriss, *Public Finance*, pp. 208–508. See Chapter 7, pp. 100–6.

the end of Edward III's reign. Unlike the individual and group pardons, this was a comprehensive amnesty, which offered protection to all of the king's subjects. This form of pardon was designed to strike a chord with the political community, particularly at times of dissent and disharmony within the echelons of government. Despite the prominent role it came to assume in the political culture of the later Middle Ages, the emergence of general pardons in the fourteenth century has gone largely unacknowledged.[10] Legal theorists and historians of the law noted the place of the general pardon in the evolution of the medieval judicial system, but the political context of these pardons, in the aftermath of governmental crises on the scale of the Good Parliament of 1376 or the 1381 Peasants' Revolt, warrants attention.[11] These pardons provided tangible evidence of the Crown's obligation to reconcile with its subjects. As public acts of mercy, they were to become a trademark of the English Crown. The work of Edward Powell has demonstrated that by the time of Henry V's reign, general pardons had become an important means of reconciling political society to the government, in a public display of their commitment to the regime.[12] The cost of the pardons lent them an exclusivity that suggests they were granted with the expectation of a favour in return; the recipient would provide military service or ensure the smooth running of the Crown's administrative system in the shires. Powell also convincingly maintained that the success of Henry V's pardons, compared to those issued under different regimes, was in large part owing to his ability to present them as an assertion of royal authority rather than an admission of weakness. General pardons could be combined with remedial legislation in a constructive policy of reconciliation. This impression has been reinforced by John Watts's examination of monarchical ideology: to be deployed effectively, the pardon needed to be seen to issue from a king who was acting on his own initiative, independent of external pressures.[13] In the second half of the fourteenth century, this form of royal mercy was still a novel expe-

---

[10] The only work to discuss the political context of fourteenth-century general pardons has been: W. M. Ormrod, ' "Fifty Glorious Years": Edward III and the First English Royal Jubilee', *Medieval History*, n.s. 1 (2002), 13–20; C. M. Barron, 'The Tyranny of Richard II', *BIHR* 41 (1968), 1–18 (pp. 7–9); H. Lacey, '"Mercy and Truth Preserve the King": Richard II's Use of the Royal Pardon in 1397 and 1398', in *Fourteenth Century England IV*, ed. J. S. Hamilton (Woodbridge, 2006), pp. 124–35; H. Lacey, 'Grace for the Rebels: The Role of the Royal Pardon in the Peasants' Revolt of 1381', *Journal of Medieval History* 34 (2008), 36–63.

[11] Bellamy, *Criminal Trial*, pp. 144–8; A. L. Brown, *The Governance of Late Medieval England 1272–1461* (London, 1989), pp. 137–9; Bellamy, *Public Order*, pp 191–8. For the 1377 and 1381 pardon, see below, Chapters 8 and 9.

[12] Powell, *Criminal Justice*, pp. 229–46; Powell, 'Law and Order', pp. 53–74; Storey, *House of Lancaster*, pp. 215–16. Powell's approach is endorsed by Musson and Ormrod, *Evolution*, p. 82. See also Krista Kesselring's recent work on the sixteenth century: Kesselring, *Mercy and Authority*.

[13] Watts, *Henry VI*, pp. 57–9.

dient. In the difficult political circumstances from the 1370s to the 1390s the government faced direct criticism from the expanding political community. The first general pardons demonstrated some awareness, on the part of the government, that it would now have to reconcile a broader cross-section of the population to its authority.

The first general pardon was granted on 22 February 1377, to mark the completion of Edward III's jubilee year. It incorporated many of the characteristics of the amnesties on judicial and feudal fines that the government had been issuing since 1316.[14] The 1377 general pardon, however, was a new development. Not only had the terminology evolved; the statute recorded that the king had 'generally pardoned' his people and the *Anonimalle Chronicle* mentioned the grant of a 'general charter of pardon', but the material clauses of this charter had also changed.[15] This grant was more expansive in scope than any previous example, covering 'all manner of felonies' as well as all trespass and offences against the royal prerogative, although it excluded treason, murder, rape of women and common thefts. In addition, the recipient was still excused offences against the king's feudal, statutory and administrative rights, such as marrying the widow of a tenant-in-chief, buying and selling land without his licence, or failing to pay debts to the Crown. It was declared that this pardon would be open to any individual who wished to purchase a copy, and the Chancery clerks duly recorded the names of each recipient on a newly created roll, which they kept separate from the main patent roll series.[16] All future general pardons would follow this procedure. The context of this grant is discussed further in Chapter 8 below, but it is important to note that the 1377 pardon was the first of its kind.[17]

---

[14] These amnesties had been increasing in scope, and by 1362 the amnesty used the terms 'pardon a sa dite commune generalment' and 'pleine pardon' (*SR*, I, 376–7).

[15] 'pardonez gereralment' (*SR*, I, 397); 'une chartre generale de pardoune' (*Anonimalle Chronicle*, ed. Galbraith, p. 95). J. G. Bellamy dates the introduction of the general pardon to the late fourteenth century, although he suggests that the 1327 political amnesty also has a claim. A. L. Brown places its arrival in the mid-fourteenth century, but does not specify a particular pardon (Bellamy, *Criminal Trial*, p. 144, n. 51; Brown, *Governance*, pp. 137–9).

[16] The standard fee for a general pardon, including the 2s. payable to Chancery, stood at 18s. 4d. Payment was made after the engrossment, usually in the Hanaper but sometimes in the Wardrobe. However, if the defendant could not afford the fees, or had given the king good service, the fee for the seal might be waived: see Maxwell-Lyte, *Great Seal*, p. 332; Wilkinson, *Chancery*, pp. 59–64; Brown, 'Great Seal', pp. 136–55.

[17] TNA C 67/28B onwards. Future general pardons continued to exclude treason, murder, rape of women and common thefts, and to encompass all other felony, trespass, contempt, evasion or abuse of the law committed before a certain date, together with any resulting sentences of outlawry, confiscation or fine. Bellamy asserts that sixteenth-century general pardons contained longer lists of exceptions. That of 1529 exempted murder, robbery, burglary, felonious theft of over 20s. value,

Significantly, it was the king, rather than his justices or an individual defendant, who publicly took the initiative in offering a general pardon. It was in the forum of Parliament that the precise terms of the grant were then formulated. A royal representative would indicate to Parliament the king's willingness to show mercy to his people. In 1377 this suggestion was made in Bishop Houghton's opening sermon to Parliament; in 1381 the point was conveyed by the treasurer, Sir Hugh Segrave, in his rehearsal of the reasons for summoning Parliament.[18] Presented with such an offer, the parliamentary Commons would submit a petition requesting a general pardon, and draw up an appropriate template, with little delay.[19] The Crown usually amended this template, often substantially altering its terms, before finally sanctioning the pardon. This procedure cast the Commons in the role of petitioners for pardon, and they tended to justify their requests for general pardon with reference to the suffering of the 'common people'. In 1377 this suffering and the new demands for taxation, as well as the need to mark the completion of the king's jubilee year, were all mentioned in their petition. The resulting statute made no reference to the tax, but it did acknowledge the wars, plague and famine with which the king's subjects had been afflicted.[20] The Crown often made the final grant conditional on the Commons' consent to taxation: in 1377 they agreed to the first of the poll taxes, and in 1381 to a wool subsidy.[21] In 1398, at the height of Richard II's 'tyranny', the terms of the pardon were designed to force the Commons to concede a subsidy; the pardon, it stipulated, would be annulled if Parliament made any 'let or disturbance contrary to the grant of the said subsidy of wools'.[22] The terms of such pardons were therefore the subject of negotiation, but the grant itself remained a matter of grace; they were not, in any sense, concessions extorted by an antagonistic parliamentary Commons. On occasion, the terms of the pardon also named particular individuals who were to be refused pardon; in 1377, for instance, William Wykeham, bishop of Winchester, was singled out for his opposition to the Crown. The statutes of pardon therefore served to publicise the names of those who were to be denied royal favour.[23] Ultimately, the Crown had an obligation to reconcile the expanding political community to its authority,

---

arson of houses, rape and escape of felons from custody. Piracy was then added in the 1540s, witchcraft in 1566: see Bellamy, *Criminal Trial*, p. 145.

[18] For Houghton's speech, see *PROME*, 'Parliament of January 1377', items 6–11; for Segrave's speech, see *PROME*, 'Parliament of 1381', item 8.

[19] *PROME*, 'Parliament of January 1377', item 24; *PROME*, 'Parliament of 1381', items 31–4; R. B. Dobson, *Peasants' Revolt of 1381*, 2nd edn (London, 1983), pp. 331–3.

[20] *SR*, I, 396–7.

[21] *PROME*, 'Parliament of January 1377', item 19; *PROME*, 'Parliament of 1381', item 39.

[22] TNA C 67/30, m. 3.

[23] *SR*, I, 397. In 1398 fifty unnamed persons were to be excluded from the pardon (see Chapter 10, pp. 164–5).

and the general pardon was an effective means of signalling this, but it would do so only in the form of an unforced dispensation of royal mercy.

For the recipients of general pardons, the letter they were issued only ever protected them against prosecution in the name of the king. Strictly speaking, the recipient of a letter of pardon was meant to appear with it in court in order to allow anyone to initiate a private prosecution against them. The court was also to verify that the holder of the pardon was indeed the person named in the indictments. Finally, all those with charges against them had to give security for good behaviour.[24] In the aftermath of the Peasants' Revolt several cases concerning the rising were adjourned into King's Bench in order to rubber-stamp pardons in this way. However, a surprisingly low number of people who purchased general pardons actually presented them in the royal courts. In 1377 only fifteen such instances can be identified in King's Bench, although 2,439 pardons were issued in total.[25] This might in part be explained by the death of Edward III in June of 1377, although the minority government of Richard II was quick to issue a confirmation of the pardon. For the Peasants' Revolt general pardon Andrew Prescott found a total of forty cases out of a possible 2,910 in which such a charter was presented, and after the general pardon of 1398, 134 can be identified on the rolls from the 4,196 issued.[26]

Given these low figures, it seems that a large number of general pardons were being purchased as a precaution, and were never actually presented in court. For many, purchase of a pardon might have been regarded as protection against malicious accusation, which never in fact materialised; it is possible, of course, that the mere act of obtaining a pardon was enough to prompt an out-of-court settlement in some instances. Certainly, not everyone who purchased a pardon did so because of outstanding criminal charges against them. Some letters of general pardon were purchased to avoid charges under the penalties of the eyre, for the escape of prisoners from gaol, for example. Charters were obtained by prelates, temporal peers, religious and civic

---

[24] *SR*, I, 257–61. Bellamy suggests that it was also common for the justices of the peace to be ordered to hold an inquisition to ascertain the reputation of the recipient (Bellamy, *Public Order*, p. 194).

[25] TNA KB 27/465, mm. 3, 7v, 10; KB 27/466, mm. 1, 1v, 11v, 13v, 18v, 19, 19v; KB 27/467, mm. 9, 10v; KB 27/468, m. 16v; KB 27/ 469, m. 23v; KB 27/548, m. 16v.

[26] A. J. Prescott, 'Judicial Records of the Rising of 1381' (unpublished PhD thesis, University of London, 1984), p. 355. 1398: TNA KB 27/547, mm. 16, 16v, 17, 17v, 19v (two), 21, 21v, 22v, 23 (two), 24, 24v, 25 (two), 26, 26v; KB 27/ 548, mm. 1, 1v, 2, 2v, 3 (four), 4, 5v (two), 6v (two), 7, 7v, 8v (two), 10, 10v, 11v, 12 (two), 13, 13v, 14v (two), 15, 17 (two), 17v, 18, 20 (two); KB 27/549, mm. 1, 3 (two), 3v (two), 4 (two), 4v, 5, 5v, 6 (two), 6v, 7 (two), 7v (two), 8, 8v (two), 9 (two), 9v (two), 10 (two), 10v (two), 11, 12 (two), 14 (two), 14v (two), 15, 20v, 21, 22 (two), 22v (two); KB 27/ 550, mm. 1 (two), 1v, 2v (two), 4, 4v, 5v, 8v, 9, 9v, 13 (two), 13v (two), 14, 14v, 16, 16v (four), 18v, 20, 20v (two), 21, 26 (two), 27, 30, 30v; KB 27/551, mm. 1v, 2, 4 (two), 7, 8, 11, 15, 18.

corporations, and groups of trustees and executors, for whom the clauses relating to crime were of least interest. Their aim was to avoid inconvenience and financial loss should royal officers investigate their business transactions. Thus a group of trustees covered themselves by buying a pardon, and then produced it when exchequer officials confiscated land that they had granted without the king's licence.[27] When a general pardon was available, it was quicker and much cheaper to obtain one than to apply for a licence to buy or sell land, submit to an official enquiry into its value, and pay a fine relative to this valuation, as well as fees for royal warrants and letters patent. For others among the polity, it was politically astute to purchase a pardon, and thus be seen to support a rapprochement with government. For these people there would be little need to prove the pardon in the royal courts. General pardons therefore represented something more than an admission of the limits of the judicial system.[28] Indeed, the strategic issue of a general pardon allowed the political community to symbolise reconciliation and demonstrate their support for the regime. It is this interaction of government with the polity, and, through the pardon, with the rest of society, that will be addressed in the chapters that follow.

---

[27] Storey asserts that the Abbot Wheathamstead purchased a general pardon for his abbey of St Albans in 1452 'for greater security', and in 1458 to avoid the legal consequences of thieves escaping from his gaol (Storey, *House of Lancaster*, p. 213). See also TNA E 404/57, no. 144.

[28] Bellamy, *Public Order*, p. 194. Storey argues that 'the general pardon was to some extent an admission of the failure of the legal system to bring accused people to trial' (Storey, *House of Lancaster*, pp. 215–16). However, Powell argues that pardons, at least those issued by Henry V, were not intended to punish crime but to reconcile the disaffected to the Crown (Powell, 'Restoration', pp. 67–8).

CHAPTER SEVEN

The Evolution Of Group Pardons

Political Amnesties

Throughout the fourteenth century the issue of an amnesty was becoming an increasingly important part of the act of political reconciliation. While there was no absolute shift away from the idea of reconciliation through a renewal of homage, there does seem to have been a change in emphasis away from the idea that the offender was being restored into the feudal relationship with his lord, and towards the idea that he was being readmitted into the king's peace. There were, of course, further nuances in the message that the grant of an amnesty could convey. In the aftermath of a rebellion on the scale of the Barons' Wars in the 1260s, the grant of a political amnesty could be used to rebuild the authority of the king. This was an authority based on a working relationship with the political community, and so a public act of reconciliation placated both parties and allowed them to collaborate in the running of government. The Crown could also use the grant of an amnesty to remind a recalcitrant vassal, such as the Welsh prince Llywelyn ap Gruffydd, of their place, or emphasise the guilt of the recipient in cases where the blame was disputed. Importantly, an opposition faction such as the Lords Appellants in 1387 could also, in theory, indemnify themselves against future reprisal. Central to such pardons, however, was the obligation the Crown owed to its subjects to reconcile them to its authority and to allow them to share in the benefits of its grace.

As the Crown, usually with the advice of Parliament, took the initiative in issuing these political amnesties, most were given statutory form and proclaimed in each county in order to inform the inhabitants of their availability. However, the exact procedure for obtaining pardon under the Crown's terms was not clearly defined. The 1266 Dictum of Kenilworth referred to royal officers authorised to receive supplicants back into the king's peace, which they were to do within forty days of the issue of the ordinance.[1] Whether all those who were received then pursued their claim by purchasing

---

[1] The exact procedure here is uncertain, for the statute merely alludes to 'all persons received to the peace by those that had commission thereunto ...' (*SR*, I, 17). Those most likely to have been commissioned were probably the chief justices of the King's Bench and Common Pleas.

their own copy of the pardon from Chancery is unclear.[2] The names of those pardoned were certainly recorded in the patent rolls, but they were entered under a copy of the relevant letter patent in long lists, rather than in separate entries with their own date and note of warranty. In some cases, the lists of names ran to several pages: two days after the Ordainers had apologised for the murder of Piers Gaveston, in 1313, pardons were issued to some 500 lesser offenders, a high proportion of whom were Lancastrian dependants.[3] In 1327, when the king in Parliament issued a comprehensive pardon, covering the period 24 September 1326 to 1 February 1327 (from Edward III's arrival into the realm until his coronation), to those who had supported his seizure of power, 945 names were submitted and granted pardon. A further 234 were given pardon on condition that they joined the forthcoming expedition against the Scots, and 175 of those who had held Caerphilly castle against the king and queen were also pardoned.[4]

By the beginning of the fourteenth century, the possession of a letter of pardon had become an important guarantee of future protection for those who had opposed the Crown.[5] The physical display of remorse and forgiveness, and particularly the kiss of peace, had been a feature of earlier displays of reconciliation.[6] In 1215 peace had been restored by a renewal of feudal homage on the part of the baronial opposition; King John formally received the barons back into a private feudal bond with the Crown. The amnesty that was then written into the penultimate clause of Magna Carta confirmed this rapprochement. By 1266, the Dictum of Kenilworth gave a more prominent role to the notion that individuals would receive royal pardon for their opposition. Its terms envisaged the rebels being publicly received back into the king's peace. It stated that the king would pardon all those who had 'committed any wrong or offence against him or his royal Crown' as long as they presented themselves before a royal officer authorised to receive them

---

2   It may be that this list of names was one drawn up by government at the time the grant was made, to make known the individuals who could receive a charter if they sought one. Alternatively, the lists could perhaps have been those compiled by the officers charged with receiving supplicants back into the king's peace, and then submitted to Chancery. However, if the supplicants wished to obtain their own copy of the pardon, they would still need to collect it from Chancery. The lists could therefore have been compiled by Chancery as a record of all those who actually sought out a charter. If this was the case then the Chancery clerks were presumably keeping a memorandum of pardons granted under a particular amnesty, and then writing it up in fair copy.

3   *Foedera*, II, 230–3; *CPR, 1313–17*, pp. 21–6.

4   *CPR, 1327–30*, pp. 43–57, 115–23; *CPR, 1327–30*, pp. 110–13, 161–3; *CPR, 1327–30*, pp. 13, 37–9.

5   A. Musson provides a detailed discussion of the growth in legal consciousness between 1215 and 1381 (Musson, *Medieval Law*, passim).

6   K. Petkov, *The Kiss of Peace: Ritual, Self and Society in the High and Late Medieval West* (Leiden, 2003).

within the next forty days.[7] As an official legal document the statute had to be carefully worded, but the Crown was also sensitive to the fact that it was intended for public consumption. The phrasing makes it clear that the king's peace was a specific state into which the offenders would only be readmitted if they took appropriate steps. Their guilt was emphasised, but while their rebellion had placed them outside the king's peace the onus for future action lay with them: unless they sought reconciliation they could not benefit from a bestowal of royal mercy. This emphasis was intentional; in other statutes of the period the king would actively 'take' the defendant 'into his grace, if it please him'.[8] This language therefore promoted the attempt that was being made to rebuild the authority of the Crown after the actions of the barons had presented such a fundamental challenge. It did so in terms that laid stress on the act of readmission into the protection of the common law rather than back into a private feudal bond.

The act of reconciliation between Edward I and Llywelyn ap Gruffydd in 1277 again involved both a renewal of fealty by Llywelyn, in order to assuage his defiance of Edward's lordship, and the grant of a pardon to forgive his act of treason against the Crown. Chronicle accounts of the reconciliation centred on the physical display of remorse and forgiveness. According to the Bury St Edmunds chronicler, Llywelyn 'submitted unconditionally his life, limbs, worldly honours and everything else to the will and judgement of the king', who 'gave Llywelyn the kiss of peace and brought him to London to negotiate the terms of the peace and its confirmation'.[9] While the chronicle accounts might be expected to dwell on the dramatic and ceremonial events, rather than the legal aspect of granting a pardon, they were, in the four-teenth century, giving a more prominent role to the charter of pardon itself. Knighton, writing at the end of the fourteenth century, suggested that Llywelyn's pardon was presented in a ceremony in which he prostrated himself at the king's feet and submitted to Edward's authority. The word Knighton uses here is *pardonavit*, but it must be remembered that the chronicler was writing sometime between 1378 and 1396, and seems to be using the precise and legalistic terminology of the later fourteenth century. On this occasion Edward's victory had given him a dominant position, and the public display of reconciliation therefore reinforced his status as the ultimate arbitrator and fount of royal justice.

Central to these thirteenth-century amnesties was the protection they afforded the recipient from the king taking any revenge in the future. In 1215 the Magna Carta amnesty remitted and pardoned any ill-will, grudge and rancour that had arisen between the parties since the time of the quarrel, and

---

7   The exact procedure here is uncertain: the statute merely alludes to 'all persons received to the peace by those that had commission thereunto' (*SR*, I, 17).
8   'face le Rei sa grace si lui plest' (*SR*, I, 49).
9   *Knighton's Chronicle*, ed. Martin, p. 272; *Bury St Edmunds*, ed. Gransden, p. 64.

the Dictum of Kenilworth promised that the king would not take vengeance on the offenders or punish them for past wrongs or offences.[10] The amnesty Edward I issued to his marshal and constable in 1297 again released the earls and their followers from 'all manner of rancour and indignation which we [Edward] had conceived against them'.[11] It seems that the earls were anxious to secure these protections; the document *De Tallagio non concedendo*, which is assumed to contain the demands they put before Parliament on 30 September 1297, contains a guarantee of pardon.[12] Even if they were putting pressure on the king to grant the amnesty, the authors still recognised the importance of such an act, and the king's authority to bestow it.

The need for a safeguard against future retaliation on the part of the Crown continued to be of paramount concern throughout the fourteenth century. In 1388, after the Lords Appellant had launched their wholesale attack on the minority government of Richard II, they attempted to cover themselves by drawing up a pardon that would excuse them 'all acts done against the appellees'. These acts more specifically comprised the execution of a number of royal favourites, men such as Nicholas Brembre and Robert Tresilian, as well as several other chamber knights and lesser royal officials, who were blamed for the failings of the minority administration.[13] On this occasion Richard's role was reduced to a formality and his youth and the evil counsel that had led him astray were emphasised to avoid laying blame directly at his feet.[14] Of course, Richard himself later used this allusion to

---

10 Clause 62. 'Et omnes malas voluntates, indignaciones, et rancores, ortos inter nos et homines nostros, clericos et laicos, a tempore discordie, plene omnibus remisimus et condonavimus' *Magna Carta*, ed. Holt, p. 337. 'Dictum: Ita quod nullo modo nullaque causa vel occasione, propter hujusmodi preteritas injurias vel offensas, in eosdem nullam exercet ulcionem; aut ipsius penam vite, membri, carceris, vel exilii, aut pecunie inferat, vel vindicatum' (*SR*, I, 13).

11 *SR*, I, 124; *Bury St Edmunds*, ed. Gransden, p. 141. See Prestwich, *Crisis of 1297–8*; J. G. Edwards, '"Confirmatio Cartarum" and the Baronial Grievances in 1297', *EHR* 58 (1943), 147–71; H. Rothwell, 'The Confirmation of the Charters, 1297', *EHR* 60 (1945), 16–35; R. W. Kaeuper, 'Royal Finances and the Crisis of 1297', in *Order and Innovation in the Middle Ages: Essays in Honour of J. R. Strayer*, ed. W. C. Jordan, B. McNab and T. F. Ruiz (Princeton, 1976), pp. 103–10.

12 *SR*, I, 125. At the Parliament that opened on 8 July 1297, the king received the archbishop of Canterbury into his grace: see Walsingham, *HA*, I, 66.

13 Robert Tresilian and Nicholas Brembre, close associates of the king, were executed. Simon Burley, John Beauchamp, John Salisbury and James Berners, all Richard's chamber knights, were also executed, as were two royal officials, John Blake and Thomas Usk. Alexander Neville, archbishop of York and Thomas Rushook, bishop of Chichester, the king's confessor, were sentenced to the loss of their temporalities. Finally, six judges were exiled to Ireland: see *PROME*, 'Parliament of February 1388', items 35, 37, 38–9; *Westminster Chronicle*, ed. Hector and Harvey, pp. 314–32; *Knighton's Chronicle*, ed. Martin, pp. 442–50.

14 *SR*, II, 47–8; *Knighton's Chronicle*, ed. Martin, pp. 504–5; *Westminster Chronicle*, ed. Hector and Harvey, pp. 296–306; *Adam Usk*, ed. Given-Wilson, pp. 9–10.

his youth to annul these pardons in the trials of the two leading appellants, which took place in 1397. Throughout the fourteenth century, then, political amnesties continued to include a clause pardoning the recipient all rancour that the king had conceived against the offenders, theoretically providing security against any possibility of retribution by the monarch or by his heirs in the future.

The other main clause of these amnesties pardoned the perpetrators all offences committed during the period of dispute. In 1313, for example, the amnesty extended to Thomas of Lancaster and his adherents referred to the crimes of bearing arms against the peace of the king, entering into confederacies, forcing entry into towns or castles, or besieging them, and taking prisoners.[15] They were always specific to crimes committed as a result of the particular disturbance, the 1327 amnesty stating categorically that it covered only the offences stipulated, and not any other unrelated acts of trespass or felony.[16]

In certain situations such grants also served to emphasise the guilt of the recipient, while at the same time reconciling them with government. The amnesty granted to the Ordainers by Edward II on 16 October 1313, for example, sought to suggest that while their execution of the king's favourite, Piers Gaveston, had been illegal, the king's pardon would absolve them and remove the threat of due punishment under the law. The terms of this amnesty were legally precise. Rather than alluding to the 'king's peace' it was clear that no one was to be appealed for the death of Piers Gaveston, nor to be brought to judgment by the Crown, 'nor by any other [person] at our suit, nor at the suit of any other whomsoever, in our court nor elsewhere'.[17] Its precise legal phrasing was certainly prompted by the complex negotiations involved in the case, but it does perhaps signal an evolution in the form of the amnesty, towards a document that drew on the vocabulary and concepts of the common law. In this particular case, as May McKisack pointed out, there had been some uncertainty over the legal position of those who killed Gaveston, and so it was of particular importance for Edward to emphasise the guilt of the Ordainers.[18] If the Ordinances were still in force, Gaveston was an outlaw and could therefore be executed without legal process. While Edward had reluctantly agreed to the Ordinances in the Parliament of August 1311, however, he maintained that on 18 January 1312 the exile of Gaveston had been proclaimed contrary to the law of the kingdom.[19] Lancaster and Warwick, the leading Ordainers, recognised that by accepting the king's offer

---

15 *SR*, I, 169, *CPR, 1313–17*, pp. 21–6; *Foedera*, II, 230–1.
16 *SR*, I, 252.
17 *SR*, I, 169.
18 M. McKisack, *The Fourteenth Century, 1307–1399* (Oxford, 1959), pp. 27–30.
19 *SR*, I, 157–67. The writs for the restoration of Gaveston's lands and castles are printed in *Foedera*, II, 153–4.

of pardon they would in effect be admitting they had been acting outside the law in murdering Gaveston.

With the two sides at an impasse, the papacy sent mediators (Cardinals Arnaud Novelli and Arnald de Auxio) to England to help find a resolution. The report they sent back to Pope Clement V stressed that the earls would find it difficult to accept pardon because this might be seen as tantamount to an admission of guilt:

> The fourth reason, that if the king orders that no-one henceforth harass anyone, at his suit or that of any other person, for the capture and death of P. de Gaveston, expressed in those terms, therefore it will be noted by the hearers that lord P. was a man under law. And thus it will be supposed and can be concluded against them that they are homicides, which stain or infamy they wish to avoid by all means, as people who lawfully and justly did what they did to the said P., as to an enemy of the king and of the realm and, as has been said before, an exile.[20]

The earls, it seems, had a keen appreciation of the legal position surrounding the case, and assumed that the implications of guilt associated with a pardon were widely appreciated. On 14 October 1313, the recalcitrant lords consented to make a public apology at Westminster Hall, and in his chronicle Walsingham recorded that a final agreement was made at the Parliament in London; the barons asked pardon of the king and the document was duly granted, although it left no doubt about their guilt.[21] Such examples of the intended recipients resisting the bestowal of a pardon are rare, but it is clear that under these circumstances the settlement represented a substantial victory for the king and signalled that he had emerged from the struggle with no new constraints upon his royal prerogative.

On occasion, kings might grant amnesties to those following royal orders. The clearest example of this was the amnesty Edward III issued to himself, to his mother, and to their supporters, for the actions they had taken in the 1327 usurpation of the throne. In this case the statute issued on 7 March 1327 attempted to indemnify those acting on behalf of the new administration against any future accusations of misconduct. No-one, it stated, would be 'impeached, molested nor grieved', for the actions taken against Edward II

---

[20] 'Quarta ratio, quia si Rex precipiat quod nullus molestet decetero aliquem ad suitam suam vel alterius cuiuscunque pro captione et morte P. de Gaveston', stando in istis terminis, ergo per audientes notabitur quod dominus P. erat homo sub lege. Et sic supponetur et conclude poterit contra eos quod sint homicide, quam maculam seu infamiam modis omnibus volunt euitare, tanquam illi qui licite ey iuste fecerunt de dicto P. quod fecerunt tanquam de inimico Regis et regni et, ut premittitur, exulato' [E. A. Roberts, 'Edward II, the Ordainers and Piers Gaveston's Jewels and Horses, 1312–1313', *Camden Miscellany* 15 (1929), 16].

[21] Walsingham, *HA*, I, 136. N. Fryde contends that the magnates demanded pardon from Edward: N. Fryde, *The Tyranny and Fall of Edward II* (Cambridge, 1979), p. 23.

in the winter of 1326–7.[22] Again the terms of the amnesty were comprehensive and legally precise. The element of wrongdoing that its issue implied would be ignored by the majority of the populace who saw in the young king's accession the herald of a brighter future, free of the unpopular policies of his father; and few would be scrutinising the implications of the pardon too closely. Indeed, the use of these pardons in the aftermath of Edward II's deposition perhaps signalled an attempt to win the support of the political community through a combination of acts of reconciliation and far-reaching legislation.[23] The posthumous pardon of Thomas of Lancaster, the restoration of the Lancastrian inheritance and the pardon of Henry of Lancaster after his stand against the government in the Salisbury Parliament of October 1328 indicated a certain desire to establish the judicial authority of the regime and, after the Lancastrian revolt, to revive respect for the administration.[24] These attempts were undermined, however, by the arbitrary treatment of prominent figures such as the earl of Kent, executed on charges of plotting to restore his brother to the throne.[25] After Edward III's own coup in October 1330, the same attempt to combine reconciliation with remedial legislation was more successfully implemented. Only Roger Mortimer and Simon Bereford were executed. Oliver Ingham and the bishops were pardoned, and legislation was enacted to address grievances that had long been aired in Parliament, but which had failed to find redress.[26] Alone, the issue of an amnesty might promote reconciliation, but it did not often address the root causes of the dissension. While the Crown took an important step towards reconciliation in granting a pardon, the measure was not necessarily a dynamic or innovative one. However, when combined with remedial legislation, the amnesty could form part of a coherent policy of reconciliation that might do more for relations between the Crown and the political establishment in the long term.

---

[22] *SR*, I, 252.

[23] The 1327 statute dealt with some of the complaints that had been aired in Parliament, without remedy, under the previous regime: see *SR*, I, 255; Ormrod, 'Agenda for Legislation', p. 11.

[24] For the posthumous pardon of Thomas of Lancaster, and restoration of the Lancastrian inheritance, see Ormrod, *Edward III*, p. 13; Fryde, *Tyranny and Fall*, pp. 207–27; *PROME*, 'Parliament of January 1327'. A pardon for Henry of Lancaster and his followers, with certain named exceptions, was offered by the king, to all those who would surrender to him by 7 January. *Knighton's Chronicle*, ed. Martin, p. 451, names those excepted as Henry Beaumont, William Trussell, Thomas Roscelin and Thomas Wyther. The limit for the submission passed, but soon after, Lancaster offered to surrender. He was fined, along with his most prominent followers, but these fines were later cancelled (*CPR, 1327–30*, pp. 472, 484, 547). Those excepted from the original pardon fled abroad, along with Thomas Wake: see G. A. Holmes, 'The Rebellion of the Earl of Lancaster, 1328–9', *BIHR* 28 (1955), 84–9; Fryde, *Tyranny and Fall*, pp. 222–3.

[25] Ormrod, *Edward III*, p. 15, and n. 11; Fryde, *Tyranny and Fall*, pp. 224–5.

[26] Ormrod, 'Agenda for Legislation', pp. 11–12.

Just such a policy was undertaken by Henry V at the outset of his reign and, as Edward Powell has demonstrated, it was to lay the foundations for much closer co-operation between the king and the political community.[27]

Political amnesties were obviously issued at times when relations between the Crown and an individual or group within the political community had been strained. Despite this, it seems more realistic to view them as attempts to reconcile the disaffected and ensure continued co-operation in the running of government, than to portray them as a tool wielded by the monarch or a concession forced from the Crown by an opposition faction. Their prominence in the act of reconciliation evolved over the course of the century, and on several occasions the terms of the amnesty took centre stage. This evolution seems to have been accompanied by a change, best described as a shift in emphasis rather than an absolute or radical development, away from reconciliation conceived of in feudal terms and towards one defined by the parameters of the common law. As earlier noted (p. 95), rather than restoring the feudal bond between the vassal and his lord, the amnesty brought the recipient back into the king's peace and allowed him to benefit from the protection that the law afforded. Pardoning politically important individuals their acts of defiance continued throughout the later Middle Ages. But increasingly, in the aftermath of a governmental crisis, the general pardon came to the fore. Before this evolution can be considered, however, it is important to examine the political circumstances behind the military pardons and remissions of feudal and judicial dues which began to be issued for the first time in the early fourteenth century.

Military Pardons

Military pardons appear to have been new to the fourteenth century; the first extant records of their use survive from the reign of Edward I, when he declared that they would be available to those who volunteered for service in the Gascon campaign of 1294. The terms of the pardon covered a range of crimes from felony to offences of the forest.[28] The grant of December 1298 was also wide-ranging, covering all trespasses, and all classes of felony.[29] Some grants were more limited in scope; in 1360 Edward III offered military pardons only for homicide indictments.[30] They were aimed at men who had been detained in prison to await trial, or those who had been indicted but were still at large, including those who had been outlawed. Not all recipi-

---

[27] Powell, *Kingship*, pp. 229–46; Powell, 'Restoration', pp. 53–74.
[28] *Rôles gascons*, nos. 3032–3, and *passim* (12 June); TNA C 67/26, 27, 28A. Powicke, *Thirteenth Century*, p. 648; Hurnard, *Homicide*, p. 248; TNA C 67/26 mm. 4, 6, 7–8.
[29] *CPR, 1292–1301*, p. 293.
[30] *CPR, 1358–61*, pp. 375–402.

ents, therefore, can be assumed to have been hardened criminals; they had not actually been convicted of any offence, and some innocent men might have preferred military service to the uncertainty and cost of the trial procedure. The recipient of such a pardon was also required to appear before court with the document on completion of his military service in order for it to be 'proved'.[31] While these pardons were potentially very useful to bolster the ranks of the infantry, they were only used on a large scale in a few specific instances.[32]

The king's letters patent let it be known that such pardons were available to anyone who sought them, without the need to submit an individual petition, as long as recipients were fit for military service. As with political amnesties, it seems that officers were appointed to receive men into the king's peace. The letter patent issued in 1294 stipulated that the recipient should come into the presence of the king himself, or into the presence of Roger Brabazon and William de Bereford, justices assigned by him, or to coroners appointed by the king. Recipients had to find sureties to their good behaviour before these officials, and were then to go beyond seas in the king's service, and stay there 'during his pleasure'.[33] Similarly, the pardon recorded in the patent rolls under the date 12 December 1298 referred to a proclamation that the king had recently made at Carlisle. This stipulated that all those who came into his presence by Martinmas to ask pardon would receive one, as long as they had served in his wars before that date. The king therefore either granted them to individuals who came before him, or appointed deputies to do the same. Lists of these men may, in some instances, have then been forwarded to Chancery. Most pardons of this type certainly included the clause that they had been given at the request of a particular military leader.[34]

Details of the crimes these new recruits were alleged to have committed are sparse, although in a few instances their pardons were written up on the main patent rolls as well as the supplementary series, in which case the

---

31 Some pardons drawn up in Chancery were never handed over, presumably either because the fee was not paid or because the intended recipient had since died in the king's wars. Fifty letters patent of pardon remain in TNA C 266.

32 See Appendix 2.

33 TNA C 67/26, mm. 4, 6, 7, 8.

34 *CPR, 1358–61*, pp. 375–402. Edward I's proclamation of 1294 was recorded in the Gascon rolls, rather than the main patent rolls, and the names of recipients were listed in the separate series of pardon rolls. The only other example of this use of a separate record occurred when Edward III issued a military pardon from Vannes in 1342, for his campaign in Brittany. TNA C 67/26 lists 320 pardons given in return for military service in Wales, Scotland and Gascony, between 1294 and 1298. C 67/27 names 162 recipients of pardons in return for military service in Flanders, given between 1297 and 1298. C 67/28A contains a few fragments of a roll recently identified among the 'unsorted miscellanea' of The National Archives. These appear to contain approximately twenty-six names of recipients of a military pardon that Edward III issued from Vannes in 1342. See Appendix 2.

outlines of the case against them can be gleaned. Under the terms of the 1294 pardon, for instance, a man called Gilbert le Glowere was pardoned by Reginald de Grey, Justice of Chester, for the death of Thomas de Houton. Another man, Walter Bythewater, was pardoned for the death of William 'the parson's son' of Toppercroft. In 1298, John de Tilton's pardon recorded that he was granted pardon for commanding six accomplices to murder his enemy. He found surety before the king to go overseas on royal service, but his infirmity compelled him to stay in England, and he sent another man to carry out the military service in his place.[35]

The use of these military pardons attracted a certain amount of criticism from contemporaries, particularly in the Parliaments of the mid-fourteenth century. This led Naomi Hurnard, in her 1969 study of medieval pardons, to condemn Edward I and his successors for their exploitation of the pardoning process. According to her interpretation, the king cynically abused his pardoning power, and the Crown profited financially, at the expense of law and order, as criminal gangs were able to operate with impunity.[36] Hurnard's work seemed to substantiate the impressionistic comments of earlier writers. Jean Jules Jusserand, for instance, writing in the mid-nineteenth century, had already argued that medieval monarchs willingly granted pardons to increase Crown revenue and bolster the ranks of the army, and in response the parliamentary Commons repeatedly asked for remedy, to little avail.[37] The protests of the Commons, he said, were further undermined by the great lords who obtained charters for their own men on the premise that they were abroad, occupied in fighting for the monarch.[38] This negative view of pardoning, and Hurnard's comments on military pardons in particular, were taken up by several other historians in the decades after she published her book, as part of a wider debate on standards of public order in the fourteenth century.[39] For those scholars who proposed a thesis of dramatic decline in public order during this period of intense foreign warfare, the exploitation of the royal pardon was another contributing factor. Whatever the objective reality, the fourteenth century saw an increase in complaints centred on the threats of increasing violence in everyday life, and on royal abuse of the pardon. Accordingly, several historians have viewed pardons as a contributory factor in the deterioration of public order as fourteenth-century England

---

[35] TNA C 67/26, mm. 1, 8; *CPR, 1292–1301*, p. 136.

[36] Hurnard, *Homicide*, pp. 247–50.

[37] Jusserand, *English Wayfaring Life*, p. 166.

[38] Jusserand, *English Wayfaring Life*, p. 167.

[39] Kaeuper, *Public Order*, pp. 174–83; Hurnard, *Homicide*, pp. 311–26. Both have argued that the policy of pardoning felons and recruiting them into the army typifies the tensions between the pursuit of war and maintenance of law and order. See also Putnam, 'Transformation', pp. 19–48; Harriss, *Public Finance*, pp. 354–5, 516–17; Musson, 'Second "English Justinian"', pp. 69–88.

moved from 'law state' to 'war state'.[40] Herbert Hewitt, for example, asserted that former outlaws returned from military campaigns with not only their pardons and resultant freedom of movement, but also the habits acquired by a 'rough but often exhilarating life in the chevauchée, unhampered by the restraints of "civil" life'.[41] In his view it was evident that such men could not be readily reintegrated into English society, and he sees the proof of this in frequent outbreaks of disorder, particularly by armed bands.[42] Richard Kaeuper also saw these pardons as one instance of a shift from law to war; after Edward I introduced military pardons, royal mercy merely supplied criminals with an immunity that would allow them to undermine the legal process.[43] The criticism that pardons supplied criminals with 'immunity' is widespread, but problematic. The charter would pardon the recipient past offences, and so might give him a second chance to continue a life of crime, but not with immunity for future offences. If indicted again, the offender could not present the old pardon for these new offences. The pardon was also meant to be 'proved' by the individual on their return from foreign campaign. This involved presenting the charter in court, to allow any aggrieved party the chance to bring an appeal. Only then would final peace be proclaimed.

More recently, a revisionist approach to this law and order debate has emphasised that the medieval perception of a decline in standards of public order was prompted by rising expectations and an expanding legal apparatus that gave a greater proportion of the population the chance to air their grievances and access judicial methods of redress.[44] This interpretation also allows for a more nuanced understanding of attitudes to pardoning. The medieval debate on pardoning appears more subtle when placed within the wider

---

[40] Kaeuper, *Public Order*; Hewitt, *Organisation of War*; Harriss, *Public Finance*; Nicholson, *Edward III and the Scots*.

[41] Hewitt, *Organisation of War*, p. 173. Hewitt states that it seems probable that from 2 to 12 per cent of most armies of the period consisted of outlaws (Hewitt, *Organisation of War*, p. 30).

[42] He cites instances such as the wounding of the king's bailiff in the fairs at Holderness and Wells (1347); the rescue of a criminal from the king's bailiff at Kingston-upon-Hull (1351); the attack on the justice at Eynsham (1350); the attacks on ships in the port of Bristol and Newcastle (1348, 1354); and the armed gangs in the fairs and markets of Gloucestershire (1348), *CPR, 1358–61*, p. 160, and in Cheshire (1360–1): Hewitt, *Organisation of War*, p. 174, and see M. C. Prestwich, 'Gilbert de Middleton and the Attack on the Cardinals, 1317', in *Warriors and Churchmen in the High Middle Ages: Essays Presented to Karl Leyser*, ed. T. Reuter (London, 1992), pp. 179–94; E. L. G. Stones, 'The Folvilles of Ashby Folville, Leicestershire, and their associates in Crime', *TRHS* 5th series 7 (1957), 117–36; S. L. Waugh, 'The Profits of Violence: The Minor Gentry in the Rebellion of 1321–2 in Gloucestershire and Herefordshire', *Speculum* 52 (1977), 843–69.

[43] Kaeuper, *Public Order*, p. 126.

[44] Musson and Ormrod, *Evolution*, pp. 161–93; Musson, *Public Order, passim*; Verduyn, 'The Politics of Law and Order', pp. 842–67; Powell, 'Administration', pp. 49–59.

discussion of the king's position in relation to the law. It is true that contemporaries saw military pardons as problematic, and there is a series of parliamentary petitions dating from the mid-fourteenth century, which aimed to put a stop to the use of the pardon as a tool of military recruitment. However, these petitions must be seen as part of a wider debate over the king's discretionary pardoning power, which stretched back over the previous century. While the use of military pardons for a time generated intense debate among the political community, preoccupation with this aspect of pardoning was relatively short-lived, and protest was largely confined to the sixteen-year period between 1337 and 1353. Discussion of the role of pardoning alongside the common law procedures, however, had been initiated at least a century earlier, and endured throughout the fourteenth century.

Over the period 1337–53 seven petitions were presented to Parliament, complaining that felons were unjustly receiving pardons because they agreed to military service.[45] While the main aim was to curtail the use of military pardons, however, the petitions continued to be framed in a standard fashion, stipulating, as they had done in the past that henceforward pardons would only be issued in accordance with the king's coronation oath. The 1337 petition suggested limitations to the king's power to pardon, by barring notorious offenders from being taken into royal service. In response to this idea, the king promised to grant charters of pardon 'according to his coronation oath'.[46] Petitions in 1339 and in 1346 attempted to prohibit the issuing of pardons after the king's departure abroad on campaign.[47] The others, presented in 1340, 1348, 1351 and 1353, all complained that although pardons

---

45 For discussion of these petitions in the context of the law and order debate, see Verduyn, 'Attitude', pp. 6, 21, 44–7, 104–5, 132–3, 183–6. Despite the infrequency of Parliaments in the 1340s, the Commons managed to achieve a consistency of approach towards such issues and continued to pursue them in subsequent decades. They opposed the use of general commissions of trailbaston, of the itinerant King's Bench and of the eyre. In contrast, the peace commissions, working in tandem with the assize justices, were seen as less intrusive and were promoted as a viable alternative. It was only in 1368 that the Commons gained the commissions that truly accorded with measures they sought. Similarly, agreements to restrict the use of military pardons throughout the 1340s were in practice ignored, and measures seem to have been more successful in 1353 only because the government recognised the value of tackling the problem of desertion: see Verduyn, 'Attitude', pp. 77, 193–203; Verduyn, 'The Politics of Law and Order', pp. 842–67; A. J. Verduyn, 'The Commons and the Early Justices of the Peace under Edward III', in *Regionalism and Revision: The Crown and its Provinces in England, 1250–1650*, ed. P. Fleming, A. Gross and J. R. Lander (London, 1998), pp. 87–106.

46 *RPHI*, pp. 268–9 (3). The text of the common petition survives in the Ancient Petitions series: TNA SC 8/272/13584: 'That the king should not receive into his peace notorious felons who seek his grace by undertaking to go to the wars in Scotland.' The response is given in SC 8/272/13587.

47 *PROME*, 'Parliament of October 1339', item 10; *PROME*, 'Parliament of 1346', item 28.

should only be issued in accordance with the coronation oath, felons were continuing to receive them and then committing further crimes.[48] In all but one case, the king agreed that he did not wish to grant pardons against his coronation oath, but in practice he continued to issue them at the same rate as before. The exception was the last petition in 1353, which focused on preventing abuses by recipients and petitioners, rather than restricting the use of the military pardon. The Crown possibly thought that this might go some way to addressing the problem of desertion from the royal armies; the letter of pardon would now record both the reason for the pardon and the name of the intercessor, so that if, in future a royal justice found the information to be untrue, the pardon could be annulled. A soldier who absconded from the army with a letter of pardon therefore had less of a sense of immunity from the law.[49] There does seem to have been a genuine intent to enforce this measure, and no complaints were presented in 1354 and 1355, although if the renewed hostilities later in the decade provoked further complaint, the lack of surviving parliament rolls makes it impossible to tell.[50]

In essence, petitions against military pardons were addressing the king's right to intervene in the legal process and pardon men widely regarded as criminals. In these particular complaints, the further point was made that such men were reoffending after their return from campaigns abroad, but the essential, unchanging point was that felons should not receive pardon. The overriding issue was the need to reconcile the prerogative of pardon with the dictates of the common law. Moreover, as Thomas Green has argued, the opinion of the local community was important, and to be seen as just, pardons had to reflect the views of the local men serving on juries of presentment and on trial juries. Presenting juries, after all, determined which persons were 'publicly known' to be felons, while trial juries were able to exercise discretionary justice in certain cases, even to the extent of 'nullifying' the trial.[51]

---

48 1340: *SR*, I, 286; 1348: *PROME*, 'Parliament of January 1348', item 53; 1351: *PROME*, 'Parliament of 1351', item 26; 1353: *PROME*, 'Parliament of 1353', item 41; *SR*, I, 330. The mention in such statutes of pardons given in accordance with the king's coronation oath had come to be used as a short-hand reference to mean those pardons issued in cases attended by mitigating circumstances; see Chapter 2, pp. 22–4.

49 In the January Parliament of 1340 the Crown had ordered all those with charters of pardon to proceed towards the coast and join the array of troops or face being put to answer immediately on the points contained in their charters: *PROME*, 'Parliament of January 1340', item 15.

50 One further petition in 1364 elicited the response that no pardon would be issued without the consent of the party grieved: *SR*, I, 386–7. Several scholars have attempted to assess the effectiveness of such protest in upholding standards of public order, see above, nn. 43–4.

51 The jury could try to nullify the trial if they recognised that the act was proscribed by the law but did not believe that it should be; or if they thought that the act proved was properly classed as criminal, but did not deserve the punishment

The concern of the local community to avoid granting pardons to criminals was perhaps heightened by a desire to avoid surrendering their powers of discretion to the competency of royal judgment. The protests surrounding military pardons therefore followed a long-established tradition. Not all pardons issued in return for military service were given to proven criminals, but it would be reasonable to assume that a large number of felons were receiving such letters under this policy. It seems that the common petitions to Parliament on this subject reflected a long-standing concern about the consequences for law and order if pardons continued to be issued to those widely regarded as notorious felons. If people began to fear possible reprisals from pardoned criminals, the whole basis of the judicial system, reliant as it was on individuals coming forward to present indictments, would be undermined.[52]

Debts owed to the Crown

One other form of group pardon to emerge in the fourteenth century was the pardon of debts owed to the Crown. These pardons were issued for the first time in the second half of Edward II's reign, and eventually evolved into the general pardons of the later fourteenth century. The terms of these pardons excused the inhabitants of a town or shire from paying all outstanding judicial fines to the Crown, and waived the king's right to seize the chattels of escaped felons, and to impose communal fines for such escapes, rights enshrined in the articles of the eyre.[53] The regular circuit of general eyres had ended in the first decade of the fourteenth century, but attempts to revive them were made in 1313, 1321 and 1329–30.[54] Under such circumstances

---

prescribed; or if the personal circumstances of the defendant excused them from the generally fair sanctions that the law proscribed: see Green, *Verdict According to Conscience*, pp. xvii–xix. See also A. Musson, 'Twelve Good Men and True? The Character of Early Fourteenth-Century Juries', *Law and History Review* 15 (1997), 115–44.

[52] Verduyn, 'Attitude', p. 45; TNA SC 8/119/5913; SC 8/39/1937. In September 1333 the sheriff of Yorkshire was instructed to appoint 'discreet and lawful men of the county' to hold enquiries in the matter: *CCR, 1333–7*, pp. 173–4. The king also ordered the justices to check that the service really had been performed before allowing the pardons: *CCR, 1333–7*, p. 158.

[53] For discussion of the articles of the eyre, see D. Crook, *Records of the General Eyre* (London, 1982); D. Crook, 'The Later Eyres', *EHR* 97 (1982), 241–68; R. B. Pugh, *Itinerant Justices in English History* (Exeter, 1967); A. H. Hershey, 'The Earliest Bill in Eyre: 1259', *Historical Research* 71 (1998), 228–32; 'The London Eyre of 1244', ed. H. Chew and M. Weinbaum, *London Record Society* 6 (1970), 5–9.

[54] Musson and Ormrod, *Evolution*, pp. 45, 82, n. 29; Crook, 'The Later Eyres', p. 265; J. R. Maddicott, 'Magna Carta and the Local Community', *P&P* 102 (1984), 25–65; W. N. Bryant, 'The Financial Dealings of Edward III with the County Communities, 1330–60', *EHR* 83 (1968), 760–71; Harriss, *Public Finance*, pp. 399–410.

the communities threatened with their imminent arrival were increasingly opting to purchase pardons from visitations of the eyre and from its penalties. However, even after visitations of the eyre had permanently ceased, there was no lessening in the Crown's concern with the profits of judicial penalties. Feudal dues might also be imposed by the Crown on local communities, to pay for the knighting of the king's son or the marriage of his daughter, for example.[55] These were also remitted under the terms of the pardon.

These pardons were negotiated by the parliamentary Commons, and they reflected the interests of the polity. The Commons had consistently opposed the imposition of such payments, and the levying of ancient feudal dues was becoming increasingly anachronistic. In 1316, the first remission on this type pardoned all outstanding fines imposed before 20 November 1291.[56] However, the terms of this pardon were allowed to lapse, and this prompted further complaints from the Commons in the Lent and October Parliaments of 1324. This pattern was to become a familiar one; a pardon would be granted but over time it would be ignored, eventually provoking complaint from the Commons. In 1327 the new government under Isabella and Mortimer acknowledged that Edward II's 1316 grant needed to be better enforced.[57] A regular sequence of these pardons then began to be issued in the 1320s and continued into the 1360s. They pardoned all the outstanding judicial and feudal dues owed by a community in return for payment of a set fee, and this option seems to have been preferred by the polity. Indeed, a distinct *quid pro quo* arrangement emerged, whereby the Crown attempted to draw on its fiscal reserves by collecting outstanding debts, at which point the parliamentary Commons petitioned for a remission, and paid a set fee or granted taxation in return.[58] Edward III's attempts to generate income in

---

[55] *SR*, I, 281–2.

[56] *CPR, 1313–17*, p. 532.

[57] *PROME*, 'Parliament of January 1327', item 7; *CPR, 1313–17*, p. 532. The terms of the 1327 pardon were reinforced a few months later in the clauses of the Statute of Northampton. *SR*, I, 255, 259. Harriss, *Public Finance*, p. 244, n. 2. M. Buck, 'Reform of the Exchequer, 1313–1326', *EHR* 98 (1983), 241–60 (pp. 247–8). For orders to enforce the collection of all debts due to the Crown in 1327, see *Memoranda Roll, 1326–7*, pp. 252, 266; *The Red Book of Exchequer*, ed. H. Hall, RS 99 (London, 1896), III, 937.

[58] The connection with taxation has been discussed in the work of B. H. Putnam concerning William Shareshull's use of judicial commissions to raise money for the Crown in the 1340s and 1350s, and by G. L. Harriss in his comprehensive examination of royal fiscal policy: B. H. Putnam, *The Place in History of Sir William Shareshull* (Cambridge, 1950), pp. 39, 75; Harriss, *Public Finance*; G. L. Harriss, 'The Commons' Petitions of 1340', *EHR* 78 (1963), 625–54. See also E. B. Fryde, 'Parliament and the French War, 1336–40', in *Essays in Medieval History Presented to Bertie Wilkinson*, ed. T. A. Sandquist and M. R. Powicke (Toronto, 1969), pp. 250–69; J. F. Hadwin, 'The Last Royal Tallages', *EHR* 96 (1981), 344–58; J. F. Hadwin, 'The Medieval Lay Subsidies and Economic History', *Economic History Review* 36, 2nd series (1983), 200–17.

order to pursue his claim to the French throne kept the issue on the parliamentary agenda. In July 1338 the Walton Ordinances attempted to repeal all personal exemptions from taxation, to ban the traditional granting of estallments (respites of debts owed to the Crown) and to enforce the payment of past debts.[59] Although the Walton Ordinances were suspended in October of the same year, Edward soon ordered the justices to levy all fines imposed in the eyre.[60] Discontent over the issue flared among a political community already agitated by levels of taxation and accusations of misgovernment (a situation that Gerald Harriss has examined in detail).[61]

The record of the Parliament held at Westminster in October 1339 provides the earliest evidence of negotiation on this issue. After accepting the king's necessity for an aid, the Commons implicitly connected the redress of grievances they had long harboured with their grant of supply. One of their requests concerned the collection of judicial fines, feudal aids and ancient debts levied before 1327.[62] Their offer of 30,000 sacks of wool was made 'upon certain conditions contained in indentures made thereon and sealed under the seals of the prelates and other great men; in such manner that, if the conditions were not met, they would not be required to make the aid.'[63] After further discussion, the Commons granted 2,500 sacks of wool, but stipulated that it would form part of a larger grant if the king accepted their conditions.[64] In the next session of Parliament; which opened two months later, the king requested a further aid, and the Parliament offered a ninth of corn, wool and sheep, conditional on the acceptance of their petitions. Clauses relating to these petitions were duly enshrined in the statute of 16 April 1340, which included a pardon of all ancient debts assessed before 1337.[65] The stance that the Commons had taken on this occasion was in line with their repeated assertion that all forms of financial levy beyond the strictly customary rights of the Crown should have common assent. In the Parliament of May 1357 similar arrangements seem to have been made. The Commons consented to a

---

[59] Harriss, 'The Commons' Petitions', p. 632; Harriss, *Public Finance*, p. 244. Earlier in the year the council had urged on the king the fruitlessness of these fiscal expedients except as bargaining counters for a parliamentary subsidy. Stratford had returned with authority to remit debts under £10 and compound for larger sums owed, to offer a general pardon to communities for chattels of felons and fugitives and for escapes, and to release the scutage and aids (*Foedera*, II, 1091).

[60] Harriss, *Public Finance*, p. 245.

[61] Harriss, *Public Finance*, pp. 231–93.

[62] PROME, 'Parliament of October 1339', item 13.

[63] PROME, 'Parliament of January 1340', item 7.

[64] PROME, 'Parliament of January 1340', item 9.

[65] SR, I, 281–2.

single subsidy and in return the king remitted judicial fines and amercements 'before this time fallen which be not yet judged before the justices'.[66]

Since the legality of such levies was not in question, the withdrawal of these demands could be secured only by paying for release or by concerted political opposition, and by granting pardon on a case-by-case basis, the Crown did not consent to any permanent diminution of its powers. For the communities receiving these pardons, it was important to secure a remission of the financial dues and feudal levies, which they associated with an intrusive form of central government control. Direct taxes, in contrast, at least had the advantage of being imposed after consultation with Parliament, and while they clearly stipulated what each region should pay, the collection was left to local officials. These pardons were issued as statutes, and letters patent were also sometimes recorded in the rolls. As these pardons covered an entire community, individual inhabitants were not obliged to seek personal charters.[67]

The involvement of the parliamentary Commons in negotiating these pardons might be seen as a precursor to their role as petitioners for the general pardons that emerged in the second half of the fourteenth century. Since the last years of Edward II's reign, the Commons had increasingly been voicing a distinct and consistent agenda. They began to use the common petition to put forward the concerns of the entire 'community of the realm', rather than just the specific grievances of individual members, and the political programme they espoused formed the basis for statutory legislation designed to placate the disaffected political community.[68] The legislation formulated in Edward III's first Parliament has already been mentioned in connection with the criticism of military pardons. Another of their concerns, repeatedly aired in Parliament over the previous decade, surrounded the

---

[66] No parliament roll exists for the proceedings of this session. For the pardon, see *SR*, I, 352; *Knighton's Chronicle*, ed. Martin, pp. 150–1; *CFR, 1356–68*, p. 44. As Harriss comments, the pardon from future eyres may have been the more substantial concession, as the fines already collected had to be delivered by the justices to the collectors so that they could be redistributed in support of the taxpayers, and the lay subsidy rolls show that in many shires no returns were made: *CCR, 1354–60*, p. 363; Harriss, *Public Finance*, p. 345. There had also been a subsidy granted in 1352 on condition that profits of judicial fines and penalties under the Statute of Labourers would be set against it (Harriss, *Public Finance*, pp. 340–1).

[67] Each one of these pardons covered all the inhabitants of the named town or city. Accordingly, their issue did not significantly increase the overall number of pardons granted in the particular year: see Harriss, *Public Finance*, pp. 345–6; Appendix 1 below.

[68] Ormrod, 'Agenda for Legislation', pp. 1–33; Harriss, *Public Finance*, pp. 118–21; M. Prestwich, 'Parliament and the Community of the Realm in Fourteenth Century England', in *Parliament and Community: Papers read before the [15th] Irish Conference of Historians, Dublin 27–30 May 1981*, ed. A. Cosgrove and J. I. McGuire (Belfast, 1983), pp. 5–24.

collection of these judicial and feudal dues owed to the Crown.[69] However, while there was clearly a *quid pro quo* aspect to negotiations for remissions of judicial and feudal dues, this does not necessarily indicate that the Commons were trying to curb the powers of the royal prerogative in order to strengthen their own hand. While the Crown issued remissions of these dues, they were given of the king's grace and his authority to enforce them remained unquestioned. As Gerald Harriss has argued, Edward III's government met the new demands of protracted warfare not by updating prerogative rights but by encouraging and cajoling the co-operation of the political community in a common enterprise.[70] It is also important to recognise that the adoption of too rigid an approach towards royal pardons neglects the wider cultural significance that they increasingly came to assume. Indeed, by the second half of Edward III's reign, remissions of judicial and feudal dues, and to a large extent the political amnesties that had preceded them, were being subsumed into the far more comprehensive general pardon, a pardon that was to evolve into a pervasive symbol of royal justice.

This evolution of existing forms of pardon into what came to be known as the general pardon is first noticeable in the 1362 grant, which coincided with the king's fiftieth birthday, on 13 November 1362. The Parliament in which this grant was formulated opened in October of 1362. Historians traditionally associate this assembly with the formulation of the Statute of Purveyors, and give less attention to the pardon that was issued alongside it. However, it is perhaps useful to consider the significance of issuing a pardon at such a time, and the symbolic connotations with which it was coming to be imbued.[71] This pardon was far more comprehensive in its scope than any previous example. The Commons, following the standard practice, had attempted to secure this pardon, and put an end to the contentious practice of purveyance (the compulsory purchase of supplies for the royal entourage and the king's armies), after giving their consent to a renewal of the wool subsidy.[72] However, the timing of the pardon seems to have been intended to coincide with Edward III's

---

[69] *SR*, I, 255; *PROME*, 'Parliament of January 1327', item 7. See common petitions from 1324: SC 8/108/5398. See also *PROME*, 'Parliament of January 1327', items 22, 32, 41. Ormrod, 'Agenda for Legislation', pp. 11–13, demonstrates that the parliamentary Commons were consistently presenting their agenda to Parliament in the 1320s and 1330s, and that during this time they operated largely independently of the Lords.

[70] Harriss, *Public Finance*, p. 419.

[71] Harriss, *Public Finance*, pp. 378–9, 408–9.

[72] Since the king was requesting a renewal of the wool subsidy, despite there being peace abroad, the Commons were in a relatively strong bargaining position (*SR*, I, 376–8; *PROME*, 'Parliament of 1362', item 32). The king was asked to order the issue of charters of pardon to all shires before the end of the Parliament. The pardon was later confirmed in the Parliament of May 1368 and in 1372 (*PROME*, 'Parliament of 1368', item 11; *PROME*, 'Parliament of 1372', item 17; *SR*, I, 388). See also Crook, 'Later Eyres', p. 268.

birthday; although Parliament had convened on 13 October, the parliament roll gives no account of any business being conducted between 19 October and 13 November. This suggests that considerable behind-the-scenes negotiations were taking place, as was usual procedure before the formulation of important legislation. Significantly, however, the hiatus might also indicate that the assembly was being artificially prolonged, so that its final plenary session would coincide with the birthday of the king on 13 November. This final session was therefore held on a Sunday, an unusual day for Parliament to sit, and one that further supports the idea that it was deliberately timed to coincide with the king's birthday.[73]

The connection of the idea of pardoning with an important anniversary was certainly to become an explicit feature of later general pardons, although on this occasion it was left to the chroniclers to state explicitly the link between the pardon and the king's personal jubilee: Thomas Walsingham noted that it was marked with a grant of grace, which pardoned offences against the Crown, freed people who had been imprisoned, and allowed all exiles to return to their home. The anonymous Canterbury chronicler said that the king, being in his fiftieth year, wished to act graciously to the community of his realm, and so granted graces and pardons. The chronicler then translated a section of the statute of pardon from the Anglo-Norman French into the Latin of his own text.[74]

On 13 November, the petitions of the Commons were read out to the assembly, and the king announced his answers. The Commons then declared their assent to the wool subsidy. Afterwards, Edward moved to introduce the idea of celebration by bestowing new titles on three of his sons: Lionel of Antwerp was made duke of Clarence, John of Gaunt duke of Lancaster and Edmund of Langley earl of Cambridge.[75] Finally, in response to a request of the Commons, Edward issued a comprehensive pardon, which covered all penalties, communal and personal, arising from the articles of the eyre that had been incurred before October of that year. This effectively allowed an amnesty on all outstanding and potential charges relating to previous visitations of the shires.[76] The pardon clearly drew on the precedent set by the remissions of judicial and feudal dues that Edward had granted earlier in

---

[73] Ormrod, 'Fifty Glorious Years', pp. 13–20.

[74] Walsingham, *HA*, I, 297; Walsingham, *CA*, p. 52; *Chronicon Anonymi Cantuariensis: The Chronicle of Anonymous of Canterbury 1346–1365*, ed. C. Scott-Stokes and C. Given-Wilson (Oxford, 2008), pp. 127–8. John Capgrave also says that the king 'losed prisoneris' and 'forgaf alle forfeitis', to mark the jubilee: *The Chronicle of England by John Capgrave*, ed. F. C. Hingeston, RS 1 (London, 1858), p. 222. The 1362 pardon was also referred to as a precedent in the grant of 1377, which was explicitly issued in recognition of the jubilee year (*SR*, I, 396).

[75] *CChR, 1341–1417*, p. 174.

[76] *SR*, I, 396–8; *PROME*, 'Parliament of January 1377', item 24. See also TNA C 49/8/6 for a model version of a letter of pardon under the statute.

his reign, yet this amnesty was far more comprehensive than its predecessors, and carried with it a greater symbolic resonance in light of the king's fiftieth birthday. It was made clear, however, that the pardon was a generous bestowal of royal mercy, and not in any sense a concession to the Commons. The final statute left out some of the Commons' original requests, such as pardons for the alienation of land without licence. This was seen to constitute too great a restriction of the king's prerogative powers.[77]

As Anthony Verduyn asserted, the practical value of the pardon is difficult to determine: the pardon of 1357 covered a period of eighteen years, and so would presumably have been of greater significance than that of 1362, which covered only five years.[78] Yet the latter grant also constituted something of a watershed. Firstly, it acknowledged, albeit implicitly, that a royal anniversary was a moment of formal significance in the political life of the realm, and secondly, it substantiated the relationship between jubilee and some form of redemption or symbolic emancipation.[79] This connection between the jubilee and a symbolic and substantive act of reconciliation was to assume an important role in the political culture of the later Middle Ages. The parliamentary process on this occasion also suggested that by recognising the king's authority and his need for the grant of a subsidy, the Commons could expect to benefit from a distribution of the king's grace on more comprehensive lines than anything that had gone before.

---

[77] See Verduyn, 'Attitude', pp. 144–5.
[78] See, for example, the two amounts claimed by the city of York under the two pardons: TNA SC 8/205/10240; SC 8/205/10258. Another petition requested redress for any person who suffered in contravention of the statute: *PROME*, 'Parliament of 1362', item 24; *SR*, II, 374.
[79] See below, Chapter Eight, pp. 114–15.

CHAPTER EIGHT

Pardoning and Celebration: Edward III's Jubilee

On 25 January 1377, Edward III became only the second English monarch to reach the end of his fiftieth year on the throne, and he marked the event with a grant of general pardon. The only previous king to have ruled for over half a century was Henry III, but in 1266, when he reached this milestone, the fragility of the political situation was such that the anniversary received scant attention. However, there was, in the teaching of the Roman Church, a well-established precedent for attaching significance to the fiftieth year. The notion of a jubilee year as a year of grace was enshrined in the scripture of the Old Testament as a time of personal emancipation and spiritual redemption. The book of Leviticus held that the fiftieth year was to be a special year of jubilee, in accordance with the divine commandments received by Moses on Mount Sinai. Every fiftieth year, on the Day of Atonement, the people of Israel were to recognise the year as holy and proclaim liberty throughout the land for all enslaved debtors, and cancel all public and private debts. All family estates sold to others were also to be returned to the original owners and their heirs; the land was to be left to rest and servants freed.[1]

The spirit of this commandment had been revived by the papacy in 1300, with a series of celebrations designed to honour the anniversary of Christ's birth. Pope Boniface VIII encouraged the faithful to make the pilgrimage to Rome, proclaiming in the bull *Antiquorum habet fidem* that plenary indulgences would be on offer to those who made the journey. Although he made the proclamation on 22 February 1300, it was designed to mark the anniversary on Christmas Day 1299.[2] This was the first time that the anniversary of the birth of Christ had been marked in such a way, and it was a noted success. Dante referred to the 'year of the jubilee' in the *Commedia*, describing the throng of pilgrims making their way across the Ponte Sant' Angelo towards St Peter's basilica, and it is possible that the poet was himself an eye-witness to these events.[3] The Chronicle of Bury St Edmunds also records how 'people

---

[1] Leviticus 25. 1–55. The Day of Atonement is the tenth day of the seventh month of the Hebrew calendar.

[2] H. L. Kessler and J. Zacharias, *Rome 1300: On the Path of the Pilgrim* (New Haven, 2000); Ormrod, 'Fifty Glorious Years'.

[3] Dante refers to 'l'anno del giubileo': *The Divine Comedy*, trans. A. Mandelbaum (London, 1995), *Inferno*, XVIII, lines 28–33. See also J. Miller, ed., *Dante and the Unorthodox: The Aesthetics of Transgression* (Waterloo ON, 2005), p. 58, n. 26.

of both sexes and every age from all over the Christian world hastened to the Roman court. For on account of the jubilee year the pope absolved all pilgrims, who had truly confessed and were contrite, from all their sins and punishment for sins.'[4] Rather than wait until the end of the century to repeat these celebrations, it was decided, in 1350, to mark the jubilee on the half-century as well.[5] The people of Rome had in fact petitioned Pope Clement VI to sanction this celebration, in support of their efforts to re-establish Rome as the seat of the papacy, over the recently favoured city of Avignon. In the jubilee bull Clement again echoed the Mosaic commandments of Leviticus, and referred to the Roman people as the heirs of the Israelites. He announced that plenary indulgences would be available to mark this anniversary, and encouraged pilgrims to come to Rome in order to atone for the recent scourge of the Black Death.[6] In reviving Old Testament notions of a half-century cycle the papacy now widely disseminated the idea of 'jubilee' as a time of forgiveness and pardon.

In 1362, the scriptural precedent for such an act of remission and reconciliation was translated by the English Crown into the contemporary political forum. In October 1362 Parliament was preoccupied with legislation concerning purveyance and a proposed extension of the wool subsidy, but another noticeable feature of this assembly was that its final session was prolonged, in order to coincide with the king's fiftieth birthday on 13 November. The king announced a 'full pardon' for all judicial fines previously levied by the eyre courts throughout the shires of England.[7] Historians have tended to dismiss this pardon as a standard reaction to yet another common petition asking for amnesty on all such charges; similar grants had been made in 1327, 1330, 1340 and 1357. However, it is useful to consider the significance of issuing a pardon at this particular moment, reinforcing as it did the notion of jubilee as a time of mercy and forgiveness.[8] While there was no direct reference to the king's birthday in the text of the pardon, it does seem to have been intended to coincide with the event; Parliament did not usually sit on a Sunday without a particular reason for doing so. This connection between the jubilee and an act of reconciliation was to assume an important role in the political culture of the later Middle Ages. The parliamentary process on this occasion also suggested that by recognising the king's authority and his need for consent to a subsidy, the Commons might

---

4   *Bury St. Edmunds*, ed. Gransden, p. 155.
5   D. Wood suggests that the golden gates of St Peter's and of the Lateran were ceremonially opened by the pope for the pilgrims, having been walled up since the previous jubilee: D. Wood, *Clement VI: The Pontificate and Ideas of an Avignon Pope* (Cambridge, 1989), pp. 90–3.
6   J. Sumption, *Pilgrimage: An Image of Medieval Religion* (London, 1975), pp. 236–42.
7   *SR*, I, 396–8; *PROME*, 'Parliament of January 1377', item 24. See Chapter 7, pp. 110–12.
8   Harriss, *Public Finance*, pp. 378–9, 408–9.

expect to benefit from a distribution of royal grace. Similarly, when, in 1377, Edward III completed his fiftieth year on the throne, the royal government looked to draft the terms of a new pardon, and in doing so it referred back to the grant of 1362, stating explicitly that it had indeed been granted to mark the king's fiftieth birthday.[9]

By the beginning of 1377, however, there had also been a marked change in the political climate. The 'Good Parliament' of April–July 1376 had witnessed an outright attack on the Crown, led by the parliamentary Commons, which represented one of the most serious challenges to government in the later Middle Ages. This chapter therefore examines the 1377 general pardon in the context of political reconciliation and celebration. The two sections that follow focus on the political tensions in the months prior to the opening of the January 1377 Parliament, and then on the terms of the pardon and the language used by the representatives of the Crown and the Commons, in seeking to portray the pardon as an unforced and celebratory act, for a king who had achieved fifty years on the throne of England.

Parliament

The Parliament of 1377 convened on 27 January, and the spokesman for the Crown, Bishop Houghton, set out the issues to be addressed in his opening sermon to the assembled Lords and Commons. In the course of his speech, Houghton intimated the king's willingness to bestow mercy on his people. The statute of pardon that emerged by the end of the session was unprecedented in the scope of its terms, and explicitly stated that the king was willing to do his people 'greater grace than ever he did before, for as much as this year is rightfully the year of [his] jubilee'.[10] For the first time, the king pardoned the recipient 'the suit of his peace, for all manner of felonies'. The terms did then exclude treasons, murders, common thefts and rapes of women, but other felonious offences such as wounding and arson were presumably forgiven.[11] This was an extremely significant expansion of the terms of a pardon, and the king's subjects certainly recognised the value of such a grant – close to 2,500 people were to purchase copies from Chancery

---

9 *SR*, I, 396.

10 'faire greindre grace qil ne leur fist unqes devant, a cause qe cest an si est droitement lan de Jubile' (*SR*, I, 396).

11 The general pardon also stipulated, at the request of the Commons, that actions arising from the Dordrecht bonds promulgated by Walter Chiriton and his merchant company in the 1340s should be annulled: see E. B. Fryde, *Studies in Medieval Trade and Finance* (London, 1983), ch. 1–10, pp. 1–17. It also contained the qualification, inserted by the government, that William Wykeham, the leader of the opposition in the Good Parliament, should be specifically excluded from the protection of the pardon.

by the end of the summer. This innovation in the terms of the pardon clearly indicates that this was a new departure for the Crown in its use of royal mercy.

In part the pardon was a celebratory act, designed to commemorate the Jubilee. But it also carried with it clear political overtones. Over the course of the previous year long-held tensions among the political community had come to the surface. The Prince of Wales, the heir to Edward's throne, had died, leaving the ten-year-old Prince Richard to succeed in his place. In April 1376 a major political crisis had erupted in the so-called Good Parliament; the Commons had refused consent to any more direct taxes, and had presented formal charges against a group of courtiers (in a process later known as impeachment). The unpopularity and suspicion of John of Gaunt's actions also increased concern over the succession, not helped by the king's departure before the end of the parliamentary session owing to illness. In the autumn and winter of 1376, the political climate remained volatile. Many of the acts of the Good Parliament were annulled, but the stand that the Commons had made could not be entirely ignored.[12] Sermons were preached on the corruption that was perceived to exist at the heart of government; Bishop Brinton of Rochester delivered a sermon denouncing royal ministers and the excesses of the court before the clerical convocation at St Paul's, even as the Good Parliament sat in session at Westminster.[13] Brinton voiced a commonly held belief that the governing classes were not fulfilling their role; the king was impoverishing his own children to reward his favourites, and had handed over the keys of the kingdom to the charge of his mistress, Alice Perrers. The sins of the upper classes, Brinton said, had brought down divine punishment on the realm of England:

> it is patent to all men that the kingdom of England, which of old abounded in riches, is now poor and needy: which of old was radiant with God's grace is now graceless and despicable: which of old regulated all things according to justice, is now without law of any sort.[14]

Brinton was preoccupied with the monarch's role as protector of his people, and declared the need for a public performance of penance, with the king and his nobles at the head of the procession. In 1375 he had urged the king

---

[12] G. Holmes, *The Good Parliament* (Oxford, 1975); Ormrod, *Edward III*, pp. 42–5.

[13] The surviving collection of his sermons, of which there are 105 in all, is published in *Sermons of Thomas Brinton*, ed. M. A. Devlin, 2 vols., Camden Society, 3rd series 85, 86 (1954).

[14] 'quia tamen constat euidenter quod regnum Anglie quod olim diuiciis habundauit modo est pauper et impecuniosum, quod olim gracia rediauit iam est ingraciosum et ignominiosum, quod olim se per iusticiam regulauit iam est sine regula viciosum' (*Sermons of Thomas Brinton*, ed. Devlin, vol. II, 318).

and his nobles to join the people in public prayer; recent events now made this imperative:

> it is truly against all rules of justice and equity that when processions are ordered to avert common tribulations there should be present at them ecclesiastics and religious only, and some few of the middle order who, in comparison, have but slightly offended God by their sins, whilst the rich people and the nobility, who are the main cause of these afflictions, neither come, nor pray, nor do penance for their iniquities, but lie in their beds and enjoy their other luxuries to their heart's content.[15]

For Brinton, the divisions within society distracted from the common obligation to do public penance before the eyes of God. Importantly, Brinton downplayed the role of the parliamentary Commons in providing a remedy. While he argued that they were less sinful than the nobility, he did not think they could take an active role in reforming the realm. It might seem odd that Brinton, a vocal opponent of government corruption, did not give a more active role to the Commons, who were, at the very moment he was speaking, launching their attack on government at the Westminster Parliament. But for Brinton it was the duty of the bishops, lords, confessors and even preachers to speak out against corruption rather than the Commons, who were not powerful enough to circumscribe the actions of the king and his favourites. Brinton emphasised his point by retelling the fable of the rat Parliament, which also appears in *Piers Plowman*, using the analogy of mice attempting to put a bell around the neck of the cat to illustrate the futility of the Commons attempting to restrain the will of the king.[16] It seems that the views he expressed were in wider circulation, at least in the capital. By the time that Parliament convened in January 1377, therefore, the Crown was looking for a way to placate the disaffected political community.

Bishop Houghton's opening sermon to Parliament on 27 January 1377 sought to deal with several of the themes raised by Brinton. Unusually for this period, the parliament roll gives the full text of his address.[17] The speech was remarkable in its content and novel in the form that it took: it appears to have combined the sermon, usually preached by a member of the episcopal bench, and the 'charge' to Parliament, delivered by the chancellor. This was perhaps because Houghton, as a clerical chancellor, could perform both functions and establish from the outset that the Crown would be taking the lead

---

15 'Qualis est igitur regula iusticie et equitatis quod ad processions pro tribulacione communiter imminente veniunt ecclesiastici, reigiosi, et pauci mediocres, qui respectiue modicum deliquerunt, et duites et magnates, qui tribulacionis precipua extant causa, non veniunt nec orant nec penitenciam faciunt pro peccatis, sed lasciuiunt in lectis et aliis solaciis ad sue libitum voluntatis' (*Sermons of Thomas Brinton*, ed. Devlin, vol. II, 320).

16 Dodd, 'A Parliament Full of Rats?', pp. 21–49.

17 *PROME*, 'Parliament of January 1377', items 4–12.

in proceedings. In his speech Houghton expounded on the need for reconciliation, and suggested the course of action to be followed to heal the divisions within society. He also used the idea of general pardon to reinforce the sense of reciprocal obligation between the king and commons; the monarch would protect his subjects from injustice, in return for their support and obedience. A detailed examination of his words helps to shed light on the response of the Crown to the recent political crisis.

Houghton began by referring to the young Prince Richard, who had recently been created Prince of Wales, and who, in the absence of his grandfather owing to ill-health, was presiding over the Parliament as its president. However, he swiftly moved the focus of his speech to the authority of the king and the protection offered by the Crown, as a key means of restoring harmony among the political community; it seems that the government attached considerable importance to promoting this sense of royal protection. He alluded opaquely to the recent ills that had beset government and the king's incapacity through illness with a reference to Psalm 127, 'the Lord disciplines those he loves'. Developing his theme, he compared the old king to St Paul, who, before his conversion was

> vile and cruel as a result of sin, and was then visited by the grace of God and fell to the ground blind, and ate and drank nothing for three nights, and was then raised up and revived …[18]

None of the parliamentary representatives who were listening to Houghton's address could fail to understand his meaning; his attempt to put a positive gloss on recent events, including the king's illness and confinement. He said that the realm of England had been uniquely blessed by God (using the past tense to refer to a time before the recent division and animosity). Like Bishop Brinton six months previously, Houghton was suggesting that the recent troubles had ensued from a withdrawal of God's grace from the realm of England, in order to punish and reform the governing classes. But Houghton now argued that this punishment had cleansed the government, and given it new purpose. In contrast to Brinton, he directed his speech above all at the parliamentary Commons, and aimed to persuade them that they needed to act; by making a gesture of reconciliation towards the Crown they might heal the divisions within the political community.

The aim of Houghton's speech was to persuade Parliament of the king's ability to resume his position of authority, and offer them the royal protection that had been so obviously lacking over the last year. Here, he was able to develop his earlier analogy to the conversion of St Paul; like Paul, the

---

[18] 'orde et cruel par pecchie devant sa conversion, et puis estoit visitez par la grace de Dieux, et chai en terre voegle, et rienz ne mangeast nene bust trois jours et trois noetz, et apres fuist relevez et resuscitez' (*PROME*, 'Parliament of January 1377', item 6).

king had been afflicted with an illness, but this illness had purified him from any trace of past sin. In referring to the king's recent recovery from illness Houghton located this idea of renewal and conversion within the present time, and importantly, since the events of the Good Parliament. Houghton was suggesting that the king's recent illness and recovery had brought about a reformation, and marked the king out as the special recipient of divine grace:

> our said lord the king [is] now revived and purified from all filth of sin, if there was any, and if God pleases, he is, and always will be, the vessel of grace or the vessel of God's choosing.[19]

This alone was reason enough for celebration: 'And thus in every way it is demonstrated by the same Scripture that our same lord the king is gracious and blessed of God, for which we all should make great joy and celebration.'[20] Added to this was the achievement of completing fifty years on the throne of England. Houghton's emphasis on the king's new-found health allowed him to reinforce the sense of imminent royal authority. The king was now in a position to offer protection to his subjects from the troubles that would ensue if the political community remained divided.

In reality, the king was far from being fully recovered, and indeed he died only a few months later, on 21 June. But the sense of optimism expressed by Houghton was nonetheless substantiated in the *Anonimalle Chronicle*. The chronicler reported that by the beginning of February 1377 the king had recovered sufficiently to be taken from the royal manor of Havering in Essex to his palace at Sheen in Surrey. At the sight of the royal barge, the Lords and Commons came out of Parliament to acknowledge the king, taking heed of Houghton's words on royal authority.[21] Bishop Houghton took his point about the king's revival still further, when he went on to paraphrase Psalm 128, a psalm that describes the Israelites as a people uniquely blessed by God, worthy of the divine inheritance. In doing so he was also conveying the idea that the entire realm of England might be a special recipient of divine grace. Houghton suggested that England had experienced a kind of reformation under the leadership of Edward III and had been honoured by God as never

---

[19] 'Issint est ores nostre dit seignur le roy resuscitez et purifiez de toute ordure de pecchie, si nul y fust, et si Dieux plest, il est, et toutdys mais serra, le vessel de grace, ou le vessel de eleccion Dieu' (*PROME*, 'Parliament of January 1377', item 6). Scriptural reference: Acts 9. 15.

[20] 'Et issint par toutes voies est concluz par meisme l'escripture qe mesme nostre seignur le roy soit gracious et benoit de Dieu, de qoy nous touz doions faire grant joie et feste' (*PROME*, 'Parliament of January 1377', item 6).

[21] *Anonimalle Chronicle*, ed. Galbraith, pp. 95, 103. Corroborated by evidence summarised in *Anonimalle Chronicle*, ed. Galbraith, p. 185. For further details, see M. Bennett, 'Edward III's Entail and the Succession to the Crown, 1376–1471', *EHR* 113 (1998), 586–90.

before. His references to the psalm compared England to Israel. Drawing these ideas to a conclusion, he even compared the king's young heir, Prince Richard, to Christ himself, sent to England by God in the same way that God sent his only son for the redemption of the chosen people.[22] Houghton represented Richard as a new messiah, clearly intending to persuade the political community that he would be fit to succeed to the throne, despite his young age.

Houghton's allusions to England as a chosen land have already been noted by Michael Wilks, and for Wilks they were particularly important as the kind of anti-papal statement that might have been supported by Wyclif and his followers.[23] What Wilks's work makes clear is that Houghton was dealing directly with notions of Old Testament kingship; the idea that God's grace would be bestowed on an identifiable promised land. Late medieval national sovereignty fitted the Jewish notion of a particular territory and a people elected by God. It may be that Houghton was attempting to play on the overtly anti-papal stance that the Commons had taken in recent years. But he was also developing this theme for a more immediate political purpose; he wanted to make the link between the idea of England as a recipient of God's grace, and the king as the mediator who could in turn bestow this divine protection on the subjects of his realm. This theme sent a clear message to the representatives assembled in Parliament that now, at the beginning of 1377, the king's recent recovery and his accomplishment of fifty years on the throne could be marked by a reassertion of royal leadership and a healing of the divisions among the political community.

The remedy for the recent hostility and division, then, lay in the willingness of the parliamentary representatives to reaffirm their obedience to, and support for the king himself. This shifted focus from the hostility towards the nobles and gave the Commons the sense of royal leadership that they felt had been lacking. Moreover, Houghton's speech suggested that this sentiment could be given tangible form, in the guise of a general royal pardon, which the king would bestow on his subjects for past offences, and which they would purchase, as a sign of their loyalty and in the spirit of reconciliation. According to Bishop Houghton, then, the key to reconciliation was the direct relationship between the king and the parliamentary Commons. In this way, the first of Houghton's themes was directly linked to the second; the king, in recovering from his illness, had been favoured by God, and the Commons

---

[22] He also referred to Prince Richard in the context of the feast of the Epiphany (6 January, also Richard's birthday), and the feast of the Presentation at the Temple (2 February, Candlemas).

[23] Wyclif was at the time preaching in London against Gregory XI's claim to jurisdiction in England: see M. J. Wilks, *Wyclif: Political Ideas and Practice; Papers by Michael Wilks*, selected and introduced by Anne Hudson (Oxford, 2000), pp. 117–45.

might share in this if they reconciled with the Crown and demonstrated their support for the unity of the realm, by abandoning past sins and vices:

> But if we, his subjects, desire and would have his grace in this jubilee year, and great comfort from him who thus is the vessel of God's grace or choosing, we must of sheer necessity undertake through good virtues to be fit to receive the grace of the same vessel, and to abandon all vices.[24]

Houghton's earlier stress on the divine favour bestowed on the king had provided justification for this pardoning power; Edward III had received purification and the grace of God, and could in turn grant this to his people. To return to Michael Wilks's point about an anti-papal sentiment common among the parliamentary representatives, this idea of a royal pardon omitted any notion of applying to the papacy for forgiveness through the dispensation of indulgences. The papal celebrations on the half-century had seen many Englishmen and women make the pilgrimage to Rome to receive such indulgences. Now, in 1377, the king's own jubilee would be marked with royal, not papal pardons.

Commons

Implicit within Houghton's sermon was a particular conception of how the political community should operate; it stressed the central relationship between the Crown and the parliamentary Commons, reaffirming the need for leadership from the former and obedience from the latter. It is worth remembering that Bishop Houghton was named as adviser to the Commons in the Good Parliament (although Thomas Walsingham substitutes his name for that of Bishop Brinton).[25] Houghton was certainly concerned with impressing on Parliament the responsibility it had to recognise the power of the Crown, and accept the protection offered by the king in the form of the royal pardon. His words were not lost on the Commons, who proved acquiescent to his wishes. In the past, historians have questioned this change in the mood of the Commons, and have, on the whole, concluded that it resulted from a change in personnel. Thomas Walsingham claimed, in his chronicle account, that John of Gaunt rigged the elections to ensure that his own supporters were returned to this assembly. In this claim, the chronicler perhaps says more about his animosity for Gaunt than the true composition

---

[24] 'Mais si einsi soit qe nous ses subgitz disirons et vorrions avoir sa grace en cest an jubile, et trereconfort de luy qi issint est vessel de grace ou de eleccion Dieu, il nous covient a fyne force de nous conformer d'estre hables par bones vertuz de resceivre grace de mesme le vessel, et lesser toutes vices' (*PROME*, 'Parliament of January 1377', item 7).

[25] See *Sermons of Thomas Brinton*, ed. Devlin, I, xxvi.

of the Commons; modern prosopographical research has demonstrated that there were not more than a dozen or so Lancastrian retainers in attendance.[26] Other historians have ascribed it to the absence of some of the leaders of the earlier opposition movement or to a tacit acknowledgement from the parliamentary representatives that the king was entitled to annul any acts forced on him against his will.[27] It is true that there was a change in personnel, but it may be that historians have underestimated the extent to which Houghton's words struck a chord with the representatives, who were looking for royal leadership at a time when fears of a full-scale French naval assault on the south coast appeared well-founded.[28]

Presented with Houghton's offer of royal mercy, the Commons submitted a petition to request a general pardon with little delay.[29] They justified their request with reference to the suffering of the common people and the new demands for taxation, as well as the need to mark the completion of the king's jubilee year. The Crown's reply made no reference to the burden of tax, but it did acknowledge the suffering imposed by wars, plague and famine:

> Our lord the king, having consideration for the very great charges and losses which his said people have had and borne previously, as a result of the wars as well as otherwise through the pestilence of people, the murrain of beasts and the fruits of the soil having generally failed in bad harvests before this time, for which things our lord the king has very great compassion; and therefore willing now in this present fiftieth year of his said reign of England to make them greater grace than he ever made before, because this year is indeed the conclusion of the jubilee year or year of grace of his aforesaid reign, so that his said commonalty can be the better comforted and take heart to do better in times to come.[30]

---

26 Walsingham, *CA*, p. 112. Thomas Hungerford, the speaker for the Commons, was a Lancastrian steward: see J. S. Roskell, *Parliament and Politics in Late Medieval England* (London, 1981), II, 15–44.

27 S. Armitage-Smith, *John of Gaunt* (London, 1904), p. 137; J. C. Wedgwood, 'John of Gaunt and the Packing of Parliament', *EHR* 45 (1930), 623–5; and H. G. Richardson, 'John of Gaunt and the Parliamentary Representation of Lancashire', *Bulletin of the John Rylands Library* 22 (1938), 175–222; Ormrod, *Edward III*, p. 45; S. K. Walker, *The Lancastrian Affinity 1361–1399* (Oxford, 1991), p. 239.

28 Ormrod, *Edward III*, pp. 44–5.

29 *PROME*, 'Parliament of January 1377', item 24.

30 'Nostre seignur le roi eant consideracion a les tresgrandes charges et perdes les queux son dit people ad euz et portez cea enarere, auxibien parmy les guerres come autrement par pestilence des gentz, moryne des bestes et les fruitz de la terre communement failliez par malvais ans devant ces heures, dont nostre seignur le roi si ad grant compassion; et par tant leur veulliant ore en cest present an cynquantisme de son dit regne d'Engleterre faire greindre grace q'il ne lour fist unqes devant, a cause qe cest an si est droitement l'an jubilee, ou l'an de grace de son regne avantdit acomply, paront sa dite commune se purra le mieltz recomforter, et ent aient le greindre coer de bien faire en temps avenir' (*PROME*, 'Parliament of January 1377', item 24).

In their mention of the wider problems that afflicted the realm, the Commons were perhaps mindful of their duty to speak on behalf of those lower down the social order. It should be noted that those without a direct voice in Parliament had increasingly been bringing their plight to the attention of the polity, in the form of labour service dissent. Indeed, the 'great rumour' of 1377 represented widespread social protest, out-done four years later in the rising of 1381.[31] In the aftermath of the Peasants' Revolt, the Commons again suggested that a general pardon should be issued as a reward to those 'good and loyal commons' who had refused to join the rebels, echoing the sentiment that this would encourage them 'to take heart to do better in times to come'.[32]

The Crown granted their request in full Parliament on 22 February, making explicit reference to the fiftieth anniversary of the king's accession in the text of the pardon itself.[33] As in 1362, the Commons responded to the grant of pardon by giving their assent to a subsidy, in the form of the first of the four-teenth-century poll taxes. But the Crown still made clear that this grant was a generous and unforced gift of royal grace. The initiative in this process had clearly been taken by the Crown, through the speech of Bishop Houghton, and the general pardon that emerged was more than just a redrafted set of Commons' petitions. Most of the Commons' requests were included in the pardon but were amended, and in some cases the pardon was only extended to the fortieth year of Edward's reign instead of the fiftieth.[34] The parliament roll also records that the schedule of pardon was taken to the king at Sheen in order to be given royal approval, emphasising its status as a royal power that could only be granted as the free act of the monarch himself:

> And then, on 22 February in the present year, some of the prelates and lords, the chancellor, treasurer, keeper of the privy seal and all the justices, by the order of our lord the king, went to Sheen where our said lord the king lay very ill; and there in his presence … the manner and the articles of the general pardon and grace which the same king had made to his commonalty were recited. … And when this had been done, the king said that he fully agreed with the same and was well content; and he ordered that these answers and graces be read in Parliament on the morrow as it is

---

[31] R. J. Faith, 'The "Great Rumour" of 1377 and Peasant Ideology', in *The English Rising of 1381*, ed. R. H. Hilton and T. H. Aston (Cambridge, 1984), pp. 43–73.

[32] *PROME*, 'Parliament of 1381', items 31–4; *SR*, II, 29.

[33] *SR*, I, 396.

[34] *PROME*, 'Parliament of January 1377', item 24; *SR*, I, 396–7. In 1362, despite the requests of the Commons, the Crown had similarly refused to extend the pardon to the fiftieth, rather than the fortieth year of the reign, and had refused to issue copies of the pardon free of the Chancery fines. The government also rejected any attempt to associate limitations on the king's right to tax overseas trade with the grant of the general pardon.

customary to do on the last day of Parliament, and that this Parliament be brought to an end.[35]

Moreover, one new section was added by the council. The king was to pardon felonies committed up to his fiftieth year, and outlawries for felonies, in all cases except treason, murder, common theft and rape.[36] While this may have aided the rehabilitation of some of the disgraced courtiers, it also had a wider application, and represented a substantial new addition to the power of the king's pardon. It remained clear in 1377 that the issue of a general pardon was the prerogative of the Crown, but it was also evident that the government was ready to expand its scope beyond even the parameters that the Commons had envisaged in order to reconcile the disaffected political community. This offer of mercy demonstrated the extent to which circumstances had changed since the last Parliament, when the Commons had in fact requested a general pardon, but had been refused one.[37]

The terms of the pardon, together with the timing of the grant, indicate that it was intended as a political act, and one that would strike a chord among the parliamentary representatives. Significant financial benefits also accrued to the Crown; the royal government might well have foreseen a profitable return on the grant, contributing badly needed revenue at a time when a French invasion was thought to be imminent. In 1377 each letter of pardon cost 18s. 4d., and on this occasion 2,439 people purchased copies, giving the Crown over £2,000 of extra revenue.[38] But this financial benefit can only have been part of the rationale. The political overtones of this grant are further emphasised in the Chancery 'pardon roll', a source that historians have in the past neglected. As the name suggests, this roll recorded individual recipients of pardon after the issue of the statute. Separate pardon rolls were only created at times of high demand; otherwise the names would simply be recorded on the main series of patent rolls. Only three earlier rolls are extant, and all were created to record military pardons.[39] In creating a new roll for the 1377 grant, it seems that the Chancery clerks were antici-

---

35 'Et puis apres, le .xxij. jour du moys de Feverer l'an present, aucuns des prelatz et seignurs, chanceller, tresorier, gardein du privee seal et touz les justices, par comandement nostre seignur le roi alerent a Shene, ou nostre dit seignur le roi gysoit trop malades; et illoeqes, en sa presence … estoient rehercez la manere et les articles de general pardoun et grace qe mesme le roy ad fait a sa commune. … Et ce fait, le roy y dist q'il s'agreast bien a ycelles et ent fust assez content; et comandast qe celles responses et graces furent lendemain lues en parlement, come la manere est de faire al darrain jour de parlement, et qe fin fust fait de ce parlement' (*PROME*, 'Parliament of January 1377', item 22).

36 *PROME*, 'Parliament of January 1377', item 24; *SR*, II, 397. Individual charters of pardon were to be sued out before 24 June.

37 *PROME*, 'Parliament of 1376', item 122: see also Verduyn, 'Commons', pp. 183–6.

38 TNA C 67/28B.

39 TNA C 67/26–28A.

pating high demand, and recognised the need for an accurate record to be kept. The roll is also important for the verbatim record it gives of the terms of the letters patent that were issued to everyone who paid the requisite fee. In fact, two distinct forms of the letter patent were made available. The 'great form', as it was called, was a copy of the entire pardon (later publicised in the form of a statute).[40] What made the 'great form' relevant to the politics of the moment was that it was purchased by several prominent members of the political community, including John Pecche and Richard Lyons, the two merchants impeached in the Good Parliament. In all 438 people are listed as recipients, including the Bishop of Lincoln, two lords, and at least fifty-four knights. Several towns also sought charters, including Northampton, Beverley, Kingston-upon-Hull, Huntingdon and Winchester. The implication seems to be that this was in part an act of political reconciliation to smooth over divisions and hostility among the polity. Pardon also offered protection against any future retribution, for those who had spoken out against the Crown. A shortened form of the charter was available to the rest of the king's subjects. This included only those clauses that pardoned suits of peace and certain felonies.[41] Copies of this form were purchased by just over 2,000 individuals.[42] The first of the shorter charters was issued on 6 March, four days after Parliament had ended, and the first of the great form on 23 March, to John de Meaux. The issue of both forms was brought to a premature halt on 21 June by the death of the king, three days before the intended final date of issue, and was preceded by a last-minute rush of purchases. In the first Parliament of Richard II's reign, convened on 13 October 1377, the general pardon was confirmed and expanded. It had clearly been a valuable concession to the Commons, and one greeted with enthusiasm.

By using a general pardon at this time, the revocation of the acts of the Good Parliament could be represented as a gesture of reconciliation that restored the unity of the polity. The grant of a pardon now emphasised the Crown's role as the protector of its people, and importantly, as an act of royal grace, it clearly demonstrated that the king's will could not be circumscribed. The general pardon therefore represented a comprehensive act of reconciliation, but an act made on the Crown's own terms. However, the use of a new, more inclusive form of pardon did give some suggestion that the government had recognised the unprecedented scale of criticism it faced from the new

---

[40] *SR*, I, 396–7.

[41] TNA C 67/28B. Enrolments under the great form are given on mm. 11–13 (the title 'de magna forma' is used at the top of m. 11). The only place in which the 'great form' differs from the statute is on the clause concerning the exclusion of William Wykeham. This clause is present in the parliament roll and in the statute, but is missing from the letter patent copied into the pardon rolls. Enrolments under the shorter form are listed on mm. 1–10.

[42] A. J. Verduyn suggests that the great form would probably have been more expensive (Verduyn, 'Attitude', p. 185).

political voice of the Commons, and the need to respond with a more public, corporate act of mercy than it had ever issued before. The use of the general pardon acknowledged the demands of a more inclusive polity; reconciliation now had to be public and accessible to a wider cross-section of the population. This practice of offering protection in the form of a general pardon was to become standard practice in later centuries. In 1377 the link between the general pardon and the need for political reconciliation after the events of the Good Parliament was implicit, and the evocation of ideas of spiritual renewal and regeneration elevated the debate above pragmatic political concerns. In 1381, however, the level of disaffection demonstrated in the Peasants' Revolt clearly necessitated an unprecedented gesture of reconciliation. This grant is the subject of the following chapter.

CHAPTER NINE

Pardoning and Revolt: The Peasants' Rising of 1381

Only four years after the jubilee celebrations of 1377, Richard II's government issued a general pardon, but this time there were no references to celebration; rather it was a response to the unprecedented crisis of the Peasants' Revolt.[1] The terms of the pardon were presented to Parliament on 13 December 1381; all the king's subjects were to be granted mercy, both those accused of rebellion and those who had remained loyal. Considering the volume of scholarship generated on the Peasants' Revolt, the subject of pardon has only ever been given fleeting reference. This is somewhat surprising in light of the long-running debate on how best to characterise government reaction to the rebels and their demands; did the Crown exercise commendable moderation in dealing with the rebels, as Barrie Dobson claimed, or was there in fact a vindictive campaign of repression?[2] J. A. Tuck's work on the Parliament held after the revolt in the autumn of 1381, highlighted the divide between the Lords and Commons, the latter championing the policy of moderation that was eventually adopted.[3] More recently, Andrew Prescott has suggested that we have glossed over the events in London in the immediate aftermath of the revolt, because of the absence of the relevant legal records. He argues that chronicle accounts give a true picture of the devastation in London, with rebels being put to the sword or hanged in their thousands.[4] Rather than enter into the debate about the number of rebels sentenced to death, this

---

[1] The substance of this chapter relates closely to my article in *Journal of Medieval History*, and is reproduced here with the kind permission of the editor: Lacey, 'Grace for the Rebels', pp. 36–63.

[2] *Peasants' Revolt*, ed. Dobson, pp. 303–4. This question has also been addressed by W. M. Ormrod, 'The Peasants' Revolt and the Government of England', *Journal of British Studies* 29 (1990), 1–30 (p. 22); Kaeuper, *Public Order*, p. 362; J. A. Tuck, 'Nobles, Commons and the Great Revolt of 1381', in *English Rising*, ed. Hilton and Aston, pp. 194–212. Attention has also been given to the government response in the more general works of N. Saul, *Richard II* (London, 1997), pp. 56–82; Musson and Ormrod, *Evolution*, pp. 96–101. For the traditional view, see T. F. Tout, *Chapters in the Administrative History of Medieval England* (Manchester, 1920–33), III, 356–84; A. Tuck, *Richard II and the English Nobility* (London, 1973), pp. 1–57. Andrew Prescott's unpublished doctoral thesis includes a valuable analysis of the pardons granted in the aftermath of the revolt: Prescott, 'Judicial Records', pp. 350–62.

[3] Tuck, 'Nobles, Commons', pp. 205–12; Ormrod, 'Government', p. 23.

[4] Prescott, 'The Hand of God', pp. 317–41.

chapter examines some of the ideas about the nature of royal mercy that were thrown into relief by the events of 1381. Several of the chroniclers noted that, at the height of the revolt in London, the rebels and the government representatives both referred to the notion of royal grace. The idea of pardon also played a prominent role in the subsequent judicial proceedings and in the parliamentary debates. The surviving records of the revolt thus shed light on some of the late medieval assumptions about the nature of royal mercy, assumptions it was perhaps only necessary to articulate at a time of such unprecedented crisis.

Events in London

The chronicle accounts of Walsingham, Froissart and the *Anonimalle Chronicle* are the main sources for the early stages of the revolt, from the first localised expressions of discontent in late May and early June 1381 through to the famous meetings between the king and Wat Tyler and his band. Historians have primarily been interested in these texts in so far as they are useful in reconstructing a picture of 'what actually happened' during the summer of 1381, comparing the narratives against one another in the search for authenticating detail. However, several recent studies have shifted the focus towards the voice of the author – the role of the chroniclers in crafting their own narratives, and the textual conventions behind their accounts.[5] The fact that several chroniclers mentioned concepts of mercy and pardon in the context of the revolt is interesting as much for what it says about the approach of these writers and the way they constructed their narratives of the rising, as for anything it might reveal about the attitude of those who participated in the revolt. According to Froissart's chronicle, for example, the council began to debate the virtues of showing mercy to the rebels even as they began massing outside London, at the same time as the insurgents were busy declaring their loyalty to King Richard, and their desire to secure his pardon.[6] At one level

---

[5] D. Pearsall, 'Interpretative Models for the Peasants' Revolt', in *Hermeneutics and Medieval Culture*, ed. P. J. Gallacher and H. Damico (New York, 1989), pp. 63–70; Ormrod, 'Joan of Kent', pp. 277–92. For a later context, see Grummitt, 'Cade's Rebellion', pp. 107–22.

[6] *Peasants' Revolt*, ed. Dobson, pp. 189–90 (Froissart). The *Anonimalle Chronicle* notes that the rebels in Kent met at Dartford on 5 June, and 'said among themselves ... that they would neither suffer nor have any king except King Richard'. A few days later they had arrived in Canterbury, and forced the mayor, bailiffs and commons to swear to be 'faithful and loyal to King Richard and the loyal commons of England'. By the time they arrived at Blackheath on 11 June they were declaring to the king's messengers that they had risen 'to save him [the king] and to destroy traitors to him and the kingdom'. Walsingham notes that the Kentish rebels blocked the pilgrimage routes into Canterbury, stopping all the pilgrims and forcing them to

we can examine Froissart's comments in light of the literary conventions to which he conforms. At another level we can explore the context of these ideas in other texts, not only in other chronicles but also in the documents produced by the rebels, by the government and by the royal courts, to understand better how these concepts evolved and circulated among different social groups. It may be that we should view overtures to reconciliation on the part of the Crown and the rebels in a cynical light; as rhetoric that both sides were obliged to utilise in order to avert crisis, and to avoid charges of treason. However, it is worth exploring the context of such ideas in more detail, before dismissing them too readily out of hand.

Looking first at the motives the insurgents expressed for their march on London, it is clear that we should not strive to separate the 'authentic voice' of Wat Tyler and his followers from that of the chronicler – even the vernacular letters that circulated among the rebels survive because of their insertion into the narratives of Walsingham and Henry Knighton.[7] Similarly the actions taken by the rebels are reported to us via the chronicles. Rather than assuming that one narrative stands in the way of our understanding of the other, however, it is perhaps more helpful to recognise the degree to which the two are mutually dependent, and draw on concepts of mercy or of corruption, for example, that were common to both. One idea promoted in these narratives is the sense that the rebels had been forced to bring their grievances to the attention of the king and council because of the corruption and inertia of the Crown's officers in the localities. This was a familiar concept – complaint about the corruption of local officials had long featured in so-called 'protest literature', in outlaw ballads and in petitions to Parliament.[8] The *Anonimalle Chronicle* brought to mind such ideas by claiming that the people of Kent had been angered by false accusations made against them concerning non-payment of the poll tax. When Robert Bealknap, chief justice of the Common Bench, was sent to enquire into the situation, the commons reportedly declared he was 'maliciously proposing to undo them by the use of false inquests taken before him.'[9] Similarly the rebels' consistent declara-

---

swear that they would be faithful to King Richard. Again, Froissart reports that the rebels at Blackheath sent a messenger to the king to 'shew him how all that they have done or will do is for him and his honour': *Peasants' Revolt*, ed. Dobson, pp. 127, 129, 133, 141. Alasdair Dunn uses the term 'populist royalism' to describe these declarations of loyalty: A. Dunn, *The Great Rising of 1381: The Peasants' Revolt and England's Failed Revolution* (Stroud, 2002), p. 58.

7 *Peasants' Revolt*, ed. Dobson, pp. 381–3.
8 Poems such as *The Simonie* and *Winner and Waster* attacked the venality of the courts, as did outlaw romances such as the *Tale of Gamelyn* and the Robin Hood ballads. More specific injustices were depicted in the *Outlaw's Song of Trailbaston*, while *Piers Plowman* provided a far-reaching denunciation of judicial corruption. For discussion of such texts, see Chapters 3, 4 and 5.
9 *Peasants' Revolt*, ed. Dobson, p. 125.

tions of loyalty to King Richard were contrasted with the abuses committed by local office-holders, abuses that the rebels trusted the king to resolve once they had a chance to put their complaints before him. So, for instance, the *Anonimalle Chronicle* includes a scene in which the Kentish rebels arrive in Canterbury on 10 June, and seek out the local officials – the mayor and bailiffs as well as the commons, and force them to swear to be 'faithful and loyal to King Richard and the loyal commons of England', perhaps intending this scene to underline their grievance over the corrupt practices of such officials.[10] Again, on arrival at Blackheath outside London, one of their first actions was apparently to send a written petition to the king.[11] Whether or not the rebels truly felt themselves to be victims of mistreatment and false accusation in the law courts, they knew that to express their grievances in this way might lend coherence to their actions, and might, crucially, encourage the king to offer them pardon for their direct action in bringing such corrupt practices to his attention. It was an idea that also found expression in the vernacular letters that circulated among the rebels; one such letter articulated the idea that justice was only available to those who could pay, and that 'true love' had fled in the face of falseness and sin:

> Jack Trewman doth yow to understande that falsnes and gyle havith regned to long, and trewthe hat bene sette under a lokke, and falsnes regneth in everylk flokke. No man may come trewthe to, bot he syng si dedero. Speke, spende and spede, quoth Jon of Bathon, and therefore synne fareth as wilde flode, trew love is away, that was so gode, and clerkus for welthe worche hem wo.[12]

Sir Michael de la Pole was later to single out the same problem in the Parliament of October 1383, citing the 'acts of disobedience and rebellion which men have recently committed ... towards the lesser servants of the king, such as the sheriffs, escheators, collectors of the subsidies and others of the same type'.[13] It was a useful concept for both the Crown and the rebels, in that it brought to mind the recognised procedure for lodging such complaint through a written petition to the monarch. For the Crown it might reinforce the sense that there was a proper procedure for such complaints, a procedure that the rebels had blatantly deviated from. For the rebels, drawing parallels between their actions and the petitioning process would lend legitimacy to

---

10 *Peasants' Revolt*, ed. Dobson, p. 127.

11 'As the king ... would not come to them, the commons of Kent sent him a petition.' (*Anonimalle Chronicle*): *Peasants' Revolt*, ed. Dobson, p. 130.

12 *Peasants' Revolt*, ed. Dobson, p. 382. *Si dedero* literally means 'I will give' (a payment). 'Jon of Bathon' might perhaps refer to John Bampton, the commissioner sent to investigate the non-payment of the poll tax in Essex. It has been suggested that this verse should be viewed alongside Langland's *Piers Plowman*. For further discussion, see Musson and Ormrod, *Evolution*, pp. 172–3.

13 *PROME*, 'Parliament of October 1383', item 6.

their cause. If, as they claimed, they were victims of false accusation in the law courts, one common method of seeking redress would be to put forward a petition for pardon. This was not to admit guilt, but rather a means of appealing to the king and council to have the case against them annulled through pardon.

According to the chronicles, they succeeded in gaining their first audience with the king on Thursday 13 June, once they had made their way to the area around the church of St Katherine, to the east of the Tower. The *Anonimalle Chronicle* suggests that the rebel leaders were already seeking to agree terms, and the idea of pardon featured prominently in the reported dialogue.[14] The insurgents requested that the king hand over the traitors in the Tower, and give them charters of manumission and pardon for all offences. In response to their request, Richard instructed a clerk to write a bill in their presence, granting them 'pardon for all manner of trespass, misprisons and felonies done up to this hour'. After sealing the document with his signet in front of them he sent two of his knights to show the bill to the people who had gathered around St Katherine's:

> The king benevolently granted their requests and made a clerk write a bill in their presence in these terms: 'Richard king of England and France, gives great thanks to his good commons, for that they have so great a desire to see and maintain their king: and he grants them pardon for all manner of trespasses and misprisons and felonies done up to this hour, and wills and commands that everyone should quickly now return to his own home: He wills and commands that everyone should put his grievances in writing, and have them sent to him; and he will provide, with the aid of his loyal lords and his good council, such remedy as shall be profitable both to him and to them, and to the kingdom.' He put his signet seal to this document in their presence and then sent the said bill by the hands of two of his knights to the people around St Katherine's. And he caused it to be read to them, the man who read it standing up on an old chair above the others so that all could hear.[15]

---

[14] St Katherine's church and hospital were situated to the east of the Tower (*Peasants' Revolt*, ed. Dobson, p. 158).

[15] *Peasants' Revolt*, ed. Dobson, pp. 159–60. 'le roy les graunta bonement et fist une clerk escriver une bille en lour presence en ceste maner: Le roy Richarde Dengleterre et de Fraunce enmercy moult ses bones communes de ceo qils ount si graunde desir pur luy vere et tener lour roy, et pardone a eux toutz maners des trespas et mespressiones et felonye faitz avaunt ces houres; et voet / et comande desore en avaunt qe chescune soy hast a soun propre hostelle et voet et comande qe chescune ses grevances en escript et les facent envoier a luy et il ordenera par lavyse de ses loials seignurs et de soun bone conseil tiel remedy qe profit serra a luy et as eux et al roialme. Et a ceo mist soun signet en presence de eux, et puis envoia la dite bille od deux des ses chivalers a eux denvers seint Kateryns et le fist leir a eux; et cestuy qe list la bille estea en une auncien chare amont les autres issint qe toutz purroient oier' (*Anonimalle Chronicle*, ed. Galbraith, p. 143).

The suggestion that Richard asked the rebels to send their grievances to him in writing conveys the sense that the rebels had deviated from the legitimate procedures of complaint, but also demonstrates the magnanimity of the monarch, and the implication that their complaints would be taken seriously. The claim that the rebels requested pardon from the king at this first meeting is also interesting. Among the extant petitions for pardon from the later fourteenth century, there are a significant number of cases in which the petitioner claims to have been 'maliciously indicted' by their enemies.[16] There is no sense that the petitioner humbly seeks the king's grace; rather, it is the voice of indignation that resonates most strongly. Sometimes the petitioner complained that the case against them had been concocted by officers of the Crown.[17] In 1381, the rebels were certainly alluding to established notions of petitioning for pardon by the time they came before the king in person.

The reference to petitioning and to the charter of pardon also gives a powerful sense of the physicality of the documents, something Derek Pearsall might describe as an 'authenticating touch', a detail included to give the audience a familiar frame of reference.[18] Froissart, too, conjures up this allusion when he notes that on Friday 14 June the king ordered more than thirty clerks to write out charters, patents and letters of protection, which they were to issue to the rebels.[19] The *Anonimalle Chronicle* adds that no fines were

---

16 Thirty-five such petitions can be identified in the ancient petitions alone. Petitioners would complain of being 'maliciously', 'falsely' or 'wrongly' indicted by their enemies. Pardons explicitly stating that they had been given on grounds of malicious indictment can also be found in the patent rolls. See TNA SC 8/2/88; SC 8/18/872; SC 8/18/898; SC 8/33/1635; SC 8/36/1800; SC 8/41/2026; SC 8/46/2276; SC 8/52/2586; SC 8/59/2937; SC 8/60/2979A; SC 8/67/3304; SC 8/97/4813; SC 8/112/5584; SC 8/141/7001; SC 8/151/7537; SC 8/183/9101; SC 8/183/9106; SC 8/183/9133; SC 8/193/9643; SC 8/194/9661; SC 8/201/10009; SC 8/221/11027; SC 8/227/11306; SC 8/227/11320; SC 8/228/11383; SC 8/240/11964; SC 8/242/12097; SC 8/245/12247; SC 8/252/12559; SC 8/252/12568; SC 8/253/12615; SC 8/254/12666; SC 8/260/12990; SC 8/262/13099; SC 8/268/13388; *CPR, 1340–3*, p. 499; *CPR, 1343–5*, p. 143; *CPR, 1345–8*, pp. 479, 514; *CPR, 1350–4*, p. 489; *CPR, 1354–8*, pp. 43–4, 356; *CPR, 1358–61*, p. 165; *CPR, 1389–92*, p. 318.

17 See Chapter 3, pp. 32–4 and also TNA SC 8/60/2979A.

18 For Pearsall, this particular scene exemplifies the chronicler's use of 'authentic touches' – the detail of the 'old chair' on which the clerk stands to read the bill, for example. On the one hand, the chair, he says, has the air of something seen, not invented, yet, on the other hand, it might have been a detail included to give the 'illusion of actuality', and carries with it the impression of impropriety and indignity, a reversal of the proper order (Pearsall, 'Interpretative Models', p. 67). It might further be added that 'old chair' is only one possible translation of the chronicler's phrase 'auncien chare', which could instead be rendered as 'old cart' (*Anonimalle Chronicle*, ed. Galbraith, p. 143). Thanks to Dr Shelagh Sneddon and Prof. Jocelyn Wogan-Browne for their advice on this point.

19 *Peasants' Revolt*, ed. Dobson, p. 192.

taken for the sealing or transcription of these documents.[20] References to such documents also established links with other contexts – the reading aloud of a pardon, for instance, would have brought to mind similar contemporary scenes of 'proving' pardons in the royal courts.[21] If, as has been suggested here, the insurgents were attempting to portray their cause as legitimate protest against injustice, then references to procedures and legal documents familiar from the royal courts would lend authority to their actions.

A similar emphasis on the physical document can be found in the St Albans context. According to a petition presented by the abbot, his tenants had forced him to make them charters of their own devising, for various franchises and liberties. Although they later surrendered the documents, the abbot noted that they had made various copies through which his successors could be disseised, and asked that all such charters should be declared null and void.[22] It has been noted elsewhere that the rebels displayed an ambiguous attitude towards written documents.[23] In Essex they destroyed court rolls and manorial records, in Cambridge they burned the muniments of the University, and in London they ransacked administrative and legal archives at Westminster, Lambeth Palace, the Temple and the Tower of London. Walsingham noted that they targeted such records and the clerks responsible for producing them:

> They made it their business to burn ancient muniments; and so that no one could be found again who had the ability or the knowledge later to commit to memory things old or new, they murdered men of that sort. It was dangerous to be recognised as a clerk, but much more dangerous if an inkpot were found by anyone's side, for such men never, or scarcely ever, escaped from their hands …[24]

On the other hand, they were clearly eager to have their charters of manumission and pardon in their possession. It was even suggested that before the

---

[20] *Peasants' Revolt*, ed. Dobson, pp. 162–3.

[21] See Chapter 2, p. 25.

[22] TNA SC 8/20/955.

[23] N. P. Brooks, 'The Organisation and Achievement of the Peasants of Kent and Essex in 1381', in *Studies in Medieval History Presented to R. H. C. Davis*, ed. H. Mayr-Harting and R. I. Moore (London, 1985), pp. 247–70; Ormrod, 'Government', pp. 1–30; M. Rampton, 'The Peasants' Revolt of 1381 and the Written Word', *Comitatus: A Journal of Medieval and Renaissance Studies* 24 (1993), 45–60; S. Justice, *Writing and Rebellion: England in 1381* (Berkeley, 1994). See also, D. Grummitt, 'Cade's Rebellion', pp. 111–12.

[24] 'Munimenta uetera studuerunt dare flammis; et ne de nouo quis reperiri ualeret qui uetera siue noua de cetero posset, uel nosset, commendare memorie, huiusmodi trucidabant. Periculosum erat agnosci pro clerico, set multo periculosius si ad latus alicuius atramentarium inuentum fuisset; nam tales uix aut nunquam ab eorum manibus euaserunt,' *St. Albans Chronicle*, ed. Taylor, Childs and Watkiss, p. 496; *Peasants' Revolt*, ed. Dobson, p. 364.

men of Essex returned home, they appointed several representatives to stay behind in order to obtain the king's charter.[25] These references to the rebels targeting particular documents, and making their own copies of charters, highlights their capacity to appropriate the structures of local administration for their own ends.[26] Steven Justice has shown that the rebels articulated their complaints in vernacular idioms that were different from the conventions of royal government. But they also proposed that formal charters could be drawn up under the great seal guaranteeing them manumission and pardon.[27] As Mark Ormrod noted, there was no precedent for such a document, and the king arguably had no right to issue one – but it seems the rebels assumed one could simply be invented.[28]

It should also be remembered that the physical document of pardon had an iconographic value, of which the rebels were well aware. The idea of royal grace as the ultimate resolution for those wrongly accused was clearly represented by the king's letters patent of pardon. Pardon was, in some instances, representative of vindication rather than of implied guilt.[29] For the rebels it represented a direct link to the personal form of grace dispensed by their monarch, unmediated by law courts or royal officers. Indeed, the chronicle accounts emphasise the extent to which the rebels invested their hopes in a face-to-face meeting with the king. Froissart even gives the dialogue of a message purportedly sent by the rebels to the king:

---

[25] Walsingham. *Peasants' Revolt*, ed. Dobson, p. 176.

[26] C. Dyer, 'The Social and Economic Background to the Rural Revolt of 1381', in *English Rising*, ed. Hilton and Aston, pp. 9–42. More generally, see R. B. Goheen, 'Peasant Politics? Village Communities and the Crown in Fifteenth-Century England', *American Historical Review* 96 (1991), 42–62; I. M. W. Harvey, 'Was There Popular Politics in Fifteenth-Century England?', in *McFarlane Legacy*, ed. Britnell and Pollard, pp. 155–74.

[27] Justice, *Writing and Rebellion*, pp. 13–66, 140–92. For the vernacular letters that apparently circulated among the rebels, see *Peasants' Revolt*, ed. Dobson, pp. 381–3. For their suggestion that particular charters could be drawn up, see *Peasants' Revolt*, ed. Dobson, pp. 159–63; B. F. Harvey, 'Draft Letters of Manumission and Pardon for the Men of Somerset in 1381', *EHR* 80 (1965), 89–91. For discussion of forged charters, see Chapter 4, pp. 51–2.

[28] W. M. Ormrod, 'Robin Hood and Public Record: The Authority of Writing in the Medieval Outlaw Tradition', in *Medieval Cultural Studies: Essays in Honour of Stephen Knight*, ed. R. Evans, H. Fulton and D. Matthews (Cardiff, 2006), p. 63. In the Parliament called in the autumn of 1381, the Lords were to question the right of the Crown to issue charters of manumission, but its right to bestow royal mercy on its subjects was never in doubt (*PROME*, 'Parliament of 1381', item 13). The Lords reminded the king of their property rights over serfs. Tuck emphasises that only the king could release men from the obligation to observe due process of law in depriving even rebels of their lives (Tuck, 'Nobles, Commons', pp. 199–200).

[29] See Chapter 3, pp. 22–4.

Sir, the commons of your realm hath sent me to you to desire you to come and speak with them on Blackheath; for they desire to have none but you: and, sir, ye need not have any doubt of your person for they will do you no hurt; for they hold and will hold you for their king. But, sir, they say they will shew you divers things, the which shall be right necessary for you to take heed of …[30]

The rebels had already made the familiar accusations of corruption against royal agents. This conventional rhetoric of the 'evil councillor' trope has been noted elsewhere, as a long-standing means of criticising government without voicing treasonous condemnation of the king himself.[31] The idea of corruption among the king's officers in the localities, the gentry justices, escheators and their like, was a related and similarly familiar concept, the staple of outlaw tales such as the *Gest of Robin Hood* and *Adam Bell*. Once the king was made aware of the honourable outlaw's plight he would see the justice of their cause and pardon them for resorting to direct action.[32] It might also be true to say that the rebels in 1381 believed that their best chance stood in putting their case before the king and asking for his pardon. Nigel Saul suggested that the rebels hoped Richard would prove an ally if released from the control of his councillors.[33] But in their desire for pardon they were also expressing a long-standing and consistent view that royal mercy represented a direct link between the king and his subjects.[34] As Alan Harding has argued, Wat Tyler's reference to the 'law of Winchester' at the Smithfield meeting perhaps alluded to a similar ideal.[35] The 1285 statute had become a touchstone of the principle of community self-policing – the hue and cry acting with the authority of the Crown, without the intervention of the sheriffs and gentry justices. As Harding suggested, it is possible that the rebels looked back to an idealised situation in which the king exercised exclusive lordship, with a small number of central justices, and received the written complaints

---

[30] *Peasants' Revolt*, ed. Dobson, p. 142. 'Très redoubtés sires, li communs de vostre roiaulme m'envoie devers vous pour traitiier, et vous prient que vous voelliés venir parler à eux sus la montaigne de la Blaquehède, car il ne desirent nullui à avoir que vous; et n'aiés nulle doubtance de vostre personne, car il ne vous feront ja mal, et vous tiennent et tenront tousjours à roi; mais il vous monsteront, che dient, pluiseurs coses qui vous sont necessaires à oïr' (Froissart, *Chroniques de J. Froissart*, Société de L'Histoire de France, ed. G. Raynaud (Paris, 1897), X, 103–4). See also the *Anonimalle Chronicle*, in *Peasants' Revolt*, ed. Dobson, pp. 129–30.

[31] Tuck, *English Nobility*, p. 43; J. A. Tuck, 'Richard II's System of Patronage', in *The Reign of Richard II: Essays in Honour of May McKisack*, ed. F. R. H. Du Boulay and C. M. Barron (London, 1971), pp. 1–20 (pp. 5–6); Ormrod, 'Government', pp. 29–30.

[32] *Gest of Robyn Hode*, lines 1645–58. *Adam Bell*, lines 435–526. The texts are published in *Robin Hood*, ed. Knight and Ohlgren. See Chapter 3, pp. 40–3.

[33] Saul, *Richard II*, p. 76.

[34] See Chapter 5, pp. 68–9.

[35] *Peasants' Revolt*, ed. Dobson, p. 164; Harding, 'Justices', pp. 165–93; Musson, *Medieval Law*, pp. 250–2.

of individuals and local communities in his court of Parliament. The intervening years had seen the steady encroachment of gentry justices at the local level, and special criminal commissions in the hands of the magnates. The rebels therefore perceived a shift in judicial authority, which had 'changed the social groups in whose interests the law worked'.[36] It seems possible that the rebels petitioned for pardon as a means of bringing their complaint to the king himself, and of ensuring the case against them was annulled, a process that they viewed as exemplifying the ideal judicial relationship between the king and his commons.[37]

Of course, in marching on London with 'force and arms' and demanding an audience with the king, the rebels were themselves subverting the judicial process for their own ends.[38] However, as John Watts has suggested, Wat Tyler and his company saw themselves as representatives of that broad, yet elusive group evoked by the term 'commons', and adopted the role of 'public petitioners', with implicit political rights.[39] It has been noted before that their grievances and the political expectations they expressed were not exclusive to the lower social orders.[40] Similarly, in drawing on notions of pardon, they dealt in a shared language, familiar to all ranks of society. In the same way that the rebels alluded to the 'evil councillor' topos, and with it a whole genre of political discourse created over the previous century, so too, the idea of royal grace as a pure form of justice was echoed in a range of texts, from the work of Gower to poems such as the *Outlaw's Song of Trailbaston* in the complaint tradition and to Corpus Christi plays such as the *Killing of Abel*.[41]

It is also important to note that the idea of pardon belonged as much to the government in 1381 as it did to the rebels. In drawing on the notion of royal mercy as an answer to a violent protest of this kind, the Crown was able to downplay the extent and novelty of the challenge presented by the rebels. Their complaints could be dealt with through established methods of political reconciliation: as the followers of the Ordainers in 1313 or those

---

36 A. Harding, 'Revolt Against the Justices', in *English Rising*, ed. Hilton and Aston, pp. 165–93 (p. 168).

37 Alan Harding suggests that Wat Tyler's demands stand in a tradition of debate between the king and the people on the proper administration of justice – a debate that had been aired in Parliament eighteen months before the revolt: Harding, 'Justices', p. 174.

38 References to the rebels using 'force and arms', being 'arrayed as if for war' and raising banners, brought to mind the precise definition of treasonous activity outlined in the Treason Law of 1352: J. G. Bellamy, *The Law of Treason in England in the Later Middle Ages* (Cambridge, 1970), pp. 103–5, 143, 183, 207.

39 Watts, 'Public', p. 161.

40 Harriss, 'Political Society', p. 56; Ormrod, *Political Life*, pp. 56–8. See also C. Valente, *The Theory and Practice of Revolt in Medieval England* (Aldershot, 2003), pp. 3–4, 167–70.

41 *Confessio Amantis*, Book 7, lines 3103–17; *Rymes of Robin Hood*, ed. Dobson and Taylor, p. 253; *Wakefield Pageants*, ed. Cawley; Watts, 'Public', pp. 168–9.

involved in the 1327 coup had been granted amnesty, now the pardon could be extended down the social order to the insurgents of 1381.[42] Indeed, if we return to the chronicle accounts of the revolt, there is the suggestion that the government had begun to discuss a possible grant of mercy as soon as it was known that the insurgents were massing outside the city. Froissart gives an account of an emergency meeting held in the Tower on the evening of 13 June.[43] He suggests that some of those present favoured a military riposte to the rebels, the mayor putting forward a plan to leave the Tower under cover of darkness and enter the city, 'so to slay all these unhappy people, while they were at their rest and asleep'. He suggested that they could call on others who lived in the city to support them, in particular Sir Robert Knolles, who was guarding his lodging with a force of more than 120 men. However, Froissart reports that several others present feared that military action would provoke the rest of the commons of London to rise in rebellion. The earl of Salisbury supposedly articulated this view when he advised the king

> if you can appease them with fairness, it were best and most profitable, and to grant them everything that they desire, for if we should begin a thing the which we could not achieve, we should never recover it again, but we and our heirs ever to be disinherited.[44]

Froissart's account here gives a sense of continuity, from Salisbury's counsel to the king's proclamation to the rebels that he would pardon them all their different offences. When this was not enough to halt the violence the council persevered with mediation. After discussing the matter early on Friday morning it decided that the king should meet the rebels at Mile End later the same day.[45] It was at this meeting that Richard agreed to issue the famous charters of manumission to the insurgents, which have been the focus of so much scholarly debate.[46] However, less attention has been paid to the hastily drafted general amnesty that was also proclaimed: the king pardoned his subjects for all felonies and acts of treason they had performed.[47] Walsingham

---

[42] See Chapter 7, pp. 93–100.

[43] *Peasants' Revolt*, ed. Dobson, pp. 189–90; Saul, *Richard II*, pp. 66–80.

[44] *Peasants' Revolt*, ed. Dobson, p. 190. 'Sire, se vous les poés apaissier par belle parolles, c'est le malleur et le plus pourfitable, et leur acordés tout ce que il demandent liement, car, se nous commenchiens cose que nous ne peuissiens achiever, il n'i aroit jamais nul recouvrier que nous et nos hoirs ne fuissons desert' (Froissart, *Chroniques*, ed. Raynaud, X, 110).

[45] *Peasants' Revolt*, ed. Dobson, p. 190.

[46] Harvey, 'Draft Letters', pp. 89–91; E. B. Fryde, *Peasants and Landlords in Later Medieval England* (Stroud, 1996), pp. 39–53; R. H. Hilton, *Bond Men Made Free* (London, 1973), p. 224; Dyer, 'Social and Economic Background', pp. 9–42; Dunn, *Great Rising*, pp. 96–7.

[47] Ambiguity exists over whether Richard issued the charters at Mile End, or whether he simply agreed to have them drawn up, and actually issued them at Smithfield.

states that the terms of this charter were confirmed to the rebels the next day at Smithfield, and again at Clerkenwell, and this, coming after the death of their leader Wat Tyler, was enough to persuade them to disperse and return to their homes.[48]

What do these references to reconciliatory overtures on the part of the Crown amount to? One line of argument would be to say that the promise of pardon was a cynical means of placating the rebels and encouraging their dispersal from the capital, so that the Crown could then initiate its favoured policy of repression. This seems to be supported by the revocation of the charters of manumission on 2 July.[49] For the author of the *Anonimalle Chronicle* such references could be used to suggest that the young king himself took the initiative in placating the rebels, in the absence of any leadership from his councillors.[50] In this sense it fits into the chronicler's broader objective of promoting Richard's own role in saving the day. The association of the king himself with the policy of conciliation seems to have been in the mind of the chronicler, if not also the royal advisers. The narrative of events suggests that Richard ordered the pardon to be proclaimed in front of the rebels himself, and that he sealed the charter with his own signet – a seal normally used to communicate the king's personal orders to his Chancery office, and to warrant their issue of a charter under the great seal.[51] There is perhaps something to be said for the fact that the grant of royal grace allowed the governing elite to claim a leading role for the young king. Accordingly the pardon had the seal of royal authority and thus stressed the reciprocal obligation on the part of the king's subjects. It also acknowledged the active role

---

Froissart clearly states that letters were given on the same day as the Mile End meeting (*Peasants' Revolt*, ed. Dobson, p. 192), but Walsingham believed that no charter was delivered to the rebels before the meeting at Smithfield. The only copy of the text is that transcribed by Walsingham (*Peasants' Revolt*, ed. Dobson, pp. 180–1). Three of the letters issued to specific counties were recorded: Walsingham transcribed the letter for Hertfordshire (*Peasants' Revolt*, ed. Dobson, p. 275); the letter for Kent is in BL, Cotton Charter 4, fol. 51; and a draft drawn up by the men of Somerset is published in Harvey, 'Draft Letters', p. 90. According to Harvey, no warrant for any has been found, although even on 15 June the king gave warrants for some conciliatory measures: TNA C 81/471/1833 contains a warrant for letters patent issued to the mayor of Oxford (later cancelled, *CPR, 1381–5*, p. 16).

48 *Peasants' Revolt*, ed. Dobson, pp. 177, 180.

49 Revocation dated 2 July: Walsingham, *HA*, II, 20–2; Walsingham, *CA*, 318. The revocation was confirmed in the November Parliament: *PROME*, 'Parliament of 1381', item 13; *SR*, II, 20.

50 *Peasants' Revolt*, ed. Dobson, p. 159; Saul, *Richard II*, pp. 67–8.

51 Richard's use of the privy seal in this context might signify that the document he was holding up to the rebels was intended to be a warrant, which would later be sent to Chancery to authorise the issue of individual charters to the rebels under the great seal. This is supported by references in Froissart's account and in the *Anonimalle Chronicle* to Chancery clerks being ordered to write out large numbers of charters, patents and letters of protection. See nn. 19–20 above.

of the monarchy in guaranteeing their rights. The grant of a pardon perhaps allowed Richard's ministers to present the king at the head of the response, while still retaining control of policy.[52] Walsingham also includes a scene in the wake of the Smithfield meeting, when the knights surrounding the king request permission to decapitate 'at least one or two hundred of the criminals as a warning to posterity'. But, according to the chronicler, the king refused them the request, saying that 'many of the commons had followed the mob out of fear; if he assented to the proposal, it might well be that the innocent would be punished and the guilty escape unharmed'.[53] This recognition of the dangers of condemning the innocent along with the guilty chimed with later protests put forward by the parliamentary Commons (discussed below). The scene clearly bestowed on the young king the sense of fairness and equity required of an adult medieval monarch. Froissart's details on the meetings in the Tower also give the impression that the council was able to contemplate the idea of reconciliation, although it had not decided whether negotiations with the rebels should be binding.[54]

The question of sincerity aside, it is interesting that the chroniclers did allow for ideas of mercy to be associated with the young king from the early stages of their narratives. While it is true that for writers such as Walsingham the idea of the violation of divinely inspired social hierarchy was the dominant frame of reference, it is clear that the chroniclers also wove into their accounts the model of royal mercy.[55] Moreover, the Crown and commons shared this common language of pardon, and understood that it signified a particular relationship between the king and his subjects. By the beginning of October, letters of pardon began to be issued from Chancery. It is worth noting from the outset that the Crown had sanctioned the issue of these letters only a few months after the insurrection. Importantly, these moves were made before Parliament had convened and therefore before the parliamentary Commons had a chance to express their views on the matter.

---

[52] Musson and Ormrod, *Evolution*, p. 170. Letters patent on the pardon roll were warranted 'by the king in parliament', referring to the November 1381 ordinance, or 'by the king and council', suggesting that Richard was still expressing his authority only in association with his advisers. In 1380 plans had been aired for the king to lead an overseas military expedition. Watts mentions a similar proposal for Henry VI to head the Calais army: Watts, *Henry VI*, p. 130, and n. 24. This suggests that both administrations sought to demonstrate the leadership, although not the coming of age of the king.

[53] *Peasants' Revolt*, ed. Dobson, p. 180. The suggestion that some participants had been forced to follow the rebels was echoed in later judicial proceedings: see, for example, the case of Osbert de Mundford in Norfolk, who was forced to join the rebel contingent under the leadership of John Gelder (TNA KB 9/166/1, mm. 53, 78), discussed in H. Eiden, 'Joint Action against "Bad" Lordship: The Peasants' Revolt in Essex and Norfolk', *History* 83 (1998), 5–30 (p. 9).

[54] Saul, *Richard II*, p. 68.

[55] Pearsall, 'Interpretative Models', pp. 64–5; *Peasants' Revolt*, ed. Dobson, pp. 367–72.

Government Reaction

The debate surrounding the nature of the government reaction in the weeks after the revolt has centred on the judicial commissions sent into the Home Counties, and the numbers of rebels executed as a result of these proceedings.[56] One source that has been somewhat overlooked in this scholarship has been the Chancery pardon roll. As the name suggests, this roll recorded the recipients of pardon in the wake of the revolt.[57] Not all recipients of pardon listed in the roll were actually involved in the rebellion, and therefore the roll does not necessarily help to identify prominent rebels.[58] Despite this, the pardon roll is of some use for a number of reasons. At the most basic level, the very creation of a new supplementary roll suggests an early assumption that the Crown would authorise the issue of pardons in significant numbers, and that an accurate record needed to be kept. Separate pardon rolls were rarely created in this period; normally pardons would simply be added to the main patent roll.[59] The roll is also useful in highlighting the continuity between the themes present in the narrative sources discussed above, and the administrative and legal records, so often treated entirely separately.

The first entries on the roll demonstrate that pardons began to be issued soon after the revolt. The very first was issued to Paul Salesbury on 22 July, but this seems to be an exception; his case had been promoted by Sir Aubrey de Vere, the king's chamberlain.[60] The next pardon was issued on 18 October, and was followed by 114 others over the next month alone. In

---

[56] See n. 2 above.

[57] TNA C 67/29. In the aftermath of the Peasants' Revolt, there was some duplication of names between the pardon roll and the main patent roll: Prescott suggests that this is because a petitioner might pay to have another record of their pardon entered on the main roll (Prescott, 'Judicial Records', p. 355).

[58] See below, pp. 151–3, for further discussion. The task of identifying individual members of the rebel band has been undertaken by several scholars: see Prescott, 'Judicial Records'; Eiden, 'Joint Action'; Hilton, *Bond Men*; Dyer, 'Social and Economic Background'; C. Dyer, 'The Rising of 1381 in Suffolk: Its Origins and Participants', *Proceedings of the Suffolk Institute of Archaeology and History* 36 (1988), 274–87; A. Prescott, 'London in the Peasants' Revolt: A Portrait Gallery', *London Journal* 7 (1981), 125–43. Prescott suggests that the pardon roll is overrated as a source of information about the revolt (Prescott, 'Judicial Records', p. 334). He also points out that the list of exclusions from the general pardon (*PROME*, 'Parliament of 1381', item 63) is not a reliable guide to the identity of leading insurgents (Prescott, 'Judicial Records', p. 361).

[59] See Chapters 7 and 8.

[60] Aubrey de Vere's name is endorsed on Salesbury's pardon. This pardon, and one other issued at the beginning of October, appears in the main patent roll: TNA C 66/311, m. 31; *CPR, 1381–5*, pp. 30–1; *Peasants' Revolt*, ed. Dobson, p. 228; Thomas de Wycresley: *CPR, 1381–5*, p. 43. For further discussion of Salesbury's role, see Dunn, *Great Rising*, p. 65 and Prescott, 'Judicial Records', p. 350.

total the pardon rolls associated with the Peasants' Revolt contain close to 3,500 names.[61] However, this first group of 115 pardons issued in October and November 1381 seem to form a discrete group on the roll. The wording of the pardon in these cases is different from all subsequent pardons, and crucially writs were issued before Parliament had met to officially sanction a pardon. It was not, in fact, until 13 December 1381 that Parliament drew up a standard form of pardon for involvement in the rebellion. These early pardons are also different from the ones that followed because of the widely varying amount that recipients paid for them. One column on the roll gives the assessed value of each person's possessions, and the fine to be paid into the hanaper. Normally, a pardon would have cost 18s. 4d. However, payments for these pardons varied considerably. Most were between 25s. and 30s., but some were far higher: two men paid as much as £40. At the other end of the scale one man was granted pardon free of any fine.[62] After the pardon was issued by Parliament, the price was fixed at 16s. 4d., until a later proclamation made it free to all those who wanted one.[63]

This raises the question of who these early recipients were. Herbert Eiden noted that not everyone who bought a pardon can be proved to have been involved in the insurgency.[64] This in itself is surely interesting; that people were buying pardons as a form of insurance against the possibility of malicious indictment, a concern which, according to certain of the chroniclers, had been prevalent since the early stages of the revolt.[65] Prescott also pointed out the inconsistencies in the issue of pardons, drawing his evidence from Walsingham's account of the St Albans' trials. Walsingham gives details of the execution of leading insurgents, men such as William Grindcobbe and William Caddington. Nevertheless, another leading St Albans rebel, Richard Wallingford, was one of the first to receive pardon. According to Walsingham, the judicial sessions held in the town throughout October by Chief Justice

---

61 There are 115 names on the first three membranes of the roll (TNA C 67/29, mm. 41, 40, 39). In total, 2,253 pardons were issued before October 1382. At this point the benefits of the amnesty were extended to all the king's subjects, free of the requirement to sue out a letter of pardon. Even so, a further 588 names were added to the roll as receiving pardon, from May 1383 until the end of the reign. This gives a total on the roll of 3,429.

62 Geoffrey Cobbe and John Refham both paid £40 (TNA C 67/29, m. 41). In Cobbe's case, the recognisance he made to pay the sum in the hanaper is noted in the close rolls (*CCR, 1381–5*, p. 92). William Punchon of Dartford was granted pardon without fine (C 67/29, m. 41).

63 The writ for proclamation of the 1381 pardon stipulates that a pardon could be procured 'for payment only of the fee for the great seal' (*CPR, 1381–5*, p. 105). This therefore indicates that the price stood at 16s. 4d. (without the 2s. usually payable to the chancellor). The pardon was declared free of charge in October 1382: *SR*, II, 29–30. Discussed further below, pp. 155–7.

64 Eiden, 'Joint Action', pp. 8–9.

65 See above, pp. 129–31.

Tresilian resulted in the execution of fifteen people and the imprisonment of a further eighty men.[66] However, we can add to this picture the forty-four pardons granted to inhabitants of Hertfordshire by the end of November 1381, ten of whom were residents of St Albans. Eleven of these recipients later proved their pardons in King's Bench.[67] Looking just at the recipients of these early pardons, then, there does seem to be a considerable range of people. A few were leading rebels, and for them to pursue a pardon was clearly a prudent course of action, so well known were they in the local area. In St Albans, for example, Richard Wallingford and Edmund Cook were known to be leading rebels, and both were quick to seek out a pardon.[68] Similarly Geoffrey Cobbe played a leading part in the rebellion in Cambridge, and had already been indicted by the time he received his pardon on 20 October.[69] Again, Richard Denarston was one of the leading Suffolk insurgents, and got his pardon on 23 October.[70] These four men were also among the wealthiest on the list. Denarston's goods were valued at £6, Wallingford was assessed at over £13, Cook at £20 and Cobbe at over £28.[71]

Another of the wealthiest on this list was Richard Martyn of Cambridge, assessed at over £20. He received his pardon on 23 October 1381, but in his case it was recorded again in the main patent roll the following year, with the note that it was granted at the special request of Queen Anne. Seeking a pardon in his case was prudent; later, on 24 May 1382, a judicial commis-

---

[66] Prescott, 'Judicial Records', pp. 350–1; Walsingham, *HA*, II, 35–8: see also Dunn, *Great Rising*, pp. 139–41.

[67] TNA C 67/29, mm. 39–41; KB 27/482 *rex*, mm. 26, 26v, 27, 27v, 28, 37 (pardons granted to inhabitants of Cambridgeshire, Northamptonshire, Yorkshire and Kent were also proved in King's Bench: KB 27/482, m. 47; KB 27/483, m. 27v; KB 27/486, m. 15; E 153/530, mm. 9–17).

[68] TNA C 67/29, mm. 40, 41; Walsingham, *HA*, I, 475 and Appendix B, p. 394. Two other St Albans men were well-known rebels, and were both quick to seek pardon: John Tyler was indicted for burning the house ('called le Thwethonerhous') of the abbot, and John Garlek for freeing prisoners from the abbey and accompanying Wallingford in marching on the abbey 'arrayed for war' with the banners of St George and demanding to speak to the abbot. Tyler received an early pardon on 23 October (C 67/29, m. 40) and later proved the pardon in King's Bench (KB 27/485, mm. 33, 33v). Garlek received his pardon on 20 October (C 67/29, m. 39) and again proved it in King's Bench (KB 27/482, m. 28). These events are described by Walsingham: *Gesta abbatum monasterii Sancti Albani*, ed. H. T. Riley, 3 vols., RS 28 (London, 1867–9), III, 301–2, 304–5: see also A. Réville, *Etude sur le Soulèvement de 1381 dans le Comtés de Hertford, de Suffolk et de Norfolk* (Paris, 1898), pp. 13, 17, 18, 33, 152.

[69] Cobbe's indictment is transcribed in E. Powell, *The Rising in East Anglia in 1381* (Cambridge, 1896), p. 137. Cobbe received his pardon on 20 October, and by 24 October the king had ordered that his confiscated lands be restored to him: *CCR, 1381–5*, p. 14.

[70] Réville, *Soulèvement*, pp. 78, 123: see below, n. 76.

[71] TNA C 67/29, mm. 40, 41.

sion was sent to Cambridge to investigate the complaint of the master of Corpus Christi College. Interestingly, the complaint was framed in terms familiar from the chronicle accounts of the rebels and their activities; the master accused Martyn and several others of breaking into the college close, having first proclaimed that the townsfolk should come to the college and help them to destroy it. They were then said to have carried away timber, doors and windows, books and jewels. They also tore up charters, assaulted the servants and hunted for the master and scholars, threatening to kill them. The call to the townsmen for support and the targeting of charters were both common themes in narratives of the rising.[72]

A few of those receiving pardons in October and November had definitely already been indicted at the judicial sessions held in the Home Counties in July.[73] They had a clear incentive to secure pardon as quickly as possible. Among the men indicted in the Rochester hearings before Thomas Holand, the king's half-brother, was Richard Poser. He was accused, again in terms common to chronicles and to petitions, of burning records and harassing officers of the Crown, in this instance the escheator of Kent, but was able to secure a pardon by November.[74] Also in Kent, John Wryde had been accused of extorting money from two men of Canterbury and William Brown of killing two men in Maidstone. Both had received a pardon by November.[75] In Norfolk three men – Richard Denarston of Suffolk (discussed above), Robert Herde of Toft Monks in Norfolk and William Metfeld of King's Lynn – were indicted before William de Ufford, earl of Suffolk.[76] As Herbert Eiden noted, we cannot assume these men were rebels from the indictment and the pardon alone; they might have been victims of malicious indictment. Indeed, Eiden demonstrated that some prominent victims of the rebels procured pardons: John Butterwick, under-sheriff of Middlesex, and the knight Andrew Cavendish in Suffolk, a relative of the murdered chief justice, both bought pardons

---

[72] It is also worth noting that another of the men accused by the master of involvement, Robert Brigham, was also among the first to receive a pardon, and in this case he was not wealthy: the value of his goods was assessed at just over 2*s*. (TNA C 67/29, m. 41; *CPR, 1381–5*, pp. 143, 203), and see below, n. 81.

[73] For a list of references to the surviving original commission records, see Prescott, 'The Hand of God', p. 325, n. 40.

[74] E. Powell and G. M. Trevelyan, ed., *The Peasants' Rising and the Lollards* (Cambridge, 1899), p. 6 (transcription of the indictment); TNA C 67/29, m. 41.

[75] TNA C 67/29, mm. 40, 41; W. Flaherty, 'The Great Rebellion in Kent of 1381 Illustrated from the Public Records', *Archaeologia Cantiana* 3 (1860), 65–96 (p. 71). These are transcriptions of the indictments in JUST 1/400.

[76] TNA KB 9/166/1, mm. 15, 22, 39, 41, 51, 64, 65. The commission's records had been returned into Chancery, and then to King's Bench in pursuance of a *mandamus* dated 13 May 1382 (m. 1): see also C 67/29, m. 41. H. Eiden, '"In der Knechtschaft werdet ihr verharren …"': Ursachen und Verlauf des englischen Bauernaufstands von 1381' (unpublished PhD thesis, Trier, 1995), p. 327, gives details of the 'Geledere–Metfeld group' and their activities in this area.

although they took no part in the rebellion.[77] False indictment, as has already been noted, was a widespread concern. The burgesses of Scarborough were even moved to petition the king and request that individuals falsely indicted before the earl of Northumberland be pardoned.[78]

Several more of the recipients of early pardons were to come before King's Bench in the months after they received pardon.[79] The court of King's Bench had not been in session on the days when the insurgents had occupied the capital. It had been due to reopen for Trinity term on 17 June, but the revolt forced its postponement until Michaelmas term. When it did open, in the second week of October, one of its main functions seems to have been the processing of pardons.[80] Three men in Cambridge, for example, had been indicted in July, but the record of their case was postponed into King's Bench and did not come before the justices until Trinity term, in the summer of 1382, by which time the men had secured pardons.[81] Another two men, Jordan de Bladington and Robert Draper, had been named as rebels in the Kent sessions of September 1381 by another suspected rebel, who had turned approver and had given the justice their names.[82] One man, Stephen Sunday of Hackney, had been accused on 20 July 1381 of misdeeds at the house of the Treasurer, Robert Hales, at Highbury. Again, his case was adjourned into King's Bench, perhaps because of its high profile, and it was not finally resolved until November 1384.[83] On occasion it was noted in the record that the court had not yet been advised to allow a charter of pardon. This occurred when William Chaundler of Prittlewell in Essex came before King's Bench in Michaelmas term 1381. The date of his appearance in court was given as

---

77 Eiden, 'Joint Action', p. 9.
78 TNA SC 8/139/6949.
79 Of the 115 recipients of 'early' pardons, twenty-three have been identified in the King's Bench rolls: TNA KB 27/482, mm. 15, 26, 26v, 27, 27v, 28, 29v, 31v, 32v, 34, 36, 37, 37v, 39, 43v, 46v; KB 27/483, m. 23v; KB 27/ 485, mm. 18, 27, 27v, 28v, 33, 33v; KB 27/486, mm. 11, 27: see also Réville, *Soulèvement*; Eiden, 'Knechtschaft'.
80 Many of these represent the processing of outstanding indictments from juries in the localities. Prescott notes that King's Bench records comprise a very late stage in the proceedings against the rebels, and consist largely of the formal processing of pardons: Prescott, 'The Hand of God', p. 325. Ormrod, 'Government', p. 8.
81 Robert Brigham, John Refham and John Stamford (TNA KB 27/485, mm. 27, 27v). Brigham and Refham presented two letters of pardon each before King's Bench, both purchased on the same days – 24 February 1382 and 20 October 1381 (C 67/29, mm. 28, 41). They had also both secured letters of protection dated 6 July 1382, and submitted these before the court (KB 27/485, mm. 27, 27v). The escheator of Cambridge was later ordered to restore to them their confiscated lands (*CCR, 1381–5*, p. 169). Stamford secured pardon on 4 November 1381, and a letter of protection the following October (C 67/29, m. 39; Réville, *Soulèvement*, p. 242).
82 TNA KB 27/482, m. 36; C 67/29, m. 40; Réville, *Soulèvement*, p. 205.
83 TNA KB 27/494, m. 32v. Sunday was named on the list of those to be excluded from royal grace in the 1381 Parliament: Réville, *Soulèvement*, pp. 209–10, and see below, p. 155.

21 November, and from the pardon roll it appears that he secured his letter of pardon two days later. It seems the justice was prepared to accept that the pardon was on its way, and William was dismissed after finding men willing to guarantee his appearance at a later date.[84]

From the King's Bench records, it becomes clear that there were several distinct groups among the men who were able to secure the first pardons. Some were implicated in specific incidents of rebellion. One group, already mentioned, from Cambridge was accused of rioting, extorting money and making threats against the master and scholars of Corpus Christi College.[85] Three groups from Hertfordshire sought out pardons. One group, from Tring, had been indicted for involvement in forcing entry into the archbishop of Canterbury's manor and destroying records, as well as parading banners of St George, and making proclamations in the town.[86] One group from Cheshunt were accused of rebellion in nearby Waltham Cross.[87] Another group were from St Albans, accused of attempting to take the records of the abbey.[88] Another contingent came from Kent, indicted for breaking into the houses of prominent townsmen alongside the well-known rebel Abel Ker.[89] A final group came from London, among them William Trewman, accused of attacking the former mayor Sir Nicholas Brembre.[90]

---

[84] J. Sparvel-Bayly, 'Essex in Insurrection, 1381', *Transactions of the Essex Archaeological Society*, n.s. 1 (1878), 205–19 (pp. 214–15); TNA C 67/29, m. 41.

[85] This group included Robert Brigham, John Refham, Richard Martyn and John Stamford: see also *Documents Relating to Cambridge Villages*, ed. W. H. Palmer and H. W. Saunders (Cambridge, 1926), p. 36.

[86] Richard Horsman junior was indicted before King's Bench: TNA KB 27/486, m. 27; Réville, *Soulèvement*, p. 39. Three other men from Tring also bought early pardons: William Tyngewyk, Walter Smyth and Richard Mathewe (C67/29, m. 41).

[87] Walter Parchemer came before King's Bench: TNA KB 27/482, m. 43; Réville, *Soulèvement*, p. 38. Thirteen other men from Cheshunt bought early pardons: Walter Ferrour, Richard Dalowe, Simon atte Marche, Thomas Ferrour, Gamelin Impey, Thomas Swetefote, William Carles, William Bisshop, Walter Lavendar, John Couper, William Phippe, John Everard and Thomas Cut (C 67/29, mm. 40, 41).

[88] Members of this group included Richard Walingford, Edmund Cook, William Gore, John Tyler, John Dene, John atte Grene, William Berewyk, Peter Webbe, John Wayte, John Garlek, Gilbert Beel, Thomas Payntour and Thomas Long: see Walsingham, *HA*, I, 475 and Appendix B, p. 394; Réville, *Soulèvement*, pp. 13, 17, 38, 152, 161; *PROME*, 'Parliament of 1381', item 63; TNA KB 27/482, mm. 26, 26v, 28; KB 27/485, mm. 33, 33v; C 67/29, mm. 39–41. One interesting pardon that might be associated with the St Albans judicial hearings was granted to Thomas de Wycresley, 'for having cut the cords by which certain condemned men were being hung at St Albans', for which offence he had been detained in Newgate prison: *CPR, 1381–5*, p. 43.

[89] Including John Yonge, Jordan de Bladyngton, Robert Draper, John Cheseman, John Clerk and Thomas Chaump: TNA KB 27/482, m. 36; KB 27/483, m. 27v; KB 27/486, m. 11; Réville, *Soulèvement*, pp. 183–4, 189, 205, 227; C 67/29, mm. 39–41.

[90] TNA KB 27/482, m. 39. Other Londoners included Stephen Sunday, William Peche, John Huntingdon and Theobald Ellis: C 67/29, mm. 39–41.

Yet the majority of people on the list do not seem to have been indicted before receiving pardon (although we are lacking the records for Hertfordshire). In fact only forty of the 115 names on the list of early pardons appear in court records, chronicle references or the parliamentary list of those excluded from grace.[91] People who had not been indicted were perhaps prompted to buy pardons after seeing the judicial commissions at work. Given the relative wealth of some of those on the list, one other possibility might be that these were men who wanted to safeguard themselves against charges of not having done anything to quell the rising, or of having taken matters into their own hands and seeking revenge on some of their attackers after the suppression.[92] Another possibility is that these early pardons were linked with the king's itinerary in the days and weeks after the rebellion. It is interesting that they were largely granted to inhabitants of areas that hosted the royal entourage in June or July 1381. From the itinerary W. H. B. Bird pieced together, Richard left London for Havering and Chelmsford in Essex where he stayed for a week. After returning to London he went to Hertfordshire, spending a week in St Albans and another in Berkhamsted and King's Langley. The court then went to Reading Abbey, to Eltham and to Leeds in Kent before returning to London.[93] This might account for the large group from south-west Hertfordshire; forty-four of the 115 early pardons were granted to residents of Hertfordshire, almost all of whom lived within a twenty-mile radius of St Albans. This also fits with the group from Kent, who came from the area surrounding the royal palace at Eltham. In contrast the numbers do not correlate with areas that had most recorded rebels – Norfolk and Essex were at the top of the list, while Hertfordshire had far fewer.[94] If the numbers were simply dictated by proximity to the Chancery at Westminster, it seems surprising that there are not more recipients from London itself.

The reasons for these pardons being given are not usually recorded. In two of the earliest pardons granted, there is explicit reference to the help of a patron interceding on the supplicant's behalf, so in the case of Paul Salesbury, the pardon was said to be given on the information of the king's chamberlain, Sir Aubrey de Vere. For Richard Martyn of Cambridge, pardon came at the request of Anne of Bohemia, who was soon to be crowned queen. Anne was also named in the pardon drawn up by Parliament; the king was said to have granted pardon at the special request of Anne, in order to encourage

---

91 For further discussion of the list of those excluded, see below, p. 155.
92 Eiden, 'Joint Action', p. 9. Prescott notes that of all the pardons issued in connection with the revolt, only just over forty were produced by defendants in court. He is surely right to suggest that many pardons would have been bought merely as a precaution (Prescott, 'Judicial Records', p. 355).
93 W. H. B. Bird, 'The Peasant Rising and the King's Itinerary', *EHR* 31 (1916), 124–6 (p. 125).
94 Eiden's figures: Norfolk (1,214), Essex (954), Kent (456), Suffolk (299), Cambridgeshire (242), Rest (389): Eiden, 'Joint Action', p. 10, n. 26.

his subjects to keep the peace in the future.[95] There are also three examples of letters ordering the restoration of confiscated lands, because 'men of the council learned in law' had concluded that the cause given by the escheator was not sufficient for forfeiture.[96]

It is also interesting that six of those who received early pardons were later named in Parliament on the list of those excluded from royal grace.[97] It might be that those who drew up the lists were simply unaware that these men had already been granted pardon. But it is also true to say that the pardons they had received did not excuse them if they were later implicated in the deaths of the senior government ministers, Sudbury, Hales and Cavendish, or the murder of the Prior of Bury, or of the burning of the Savoy Palace or Clerkenwell Priory. If this was the case there would be no contradiction in placing them on the list of those excluded. This can be proved true of one man, Stephen Sunday, who was granted pardon on 12 November, but was later accused of involvement in the murder of Robert Hales.[98] A final point about these early pardons is that seven of the recipients went on to sue out another pardon in the spring of 1382. Four of them came before King's Bench, and both pardons were noted in the record. Robert Brigham and John Refham of Cambridge were even able to produce two letters of pardon and letters of protection.[99]

Returning to the scholarly debate on the character of the government reaction, it has been argued that an initially harsh and vindictive campaign of repression gave way to a more moderate stance once the Commons were able to voice their concerns in Parliament.[100] However, this might be too neat a division to make. In fact, the issue of pardons before the opening of Parliament suggests that they were a recognised part of the judicial process, and

---

95 See below, pp. 154–5.
96 Salesbury: TNA C 66/311, m. 31, *CPR, 1381–5*, pp. 30–1; *Peasants' Revolt*, ed. Dobson, p. 228. Martyn: *CPR, 1381–5*, pp. 143, 203. Parliamentary pardon: *PROME*, 'Parliament of 1381', item 32. Letters to escheators: *CCR, 1381–5*, pp. 14, 169, 175.
97 *PROME*, 'Parliament of 1381', item 63. John Yonge of Herefordshire (listed under London); Richard Scott, hosier, of London; Stephen Sunday, of Hackney; Thomas Bunny, sheather and grinder, of London; William de la Stable, alias William Gore of St Albans; John le Dene, pedlar, of Ashbocking in Suffolk.
98 Another name on the list of exclusions was Thomas, servant of Paul Salesbury (see above, n. 60). While Salesbury was the first to receive a pardon, his servant was not so lucky. Prescott notes that nearly one in ten of those excluded were later found not guilty. He suggests that local commissioners adopted different criteria for deciding which names to put forward for exclusion. In London, it seems, Walworth's commission simply forwarded the names of those awaiting trial: Prescott, 'Judicial Records', pp. 358–61.
99 John Refham, Robert Brigham (n. 72 above), Gamelin Impey, William Phippe, Thomas Longe (TNA KB 27/485, m. 33), Peter Webbe and Jordan de Bladyngton (n. 89 above): C 67/29, m. 28, 26, 25.
100 Tuck, 'Nobles, Commons'; Ormrod, 'Government'.

that they could, and would, be used as part of the government's response to the revolt. While they had not yet been sanctioned by Parliament, this rubber-stamp was assumed to be only a matter of time in coming, and it was perfectly acceptable to issue pardons in the meantime.[101] In the context of the chronicle narratives discussed above, these pardons are also consistent with the sense that royal mercy would be available to those judged worthy of receiving it, and that this form of grace could be dispensed by the young king without waiting for the sanction of Parliament. Moreover, there is a suggestion from certain of the chroniclers that concerns were being expressed among sections of the local gentry communities about the activities of the royal commissioners sent from Westminster. According to Walsingham, prominent members of the gentry in Kent and Hertfordshire had offered to stand surety for the commons, rather than see a royal visitation of their counties.[102] Nigel Saul suggests that this was prompted by a growing belief that the campaign of repression had been pushed too far.[103] It might also be the case that local gentry wanted power to deal with local rebels themselves, rather than cede authority to the judicial commissions sent from Westminster. A petition of the abbot and convent of Peterborough, for example, requested authority over correction of their own tenants. They also asked for charters of pardon to be withheld until the individuals concerned had made satisfaction for their rebellion.[104] This is particularly interesting in light of the debate surrounding the social exclusivity of the law. The supposed corruption of local gentry justices was apparently a central concern of the lower social orders, and one that was articulated by the chroniclers. In this instance, however, it was the gentry suspicion of the officers of central government that Walsingham chose to articulate.

By 30 August the Crown had halted all arrests and executions and adjourned outstanding hearings into King's Bench.[105] Writs for attendance at Parliament had already been sent out, so it is possible that these measures were designed to appeal to the representatives in Parliament.[106] It is also

---

101 Parliament was originally called (by writs of 16 July) for 16 September, but was postponed until the beginning of November. It was then adjourned on 13 December to meet again between 27 January and 25 February 1382: *Peasants' Revolt*, ed. Dobson, p. 325. For further discussion, see below, pp. 149–55.

102 Walsingham, *HA*, II, 14, 22–6.

103 Saul, *Richard II*, pp. 78–9.

104 TNA SC 8/94/4698. The tenants had been indicted before Lord de la Zouche's commission.

105 *CCR 1381–5*, pp. 7–8.

106 The place-dates on the letters patent recorded on the pardon roll indicate that Richard had reached Westminster by 20 October (TNA C 67/29, mm. 41, 40, 39). This would suggest that warrants for all the 'early' pardons were issued from the time Richard arrived in Westminster until shortly before the schedule of pardon was submitted in Parliament. The only exceptions were the pardons to Salesbury and possibly that to Wycresley: Salesbury's was dated 22 July, and issued from

possible that the council themselves favoured a general pardon. A meeting of the council was held on 7 October in Berkhamsted. The main focus of attention at this meeting were plans for the king to lead a campaign to France and capitalise on the political weakness created by the death of Charles V.[107] If such a campaign were to go ahead, the nobles would be needed to lead the army, rather than to head up judicial commissions at home. It is possible that the council also considered the financial benefits of granting a pardon. The *Anonimalle* author made the point explicitly when he commented that 'everyone was to have his charter of pardon and pay the king as fee for his seal twenty shillings, to make him rich'.[108] What is clear is that the idea of pardoning the insurgents was not new to the Parliament that met in November. It is also evident that in issuing these early pardons the young king was assuming, or at least being given a central role in affairs, a role consistent with the narratives of the chroniclers.

Parliament

The discussion of pardon in the Parliament convened on 3 November 1381 has received some scholarly attention. The debate has centred on the conflicting aims of the Lords and Commons; did the peers favour a swift and harsh brand of justice that would allow them to resume the war with France, and did the Commons exert pressure to enforce a more moderate stance?[109] While these questions are pertinent, it is also important to retain the sense of these parliament rolls as texts, and to view them in a broader context, alongside the chronicle accounts and the legal records. Much of the language of the Common petitions and the terms used in the royal grant of pardon, for example, drew on a discourse of pardon familiar from earlier grants, and

Berkhamsted (*CPR, 1381–5*, p. 30), Wycresley's on 10 October from Berkhamsted (*CPR, 1381–5*, p. 43). It is unlikely that the warrants were given before this time as it was customary for letters patent to bear the date of the original royal warrant: Maxwell-Lyte, *Great Seal*, pp. 247–8. Brown, 'Great Seal', pp. 125–55, notes that the warrant 'per ipsum regem' on letters of general pardon was a fiction, indicating not that a warrant had been issued for every individual, but referring instead to the original grant: see also Wilkinson, 'Chancery Writs', pp. 107–39.

107 A. Goodman, *John of Gaunt: The Exercise of Princely Power in Fourteenth Century Europe* (London, 1992), p. 89, n. 9, citing writs of summons TNA E 403/485/14; Tuck, 'Nobles, Commons', p. 209.

108 *Peasants' Revolt*, ed. Dobson, pp. 305–6. Income from the third poll tax had been 20 per cent lower than predicted, and, as Saul comments, a main object of summoning Parliament was to address the state of royal finances (Saul, *Richard II*, pp. 79, 104): see also Tuck, 'Nobles, Commons', pp. 203–4.

109 Tuck, 'Nobles, Commons', pp. 207–9; Ormrod, 'Government', p. 22; Ormrod, 'Joan of Kent', pp. 287–91.

in this sense the Crown self-consciously sought to ground its action in the precedent set by past acts of grace.

While it might be true to say that certain of the magnates were focused on a foreign campaign, it does not necessarily follow that the grant of pardon was forced on them against their will. It is dangerous to assume that pardon was solely a policy of the Commons, designed to promote reconciliation, as a precursor to pushing forward their agenda of thoroughgoing reform. Indeed, it was the Crown's representative, the treasurer, Sir Hugh Segrave, who first mentioned the idea of pardon in the opening speech. He outlined the king's desire to make an ordinance that would bestow 'peace and tranquillity' upon the realm, and his willingness to grant a general pardon if Parliament authorised him to do so.[110] But to say that the government was ready to countenance the idea of pardon is not to say that it was earnestly looking to implement the fundamental reforms put forward by the Commons.[111] In contrast, Sir Richard Waldegrave's speech as speaker of the Commons expressed a different attitude to the pardon. He suggested that the issue of a pardon was a chance to reawaken the sense of obligation among the king's subjects, and to encourage officials to perform their duties conscientiously. The rebels, he said, had been forced to take action by burdensome taxation and mistreatment at the hands of royal officers, and the government's response should comprise reform and reconciliation.[112] These twin aims were articulated in his proposal for ministers to be appointed to implement reforms and for grace to be granted to all the king's subjects. This endorsement of the complaints of the insurgents, despite the danger of exacerbating unrest and disorder in the realm, perhaps speaks of shared political frustrations.[113]

Ultimately, the Crown would grant a pardon on its own terms. On 13 December, the king gave his assent to the ordinance of pardon in the form the Commons had devised. However, when the Commons refused to countenance an extension of the wool subsidy, the Crown used the pardon as a bargaining chip.

> ... it was replied on the king's behalf that it had not been customary in parliaments in the past for a general pardon and such grace to be had from the king, when the commons wished to grant the king nothing. ... To which the commons again replied that they would further discuss and consult on their grant to be made of the subsidy on wool, and it was then said on the

---

110 *PROME*, 'Parliament of 1381', item 8.
111 The government's failure to institute administrative reform is demonstrated in Ormrod, 'Government', pp. 25–30.
112 *PROME*, 'Parliament of 1381', items 17–27. The Commons suggested thoroughgoing reforms to the royal household, administration and judiciary.
113 *PROME*, 'Parliament of 1381', item 28; Watts, 'Public', p. 177.

king's behalf that the king would consider his said grace until the commons had done for their part that which pertained to them.[114]

The Crown's stance had the desired result: the Commons consented to the subsidies on wool.[115] Clearly, the government felt itself to be in control of the situation. It authorised the charters of pardon and every subsequent amendment. But it was prepared to use the grant as a bargaining tool when taxation was at stake. The issue of a pardon also contained the implicit assumption that the rebels wanted to be reconciled with the Crown, and that the Crown, while it could take further repressive measures if it chose, was generously exercising its prerogative of mercy. In the case of the pardon at least, the Crown could maintain that it was not pushed into a corner by a hostile parliamentary Commons. Nor was it forced to implement a desperate measure of last resort in the face of an unprecedented rebellion.

The way in which the pardons were formulated in Parliament is interesting. The schedule presented by the Commons contained three kinds of grace and pardon, only one of which concerned the rebels.[116] The first granted an amnesty to all lords who had acted 'without the due process of law' in quelling the rebellion; the second allowed for accused rebels to sue out a pardon, although there were certain named exceptions; and the final clause allowed for anyone *not* involved in rebellion to purchase general pardons as a reward for their loyalty.[117] This third type of pardon was by far the most popular, and was purchased by many people who lived in areas unaffected by revolt.[118] The distinction between these three types of pardon was also maintained on the pardon roll.[119] The roll has three distinct sections, the first

---

114 'fuist repliez depar le roi qe ce n'ad mye este custume de parlement devaunt ceste heure, d'avoir general pardoun, et tielle grace [de roi,] quant la commune riens ne voet au roi granter. ... A quoi la commune respondi autre foitz q'ils se vorront adviser et communer derechief de lour grant affaire del subside des leynes, et adonqes fuist dit depar le roi qe le roi s'adviseroit de sa dite grace tanqe la commune avoit fait de leur part ce qe a eux appartient' (*PROME*, 'Parliament of 1381', item 39). For the use of this 'supply and redress' formula elsewhere, see Ormrod, 'Agenda for Legislation', pp. 1–33; R. G. Davies and J. H. Denton, ed., *The English Parliament in the Middle Ages* (Manchester, 1981), pp. 34–87.
115 See Chapter 8, p. 123.
116 *PROME*, 'Parliament of 1381', item 30.
117 *PROME*, 'Parliament of 1381', items 30–4; *Peasants' Revolt*, ed. Dobson, pp. 331–3.
118 See Appendix 3.
119 *PROME*, 'Parliament of 1381', items 31–4; *Peasants' Revolt*, ed. Dobson, pp. 331–3. Andrew Prescott argues that it is impossible to distinguish which of the pardons listed in this roll were given to rebels, and that it does not help to identify participants in the rising (Prescott, 'Judicial Records', p. 354). However, there does seem to be three distinct sections to the roll, separating 'rebel' pardons from 'general' pardons. It is true, of course, that those buying a 'rebel' pardon were not necessarily insurgents.

of which records the 'early' pardons granted before the opening of Parliament. But at the end of this first list, the diplomatic alters considerably, indicating the change in procedure to accompany the parliamentary issue. There is a new letter patent copied into the roll at this point, which is phrased in the same way as the form of grace drawn up in Parliament and issued specifically to the rebels.[120] This pardons the individual all felonies and treasons committed during the insurrection, defined as lasting from 1 May until 1 November. The letters also repeat the terms recorded on the parliament roll in specifically excluding those who killed Simon Sudbury, Robert Hales and John Cavendish. There is also a change in the way the names are recorded; they are now divided into counties, with inhabitants of the same town grouped together. It seems that either the Chancery clerks were keeping a memorandum of the pardons grouped under geographical location, and then writing them up in fair copy, or that the names were already recorded in lists drawn up at the county level.[121] There are 547 names in this first section associated with twenty-five different regions, mostly in areas associated with the revolt. After this, there seems to be a third, distinct section, headed by a different letter patent.[122] The letter makes no mention of the murderers of the Sudbury, Hales or Cavendish. Instead it echoes the general terms of the third grace on the parliament roll. The recipient is pardoned all manner of felonies committed before 14 December.[123] The impression that this is a new section is reinforced by the run of dates, which breaks off at this point at May 1382 and begins again at December 1381. In contrast to the previous section, this group contains close to 2,500 names from thirty-nine different regions, including areas little affected by the revolt.[124] It therefore seems probable that

---

120 The 'early pardons' are listed on the first three membranes, mm. 39–41. At the head of membrane 38, a new letter patent denotes the new section. This letter is repeated on mm. 29 and 26. This section appears to end on m. 25. On m. 24 is a new letter patent denoting the third section.

121 If the latter suggestion were accurate, then the sheriff or parliamentary representative would be the most likely figure to pass on this information.

122 This begins on m. 24. The distinction is also observed in the letters recorded on the main patent roll. C. M. Barron notes a similar distinction on the 1398 rolls, between pardons given to those who had supported Gloucester and Arundel in 1386–7 and general pardons. Barron, 'Tyranny', pp. 7–10. See Chapter 10, p. 174.

123 TNA C 67/29, m. 24; *PROME*, 'Parliament of 1381', item 106, gives the recommended text of the pardon, amended at the request of the Commons to include those detained in prison for felony on 13 December. This form was adopted largely unaltered.

124 The last six membranes of this section date from May 1383 to January 1398 and list 588 names. The ordinance, however, stipulated that all pardons should be obtained before 2 June 1382. Despite this, these pardons are also headed by letters patent in the form that the ordinance prescribes. There are also thirteen general pardons recorded on the main patent roll that were issued after 2 June 1382: *CPR, 1381–5*, pp. 179, 182, 206, 211, 212, 213, 236, 242, 272.

this second section contains the names of those suing out pardons under the terms of the third grant to the 'good and loyal' commons. The numbers involved are comparable to the general pardons of 1377 and 1398. The former was again given to almost 2,500 people, while in 1398 the figure went up to over 4,000.[125]

The reason it was deemed necessary to issue this last, comprehensive pardon, and to reissue it (although this time only for trespass) in October 1382, seems to be tied to the government's desire to ground their action in precedent.[126] In adopting the machinery and language of the general pardon, the government could look back to established procedures for the solution rather than forward to fundamental administrative reform. By setting the pardons for the rebels within the context of the general pardon, the Crown and the county representatives could also adopt defined roles, one as the source of royal grace and mercy, the other as the supplicant for it. It was a discourse that had been rehearsed most recently in the general pardon of 1377, issued soon after the turmoil of the Good Parliament. A comparison of the language used in the parliament rolls of 1377 and of 1381 reveals the extent of the similarity. Edward III, it was reported to Parliament, had the utmost compassion for the 'very great charges and losses' that his people had borne, and was therefore willing to make 'greater grace than he ever made before', so that his commons could be 'the better comforted and take heart to do better in times to come.'[127] The pardon was to represent the mutual obligation between the king and his subjects. Richard's pardon echoed such sentiments:

> our lord the king considering that the lieges and subjects of his said realm, from the time of his coronation until the said insurrections and upris-ings, had conducted themselves well, governed themselves peaceably, and shown him favour and good will in all his needs and affairs ... out of rever-ence for God and His sweet mother St. Mary, and at the special request of the noble lady, the Lady Anne, daughter of the noble prince Charles, late emperor of Rome, soon, if it please God, to be queen of England; and also to the end that the same subjects should be the more strongly inclined to remain faithful and loyal in future, as they were before the said uprising; of his special grace he has pardoned the said commons.[128]

---

125 1377: TNA C 67/28B (2,439 names); 1398: C 67/30 (3,511 names) and C 67/31 (680 names).

126 *PROME*, 'Parliament of October 1382', item 43.

127 *PROME*, 'Parliament of January 1377', item 24 (answer). See Chapter 8, pp. 122–3.

128 'nostre seignour le roi, considerant coment ses liges et subgitz de son dit roialme tutdys depuis sa coronement tanqe as dites insurreccions et levees faitz se sont bien portez et peisiblement lour governez, et lour ad trovez propices et bone voluntee devers lui en toutz ses affaires et necessities ... al reverence de Dieux, et de sa doulce mere Seinte Marie, et al especiale requeste de noblee dame, dame Anne, file a noble Prince Charles nadgaires emperour de Rome, roigne

Richard recognised the enduring loyalty of his subjects, and issued the pardon to reaffirm his commitment to the reciprocal relationship between the Crown and the commons. The text of the pardon helped to give it a recognisable context, and to suggest that it was within the competence of the minority government to deal with the threat posed by the revolt. It is also worth noting that in framing the pardon in terms of loyalty and forgiveness, the Crown was drawing on a religious discourse that the rebels themselves had tried to appropriate. As Margaret Aston demonstrated, the insurgents had used the feast of Corpus Christi on 13 June to mobilise supporters and to co-ordinate their move on London.[129] But this was a festival dedicated to unity and to reciprocal obligation through the New Covenant of Christ, and the Crown now demonstrated itself to be the guardian of these values. The royal pardon reunited the king with his subjects, in return for the promise of future loyalty. In issuing a pardon at this time, the government also echoed the common practice of granting indulgences to those attending church on Corpus Christi Day.[130] The theme of pardon on this day was reinforced in the pageant cycles – the Towneley Corpus Christi play *The Killing of Abel*, for example, contained a scene in which Cain proclaimed a royal pardon for his servant.[131]

It is true to say, however, that in 1381 the Crown was using the procedures of the general pardon for a new purpose, and in so doing amended some of the familiar terms. The 1381 general pardon, for example, did not contain the detailed clauses concerning land ownership and property rights of the 1377 grant. Similarly, the 1382 statute contained a general pardon for all trespasses, but not for the treasons and felonies that the 1381 pardon had addressed.[132] A more prominent departure from precedent was the reference to Queen Anne's intercession in the text of the pardon itself. Previous grants of general pardon had not made such a reference, perhaps because this form of pardon was represented as a munificent bestowal of royal grace, a gift of grace from the monarch to reward the loyalty of his subjects. It was

---

d'Engleterre, si Dieux plest, proscheinement avenir; et auxint au fin qe mesme les subgitz eient la greindre corage a demurrer en lour foialtee et ligeance pur temps avenir, sicome ils firent devant la dite levee; de sa grace especiale ad pardonez a sa dite commune' (*PROME*, 'Parliament of 1381', item 32).

129 M. Aston, 'Corpus Christi and Corpus Regni: Heresy and the Peasants' Revolt', *P&P* 143 (1994), 3–47; M. Rubin, *Corpus Christi: The Eucharist in Late Medieval Culture* (Cambridge, 1991).

130 Urban IV instituted indulgences for all who attended church for matins and evensong on Corpus Christi Day and during its octave: see *Calendar of Entries in the Papal Registers Relating to Great Britain and Ireland: Papal Letters, 1198–1484*, ed. W. H. Bliss and J. A. Twemlow (London, 1893–1960), IV, 165; Aston, 'Corpus Christi', p. 19; Rubin, *Corpus Christi*, p. 213, n. 4.

131 *Wakefield Pageants*, ed. Cawley, pp. xiv–xvii: see Chapter 4, pp. 52–5.

132 The 1382 statute seems to have addressed specifically the issues raised by the Commons concerning the fear of false indictment.

not intended to be seen as royal forgiveness for a particular act of defiance or disobedience, and therefore it did not require the legitimising use of the feminine intercessor to justify the setting aside of masculine ideas of vengeance. The 1381 pardon similarly evokes this idea of mutual obligation and the loyalty of the king's subjects. In this instance, however, it seems that further justification is needed – the pardon is granted out of 'reverence for God and His sweet mother St. Mary' and 'at the special request of the noble lady, the Lady Anne'. The novelty of the situation and the insecurity of the minority regime were, perhaps, coming to the surface.[133]

At the same time that the pardon was drawn up, a list of those to be excluded was also compiled. It contained the names of 287 people said to be principal instigators of revolt.[134] Also excluded were all inhabitants of Canterbury, Bury St Edmunds, Beverley, Scarborough, Bridgwater and Cambridge, all approvers and those appealed, those who killed Simon Sudbury, Robert Hales and John Cavendish, and those who had escaped from prison.[135] These terms were soon to be moderated. All the exempted towns were pardoned, apart from Bury St Edmunds. As far as Bury was concerned, the prior and convent of the town had themselves petitioned the king to ask that the townsfolk be denied a pardon until they had given sufficient security for keeping the peace in the future.[136] Further amendments saw the inclusion of those who were detained in prison for felony on 13 December and those whose approver was not still alive. It was also stipulated that charters already sealed were to be amended free of charge.[137]

One further, important amendment was made in the Parliament of October 1382. At this meeting, the Commons raised concerns about the availability of the pardon.[138] In an echo of the rebels' earlier complaints of malicious indict-

---

133 Mark Ormrod has suggested that this reference to Queen Anne allowed the government to legitimise its *volte-face* from a policy of repression to reconciliation in the November Parliament. I have portrayed the idea of pardon as less innovative and less directly related to the influence of the parliamentary Commons than has previously been supposed. But when it came to drafting the terms of the general pardon in Parliament, the novelty of the situation showed through in the elaborate justification, despite the government's attempts to ground its actions in precedent and downplay the scale of the threat (Ormrod, 'Joan of Kent', p. 288).

134 The names were submitted to Parliament: *PROME*, 'Parliament of 1381', item 63.

135 *PROME*, 'Parliament of 1381', item 32.

136 TNA SC 8/95/4703.

137 *PROME*, 'Parliament of 1381', item 106.

138 This had been preceded by the issuing of charters of pardon to York, Scarborough and Beverley: *PROME*, 'Parliament of October 1382', items 18–21. The copy for York was kept in the city archive, dated 18 October 1382. No further 'rebel' pardons are recorded on the supplementary roll after the 2 June deadline, but there are several on the main patent rolls: *CPR*, *1381–5*, pp. 158, 159, 173. Thomas Bordefeld (13 July 1382); John Mylot (16 July 1382); Thomas de Middelton (20 October 1382).

ment, the Commons now asserted that many of the people indicted for treasonous action during the uprising were innocent, but too poor to purchase charters of pardon and were therefore placed outside the protection of the king's peace. They suggested that the solution was to issue a general pardon for treason free of charge, without the need to sue out a personal copy:

> And because a large number of the people who were indicted for treason because of the said uprising are labourers and the like who have nothing, and are not in a position to purchase their charters, so that they remain without the same pardon: and because they fear that they will be placed in exigent or outlawry, or seized and put to death, they flee together into woods and other places, and what is more, a large number of others who have not been indicted fear the same plight, from which great trouble may arise. On account of which may it please you to grant a general pardon of treason in the aforesaid uprising, excepting those who were excluded, without a charter being necessary...[139]

The king's favourable reply represented an unprecedented grant of royal mercy. All the subjects of his realm were to be pardoned any treasons and felonies committed in the uprising (between 1 May and 24 June 1381). The only people excepted were those 287 on the list of principal insurgents, three additional named citizens of London, and the inhabitants of Bury St Edmunds. For the first time ever, a comprehensive general pardon had been granted free of any requirement to purchase letters patent and thus automatically extending the king's mercy to all his subjects.[140] Such a concession was remarkable since, apart from its novel nature, it meant the king conceded his rights to a potentially lucrative source of revenue in the fees charged for copies of letters patent. For the pardons already issued, the amount received

---

[139] 'Et porce grant nombre des gentz qi sont enditez de tresoun par cause de le rumour sont laborers et tielx qi riens n'ont, et ne furent pas de poair de purchacer lours chartres, issint q'ils sont hors de mesme la pardoun: et a cause q'ils se doutent d'estre mys en exigende et utlagarie, et en cas q'ils soient prises d'estre myses a mort, s'enfuent ensemble as boys et autres lieux, et auxint grant nombre des autres qi ne sont pas enditez se doutent d'estre en mesme le cas, dont purra sourdre grant meschief. Par quoy plese granter une pardoun general de tresoun de le rumour suisdit, forspris ceux qi furent forsprises, sanz chartre avoir' (*PROME*, 'Parliament of October 1382', item 43). See also a petition for the 1381 pardon to be extended: TNA SC 8/174/8684.

[140] *PROME*, 'Parliament of October 1382', item 49; *SR*, II, 29–30. They adopted the standard procedure of excepting treason, murder, robbery and the rape of women, and asked that no justice of eyre nor trailbaston be sent for offences committed before this time. Prescott notes that it was no longer necessary to purchase letters of pardon to benefit from the amnesty, but letters close could be obtained if necessary for court proceedings, and were free of charge (Prescott, 'Judicial Records', p. 356, n. 61).

must have been over £2,000.[141] In line with this blanket amnesty, there are several examples recorded on the close rolls of orders to the justices of the peace in a particular county 'not to trouble' named inhabitants because of the agreement the king had made to pardon all his subjects, 'of whatever estate or condition.'[142] This amnesty reflected the fears of the wider community concerning the threat of false indictment without the protection of a letter of pardon. In a few cases the terms of the pardon explicitly stated that the recipient had been falsely accused. In 1383, for example, two men received pardons after it was decided at King's Bench that they had been indicted by their enemies.[143] The pardon also ensured that the full resources of the judicial system could be focused on prosecuting those individuals who had been exempted from the amnesty.

The end of the amendment and reissue of the pardon seems to have been signalled in the 1383 Parliament. The Commons now requested that no one should be excluded from the amnesty except the 287 named individuals, and asked that anyone indicted because of the insurrection would be released by this pardon. They also wished to set a terminal date of 7 July 1383 for anyone to bring a suit connected with the insurrection and to allow for the acquittal of anyone who could present the testimony of three of four worthy men. The king granted these requests in a final statute promulgated on 18 May 1383.[144] New judicial proceedings were initiated against those 287 individuals who had been excluded from the pardon. The government sent these names to the

---

[141] A. L. Brown suggests that in 1433 Chancery would have been expected to produce total profits of, at most, £2,000 (Brown, *Governance*, p. 65). Instead of the charters of pardon, letters close were apparently made available after the concession of 1382, but were not recorded on the supplementary roll. These, it seems, could be obtained without payment and had the same effect as earlier charters of pardon: TNA KB 27/487, m. 19v; KB 27/488, mm. 8, 19; KB 27/489, mm. 18, 21, 24v; KB 27/490, mm. 21, 21v; KB 27/493, m. 4; KB 27/494, m. 14.

[142] *CCR, 1381–5*, pp. 165, 185–6, 258, 259, 267, 277, 372. Those who had been exempted from the amnesty, but were subsequently pardoned, were still issued individual letters patent. However, nine letters patent on the main roll were issued after the 24 October amnesty to rebels who had not actually been exempted. It is not certain why these pardons were issued, as the amnesty of 24 October removed the obligation to sue for individual letters. Three seem to have been renewals of pardons sealed at another time: *CPR, 1381–5*, pp. 203, 215, 399. Two state that they are exemplifications of the 24 October amnesty, suggesting that court proceedings had been initiated against them before this date: *CPR, 1381–5*, p. 224.

[143] TNA KB 27/501, m. 1v; *CPR, 1381–5*, p. 272; SC 8/262/13099; KB 27/488, m. 25. Prescott notes that the list of those excluded from the pardon in 1381 had been badly affected by false accusation (Prescott, 'Judicial Records', pp. 358–9). Reform of the judicial system had long been on the political agenda of the Commons, echoing the contemporary perception that the quality of the legal system was degenerating: Musson and Ormrod, *Evolution*, pp. 161–93; Powell, 'Administration', pp. 49–59.

[144] *PROME*, 'Parliament of February 1383', item 17; *SR*, II, 30–1.

King's Bench and the justices accordingly issued new orders for the arrest of the indicted.[145] However, this action merely repeated proceedings taken by local commissions, and as a result there seem to have been no additional convictions. Several of those named on the list were victims of false accusation. The names were supplied by local commissions, and it seems likely that in London at least the commission simply forwarded to Chancery the names of those against whom prosecutions were outstanding. About fifty of those excluded from the general pardon appeared in King's Bench between 1383 and 1398, but almost all were acquitted or produced special letters of pardon granted at the request of an influential intermediary such as the queen or the mayor of London.[146]

This examination of the role of pardon and mercy in the events of 1381 has suggested that a picture of government-led repression, halted only by the moderating voice of the parliamentary Commons, is perhaps too clear-cut. Similarly, the idea that pardon was commonly associated with more concrete governmental and bureaucratic reform needs to be questioned. Looking first at the chronicle accounts of events, it is true, as Pearsall says, that the dominant models or images through which the writers sought to understand the revolt were of human wickedness, and violation of a divinely ordained hierarchy, of reason and nature being overturned.[147] But another model that can be identified is that of the quality of royal mercy, the sense that petitioning the monarch in the case of false accusation or mistreatment at the hands of officials was the legitimate avenue of complaint, and would be met with a judgment from the king based on principles of equity and mercy. As already noted, this was a model that appeared not only in the court literature of advice, but also in poems such as the *Outlaw's Song of Trailbaston* in the complaint tradition and in Corpus Christi plays such as the *Killing of*

---

145 *PROME*, 'Parliament of 1381', item 63; TNA KB 27/487, mm. 5, 6, 11, 11v; KB 27/488, m. 4.

146 Prescott, 'Judicial Records', pp. 356–7. Prescott found twenty-nine such pardons in the King's Bench rolls (ibid., p. 357, n. 68). It appears that fourteen were recorded on the main patent roll, of which eleven were subsequently presented in King's Bench: Thomas Sampson, *CPR, 1381–5*, p. 226; John Awedyn, *CPR, 1381–5*, p. 238 (TNA KB 27/488, m. 23); Thomas Engilby, *CPR, 1381–5*, p. 270 (KB 27/503, m. 12); John de Spayne, *CPR, 1381–5*, p. 272 (KB 27/501, m. 1v); William de Benyngton, *CPR, 1381–5*, p. 297; John Ellesworth, *CPR, 1381–5*, p. 377 (KB 27/501, m. 15v); Thomas atte Raven, *CPR, 1381–5*, p. 409 (KB 27/490, m. 20); Richard Redyng, *CPR, 1385–9*, p. 25 (KB 27/512, m. 22v); Henry Nasse, *CPR, 1385–9*, p. 75 (KB 27/513, m. 7); Robert Wesebrom, *CPR, 1388–92*, p. 186 (KB 27/523, m. 19v); William Pypere, *CPR, 1388–92*, p. 290 (KB 27/535, m. 10v); Thomas Wyllot, *CPR, 1388–92*, p. 457 (KB 27/522, m. 13); William Pykas, *CPR, 1392–6*, p. 362 (KB 7/531, m. 14v); Robert Priour, *CPR, 1396–9*, p. 109 (despite the claim in his letter patent, he does not seem to have been on the list of the excluded).

147 Pearsall, 'Interpretative Models', pp. 64–5; *Peasants' Revolt*, ed. Dobson, pp. 367–72.

Abel.[148] It was a model, too, that was reflected in the actions of the rebels, in their evocation of an idealised judicial relationship between the king and his subjects, and in their construction of themselves as spokesmen for the commons, with implicit political rights.

The judicial and administrative records produced in the immediate aftermath of the revolt again demonstrate that ingrained notions of pardon could sit alongside repressive measures. Whether or not large numbers of rebels were executed, the idea of pardon had been in circulation since the rebels had first gathered on Blackheath, and it was assumed to be one option available to the justices who headed the first judicial commissions. The issuing of pardons to certain of the rebels at an early stage was not seen as irreconcilable with the idea of strict, even harsh justice. Recourse to pardoning was assumed to be intrinsic to the operation of the judicial system, rather than necessarily the herald of a distinct 'policy' of reconciliation. The issuing of pardons in the immediate aftermath of the revolt also gave a central role to the young king, who did not need to wait for Parliament to ratify grants of royal grace.

Finally, it is useful to view the 1381 pardon in the light of past grants of royal mercy. In 1377 Edward III issued a pardon to symbolise reconciliation between the Crown and the political elite. In 1381, it was evident that the pardon was a gesture that harked back to past grants of royal grace for the solution rather than forward to fundamental administrative reform.[149] Suggested changes to the procedures of Chancery and exchequer were never taken up, and certain of the king's favourites continued to exercise an overbearing political influence. In the light of the precedent set by earlier general pardons, it seems that the minority administration was attempting to draw on established notions of political reconciliation and routinise the issue of pardons in order to pull themselves back from the brink of crisis. The general pardon perhaps even raised public expectations for reform that the Crown had no intention of implementing.

---

[148] Gower, *Confessio Amantis*, ed. Peck, Book 7, lines 3103–17; *Rymes of Robin Hood*, ed. Dobson and Taylor, p. 253; *Wakefield Pageants*, ed. Cawley; Watts, 'Public', pp. 168–9, and see Chapter 3, pp. 40–2 and Chapter 4, pp. 52–5.

[149] Gransden refers to the disillusionment expressed by chroniclers in the 1390s who had, only a decade before, glorified Richard's stance against the insurgents: A. Gransden, *Historical Writing in England 2, c. 1307 to the Early Sixteenth Century* (London, 1982), pp. 157–93.

CHAPTER TEN

Pardoning and Revenge: Richard II's 'Tyranny'

The general pardons discussed so far were used to promote reconciliation in the face of disunity or rebellion.[1] However, in 1398 Richard II subverted the principles of granting pardon, by using it as a tool of accusation and incrimination.[2] The last three years of Richard's reign have often been set apart, in the historiography, as a distinct period of tyrannical rule. In the summer of 1397 the king ordered the arrest of his long-standing political opponents, the Lords Appellant, and two months later he convened his so-called 'Revenge Parliament', which provided the forum for their public trial and conviction.[3] This heralded Richard's intention to impose a new personal agenda on the polity of the realm. He sought to intimidate the Lords and Commons with a display of force: 2,000 members of his personal retinue of Cheshire archers were ordered to surround Parliament. He then went on to extort concessions from the Lords and Commons, which effectively curtailed the powers of Parliament, and announced a pardon, but declared that certain, unnamed persons would be excluded from its protection.[4] For the chronicler Thomas

---

1 The substance of this chapter relates closely to my article in *Fourteenth Century England*, and is reproduced here with the kind permission of Boydell & Brewer: see Lacey, 'Mercy and Truth', pp. 124–35.

2 *SR*, II, 106–7.

3 For references to the Cheshire archers, see TNA CHES 2/70, m. 7v; *CCR, 1396–9*, p. 144; *PROME*, 'Parliament of September 1397'. They are also discussed in Dodd, 'Cheshire Archers', pp. 102–18; R. R. Davies, 'Richard II and the Principality of Chester, 1397–9', in *The Reign of Richard II: Essays in Honour of May McKisack*, ed. F. R. H. Du Boulay and C. M. Barron (London, 1971), pp. 256–79; J. L. Gillespie, 'Richard II's Cheshire Archers', *Transactions of the Historic Society of Lancashire and Cheshire* 125 (1974), 1–35. For the chronicle references, see *Historia Vitae et Regni Ricardi Secundi*, ed. Stow, p. 140; *Adam Usk*, ed. Given-Wilson, pp. 22–5. There is some discrepancy in the reports of the number of archers present, discussed in Dodd, 'Cheshire Archers', p. 102, n. 3.

4 For the contemporary references to these events, see *PROME*, 'Parliament of September 1397'; 'Annales Ricardi Secundi et Henrici Quarti', *Johannis de Trokelowe et Henrici de Blaneforde, monachorum S. Albani, necnon quorundam anonymorum chronica et annales, regnantibus Henrico Tertio, Edwardo Primo, Edwardo Secundo, Ricardo Secundo, et Henrico Quarto*, ed. H. T. Riley, RS 28 (London, 1866); *Vitae et Regni Ricardi Secundi*, ed. Stow, pp. 137–51; *Eulogium Historiarum Sive Temporis*, ed. F. S. Haydon, RS 9 (London, 1858), III, 371–9; *Adam Usk*, ed. Given-Wilson, pp. 28–35; *Traison et Mort: Chronique de la Traison et Mort de Richart Deux Roy Dengleterre*,

Walsingham these events were a portent of worse to come, and he made the well-known comment that, in the summer of 1397 the king 'began to tyrannise and burden his people'.[5] Historians have generated a considerable body of scholarship in their attempt to elucidate the events that led ultimately to Richard's deposition.[6] However, one central element of Richard II's 'tyranny' has been overlooked: namely his view of the role and significance of the royal pardon. Beyond the drama of parliamentary proceedings, scant attention has been paid to the way in which Richard actually used the royal pardon in these years to bring pressure to bear on his political opponents. While the chroniclers dwell on the set-piece show trials of Arundel and Warwick, they allude only briefly to events occurring outside the limelight of Parliament. Walsingham refers to a vague atmosphere of suspicion, and to secretive activities carried out by royal agents in order to secure forced loans for the king.[7] The administrative records of government, however, contain a whole series of veiled references to arrests, imprisonments and council meetings, which, when pieced together, reveal a sequence of events revolving around the use of the royal pardon as a political bargaining tool. Richard was using the very concept of pardon to justify his move against the supporters of the Lords Appellant in the autumn of 1397. This chapter therefore examines Richard II's use of the royal pardon in the final, 'tyrannical' years of his reign. The king, it seems, was able to use the prerogative of mercy to achieve specific political ends: to bring opponents of the regime to account and to send a clear signal that royal mercy would be exercised by the monarch, of his own free will.

ed. B. Williams (London, 1846), pp. 117–27; *Kirkstall Abbey Chronicles*, ed. J. Taylor, Publications of the Thoresby Society (1952), pp. 118–20; 'Chronicles of Dieulacres Abbey, 1381–1403', in 'The Deposition of Richard II', ed. M. V. Clarke and V. H. Galbraith, *Bulletin of the John Rylands Library* 14 (1930), 164–70; C. Given-Wilson, *Chronicles of the Revolution, 1397–1400* (Manchester, 1993), pp. 54–102.

5   Given-Wilson, *Revolution*, p. 71.

6   J. G. Edwards, 'The Parliamentary Committee of 1398', EHR 40 (1925), 321–33; Saul, *Richard II*, pp. 375–81; Tuck, *English Nobility*, pp. 187–92; M. Bennett, *Richard II and the Revolution of 1399* (Stroud, 1999), pp. 98–108, 118–20; M. Giancarlo, 'Murder, Lies and Storytelling: The Manipulation of Justice(s) in the Parliaments of 1397 and 1399', *Speculum* 77 (2002), 76–112; T. F. T. Plucknett, 'Impeachment and Attainder', *TRHS*, 5th series 3 (1953), 145–58; Barron, 'Tyranny', pp. 1–18.

7   Walsingham states that the king began to burden his people with great loans, and that the king's agents made secret enquiries into the wealth of particular citizens, before endorsing blank charters with their names (Given-Wilson, *Revolution*, p. 71). The author of the continuation of the *Eulogium Historiarum* refers to individual messages sent out to every bishop, abbot, gentleman and merchant, from whom the king then extorted large sums of money (ibid., p. 65).

Summer and Autumn, 1397

The first phase of Richard's period of tyranny is usually associated with the events of the summer and autumn of 1397. Two episodes in particular have been singled out for attention: the imprisonment of the Lords Appellant, and their trial and conviction before the representatives assembled in the Revenge Parliament. On 15 July the king proclaimed the arrest of the Lords Appellant. Three days before, the constable of the Tower of London had been ordered to receive Thomas, earl of Warwick and to keep him in custody. By 28 July it was deemed necessary to send out orders to the guardians of the peace in Sussex, Surrey, Kent and Essex to arrest those stirring discontent against the imprisonment of Gloucester, Arundel and Warwick. The arrest of the Lords Appellant and the seizure of their property were the first indications of Richard's intentions.[8] By 17 September Parliament had convened, and it witnessed the dramatic trials of Arundel and Warwick (Gloucester having already died while in captivity in Calais). These high-profile events have attracted the attention of historians, but it seems that scholars have overlooked the actions Richard also took against a number of lesser men throughout the summer and autumn of 1397, men who were suspected of involvement with the conspiracy of the Lords Appellant. A series of entries in the Chancery rolls and in the records of the council suggest that some of these men were arrested and held in custody, before appearing before specially convened meetings of the council. Shortly after the date of their appointments these men then sued for pardon and paid substantial fines to the Exchequer. Their example was followed by other individuals who, while not yet summoned before the council, clearly feared that they might be next.

Before Parliament convened, then, Richard had issued orders to arrest certain men, and to hold them in custody until he sent word to bring them before a specially convened meeting of the council. These men were suspected of involvement with the Lords Appellant and were to be brought before the council to explain their actions. Twenty-nine individuals were arrested in this way, the majority of whom were taken in the first wave of arrests, which occurred between September and November 1397.[9] Of these individuals

8   *CCR, 1396–9*, pp. 140, 147, 208. Inquests were then made into the property of the earls, and orders for its seizure were sent out after they had been tried and convicted in Parliament: *CCR, 1396–9*, pp. 154, 157, 159, 160, 162.

9   Twenty-two men were arrested between September and November 1397: John Cobham, John Wiltshire, Thomas Feriby, John Aspall, John Lacy, Robert Jugler, Hugh Grenham, Robert Rikedon, John Bullocke, John Catesby, John de Boys, Thomas Lampet, William Castelacre, William Clipstone, John Faunessoun, Thomas Armurer, Richard Armurer, Edward Charleton, John Tracy, Richard Chamberlayn, John Bray and John Bakere. A further seven were arrested between February and May 1398: John Broun, Walter Stywarde, John Saymour, Richard Herefelde,

John Cobham is the most well known because of his eventual conviction and banishment before Parliament in 1398. Prior to this he had been held in custody at Donnington castle from 8 to 26 September 1397, before being ordered to come into the king's presence. It seems he was then held prisoner by the duke of Surrey, before finally being brought before Parliament on 28 January 1398, and banished for his association with the Lords Appellant and his treasonable activities as a member of a parliamentary commission in 1386.[10] However, none of the others were given a public audience in Parliament. Seven of them were definitely summoned before the king's council, all between 30 September and 5 November, at meetings that were perhaps intended to attract little public attention. The allegiance of these seven men was clear: all were prominent associates of the Lords Appellant. John Wiltshire had been a councillor to the earl of Arundel; Thomas Feriby had been the duke of Gloucester's chancellor since 1394; and Robert Rikedon, Thomas Lampet, William Castleacre, John de Boys and Hugh Grenham were all associates of the duke of Gloucester.[11] Whether or not the king and his ministers actually ordered these men to pay fines and to sue out pardons when they were brought before the council, all of them understood the message given. All but Grenham and de Boys immediately sought a copy of the Appellant pardon as soon as it was proclaimed in the opening session of the September Parliament. Their names are recorded together, along with eight others, on one membrane of the pardon rolls.[12] This membrane is the only one to record

---

Lawrence Bright, John Fesaunt and William Wetheresfelde: *CCR, 1396–9*, pp. 149, 151–4, 157–9, 164, 222, 238, 243, 246, 254, 262; *PPC*, I, 76–7.

[10] *CCR, 1396–9*, pp. 157, 159, 245; *PROME*, 'Parliament of September 1397', item 10; J. S. Roskell, L. Clark and C. Rawcliffe, *The Commons, 1386–1421*, History of Parliament (Stroud, 1993), II, 607–8.

[11] Their individual summonses to the Council are recorded in *CCR, 1396–9*, pp. 153, 155, 159, 222, 225, 234; *PPC*, I, 76–7. For details of their careers, see A. Goodman, *The Loyal Conspiracy: The Lords Appellant under Richard II* (London, 1971), pp. 94–104; Roskell, Clark and Rawcliffe, *The Commons*, pp. 232–3, 320–1, 874–5.

[12] TNA C 67/30, m.3. All are dated between 18 October and 28 November 1397. The eight other men were Giles Malory, Nicholas Lilling, Hugh de la Zouche, Thomas Coggeshalle, Richard Monk, John Estephus, Walter Roo and Thomas Walwayn. They were all prominent associates of the Lords Appellant. The king's warrant for two of these pardons (as writs under the privy seal) survive: John Estephus: C 81/570/11739; John Wilteshire: C 81/570/11745. They also survive for several pardons granted in 1398: John Keleryan, C 81/579/12649 (6 February 1398), enrolled on C 67/31, m. 13; John Chapman: C 81/579/12693 (2 March 1399), enrolled on C 67/31, m. 7; John atte Wode: C 81/581/12839 (12 April 1399), enrolled on C 67/31, m. 10; John More, C 81/573/12038 (24 April 1398), enrolled on C 67/30, m. 19. Barron comments of these writs that 'in at least five further cases the chancellor was instructed to issue charters of pardon under the great seal which have not been enrolled' (Barron, 'Tyranny', p. 9, n. 1). However, as shown above, all are in fact enrolled on the supplementary patent rolls: see R. Storey, *Index to Pardons*, unpublished typescript, TNA.

any pardons issued as early as September–November 1397, several weeks before any other such letters were granted. Seven of those so pardoned also paid substantial fines to the exchequer at this time. Their names are listed together on the receipt rolls in an entry dated 4 December 1397, and described as 'fines made in the presence of the king's council'.[13] Thomas Coggeshalle and Hugh de la Zouche each paid £133 6s. 8d.; Thomas Feriby £100; Richard Monk £20; Robert Rikedon and Thomas Lampet paid £13 6s. 8d. each and Walter Roo £10.

While the existence of these fines has been noted before, historians have not recognised that they were paid by a distinct group of men, whose fortunes in the autumn of 1397 can be traced through their individual summonses before the council, their procurement of pardons and their payment of fines to reveal that Richard had singled them out for special treatment even before he presided over the first session of the Revenge Parliament.[14] This is interesting when considered in light of the statement Richard had made on 15 July 1397, proclaiming the arrest of the Lords Appellant. He stated that their arrest was not connected with the uprising of 1387–8 and he assured any associates of Arundel, Gloucester and Warwick that they should not fear 'impeachment or hurt' for their part in the rising.[15] Despite this reassurance, it seems that associates of the Appellants were right to fear Richard's future intentions towards them. By early September, the king had already gone back on his word and singled out certain of these men for special treatment. The existence of this distinct group is even more significant in light of the fact that, at the opening of Parliament on 17 September, Richard directed his chancellor not only to proclaim a wide-ranging pardon, but also to stipulate that fifty unnamed men would be exempted from its terms. Were these fifty men perhaps the same group that Richard had taken into custody shortly before the opening of Parliament? If so, it would seem that the king's intention was to deny them the amnesty of this comprehensive pardon until he had brought them before the council (which, as we have seen, he did between 30 September and 5 November) and, in many cases, impose on them substantial fines. Whether or not this group of men can be associated with the 'fifty unnamed persons'

---

13 TNA E 401/608. From the wording of the entry, it therefore appears that Cogge-shalle, Monk, de la Zouche and Roo were also in fact brought before the council, although their individual writs of summons do not survive. Another entry on the same roll records that Thomas fitz Nicole paid £100 on 16 November 1397 'pro mora sua penes Ricardum comitem Arundell', and a further £50 in March 1398. The king also later granted the men of Essex and Hertfordshire a collective pardon, in return for the sum of £2,000, and anyone who refused to contribute his share of what was in effect a huge collective fine was liable to be imprisoned: *CPR, 1391–6*, pp. 311–12; *CFR, 1391–9*, pp. 250–2; Tuck, *English Nobility*, p. 197.

14 Barron, 'Tyranny', p. 8; A. Steel, *The Receipt of the Exchequer, 1377–1485* (Cambridge, 1954), p. 118.

15 *CCR, 1396–9*, p. 208; *Foedera* [First edition], VIII, 6–7.

mentioned by the chancellor, they were certainly key targets for Richard's programme of revenge. Almost all of them went on to purchase yet another letter of pardon in May and June 1398.[16] Moreover, their fate lends credence to the charges of 'unjust fines and exactions' laid against Richard at his deposition, an issue to which we will return.

It must be made clear that not all those arrested between September and November 1397 were immediately brought before the council. For some individuals, their cases dragged on into the spring of 1398, and some were arrested, fined and released, before being brought back yet again to face the council. Four of the men were released soon after arrest, following orders from the king.[17] In one case it was specified that the individual concerned, one Edward Charleton, was to be set free on certain conditions: he was to pay a fine of 500 marks; to sue with the king for his grace by 21 April 1398; and to remain ready to come before the council if summoned. It was later recorded that Charleton had paid the fine, 'as the treasurer had borne witness by word of mouth'.[18] Scme of these men, it seems, were initially allowed to go free without having to come before the council. However, even this decision was soon to be repealed, and a number of individuals initially exempted from attending the council were now summoned before the tribunal. This seems to be the implication of an enigmatic entry into the minutes of an undated council meeting. It states that certain persons, who were initially exempt from attending the council, were now to be ordered to 'treat with the council' and, if they failed to co-operate, they were to be imprisoned. It also refers to certain fines to be made by these individuals, which, it states, should be delivered to the treasurer and placed in a special bag (rather than being processed through the official channels of the exchequer). Finally, it stipulates that none were to be present in the council at the exaction of the fines except the chancellor, the treasurer, the keeper of the Privy Seal, Sir John Bussy, Sir Henry Green and Sir William Bagot.[19] The date of this entry is unclear. Tout

16 Giles Malory purchased a second pardon on 10 June, TNA C 67/30, m. 10; Nicholas Lilling on 16 June, C 67/30, m. 6; Thomas Coggeshalle on 15 May, C 67/30, m. 23; Robert Rikedon on 1 May, C 67/30, m. 25; Thomas Lampet on 10 June, C 67/30, m. 17; Thomas Walwayn on 12 June, C 67/30, m. 15; Richard Monk on 15 June, C 67/30, m. 15; William Castelacre on 6 June (and Elizabeth his wife), C 67/30, m. 9; Walter Roo on 10 June, C 67/30, m. 13. Two different forms of the pardons were in fact available.

17 John Catesby, Edward Charleton, Richard Chamberlayn and John Bray: *CCR, 1396–9*, pp. 157, 159, 164. Catesby was steward to the earl of Warwick and Bray was an associate of the duke of Gloucester: see Goodman, *Loyal Conspiracy*, p. 97; Roskell, Clark and Rawcliffe, *The Commons*, pp. 501–2.

18 *CCR, 1396–9*, p. 286.

19 'certains persones exemptz de venir devant le consail du roy au fin quils tretent avec mesme le counsail et que sur le dit tretee report soit fait au roy et que mesmes les persones soient commys a prisone en cas quils ne purront accorder ovec le dit counsail. … Item que les sommes que serront pris des fins des dites persones

believed that it could not have been written before the end of 1398, while Caroline Barron dated it to September 1397.[20] While its date cannot be determined precisely, it seems likely that this decision in fact relates to an order, issued on 3 April 1398, to twenty-eight named men, who were instructed under pain of a £200 fine, for 'particular causes specially moving the king and council', to cease all other activities and to present themselves before the king and council at Westminster on 21 April 1398.[21] Included among this list of twenty-eight names were Edward Charleton, who had already been arrested and set free once (see above), and Giles Malory, Hugh de la Zouche, Thomas Coggeshalle, Thomas Walwayn, John Stevens and Richard Waldegrave, all of whom had already purchased pardons or paid fines in October–November 1397.[22] The other men summoned to the council on 3 April followed this example and most sued for pardon in April–June 1398.[23] Several also paid sizeable fines to the exchequer on 13 July 1398, and these were again recorded as 'fines paid in the presence of the king's council'.[24] John More, a London mercer, was among those summoned, but, in a pardon of 24 April 1398, he was forgiven a fine of 100 marks which had been imposed on him by the council for having 'ridden with the condemned lords, contrary to his allegiance'.[25] The fate of these men certainly lends credence to the charges

exemptz soient delivrees au Tresurer Dengleterre et mys en une bagge. Item que cellui soit paient en counsail a la taxacion des fins affaire par les persones exemptz forspris les Chancellor, Tresoror, Garde du prive seel, Monsieur John Bussy, Monsieur Henry Green et Monsieur William Bagot' (*PPC*, I, 75–6).

20 Barron, 'Tyranny', p. 8, n. 1.
21 *CCR, 1396–9*, p. 277. The men summoned were Hugh de Zouche, Payn Tiptoft, Edward Charleton, Arnald Savage, Giles Malorye, John Trussell, Richard Waldegrave, Thomas Herlyng, Philip Milstede, David Holbech, Thomas Coggeshalle, Richard Whityngton, Thomas Oldcastell, Thomas Walweyn, John Stevens, John Hende, John Shadworth, Robert Plesyngton, John Harwedoun, John Tauk, John More, John Saymore, William Echyngham, Richard Cralle, John Frome, John Bonham, John Mewe and John Whethales.
22 TNA C 67/30, m. 3; E 401/608.
23 Payn Tiptoft, 30 April 1398, TNA C 67/30, m. 2; Edward Charleton, 20 May 1398, C 67/30, m. 23; Giles Malorye, 18 October 1397, 10 June 1398, C 67/30, mm. 3, 10; John Trussell, 27 April 1398, 5 June 1398, C 67/30, mm. 3, 18; Richard Waldegrave, 12 June 1398, C 67/30, m. 15; Thomas Coggeshalle, 7 November 1397, 15 May 1398, C 67/30, mm. 3, 23; Thomas Oldcastell, 14 June 1398, C 67/30, m. 14; Thomas Walweyn, 18 November 1397, 12 June 1398, C 67/30, mm 3, 15; John Hende, 10 June 1398, C 67/30, mm. 14, 15 (possibly also 3 September 1398, C 67/31, m. 7); John Harwedoun, 12 June 1398, C 67/30, m. 12; John More, 21 May 1398, C 67/30, m. 19; William Echyngham, 5 May 1398, C 67/30, m. 3; Richard Cralle, 15 June 1398, C 67/30, m. 15; John Bonham, 17 May 1398, C 67/30, m. 19.
24 TNA E 401/609. John Frome paid £66 13s. 4d.; William Echyngham £33 6s. 8d.; Edward Charleton £266 13s. 4d.; John Seymour £33 6s. 8d. Richard Crowe [Cralle] 'nuper de retencione comitis Arundell' £13 6s. 8d.; David Holbech £100.
25 TNA C 81/573/12038; C 67/30, m. 19. Caroline Barron connects John More's pardon with the minutes of the undated council meeting referred to above (*PPC*, I,

of 'unjust fines and exactions' laid against Richard at his eventual deposition, as Caroline Barron concluded in the only previous study to examine these events in any detail.[26] Richard clearly forced many of those who supported the Appellant uprising to sue for pardon, despite his earlier assurance that they would not have to do so. A large proportion of these men were also forced to pay fines far higher than the standard charge for a pardon, and many, it seems, had to purchase more than one of these letters patent before they were in any sense reconciled with the regime.[27]

It is clear that Richard sought to intimidate political opponents into purchasing a pardon, through the threat of enigmatic summonses before the council, but also by refusing to name those who would be refused mercy. At the outset of the Revenge Parliament, on 17 September 1397, the chancellor, Bishop Stafford, delivered his opening address, and declared that a general pardon would be available to all who sought the king's grace, but he then went on to stipulate that fifty unnamed men would be excluded from the king's peace. In fact, there are two different versions of the Stafford's speech – one in the parliament roll and one given in the chronicle of Adam Usk. Both refer to the fifty unnamed men, but the parliament roll describes the pardon in far more expansive terms than does Usk. According to the parliament roll, Stafford made the point that if the king's subjects were duly obedient and upheld the king's prerogative powers and laws, they would ultimately reap the reward.[28] To demonstrate this, and to strengthen his subjects' goodwill towards him, Richard intended to bestow on them a grant of general pardon as evidence of his gracious mercy, with the proviso that certain individuals would be excluded. Adam Usk's report, on the other hand, says nothing of a generous bestowal of grace, but instead reports that the king declared his intention to pardon all those who had schemed to undermine his power and regality.[29] This was clearly a reference to the actions of the Lords Appellant. According to Usk, then, this was not a generous bestowal of grace to all the king's subjects for any past misdeeds. It was instead only intended to cover the offences committed in fighting for the Appellant cause in 1388.[30] This latter version of events is supported by the rubric of the pardon rolls. It

---

75–6), but does not connect the twenty-seven other men, who were mentioned in the summons of 3 April (*CCR, 1396–9*, p. 277). Barron, 'Tyranny', p. 8 and n. 2.

[26] Barron, 'Tyranny', pp. 6–9.

[27] *PROME*, 'Parliament of 1399', items 23–4.

[28] *PROME*, 'Parliament of September 1397', opening address.

[29] *Adam Usk*, ed. Given-Wilson, p. 21.

[30] The need to sue for a pardon after the 1397 Parliament, but before the beginning of the 1398 session, was widely known. See the warrant for a letter patent sent by the king to the chancellor under the privy seal: TNA C 81/571/11819. The king sent this letter from Coventry on 1 January 1398. It orders that the chancellor send letters to the sheriffs of England to publicly proclaim that those seeking such pardons were to do so by 24 June. However, the warrant does not shed further light

records a copy of the letter patent issued to those who sued for pardon in the autumn and winter of 1397. This letter of pardon is clearly concerned only with offences committed in riding with the Lords Appellant, and does not grant pardon in any more general sense:

> we have pardoned by our special grace [name of recipient] the suit of our peace and that which relates to us against himself in the matter of the said commission and the same, congregating, rebelling, riding, committing depredations, imprisoning, killing and arson by himself in the company of the said duke and earls.[31]

This declaration of pardon, then, seems to have been aimed solely at forcing those implicated in the Appellant uprising to make themselves known to the king and seek his grace. The desire to secure such a pardon was clearly heightened by the secrecy surrounding the list of exempted persons. Although the chancellor had said that the king would name these people in Parliament, no list was forthcoming. The Commons remained anxious to hear the names and their speaker, Sir John Bussy, went as far as to protest against the secrecy surrounding these exempted persons.[32] If, as suggested above, Richard intended this exemption to apply to the group of men he had recently taken into custody, there was an obvious reason for such subterfuge. It was clear that the king did not intend to adopt the conciliatory tone of previous general pardons, but rather to manipulate the pardon into a tool of intimidation with which to highlight the guilt of the former Appellants and their adherents.[33]

The royal pardon played a central role in Richard's opening moves against the supporters of the Appellants in the autumn of 1397. With these events properly elucidated, it also becomes clear that the declarations of pardon made in the Revenge Parliament were not simply isolated gestures of grace. They were in fact part of a comprehensive scheme to use the prerogative of mercy to force political opponents to answer for their actions. Richard's use of the prerogative did not end here, however. Once the trials of Arundel and Warwick commenced in the first session of Parliament, the very definition of royal pardon and mercy came under intense scrutiny. Richard wanted to make clear to all that the pardons he had granted the Lords Appellant in 1388 had been extorted from him under duress, and could not, therefore, be

---

on whether this was a general pardon, or a pardon only to those associated with the Appellants.

31 'pardonavimus Egidio de Malorre chivalier sectam pacis nostre et id quod ad nos versus ipsum pertinet occasione dicte comissionis et exercisii euisdem ac congregacionis insurrecctionis equitataciones depredacionis imprisonamenti interfecionis et arsure per ipsum in comitiva predicoram ducis et comitum' (TNA C 67/30, m. 3).

32 *Adam Usk*, ed. Given-Wilson, p. 25.

33 *SR*, I, 396–8; *PROME*, 'Parliament of January 1377', item 24; *PROME*, 'Parliament of 1381', item 28; *SR*, II, 20, 29–30.

allowed to stand. Conversely, Arundel and Warwick both defended themselves from the charges laid against them on the basis of these pardons. The exact definition of royal grace therefore came to play a crucial role at the forefront of national politics. What follows is an examination of the concept of pardoning articulated in the trials of Arundel and Warwick. It must be emphasised that, in using arguments surrounding the prerogative of mercy against the two lords, Richard was pursuing a course of action that he had, in fact, initiated in the first arrests of autumn 1397 and had consistently used against his political opponents thereafter. It is also important to note that the trials of Arundel and Warwick were reported extensively by chroniclers, who themselves understood the significance of pardoning, and drew on well-established literary traditions in their descriptions of these 'pardon scenes'.

The Trials of Arundel and Warwick

In essence, the key issue in the trials of Arundel and Warwick was the validity of the amnesties that Richard had granted them back in 1388. Immediately after the Lords Appellant had been formally accused of treason, Parliament took the step of revoking the 1388 pardon.[34] However, the earl of Arundel challenged the fundamental legality of such an annulment, and based his entire defence on the argument that he could not be tried for misdeeds that the king had already pardoned.[35] He claimed that his pardons were still valid because they had been granted by the king within the last six years, when he was of full age and free to act as he wished: 'I still claim the benefit of my pardon, which you, within the last six years, when you were of full age and free to act as you wished, granted to me of your own volition.'[36] The earl's case rested on the fact that the pardons that Richard had granted him in 1388 and 1394 were still valid, and in order to claim this, it seems, he had to make the case that they were granted by an adult monarch of his own free will. Indeed, Arundel argued, he put no pressure on the king for a pardon in 1388, and knew nothing of it until the king actually gave it to him. Arundel's point about Richard's age at the time the pardons were granted was hard to dispute. The earl stressed that the king had attained his majority by the time he granted him a pardon in 1394. Richard had indeed declared himself of age five years before, on 3 May 1389. Interestingly, however, Richard had still technically been a minor during the Merciless Parliament of 1388. At

---

[34] *PROME*, 'Parliament of September 1397', items 12–13. All the members of the 1386 commission except Gloucester, Arundel and Warwick, and the archbishop, were, however, immediately exempted from the revocation of the pardon: Tuck, *English Nobility*, p. 188.

[35] Given-Wilson, *Revolution*, pp. 58–9.

[36] Given-Wilson, *Revolution*, p. 58.

this assembly the Appellants had emphasised Richard's youth and the evil counsel that had led him astray. Yet they had still recognised his authority to grant them an amnesty for their actions.[37] It was clear that to some extent the Appellants wanted the best of both worlds: to claim that Richard's youth had lain him open to manipulation, but also to assert that he could grant them a pardon of his own free will. The age at which a monarch could grant mercy was not clearly defined. As a ten-year-old at his accession, Richard II had always exercised the power to pardon under the authority of the privy seal. However, when the infant Henry VI acceded to the throne the use of the prerogative of mercy fell into abeyance. Interestingly, one of Henry's first acts on coming of age was to issue a general pardon, at the request of the parliamentary Commons, suggesting perhaps that the ability to grant mercy was widely regarded as a power that rested on the decision of an adult monarch.[38] Since pardon was a matter of royal grace, it was clearly important that it should be issued by the king himself, as a personal contract between recipient and monarch.

The legality of revoking a pardon was fundamental to Arundel's trial. Richard himself countered the earl's claims with the assertion that he had granted mercy provided that it was not to his prejudice, a get-out-clause that previous monarchs had invoked in order to renege on disadvantageous legislation. Richard's claim therefore at least had well-known precedent. The same logic had been used in 1377 to justify the repeal of the acts of the Good Parliament.[39] Interestingly, the speaker of the Commons, Sir John Bussy, clearly thought that the assent of the Lords and the Commons had added an extra air of legality to the revocation of the pardon: 'That pardon has already been revoked by the king, the lords, and us, the faithful commons.'[40] Ultimately, however, by claiming that the act had proved prejudicial to the Crown, Richard could revoke it on his own authority. This demonstrates the extent to which a grant of pardon was dependent on the king's prerogative and goodwill, although the charges made against Richard at his deposition made it clear that misuse of this power would provoke resentment.[41]

John of Gaunt, presiding over the trial as high steward of England, introduced a different interpretation of the pardon by asking the earl why, if he was innocent of treason, he had sought a pardon at all. To this Arundel is reported to have responded with the famous remark: 'To silence the tongues

---

37 *SR*, II, 47–8; *Knighton's Chronicle*, ed. Martin, pp. 504–5; *Westminster Chronicle*, ed. Hector and Harvey, pp. 296–306; *Adam Usk*, ed. Given-Wilson, pp. 9–10: see also Goodman, *Loyal Conspiracy*, pp. 36–41; J. L. Leland, 'Unpardonable Sinners', *Medieval Prosopography* 17 (1996), 181–95.

38 On 27 March 1437. Storey, *House of Lancaster*, p. 213.

39 See above, Chapter 8, p. 116.

40 Given-Wilson, *Revolution*, p. 59.

41 The revocation of the pardon that the king issued to the Lords Appellant in 1388 is given in Given-Wilson, *Revolution*, pp. 173–4.

of my enemies, of whom you are one, and to be sure, when it comes to treason, you are in greater need of a pardon than I am.'[42] Arundel's defiant stance failed to sway his judges, and, convicted of treason, he was taken to Tower Hill for execution. But Gaunt's question to Arundel about why he had sought pardon if he was in fact innocent raises a further point about the common understanding of the king's pardon: the issue of whether or not it necessarily implied guilt. In this period a pardon could be purchased before trial, and pleaded by the suspect on his arraignment before the justices.[43] If this was the case the recipient would not actually have been convicted before the king's courts. Indeed, an individual innocent of the charges against them might seek pardon in order to avoid relying on the justices to reach a favour-able verdict, and to save themselves the considerable expenses that might be incurred during the trial procedure. It is clear, however, that high-profile grants of mercy often served to emphasise the guilt of the recipient, while at the same time reconciling them with government. The amnesty granted to the Ordainers by Edward II on 16 October 1313 is a case in point; the king left no doubt about their guilt in the text of the pardon.[44] Gaunt clearly felt Arundel's acceptance of a pardon carried with it similar connotations. On this point, the interpretation of a pardon was clearly flexible. At times, a royal pardon could vindicate an individual who felt he or she had been wrongly accused in the royal courts. On other occasions, accepting pardon was tanta-mount to an admission of guilt.

Richard had clearly abused his power to pardon by using it as a tool of accusation and incrimination. However, in the case of the earl of Warwick, he was able to show himself capable of mercy.[45] In Warwick's trial, Richard was able to exercise clemency because of the earl's willingness to admit his guilt and throw himself on the king's mercy. The Monk of Evesham described the scene of supplication for mercy:

> On the Friday Thomas earl of Warwick was put on trial. Once his hood had been removed and the appeal read, he foolishly, wretchedly and pusillani-mously confessed to everything in the appeal, weeping and wailing and whining that he had indeed acted traitorously in all these matters, submit-ting himself to the king's mercy in all things and bemoaning the fact that he

---

[42] Given-Wilson states that the descriptions of the trials of Arundel and Warwick, given by Adam Usk and by the Monk of Evesham, were probably based on a tract written by a clerk of the royal Chancery present at the proceedings. Their accounts accord with the Rolls of Parliament: Given-Wilson, *Revolution*, pp. 58–9; *Adam Usk*, ed. Given-Wilson, pp. 28–35; PROME, 'Parliament of September 1397', items 12–22. See also C. Given-Wilson, 'Adam Usk, the Monk of Evesham, and the Parliament of 1397–8', *Historical Research* 66 (1993), 329–35.

[43] The ability to obtain pardon before arraignment was somewhat controversial, and was finally outlawed in the Tudor period.

[44] See Chapter 7, p. 98.

[45] Tuck, *English Nobility*, p. 190; Given-Wilson, *Revolution*, p. 17.

had ever associated with the appellants … so at length, since almost everybody there felt moved by his tears and was begging and pleading with the king to show mercy to him, the king granted him his life.[46]

Warwick's ostentatious display of contrition gave the king the opportunity to pardon the earl with no loss of face. This description of Warwick's actions also accords with the well-established tradition of describing 'pardon scenes' in a particular way, emphasising the physical appearance of the supplicant and the intercession of onlookers, for instance.[47] There were established literary traditions for the Monk of Evesham to draw on in describing Warwick's trial. This is not to say the earl did not act in the manner described – behaviour and literary construction were surely mutually dependent.

The third of the leading Lords Appellant, the duke of Gloucester, had been summoned before Parliament on 24 September, but by this time he was already dead, having been secretly murdered while in the custody of the earl of Nottingham in Calais.[48] Parliament was informed of his 'natural' death by Nottingham, and the Lords took the decision to pass a posthumous sentence of treason against the duke.[49] The parliament roll contains a supposed transcription of the confession that Gloucester made just before he died to a royal commission headed by Sir William Rickhill, a judge of the Common Bench. The terms of this confession have been the subject of scholarly debate, due largely to the testimony Rickhill later gave in Henry IV's first Parliament. Rickhill claimed that Richard had edited the confession before having it read aloud to Parliament: 'some of the said articles, those which suited the king, were read out, and some of the said articles, those which were contrary to the king's aim and purpose, were not read or made known'.[50] The final section of the written confession was omitted, presumably because of the plea for the king's mercy that it contained:

---

46 Given-Wilson, *Revolution*, p. 61. 'Die Veneris Thomas, comes Warwic', sistabatur in iudicio, ablatoque capicio, et lecta appellacione, quasi pusillanimous, miser et uecors, fatebatur omnia, in appellacione contenta, plorando, gemendo et ululando per ipsum proditore esse perpetrate, Regis gracie se in omnibus submittendo, dolensque, quod unquam extitit appellatis associatus. … Et tunc, quasi omnibus pro se plorantibus, ac sibi graciam Regis petentibus, motis his fletibus rex concessit ei uitam' (*Historia Vitae et Regni Ricardi Secundi*, ed. Stow, p. 145).

47 See Chapter 3, pp. 38–43.

48 He was widely believed to have been killed on the king's orders: see A. Tuck, 'Thomas, Duke of Gloucester (1355–1397)', *Oxford Dictionary of National Biography* (Oxford, 2004), online edn, May 2007. J. Tait suggested a chronology of events in his article of 1902: J. Tait, 'Did Richard II Murder the Duke of Gloucester?', *Historical Essays by Members of the Owens College, Manchester*, ed. T. F. Tout and J. Tait (1902), pp. 193–216.

49 *PROME*, 'Parliament of September 1397', item 7.

50 *PROME*, 'Parliament of 1399', item 92; Tait, 'Duke of Gloucester', p. 204.

I beseche my lyege and souverayn loord the Kyng, that he wyll of his heygh grace and benyngnytee accepte me to his mercy and his grace, as I that putt my lyf, my body, and my goode holy at hys wyll as lowlych as mekelych as any creature kan do or may do to his lyege loord. Besechyng to hys heygh lordeschipp that he wyll, for the passion that God soffred for all mankynde and for the compassion that he hadde of hys moder on the cros and the pytee that he hadde of Marye Maudelyne, that he wyll vouchesauf for to have compassion and pytee; and to accepte me unto his mercy and to his grace, as he that hathe ever bene ful of mercy and of grace to all his lyeges and to all other that have naght bene so neygh unto him as I have bene, thogh I be unworthy.[51]

Such an abject plea for royal mercy, with its evocation of Christian virtues, was judged too sensitive to be read aloud before Parliament, only the day after Richard had endorsed a posthumous conviction for treason against the duke. As James Tait commented, this confession was intended to legitimise the conviction for treason, not to arouse the sympathy of the commons. The popularity of the duke was such that there remained a risk of popular demonstrations in his favour.[52] This plea for royal mercy would also have been uncomfortable for Richard, in the knowledge that he had ordered the murder of his uncle. He would presumably have known of the circumstances, which were later retold by the man charged with Gloucester's murder in the first Parliament of Henry IV's reign. The duke had apparently been taken to a house in Calais where he had confessed himself to a chaplain before being suffocated on a feather bed.[53]

Finally, on 29 September, the parliamentary Commons asked the king to pardon other prominent individuals implicated in the plot of the Lords Appellant, having been named in the Appellants' commission of October 1386.[54] Of those named in the commission, the duke of York, the bishop of

---

[51] Tait, 'Duke of Gloucester', pp. 207–8; Given-Wilson, *Revolution*, p. 82. Tait explains that Rickhill had his own 'full' copy of the confession, which was exemplified in the patent rolls. A copy of this full version survives, because it was 'placed improperly in one of the Rolls of Parliament of the eleventh year of King Richard II'. This version can be compared against the amended one that was recorded in the rolls of the September 1397 Parliament, having been read out to the assembly (Tait, 'Duke of Gloucester', p. 204).

[52] Tait, 'Duke of Gloucester', p. 208.

[53] For details, see the confession of John Hall for his part in Gloucester's murder, given in the first Parliament of Henry IV's reign: *PROME*, 'Parliament of 1399', item 11.

[54] This commission had already been read aloud before Parliament at the start of the session: *PROME*, 'Parliament of September 1397', item 11. The commission named: William archbishop of Canterbury, Alexander archbishop of York, Edmund duke of York, Thomas duke of Gloucester; William bishop of Winchester, Thomas bishop of Exeter, and Nicholas abbot of Waltham; Richard earl of Arundel, John Lord Cobham, Richard le Scrope and John Devereux.

Winchester and Sir Richard le Scrope were still alive and were pardoned. Posthumous pardons were declared for the late archbishop of Canterbury, archbishop of York, bishop of Exeter and abbot of Waltham.[55] The two junior Appellants, the earl of Derby and the earl of Nottingham, were also granted pardon after a plea from the Commons, in which they were given credit for foiling the plot of Arundel, Gloucester and Warwick.[56] The individual Appellant supporters had now been dealt with, but one last act of pardon was to be declared in January 1398.

On 30 September 1397 the Revenge Parliament was adjourned, to meet again on 27 January 1398, at Shrewsbury. This Shrewsbury session only lasted from 28 to 31 January, but it drew up and issued a general pardon, this time to all the king's subjects. They were pardoned any misdeeds committed before 31 January 1398, and not just those concerning the Appellant revolt.[57] The pardon was also made conditional on the grant of a wool subsidy.[58] The representatives duly agreed to give their consent and handed over the customs revenue for life to the king, a grant that had the potential to weaken their bargaining power in future negotiations with the Crown. However, their generosity was rewarded with a pardon that still excluded those who had rebelled against Richard in 1388. These men, although unnamed, were to sue for pardon separately.[59] The take-up of this pardon was far greater than for any previous amnesty. Over 4,000 pardons were issued in total, almost double the number granted in 1377 to celebrate Edward III's jubilee year. Clearly, the anxiety generated by Richard's use of the pardon allowed the king to discover who his enemies were, and enabled the exchequer to profit from their insecurity. Throughout the whole series of measures Richard initi-

---

55 *PROME*, 'Parliament of September 1397', item 26. The only people mentioned in the 1386 commission who were not pardoned at this time were the two knights, John Cobham, who was subsequently banished in the 1398 session of Parliament (*PROME*, 'Parliament of September 1397', item 10), and John Devereux, who had died in 1393.

56 *PROME*, 'Parliament of September 1397', item 27.

57 *PROME*, 'Parliament of September 1397', item 77; *SR*, II, 106–7. The names of the recipients are recorded on the supplementary patent rolls, TNA C 67/30, mm. 5–18, 20–34; C 67/31, mm. 1, 3, 5–11. The practice of issuing two forms of pardon followed the procedure instigated in 1377 (see Chapter 8, pp. 124–5). A few had their pardons duplicated in the patent roll and pardon rolls, for instance, Sir William Bagot: C 67/31, m. 13. A few were only entered into the patent roll and not the pardon roll, and at least five others received pardons that have not been enrolled, the chancellor being instructed to issue them under the great seal: C 81/570/11739, 11745; C 81/579/12649, 12693; C 81/581/12839.

58 *PROME*, 'Parliament of January 1377', item 19; *SR*, II, 106–7.

59 According to the pardon rolls, 596 people were granted pardon for association with the Lords Appellant, between September 1397 and September 1399: TNA C 67/30, mm. 19 (42 names), 4 (3), 3 (99), 2 (124), 1 (117); C 67/31, mm. 13 (53), 12 (133), 4 (2), 2 (23).

ated against the Appellants and their supporters, from the first arrests and council meetings of autumn 1397, to the trials of Warwick and Arundel and the reissue of the general pardon in 1398, the king used the royal pardon as a tool with which to manipulate his political opponents. He subverted the traditional uses of pardon, and proved that his grants of mercy were not to be relied upon.

However, it must be noted that throughout the fifteenth century grants of royal mercy were once again used as symbolic acts of political reconciliation. On one level these acts of clemency can be seen as a pragmatic concession by the Crown – an acknowledgement of its inability to enforce all the judicial penalties it prescribed.[60] But they can also be seen as an important representation of the Crown's responsibility to reconcile its subjects to its authority. Despite Richard's misuse of the prerogative, the general pardon remained at the heart of the Crown's judicial policy. The general pardon had emerged, in the final months of Edward III's reign, in part as a response to a specific political emergency. But it also fulfilled a more general need for the late medieval monarchy to be seen to be taking an active part in the common enterprise of the realm: the monarchy needed to demonstrate its willingness to take the initiative in reconciling the expanding political community to its authority in times of crisis. In using the pardon, which remained an act of royal grace, there was no sense in which the monarchy was acknowledging a permanent shift in the balance of political power. In fact, the use of royal grace reinforced the central role of the will of the king in the medieval constitution. If pardon implied some guilt on the part of those who bought a copy, the members of the polity who paid for a writ from Chancery each implicitly acknowledged some culpability in the deterioration of relations with the Crown. But it did at least indicate that the Crown understood that the procedures of government would eventually stall without the support of those lower down the ranks of the political community. By the end of Richard II's reign, the concept of reconciliation through pardon was familiar enough for it to be the focus of debate between the Crown and the Lords Appellant. Richard's manipulation of the pardon shows that it was eminently possible for an individual king to abuse the powers of royal grace at his disposal. But this imbalance in the medieval constitution could not be perpetuated for long, as the charges laid against Richard II at his deposition clearly demonstrated.

---

[60] Hurnard, *Homicide*, p. vii.

CHAPTER ELEVEN

Conclusion: Attitudes to Pardoning

This study has been predicated on the notion that the role of the pardon in fourteenth-century England deserves further attention, and that it is a subject uniquely suited to uniting much of the new work on the legal, political and cultural contexts of the later Middle Ages. Since Naomi Hurnard's study of pardoning was published in 1969, work on the use of the pardon in the eighteenth century and the renewed interest of historians in medieval political culture has provided an entirely new context and methodology through which to view the role of the royal pardon. In the 1970s the 'Warwick school' of historians, including Thompson and Hay among others, led the way in demonstrating how the use of the pardon should be understood in the light of a more general perception of the law as a malleable tool of the propertied classes. Pardon might provide welcome leniency in the strictures of the law, but it was a leniency that was bestowed at the discretion of judges and monarchs, rather than accorded as of right, according to a transparent legal code. It therefore reinforced the view of the dispensation of mercy as a paternalistic act that would uphold the prevailing social hierarchy.[1] These lessons have been heeded in more recent work, although scholars over the last twenty years have been keen to accord a greater role to individual agency in shaping people's experience of the law and the system of pardoning in particular. For those who played an active part in the political community at least, historians have demonstrated the degree to which they were able to use and adapt the language of pardon to suit their own purposes.[2]

Similarly, the work on later medieval political culture since the 1960s has provided an entirely new context for understanding the dispensation of royal mercy. This work has offered new insight into the way in which historians should interpret medieval prescriptive texts on law and kingship, and employed new methodologies to bring together a greater range of material, such as parliamentary records, petitions, vernacular literature and legal tracts, to further inform our understanding of relations between the Crown and the political community. Recent work by John Watts, Gwilym Dodd and others has also focused attention on the language of medieval politics and

---

[1] See above, Chapter 1, pp. 5–6.
[2] See above, Chapter 1, n. 13.

the common rhetorical devices that appeared in a variety of different genres of texts and were adopted by the Crown and its subjects alike.[3] Dodd's study of private petitioning demonstrates how this approach sheds light on the application and reception of royal authority throughout the realm. This methodology has been applied here to the study of pardoning in the fourteenth century, in an attempt to show the variety of ways in which people experienced and interpreted royal mercy.

This book has made a clear division between individual, group and general pardons, in order to analyse the different facets and contexts for each type of grant. However, this should not serve to promote too rigid a distinction; one of the points of this concluding chapter is to reinforce the sense that people in the Middle Ages experienced the operation of royal mercy in a number of different contexts, but that they overlapped and informed each other in shaping attitudes to this royal prerogative power. The first main section of this book examined the use of individual pardons, and the separate chapters on the role of the petitioner, intercessor and the monarch directed attention to the individuals involved in the pardoning process, and the variety of ways in which people experienced and had access to royal mercy. In basing these chapters on the people involved in the process, it is hoped that the range of opinions and experiences of pardoning to which people were exposed has been more fully elucidated. Individuals who petitioned for pardon were aided by county lawyers to frame their appeal in a commonly accepted language of supplication. But the same people who succeeded in purchasing their own pardons from Chancery might also be aware of the protests put forward in Parliament over the use of pardons as a reward for military service, and they may also have watched the process of intercession for pardon being satirised in a Corpus Christi play. Moreover, a range of different people might intercede for pardon on behalf of associates or retainers. Nobles might recommend a case direct to the king, while those who were less well-connected might purchase a fake writ from a forger of royal documents. The monarch himself would also interact with the procedures of pardoning in different ways; on occasion exercising the power in public displays of mercy; dispensing pardons alongside cramp rings to aid those afflicted with epilepsy and using the healing properties of the royal touch to cure scrofula. However, he might also withhold pardon, when it was politically expedient to do so.

The role of the monarch in the pardoning process was the aspect that attracted most comment and attention from a variety of different writers: legal theorists emphasised the need to remind the monarch of the promise to use pardon in accordance with the terms of his coronation oath, while those who penned the outlaw ballads portrayed the idealised vision of a monarch

---

[3] See above, Chapter 1, pp. 7–8.

dispensing mercy with the equitable insight that only a divinely appointed king could hope to attain. Aspects of this royal power might be more closely defined, but the king's authority to pardon was not fundamentally challenged; the power to exercise royal grace placed the monarch outside the legal system that operated in his name. Although, in practice, he would not often make judgments in direct contradiction to the law, his prerogative of grace was not entirely bound by its conventions. The idea that the king's subjects ultimately had access to mercy, in the person of the monarch, was too important and pervasive to be fundamentally challenged.

The analysis presented in Part I of this book therefore reinforced the sense that the importance of the pardon was not confined to the law courts; the notion of royal mercy went far beyond legal classifications and resonated throughout medieval culture. Even within the judicial sphere, it was recognised that the pardon stood for more than a method of mitigating prescribed sanctions in certain cases. In the thirteenth century, *Bracton* had criticised the effect of the pardon on the authority and status of the common law, but recognised that the royal prerogative of mercy embodied the king's moral duty to provide equitable justice, and even advocated that subjects should be able to bring an appeal to the monarch himself. Accordingly, texts such as *Bracton*, *Fleta* and the 1278 Statute of Gloucester sought to clarify the procedure of pardoning, but continued to express an underlying belief in the value of the prerogative.[4] For petitioners, too, the pardon was more than merely a mechanism of the law, confined in importance to the courtroom. It represented their right to appeal to the king as the head of the judicial system, for a judgment of grace. The physical object of the letter patent of pardon embodied the promise of protection they had received from the Crown.[5] These ideas were part of the wider notion that the legal system itself was not a discrete and self-governing entity. The processes of the law could be moderated from above by the dictates of the monarch or from below by juries and local communities, or by the Church through the ecclesiastical privileges of sanctuary and benefit of clergy.[6] The notion that informal standards would be applied in passing judgment, and that the process of personal arbitration moderated the strict application of legal categories, was entrenched in medieval thought.[7]

Part II of this book examined the use of group pardons, and the evolution of the general pardon in the second half of the fourteenth century. The focus here on three particular contexts, the Good Parliament and royal jubilee of Edward III in the last year of his reign, the Peasants' Revolt of 1381 and

---

4 See above, Chapter 2, pp. 22–4.
5 See, for example, the use of the physical charter of pardon in the Towneley Corpus Christi pageant: Chapter 4, p. 55.
6 See above, Chapter 1, pp. 11–16.
7 See above, Chapter 1, pp. 11–12.

Richard II's actions against the Lords Appellant in the late 1390s emphasised the political role of the general pardon and the part it played in shaping relations between the Crown and the political community. The evolution of the general pardon signalled that the royal prerogative of mercy was to occupy a permanent position in the political sphere. Grants of amnesty to opponents of the Crown had long occupied a less official political role in reconciling disaffected factions to the regime.[8] The general pardon now supplanted these amnesties, and allowed the government to portray the use of the prerogative as an unforced act of mercy, rather than merely a reaction to a political crisis on the scale of the Good Parliament or the Peasants' Revolt. These pardons were formulated as a statement of royal authority rather than an admission of weakness.

This point has important implications for our understanding of the king's own exercise of his prerogative rights during the later fourteenth century and beyond. While the monarch consented to issue a general pardon, he always did so of his own free grace. He could, therefore, rescind the grant by another assertion of the royal will. Importantly, this protected the feudal rights of the Crown intact and did not allow Parliament to assume any power over future grants of pardon.[9] In one very real sense, then, the continued exercise of the royal prerogative of mercy represented the unilateral capacity of the Crown to take decisions and to issue orders on its own authority. This survival serves to qualify, rather than support, any notion of the development of consensual government in Parliaments of the later fourteenth century. The grants of royal mercy offered by the Crown in 1362 or 1377, for example, represented the development of a reciprocal relationship between the king and Commons, but not one in which the Commons encroached, in any sense, on the feudal and prerogative rights of the Crown. In issuing a general pardon, the royal government also extended its influence to those outside the immediate circle of the polity, and in taking the recipients of pardons back into the king's peace it gave them a vested interest in upholding the working of the law.

A study of general pardons inevitably focuses attention on the more sympathetic and moderate aspects of Crown policy in the face of political crises, steering discussion towards issues of reconciliation and inclusivity. At the same time, however, 'structuralist' arguments have propounded the view that in the years after the Black Death, the governing classes were united in a desire to impress upon the commonalty a renewed sense of obedience and obligation.[10] In this light, general pardons can be viewed as a mechanism

---

[8] See above, Chapter 7, pp. 93–100.

[9] This point has been made by Mark Ormrod in relation to the 1362 Statute of Purveyors: see *PROME*, 'Parliament of 1362', introduction.

[10] In the October 1383 Parliament Sir Michael de la Pole's address emphasised the subject's duty of obedience. Tuck suggests this echoed a view dominant among the king's advisers in the early 1380s (Tuck, 'Nobles, Commons', pp. 206–7). The

with which to reawaken the sense of duty among the polity and reconcile them to their public duties.[11] However, these pardons should not be portrayed simply as evidence of a restoration of perceived norms in social relations. Royal mercy was accessible to those lower down the social order, and relied on their co-operation to remain effective. Musson and Ormrod have argued that royal justice in the fourteenth century 'regulated or provided redress for considerably more areas of life – including areas of relevance to peasant society – than had been the case a hundred years before'.[12] The idea that all of the king's subjects had access to royal mercy was a pervasive one, and it was not one entirely divorced from reality. As this study has shown, a whole range of people sought, and received, the king's pardon. Similarly, the rebels in 1381 were as well-versed in the language of pardon as the Lords Appellant. Both used the idea of pardoning to further their political objectives.

It is clear that attitudes towards royal pardons were far from uniform. Opinions surrounding pardoning did not follow a clear trajectory from exclusive support for the exercise of mercy to increasing disillusionment and criticism of royal pardons as the fourteenth century wore on. It is true, for example, that the parliamentary Commons attacked the use of pardons for military service in the middle years of Edward III's reign. But they also requested the issue of comprehensive pardons to all the king's subjects on several occasions from the 1360s to the end of the century and beyond. It is clear that the debates on pardoning cannot be viewed in isolation: they influenced, and were in turn informed by, the views of a variety of commentators, whether they were legal theorists, theologians or writers of satire or advice. The purpose of this book has been to present a more subtle exposition of such perceptions in the context of the judicial and political developments that occurred throughout the fourteenth century. At the centre of such an analysis must be the fundamental contemporary concern with the king's position in relation to the law. This concern motivated efforts to define the authority of the king's power of mercy over the jurisdiction of the common law courts. On the one hand, legal theorists and members of the polity were anxious to limit the potential for a monarch to abuse such a prerogative by pardoning undeserving felons. On the other, commentators praised the equitable justice dispensed by the monarch, and many acknowledged the right of his subjects

---

structural thesis advocated by Palmer, Putnam and others suggests the county gentry increasingly appropriated the machinery of local justice: R. C. Palmer, *English Law in the Age of the Black Death 1348–1381: A Transformation of Governance and Law* (Chapel Hill NC, 1993); Putnam, 'Transformation'; Harriss, *Public Finance*, pp. 354–5, 516–17; Kaeuper, *Public Order*, pp. 386–7. For further discussion, see S. H. Rigby, *English Society in the Later Middle Ages: Class, Status and Gender* (Basingstoke, 1995), pp. 124–44; Fryde, *Peasants and Landlords*, pp. 113–35; Ormrod, 'Government', pp. 19–30.

11 See above, Chapter 8, pp. 120–1.
12 Musson and Ormrod, *Evolution*, p. 179.

to have access to such a process of appeal. Indeed, by the end of the century courts of conscience had developed to formalise the process of an appeal to equity that had persisted in the royal judicial system, providing a defined and quick method of access to the king's discretionary justice.[13] Within this context, it is important to recognise that while the use of military pardons for a time generated intense debate among the political community, preoccupation with this aspect of pardoning was relatively short-lived and protest largely confined to the sixteen-year period between 1337 and 1353. Discussion of the role of pardoning, however, had been initiated at least a century earlier, and was to continue throughout the later Middle Ages.

The royal pardon occupied a unique place in medieval culture. Its role was variously criticised, extolled and debated by the authors of legal texts, parliamentary petitions and statutes, and literary works of advice or protest. It was a pragmatic means of mitigating the severity of the law, but also stood as a symbol of royal mercy and of the Crown's obligation to provide effective justice. Access to this ultimate form of appeal reinforced the reciprocal relationship between Crown and commonalty. In this sense, the role of the royal pardon has a vital part to play in our considerations of the nature of later medieval political culture.

---

[13] H. J. Berman, *Faith and Order: The Reconciliation of Law and Religion* (Atlanta, 1993), pp. 55–82.

APPENDICES

Introduction

The statistics given in the appendices that follow are drawn from several different series of documents in the National Archives. The majority of the records relating to pardons were kept by the Chancery. The letters of pardon were drawn up by the Chancery clerks and recorded on the patent rolls (TNA, C 66). Inevitably there are a few examples of pardons that were entered on the patent rolls incorrectly, or omitted altogether, presumably because of a clerical error. Pardons might also be entered onto the Gascon and Scotch rolls (C 61; C 71) when the grant related to these particular areas. Sometimes, when a pardon had been approved by the king himself, rather than being issued solely on the authority of the chancellor, the writ of privy seal also survives. This was the document used to convey the monarch's decision to the Chancery, and it would then serve as a warrant for the clerks to issue the pardon (TNA, C 81). Most of these warrants can therefore be matched to the record of the pardon subsequently issued, but in some instances no corresponding enrolment can be identified (examples can be found in the *Calendar of Chancery Warrants*).[1] The Chancery also kept records of those who volunteered to act as sureties for the future good conduct of a recipient of pardon (C 237). In 1336 there was an attempt to make the finding of sureties a legal requirement, but in practice this requirement was increasingly waived or ignored (see Chapter 4 for further details). A final category of useful Chancery documents comprises the 'cancelled letters patent'. Among them are letters of pardon that were drawn up, but never collected, perhaps because the recipient had died while on a military campaign (C 266). These documents all record the issue of the pardon itself. Petitions for pardon, where they survive, are found predominantly in the series of 'ancient petitions to the crown' (SC 8).[2] The financial records of the Hanaper also record payment for pardons, although these records are not complete for the fourteenth century (E 101/211–13). When the first general pardons began to be granted, the Chancery clerks recorded the names of those who came to purchase a copy on a separate roll

---

[1] *Calendar of Chancery Warrants Preserved in the Public Record Office, A.D. 1244–1326*, ed. H. C. Maxwell-Lyte (London, 1927).
[2] See Dodd, *Justice and Grace*, pp. 326–34 for a thorough survey of the archival material relating to parliamentary petitions.

supplementary to the main patent roll series (TNA, C 67/28B–31).[3] However, there is some overlap between the patent rolls (C 66) and the supplementary patent rolls (C 67), when the name of an individual recipient of general pardon appears in both places.

The statistics relating to pardons must, therefore, be regarded as approximations. It is impossible to calculate the exact number of pardons issued, but we can say that, from the accession of Edward I to the deposition of Richard II, close to 40,000 were recorded on the patent rolls and another 20,000 were entered under the general pardons on the supplementary rolls. Of course, these pardons were not evenly distributed over the period; grants of military pardons or general pardons caused peaks in particular years.

---

3   Three separate fragmentary rolls of military pardons also survive in this series: TNA C 67/26–28A.

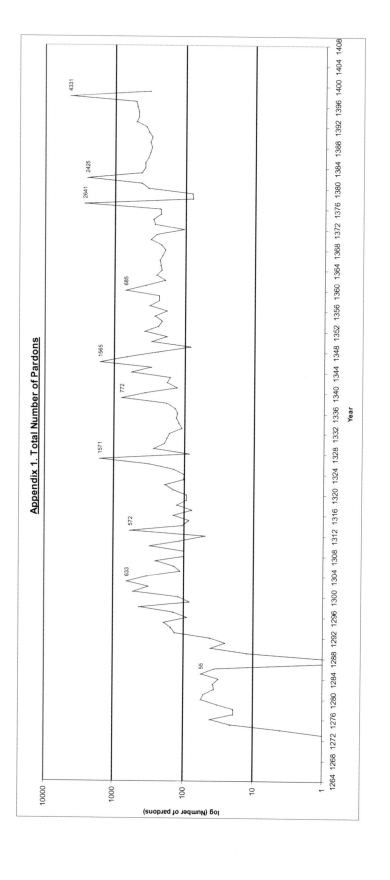

Appendix 1. Total Number of Pardons

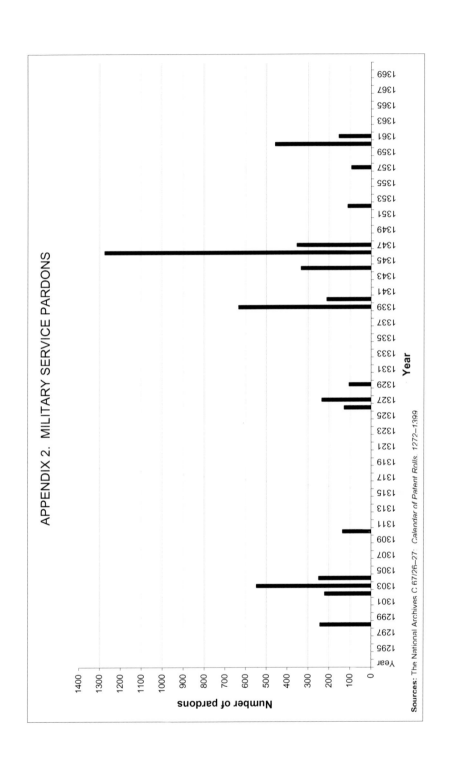

APPENDIX 2. MILITARY SERVICE PARDONS

Number of pardons

Year

Sources: The National Archives C 67/26–27. Calendar of Patent Rolls, 1272–1399

APPENDIX 3. REGIONAL DISTRIBUTION OF PARDONS

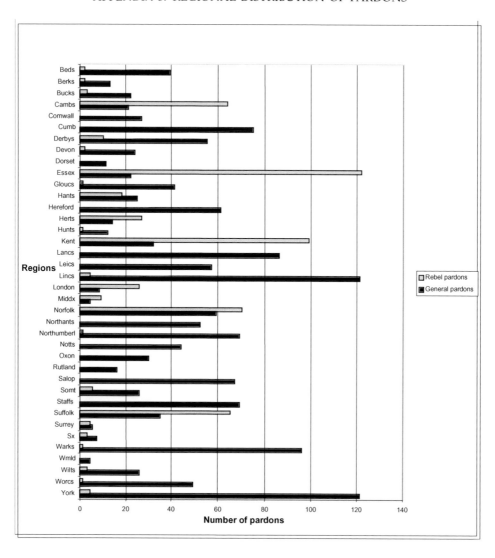

187

APPENDIX 4.i INTERCESSORS FOR PARDON: EDWARD II, 1307–1327

Intercessor	Total	Sub-total for year
Apelby, Robert	1	(1) 1315
Archer, Thomas le, prior of the Hospital St John of Jerusalem	1	(1) 1322
Argenteym, Giles	1	(1) 1307
Arundel, Edmund Fitzalan, earl of	5	(1) 1320
		(2) 1323
		(1) 1324
		(1) 1326
Athy, John	2	(2) 1326
Audley, James, king's yeoman and kinsman [Daudele]	1	(1) 1312
Ayreminne, Richard [Airmyn, Ayremynne]	1	(1) 1321
Ayreminne, William, king's clerk [Airmyn, Ayremynne]	10	(2) 1322
		(8) 1324
Badlesmere, Sir Bartholomew [Baddlesmere]	9	(1) 1314
		(2) 1316
		(1) 1317
		(3) 1318
		(2) 1319
Baldock, Robert	15	(1) 1320
		(2) 1321
		(8) 1322
		(4) 1323
Beaumont, Sir Henry [Bello Monte]	10	(1) 1308
		(1) 1309
		(3) 1310
		(2) 1312
		(1) 1313
		(1) 1314
		(1) 1316
Bek, Anthony, bishop of Durham	1	(1) 1309
Burdegala, Oliver	2	(2) 1312
Bykenore, Alexander, king's clerk, treasurer of Ireland	1	(1) 1311
Carlisle, Andrew Harcla, earl of	1	(1) 1322
Certain persons in parliament	1	(1) 1321
Charleton, John, Lord	4	(1) 1310
		(3) 1316
Cherleton, Thomas, bishop of Hereford	5	(1) 1316
		(2) 1317
		(1) 1318
		(1) 1319
Clifford, Henry	1	(1) 1325
Clifford, Robert	3	(2) 1307
		(1) 1310
Clifford, William [Clyfford]	2	(2) 1325

Colby, William	1	(1) 1326
Controne, Pancius, king's clerk and doctor	4	(4) 1325
Cornwall, Piers Gaveston, earl of	5	(2) 1308
		(1) 1309
		(1) 1310
		(1) 1311
Cromwell, John [Crombewelle]	3	(2) 1307
		(1) 1316
Damory, Sir Roger, steward of the household [Dammory]	6	(1) 1312
		(1) 1317
		(3) 1318
		(1) 1320
Darcy, Sir John, justiciary of Ireland	1	(1) 1326
Darcy, Robert and John Darcy	1	(1) 1312
Despenser, Hugh, the younger, Lord	9	(2) 1313
		(4) 1322
		(2) 1324
		(1) 1326
Echingham, Robert	2	(1) 1322
		(1) 1323
Edmund of Woodstock, earl of Kent	2	(1) 1318
		(1) 1325
Ergadia, John	1	(1) 1310
Felton, Roger	1	(1) 1314
Feraria, John and Gaillard of Gazaco, papal nuncios	1	(1) 1307
Ferre, Guy	1	(1) 1308
Foxton, Robert	1	(1) 1313
Frescobaldi, Amerigo dei, Italian banker	1	(1) 1308
Gloucester, Gilbert de Clare, earl of	2	(1) 1309
		(1) 1311
Gloucester, Hugh de Audley, earl of [Daudele]	2	(1) 1316
		(1) 1318
Gray, Sir Thomas	2	(1) 1322
		(1) 1323
Greenfield, William, archbishop of York	1	(1) 1314
Grendon, Robert, marshal of the king's hall	3	(3) 1323
Griffith, Res ap, king's yeoman	1	(1) 1325
Hainault, Alice of [late the wife of Roger Bigod]	1	(1) 1316
Hastings, Isabel	2	(1) 1325
		(1) 1326
Hastings, John, Lord	4	(4) 1307
Hastings, William	1	(1) 1307
Hereford and Essex, Humphrey Bohun, earl of	5	(1) 1307
		(1) 1316
		(1) 1317
		(2) 1318

Herlaston, William	2	(2) 1326
Hothum, John, bishop of Ely	4	(2) 1312
		(1) 1316
		(1) 1319
Inge, Sir William	3	(1) 1307
		(1) 1312
		(1) 1316
Insula, Warren	1	(1) 1310
Isabella, queen of England	21	(5) 1308
		(1) 1309
		(1) 1310
		(1) 1311
		(5) 1313
		(4) 1314
		(1) 1316
		(1) 1317
		(1) 1319
		(1) 1320
John, son of Thomas and other magnates of Ireland	1	(1) 1316
Kendale, Robert	2	(1) 1313
		(1) 1322
Lancaster, Thomas, earl of	4	(2) 1307
		(1) 1315
		(1) 1316
Langton, Walter, bishop of Coventry and Lichfield	1	(1) 1312
Lech, John, archbishop of Dublin	1	(1) 1313
Lenham, brother J.	1	(1) 1308
Lestrange, Fulk	1	(1) 1322
Lestre, Henry, king's yeoman	1	(1) 1314
Lincoln, Henry de Lacy, earl of	4	(1) 1307
		(1) 1309
		(2) 1310
Lovel, Richard	1	(1) 1316
Lucy, Sir Anthony	2	(2) 1323
Maidstone, Walter, bishop of Worcester	3	(3) 1314
March, Roger Mortimer, earl of	2	(1) 1308
		(1) 1310
Marmyoun, William	1	(1) 1310
Martyn, William	1	(1) 1310
Mauleverer, John	1	(1) 1314
Mauley, [Malo Laco], Edmund, steward of the king's bench	12	(2) 1311
		(9) 1312
		(1) 1313

Melton, William	19	(7) 1308
		(2) 1309
		(2) 1310
		(2) 1311
		(5) 1314
		(1) 1315
Merlawe, Drogo	1	(1) 1314
Middleton, Gilbert, king's clerk	2	(2) 1322
Montacute, William	4	(1) 1316
		(2) 1317
		(1) 1318
Montboucher, Bertrand	1	(1) 1308
Monthermer, Ralph, Lord [Monte Hermerii]	1	(1) 1314
Norfolk, Alice, countess of (Alice de Hales), king's sister	1	(1) 1327
Norfolk, Thomas Brotherton, earl of	2	(1) 1321
		(1) 1323
Northburgh, Roger	7	(1) 1312
		(1) 1314
		(3) 1316
		(1) 1318
		(1) 1321
Ormond, James de Butler, earl of [Botiller]	1	(1) 1326
Oxford, Robert de Vere, earl of	1	(1) 1308
Pembroke, Aymer de Valence, earl of	22	(1) 1307
		(3) 1312
		(2) 1313
		(1) 1314
		(1) 1315
		(1) 1316
		(6) 1318
		(4) 1319
		(1) 1321
		(1) 1322
		(1) 1324
Percy, Eleanor, king's kinswoman	1	(1) 1322
Pessaigne, Anthony	1	(1) 1316
Pouer, Arnald le	1	(1) 1326
Ralph, son of William	1	(1) 1314
Raundes, Eleanor	1	(1) 1311
Reynolds, Walter, bishop of Worcester, archbishop of Canterbury	7	(1) 1307
		(1) 1308
		(1) 1311
		(2) 1314
		(1) 1315
		(1) 1317
Richmond, John, earl of	3	(1) 1307
		(1) 1321
		(1) 1322

Robert, son of Payn [steward of the king's household]	4	(1) 1310
		(3) 1311
Ros, William	1	(1) 1318
Salmon, John, bishop of Norwich	1	(1) 1322
Sandale, John, bishop of Winchester, treasurer	6	(1) 1310
		(1) 1311
		(1) 1313
		(1) 1314
		(1) 1316
		(1) 1317
Sapy, John, king's yeoman	1	(1) 1309
Scrope, Sir Geoffrey le	4	(1) 1323
		(1) 1324
		(1) 1325
		(1) 1326
Segrave, John and Geoffrey Segrave	1	(1) 1308
Segrave, Nicholas	2	(1) 1312
		(1) 1313
Senche, Martin	2	(2) 1307
Somery, John	3	(1) 1310
		(1) 1311
		(1) 1314
Stapeldon, Walter, bishop of Exeter, treasurer	3	(1) 1322
		(1) 1323
		(1) 1326
Stratford, John, bishop of Winchester	3	(1) 1320
		(2) 1322
Surrey, John de Warenne , earl of	3	(2) 1310
		(1) 1320
Swynnerton, Roger	1	(1) 1317
Touney, Robert	2	(1) 1308
		(1) 1309
Tybetot, Payn	2	(2) 1307
Verdun, Nicholas	2	(2) 1322
Vienna, William, archbishop of, and Hugh, bishop of Orange, envoys of the pope	1	(1) 1326
Walewayn, John, king's clerk	2	(2) 1319
Walkefare, Robert	1	(1) 1327
Warle, Ingelard	2	(1) 1311
		(1) 1314
Wateville, Robert	3	(1) 1323
		(2) 1326
Welle, Robert	4	(4) 1322
Welleford, Geoffrey, king's clerk	1	(1) 1319
West, Thomas	1	(1) 1323
Weston, John	1	(1) 1321

Winchester, Hugh Despenser, elder, earl of	12	(4) 1308
		(3) 1309
		(1) 1313
		(1) 1317
		(1) 1322
		(1) 1325
		(1) 1326
Wyngefeld, Roger	2	(1) 1313
		(1) 1314
	359	

Intercessor(s)	Total	Sub-total for year
Abbeville, Peter, prior of Lenton	3	(3) 1355
Alisandre, John, king's minstrel	2	(1) 1357
		(1) 1363
Appleby, Thomas, bishop of Carlisle	3	(1) 1366
		(1) 1367
		(1) 1369
Armes Richard atte, king's yeoman	1	(1) 1361
Arundel, John [Darundell]	2	(1) 1372
		(1) 1373
Arundel, Richard Fitzalan, earl of	46	(1) 1331
		(1) 1332
		(1) 1337
		(1) 1338
		(1) 1341
		(3) 1344
		(3) 1345
		(13) 1346
		(2) 1347
		(1) 1348
		(1) 1350
		(2) 1351
		(1) 1355
		(1) 1356
		(3) 1357
		(1) 1360
		(1) 1364
		(1) 1365
		(1) 1369
		(1) 1370
		(1) 1371
		(1) 1372
		(3) 1373
		(1) 1374
Arundel, Richard Fitzalan, earl of, and Geoffrey Say	2	(1) 1351
		(1) 1358
Arundel, Richard Fitzalan, earl of, and earl of Stafford	1	(1) 1357
Arundel, Richard Fitzalan, earl of, and Walter Mauny	1	(1) 1344
Arundel, Richard and John his brother, king's esquires	1	(1) 1369
Ashton, Robert	3	(1) 1368
		(1) 1371
		(1) 1377
Ashton, Robert, treasurer, and chamberlains	1	(1) 1376
Ask, Richard, king's yeoman	1	(1) 1366

Asshehurst, Adam	6	(4) 1347
		(1) 1348
		(1) 1355
Assheton, Matthew, king's clerk	1	(1) 1350
Asteleye, Thomas	1	(1) 1331
Atheles, Aymer	1	(1) 1346
Audley, Eva [Daudele]	1	(1) 1369
Aumarle, William	1	(1) 1346
Aunsel, Alexander	1	(1) 1351
Bacon, Adam	1	(1) 1346
Badeby, Thomas	4	(4) 1346
Balliol, Edward, claimant to throne of Scotland	11	(1) 1334
[1 posthumous]		(1) 1346
		(2) 1354
		(3) 1356
		(3) 1358
		(1) 1370
Banastre, Thomas	1	(1) 1376
Barnet, John, bishop of Ely	1	(1) 1370
Barry, Ralph, esquire	1	(1) 1372
Bateman, William, bishop of Norwich	2	(1) 1352
		(1) 1354
Battle, Robert of, abbot of Battle	1	(1) 1364
Beauchamp, Sir Giles	2	(1) 1338
		(1) 1349
Beauchamp, Sir John [senior]	12	(2) 1347
		(3) 1350
		(1) 1351
		(1) 1352
		(5) 1354
Beauchamp, Sir John [senior] and Thomas Brembre	2	(2) 1353
Beauchamp, Sir John [junior]	3	(2) 1370
		(1) 1371
Beauchamp, Peter, king's yeoman	1	(1) 1347
Beauchamp, Roger	9	(1) 1350
		(3) 1351
		(2) 1352
		(1) 1353
		(1) 1373
		(1) 1376
Beaumont, Eleanor, wife of John	3	(1) 1338
		(2) 1343
Beche, Nicholas	1	(1) 1338
Bedford, Enguerrand de Coucy, earl of	3	(2) 1367
		(1) 1369
Benham, John, abbot of Chertsey	1	(1) 1359

Bentley, Walter, captain of Brittany [Bentele]	6	(1) 1351
		(3) 1352
		(1) 1355
		(1) 1358
Berkeley, Maurice [Berkele]	13	(1) 1338
		(1) 1339
		(1) 1341
		(1) 1342
		(9) 1346
Berle, Thomas	2	(1) 1350
		(1) 1351
Beverly, John, king's esquire [Beverle]	7	(1) 1368
		(2) 1372
		(1) 1373
		(2) 1374
		(1) 1376
Beverly, Robert [Beverle]	1	(1) 1346
Birmyngeham, Walter	1	(1) 1347
Blacomore, William	1	(1) 1370
Blankouster, John	1	(1) 1372
Bohun, Edward	1	(1) 1329
Bohun, Eleanor	1	(1) 1327
Bosvyle, John	1	(1) 1364
Bourne, Ralph, abbot of St Augustines, Canterbury	1	(1) 1332
Bourne, Thomas	1	(1) 1345
Brabant, John, duke of	1	(1) 1340
Bradeston, Thomas, king's yeoman	7	(1) 1329
		(1) 1331
		(1) 1339
		(2) 1345
		(1) 1347
		(1) 1351
Branketre, John, clerk	1	(1) 1360
Brembre, Thomas, king's clerk	10	(1) 1346
		(1) 1347
		(2) 1351
		(1) 1352
		(3) 1353
		(1) 1357
		(1) 1359
Breouse, Peter	1	(1) 1371
Brewes, Peter, king's yeoman	9	(1) 1345
		(3) 1346
		(2) 1347
		(1) 1352
		(1) 1367
		(1) 1371
Brewes, Thomas	2	(2) 1347

Brian, Guy, Lord	15	(1) 1346
		(1) 1348
		(2) 1349
		(2) 1350
		(1) 1351
		(1) 1352
		(1) 1353
		(1) 1354
		(1) 1355
		(1) 1356
		(3) 1371
Brittany, John de Montfort, duke of, earl of Richmond	5	(1) 1359
		(1) 1364
		(1) 1367
		(1) 1373
		(1) 1374
Brocas, Bernard	1	(1) 1372
Brocas, John	15	(14) 1346
		(1) 1347
Brugge, Peter	1	(1) 1355
Buchan, Henry Beaumont, earl of	3	(1) 1327
		(1) 1333
		(1) 1334
Buckingham, John, bishop of Lincoln	5	(1) 1357
		(1) 1359
		(1) 1363
		(1) 1366
		(1) 1368
Burele, John	2	(1) 1359
		(1) 1376
Burghersh, Bartholomew, Lord	17	(1) 1344
		(4) 1345
		(5) 1346
		(1) 1347
		(2) 1351
		(1) 1352
		(2) 1353
		(1) 1354
Burghersh, Bartholomew and Roger Beauchamp	1	(1) 1351
Burghersh, Henry, bishop of Lincoln	4	(2) 1329
		(1) 1338
		(1) 1339
Burghersh, Henry, bishop of Lincoln and Thomas Bradeston	1	(1) 1338
Burgo, Elizabeth	2	(1) 1348
		(1) 1359
Bury, Richard, bishop of Durham	9	(1) 1330
		(1) 1331
		(2) 1334
		(3) 1335
		(1) 1336
		(1) 1341

Buxhill, Alan	8	(1) 1364
		(1) 1367
		(3) 1369
		(2) 1372
		(1) 1374
Calveley, Hugh	1	(1) 1375
Cantilupe, William [Cantilupo]	2	(1) 1346
		(1) 1351
Caourz, Ralph le	1	(1) 1348
Carbonel, William	1	(1) 1346
Cardinals, cardinal P. of St Praxeds and B. of St Marys in Aquiro	1	(1) 1338
Careswelle, William	1	(1) 1346
Chandos, Sir John	3	(2) 1359
		(1) 1360
Chandos, Robert, king's yeoman	1	(1) 1349
Charleton, John	1	(1) 1372
Chastel, Gregory	1	(1) 1330
Cherleton, John, of Powys	2	(2) 1372
Chesthunt, Edmund, king's falconer	1	(1) 1366
Chevereston, John	1	(1) 1346
Coloigne, John	1	(1) 1355
Clifton, Gervase	1	(1) 1364
Cloune, William, abbot of Leicester	1	(1) 1370
Cobham, John, of Kent [Cobeham]	2	(1) 1368
		(1) 1369
Cobham, Reginald, Lord	2	(1) 1337
		(1) 1346
Cokeham, John, clerk	1	(1) 1335
Colley, Thomas, king's yeoman	1	(1) 1350
Cornubia, Geoffrey	1	(1) 1328
Council, those of the council in parts beyond the seas	1	(1) 1338
Coupland, John, king's yeoman	6	(1) 1347
		(1) 1350
		(2) 1356
		(1) 1357
		(1) 1361
Courteney, Maud, Lady	2	(1) 1373
		(1) 1374
Courtenay, Philip	1	(1) 1373
Covene, Thomas	3	(3) 1370
Crabbe, John	1	(1) 1346
Crull, Robert, king's clerk	4	(2) 1369
		(1) 1373
		(1) 1374
Cusancia, William, king's clerk	1	(1) 1332

Dabrichecourt, Collard	1	(1) 1372
Dabrichecourt, Nicholas, esquire	3	(3) 1372
Dagworth, Nicholas	1	(1) 1374
Dagworth, Thomas, Lord	1	(1) 1346
Dale, Thomas	1	(1) 1368
Dallyng, Roger, brother	1	(1) 1346
Dalton, Robert	1	(1) 1346
Dalton, William, king's clerk	1	(1) 1358
Darcy, John, Lord, steward of the household	20	(1) 1332
		(1) 1337
		(13) 1346
		(3) 1347
		(2) 1348
Dautre, James	1	(1) 1346
David II, king of Scotland	5	(1) 1363
		(1) 1364
		(2) 1369
		(1) 1370
David, son of the king of Scotland and Joan, his wife, the king's sister	1	(1) 1328
David, Roger	1	(1) 1354
Dayncourt, John	1	(1) 1348
Denton, Richard	1	(1) 1362
Despenser, Edward, Lord	2	(1) 1372
		(1) 1373
Despenser, Hugh	9	(1) 1344
		(8) 1346
Dighton, William, king's clerk	1	(1) 1361
Dorkyng, Master Roger	1	(1) 1347
Driby, John, king's yeoman	1	(1) 1342
Durfort, Arnold [Duro Forti]	1	(1) 1336
Dynant, masters, burgesses, consuls and jurats	1	(1) 1339
Eccleshall, Richard, king's clerk, treasurer of Calais [Eccleshale]	1	(1) 1360
Edington, William, bishop of Winchester	13	(2) 1352
		(1) 1353
		(9) 1355
		(1) 1359
Edington, William and Thomas Brembre	1	(1) 1351
Edmund of Langley, earl of Cambridge, king's son	2	(1) 1366
		(1) 1374
Edmund of Woodstock, earl of Kent	3	(2) 1327
		(1) 1328

Edward of Woodstock, prince of Wales, duke of Cornwall	224	(1) 1341
		(48) 1346
		(13) 1350
		(1) 1351
		(7) 1352
		(1) 1353
		(1) 1355
		(3) 1356
		(103) 1357
		(26) 1358
		(5) 1359
		(1) 1360
		(1) 1361
		(1) 1366
		(1) 1367
		(4) 1368
		(4) 1370
		(3) 1371
Erchebaud, Richard, esquire	1	(1) 1370
Felton, William	1	(1) 1364
Ferrers, Henry [Ferariis]	5	(4) 1338
		(1) 1339
Ferrers, Ralph [Ferariis]	17	(15) 1346
		(1) 1360
		(1) 1373
Ferrers, Robert [Ferariis]	3	(1) 1344
		(1) 1345
		(1) 1346
Fitzwarin, William	2	(2) 1346
Flanders, Lewis, count of	1	(1) 1364
Foljambe, Geoffrey	1	(1) 1366
Foxley, John [Foxle]	7	(1) 1368
		(1) 1370
		(1) 1372
		(1) 1373
		(1) 1374
		(1) 1375
		(1) 1376
Furnivall, Joan, wife of Thomas	1	(1) 1330
Furnivall, Thomas [Fournivalle]	4	(4) 1346
Giffard, Gilbert	3	(3) 1373
Gildesbrugh, Peter	1	(1) 1346
Grandison, Sir Otto	1	(1) 1328
Grantson, Sir Thomas	3	(2) 1370
		(1) 1375
Graunceon, Thomas	1	(1) 1364
Grenacres, Robert	1	(1) 1370

Grey, John	4	(1) 1346
		(2) 1350
		(1) 1351
Grey, John and Thomas Brembre	1	(1) 1351
Grey, John and William Catesby	1	(1) 1355
Grey, Reynold	2	(1) 1361
		(1) 1370
Grey, Richard	1	(1) 1327
Griffith, Rees	4	(4) 1346
Guelders, Eleanor, duchess of, king's sister	1	(1) 1349
Guelders, Reginald III, duke of, Bavaria, king's nephew	1	(1) 1352
Gunthorp, William, king's clerk	1	(1) 1370
Gybourn, John	1	(1) 1355
Haddon, John, sergeant-at-arms	2	(1) 1347
		(1) 1350
Harewell, John, bishop of Bath and Wells	2	(1) 1373
		(1) 1374
Hatfield, Thomas, bishop of Durham	21	(1) 1345
		(20) 1346
Hauteyn, Thomas	1	(1) 1369
Hereford and Essex, Humphrey de Bohun, earl of	6	(1) 1368
		(1) 1369
		(3) 1371
		(1) 1372
Herle, Robert	2	(1) 1350
		(1) 1357
Herlyng, John, esquire	2	(1) 1347
		(1) 1369
Hertyngdon, Adam, king's clerk	1	(1) 1375
Hethe, Thomas	1	(1) 1347
Holland, John	2	(1) 1361
		(1) 1363
Huntelowe, William, king's clerk	1	(1) 1369
Huntingdon, Juliana, countess of (Juliana Leybourne)	2	(1) 1363
		(1) 1366
Huntingdon, William Clinton, earl of	10	(1) 1327
		(1) 1335
		(1) 1340
		(1) 1341
		(1) 1344
		(1) 1345
		(2) 1347
		(2) 1350
Huet, Walter [Huwet]	27	(1) 1362
		(3) 1369
		(20) 1370
		(1) 1371
		(2) 1373
Husse, James	1	(1) 1358

John of Gaunt, earl of Lancaster	26	(1) 1365
		(1) 1366
		(1) 1367
		(1) 1368
		(2) 1369
		(2) 1370
		(12) 1371
		(4) 1372
		(1) 1374
		(1) 1377
John, son of Walter	7	(7) 1346
Kendale, Edmund	2	(1) 1342
		(1) 1343
Kent, Margaret, countess of	1	(1) 1340
Keynes, Thomas	1	(1) 1362
Kilsby, William [Kildesby]	7	(7) 1346
Kilmessan, Ralph, bishop of Down [Doun], Ireland	1	(1) 1342
King's lieges	6	(4) 1344
		(1) 1347
		(1) 1359
Kirkby, John, bishop of Carlisle	1	(1) 1336
Knolles, Robert	63	(61) 1370
		(1) 1371
		(1) 1373
Knyvet, Sir John, chancellor	1	(1) 1376
Lacy, Peter	1	(1) 1367
Lancaster, Constance, duchess of, queen of Castile and Leon	4	(1) 1367
		(1) 1373
		(2) 1374
Lancaster, Henry, earl of, earl of Leicester	10	(1) 1327
		(6) 1330
		(2) 1338
		(1) 1341
Lancaster, Henry and Henry Grosmont, his son, earl of Derby	6	(2) 1338
		(1) 1341
		(1) 1342
		(2) 1344
Lancaster, Henry of Grosmont, duke of, earl of Derby	304	(3) 1341
		(1) 1342
		(3) 1344
		(98) 1345
		(37) 1346
		(88) 1347
		(11) 1348
		(1) 1349
		(32) 1350
		(7) 1351
		(5) 1352
		(2) 1354
		(6) 1355

Magnates	16	(1) 1337
		(1) 1347
		(14) 1348
Magnates and cardinals	3	(3) 1337
Maltravers, John	1	(1) 1329
March, Edmund Mortimer, earl of	3	(1) 1370
		(1) 1371
		(1) 1374
March, Roger Mortimer, earl of	8	(6) 1327
		(1) 1329
		(1) 1330
March, Roger Mortimer, second earl of	5	(1) 1350
		(1) 1354
		(1) 1355
		(1) 1356
		(1) 1357
March, Roger Mortimer, earl of, and Gilbert Talebot	1	(1) 1327
Marshal, Margaret, lady, of Segrave and Weston	2	(1) 1372
		(1) 1374
Mauleye, Robert	1	(1) 1350
Mauny, Walter, Lord	6	(1) 1341
		(2) 1344
		(1) 1345
		(1) 1347
		(1) 1355
Melton, William, archbishop of York	1	(1) 1333
Mirymouth, Richard, king's chaplain	1	(1) 1332
Mohun, Joan, Lady	1	(1) 1363
Moigne, Thomas	1	(1) 1362
Molyns, Sir John	1	(1) 1339
Montacute, Edward, Lord	3	(3) 1346
Montgomery, John	1	(1) 1346
Morle, Robert	2	(2) 1346
Mortimer, Geoffrey	1	(1) 1330
Mosdale, Thomas	1	(1) 1368
Mugge, William, dean of St George, Windsor	4	(3) 1369
		(1) 1371
Munstreworth, John	1	(1) 1370
Neville, John, Lord, steward of the household	11	(2) 1333
		(3) 1340
		(2) 1371
		(3) 1372
		(1) 1376
Neville, Ralph, Lord, steward of the household	7	(2) 1333
		(5) 1340

Neville, Robert	3	(2) 1372
		(1) 1373
Norfolk, Mary, countess of	3	(3) 1356
Northampton, William de Bohun, earl of	75	(2) 1338
		(13) 1344
		(33) 1345
		(7) 1346
		(2) 1347
		(1) 1348
		(1) 1350
		(3) 1351
		(1) 1353
		(6) 1355
		(6) 1356
Northampton, William de Bohun, earl of, Thomas Beauchamp, Robert Ufford and William Clynton	1	(1) 1346
Northborough, Michael [Northbrugh]	3	(3) 1346
Northumberland, Henry Percy, earl of	4	(1) 1369
		(1) 1372
		(1) 1374
		(1) 1376
Norwich, Richard, clerk	25	(1) 1350
		(1) 1351
		(2) 1352
		(14) 1353
		(5) 1355
		(1) 1357
		(1) 1361
Offord, John, archdeacon of Ely	1	(1) 1341
Ormond, Elizabeth, countess of	1	(1) 1352
Ormond James Butler, earl of [Butiller]	2	(2) 1351
Oxford, John de Vere, earl of	1	(1) 1346
Parliament	1	(1) 1331
Pembridge, Richard [Pembrigg, Pembrugge]	4	(1) 1352
		(1) 1363
		(1) 1370
		(1) 1371
Pembroke, Agnes, countess of	2	(1) 1359
		(1) 1365
Pembroke, Mary, countess of, St Pol	2	(1) 1346
		(1) 1374
Pembroke, John Hastings, earl of	7	(1) 1362
		(1) 1365
		(4) 1371
		(1) 1372
Percy, Henry, second Lord Percy	3	(2) 1330
		(1) 1341

Percy, Henry, third Lord Percy	11	(2) 1360
		(3) 1363
		(3) 1366
		(1) 1367
		(2) 1368
Percy, Thomas	1	(1) 1368
Philippa of Hainault, queen of England	56	(1) 1328
		(3) 1331
		(3) 1333
		(1) 1336
		(3) 1337
		(5) 1338
		(1) 1339
		(1) 1340
		(1) 1341
		(1) 1345
		(2) 1346
		(9) 1348
		(3) 1351
		(1) 1352
		(2) 1356
		(1) 1358
		(1) 1361
		(1) 1362
		(3) 1363
		(4) 1364
		(1) 1365
		(1) 1366
		(2) 1367
		(2) 1368
		(3) 1369
Philippa, queen and Edmund, earl of Cambridge	1	(1) 1367
Philippa, queen and Isabel, king's daughter, duke of Lancaster and earl of Northampton	1	(1) 1355
Ponynings, Michael, Lord [Ponyngges]	6	(1) 1347
		(2) 1350
		(1) 1352
		(1) 1353
		(1) 1355
Prelates, clerical	4	(4) 1342
Prelates and other ecclesiastical persons of the realm	4	(4) 1342
Princess [unspecified]	3	(1) 1373
		(2) 1374
Pulteneye, John, citizen of London [Pulteneye]	2	(1) 1333
		(1) 1338
Purchas, Thomas, yeoman	1	(1) 1353
Picard, Henry, king's merchant [Pycard]	2	(2) 1360
Pyk, Nicholas, king's yeoman	1	(1) 1338
Ramsey, Alexander, abbot of Barlings [Barlyngs]	1	(1) 1367

Ravenser, Richard	1	(1) 1363
Redeman, Matthew	5	(2) 1370
		(3) 1373
Restwold, Ralph, esquire	1	(1) 1373
Retford, William, keeper of the wardrobe	1	(1) 1352
Richard II, king of England [king's grandson]	2	(2) 1371
Richard, son of Simon	2	(2) 1346
Risseby, William, yeoman	1	(1) 1366
Roche, Audrouin, abbot of Cluny	3	(3) 1355
Rokeby, Thomas	2	(1) 1343
		(1) 1347
Roldeston, Thomas	2	(2) 1346
Roos, Geoffrey	4	(3) 1371
		(1) 1372
Roos, Peter	1	(1) 1374
Ros, John, steward	4	(1) 1327
		(3) 1353
Rose, Edmund	2	(1) 1350
		(1) 1351
Routhe, Peter, yeoman	2	(1) 1361
		(1) 1370
St John, Edward	2	(1) 1365
		(1) 1371
Salisbury, William Montacute, earl of	11	(1) 1333
		(1) 1334
		(4) 1338
		(2) 1339
		(2) 1341
		(1) 1342
Salisbury, William Montacute, second earl of	7	(2) 1353
		(1) 1369
		(1) 1370
		(2) 1371
		(1) 1373
Salisbury, William Montacute (first earl) and John Pulteneye	1	(1) 1338
Salle, Robert	1	(1) 1374
Salman, John	1	(1) 1368
Say, Geoffrey	1	(1) 1350
Scrope, Sir Geoffrey	4	(2) 1332
		(1) 1334
		(1) 1338
Segrave, Hugh	1	(1) 1371
Seymor, Robert, yeoman	2	(1) 1346
		(1) 1353
Shirburn, John	1	(1) 1346
Shrewsbury, Ralph, bishop of Bath and Wells	1	(1) 1346
Shyrard, Richard	1	(1) 1328

Sleford, William	1	(1) 1374
Spygernel, Thomas, esquire	2	(1) 1366
		(1) 1372
Stafford, Hugh Stafford, earl of	2	(2) 1373
Stafford, Ralph Stafford, earl of	14	(2) 1345
		(3) 1347
		(2) 1350
		(4) 1353
		(3) 1356
Stafford, Richard	1	(1) 1366
Stoke, John, clerk	2	(1) 1368
		(1) 1369
Stotevill Joan, nun of Brodholme	1	(1) 1348
Stratford, John, archbishop of Canterbury, chancellor	23	(1) 1333
		(2) 1335
		(1) 1336
		(15) 1343
		(2) 1344
		(1) 1345
		(1) 1346
Stratford, John, and Henry Lancaster	1	(1) 1339
Stratford, John, and Robert Stratford, bishop of Chichester	1	(1) 1345
Stratford, Robert, bishop of Chichester	1	(1) 1332
Strauley, Henry	1	(1) 1373
Straunge, Ebulo	1	(1) 1333
Straunge, John	5	(5) 1346
Strete, William, king's butler	4	(1) 1365
		(1) 1367
		(1) 1368
		(1) 1369
Stryveln, John [Stivelyn]	14	(1) 1337
		(13) 1346
Sturmy, Henry	1	(1) 1373
Sturmy, John, yeoman	1	(1) 1356
Stury, Sir Richard, knight of chamber	4	(1) 1369
		(1) 1370
		(2) 1372
Suffolk, Robert Ufford, earl of (Dufford)	26	(2) 1331
		(1) 1333
		(1) 1334
		(2) 1344
		(2) 1345
		(13) 1346
		(4) 1347
		(1) 1350
Suffolk, William Ufford, earl of	3	(1) 1370
		(2) 1373
Sully, Henry, Lord	1	(1) 1331

Surrey, John Warenne, earl of	3	(1) 1329
		(1) 1334
		(1) 1339
Sutton, John	1	(1) 1346
Swynburn, Adam	6	(6) 1346
Swynnerton, Roger	1	(1) 1327
Swynnerton, Thomas	3	(1) 1338
		(1) 1346
		(1) 1352
Symeon, Simon, king's yeoman	1	(1) 1346
Symon, Thomas	2	(1) 1372
		(1) 1376
Talbot, Sir John	1	(1) 1374
Talbot, Richard, Lord, steward	8	(4) 1346
		(3) 1347
		(1) 1348
Tamworth, Nicholas, captain of Calais	11	(1) 1362
		(1) 1366
		(1) 1367
		(8) 1371
Thoresby, John	12	(11) 1346
		(1) 1347
Thorpe, Robert	1	(1) 1356
Thorpe, Sir William	2	(2) 1352
Tildesle, Ralph	2	(2) 1361
Trussebut, William	1	(1) 1347
Trussel, William	3	(1) 1330
		(1) 1346
		(1) 1354
Tirrington, William, king's clerk	1	(1) 1369
Tusculum, A. cardinal, bishop of, and S. cardinal, priest of St John and St Paul	1	(1)1347
Twyford, Edward	2	(1) 1373
		(1) 1374
Ufford, Ralph	1	(1) 1339
Ughtred, Thomas, Lord	12	(7) 1346
		(1) 1347
		(4) 1350
Urswyk, Robert	1	(1) 1370
Vache, Richard la	5	(1) 1355
		(1) 1358
		(1) 1360
		(1) 1361
		(1) 1364
Veer, Elizabeth	1	(1) 1359
Verdon, John	1	(1) 1346
Wake, Blanche, wife of Lord Thomas	3	(1) 1352
		(1) 1355
		(1) 1376

Wake, Thomas, Lord [of Liddell]	2	(2) 1327
Waleis, Stephen	2	(2) 1346
Walsham, Robert	1	(1) 1369
Walssh, Walter, yeoman, king's esquire	2	(1) 1366
		(1) 1369
Warde, Roger	1	(1) 1364
Warde, Simon	1	(1) 1368
Warwick, Thomas Beauchamp, earl of	40	(1) 1342
		(2) 1344
		(7) 1345
		(11) 1346
		(6) 1347
		(4) 1350
		(1) 1351
		(1) 1364
		(1) 1366
		(1) 1369
		(1) 1371
		(1) 1372
		(2) 1373
		(1) 1374
Weston, Philip, clerk	2	(1) 1346
		(1) 1347
Wetewang, Walter	3	(1) 1345
		(2) 1346
Whitbergh, Robert, clerk of Queen Philippa	1	(1) 1357
Whithors, Isabel	1	(1) 1367
Whithors, Walter, yeoman, esquire	5	(1) 1354
		(1) 1355
		(1) 1363
		(2) 1369
Whitton, Philip, yeoman	1	(1) 1346
Windsor, William of	8	(1) 1362
		(1) 1364
		(1) 1365
		(1) 1366
		(4) 1369
Winwick, John [Wynwyk]	4	(1) 1348
		(1) 1352
		(1) 1356
		(1) 1359
Winwick, John and Henry Ingelby	1	(1) 1351
Wode, Walter atte, sergeant-at-arms	1	(1) 1357
Wode, William atte, sergeant-at-arms	2	(1) 1352
		(1) 1357
Woderove, John, king's confessor	1	(1) 1375
Wollore, David, clerk	1	(1) 1354

Wykeham, William	3	(1) 1361
		(1) 1362
		(1) 1363
Wykford, Robert	1	(1) 1373
Wyngefeld, John	1	(1) 1350
Wynklee, Richard, brother, king's confessor [Wyngle]	5	(2) 1346
		(3) 1347
Wynklee, Richard, brother, king's confessor and Richard Norwich	1	(1) 1352
Wyville, Robert, bishop of Salisbury	3	(2) 1356
		(1) 1362
Zouche, Alan la	4	(4) 1346
Zouche, Richard la	1	(1) 1364
Zouche, William	1	(1) 1356
Zouche, William, of Haringworth	1	(1) 1370
	2045	

Intercessor (s)	Total	Sub-total for year
Abberbury, Richard	1	(1) 1386
Almaly, Walter	1	(1) 1380
Alyngton, William	1	(1) 1394
Andreu, John	1	(1) 1391
Anne of Bohemia, queen of England	71	(8) 1382
		(4) 1383
		(11) 1384
		(6) 1387
		(1) 1388
		(4) 1389
		(7) 1390
		(11) 1391
		(10) 1392
		(7) 1393
		(2) 1394
Anne of Bohemia, queen of England and certain of the king's household	1	(1) 1383
Anne of Bohemia, queen of England and citizens of London	1	(1) 1392
Anne of Bohemia, queen of England and king's lieges	1	(1) 1392
Appultrewyk, Thomas	4	(1) 1391
		(2) 1392
		(1) 1393
Armesthorp, John, chamberlain of Exchequer	1	(1) 1384
Arundel, John, marshal of England [Darundell]	3	(1) 1378
		(2) 1379
Arundel, Richard Fitzalan, earl of	17	(2) 1378
		(2) 1379
		(1) 1382
		(1) 1383
		(6) 1384
		(1) 1390
		(1) 1392
		(1) 1393
		(1) 1394
		(1) 1396
Arundel, Richard Fitzalan, earl of, and Thomas Arundel, bishop of Ely	2	(1) 1380
		(1) 1388

Arundel, Thomas, bishop of Ely, archbishop of York, archbishop of Canterbury	21	(1) 1379
		(1) 1380
		(1) 1383
		(2) 1386
		(7) 1390
		(1) 1391
		(8) 1397
Ashburnham, John	1	(1) 1391
Asheton, William, clerk	1	(1) 1392
Aslak, John, serjeant-at-arms	1	(1) 1387
Aspal, John, esquire	1	(1) 1390
Asshe, William, usher of the chamber	1	(1) 1393
Aubill, John, parson	1	(1) 1390
Audley, Nicholas, Lord	1	(1) 1389
Audyn, John	1	(1) 1381
Bache, Alexander, bishop of St Asaph, king's confessor	9	(1) 1388
		(1) 1389
		(4) 1390
		(1) 1391
		(2) 1393
Bagot, William	3	(3) 1388
Bakepuz, John	1	(1) 1390
Bakpuse, William	1	(1) 1391
Baldok, Walter, prior of Launde [Lund]	2	(1) 1392
		(1) 1397
Balscot, Alexander, bishop of Meath, and Robert Waldby, archbishop of Dublin	1	(1) 1391
Banastre, Thomas	1	(1) 1379
Bardolf, Robert and Edmund Noon esquire	1	(1) 1381
Barnolby, Thomas de, clerk	2	(1) 1379
		(1) 1380
Barre, Thomas	2	(1) 1380
		(1) 1381
Basset, Ralph	1	(1) 1380
Baukewell, John, yeoman of the crown	2	(2) 1387
Bayley, Laurance of, clerk	2	(1) 1390
		(1) 1391
Beauchamp, Edward	1	(1) 1379
Beauchamp, John, steward	10	(2) 1381
		(4) 1384
		(4) 1387
Beauchamp, William	6	(2) 1378
		(1) 1382
		(2) 1383
		(1) 1388

Beaufort, John, marquess of Dorset [Beauford]	3	(1) 1390
		(1) 1392
		(1) 1399
Beaumond, Charles of, Alferis of Navarre	1	(1) 1390
Beaumont, John, king's kinsman	10	(2) 1387
		(1) 1389
		(4) 1390
		(1) 1391
		(2) 1394
Becket, Richard, esquire	1	(1) 1379
Bedford, Thomas, friar	1	(1) 1393
Belle, John, clerk	1	(1) 1390
Bereford, Baldwin	18	(1) 1379
		(2) 1380
		(1) 1382
		(1) 1383
		(6) 1384
		(1) 1387
		(2) 1390
		(4) 1391
Berkeley, Edward [Berkele]	1	(1) 1378
Berkhamstede, Henry	1	(1) 1392
Bernard, John, chaplain	1	(1) 1393
Berners, James	6	(5) 1385
		(1) 1386
Bernolby, John	1	(1) 1394
Beurle, Sir John	1	(1) 1378
Bitterley, Walter, king's esquire	2	(1) 1392
		(1) 1393
Blont, Walter	1	(1) 1379
Bokenham, Edmund of	1	(1) 1377
Bokton, Robert	1	(1) 1390
Boor, John, dean of king's chapel	1	(1) 1393
Botiller, Thomas	2	(1) 1379
		(1) 1389
Bracy, Guy, esquire	1	(1) 1395
Bradeston, Blanche	3	(2) 1394
		(1) 1395
Brak, Thomas	1	(1) 1392
Brakenhull, Hugh, clerk [Buckenhall]	9	(1) 1390
		(7) 1391
		(1) 1392
Brand, Roger, soldier of Calais	1	(1) 1386

Braybrooke, Robert, bishop of London [Braybrook]	8	(2) 1379
		(1) 1383
		(2) 1385
		(1) 1389
		(1) 1392
		(1) 1393
Brayton, Robert, clerk	3	(1) 1391
		(2) 1393
Brian, Guy, Lord	4	(4) 1379
Brittany, Joan, duchess of, king's sister	1	(1) 1383
Brittany, John Montfort, duke of	3	(1) 1378
		(1) 1379
		(1) 1396
Brocas, Bernard	1	(1) 1385
Bromwych, John of	1	(1) 1377
Brut, Thomas	1	(1) 1394
Bubwyth, Henry of, king's serjeant-at-arms	1	(1) 1389
Buckingham, John, bishop of Lincoln	1	(1) 1388
Burgh, Richard, esquire	4	(1) 1389
		(1) 1391
		(1) 1393
		(1) 1395
Burgh, William of	1	(1) 1379
Burgundy, Philip the Bold, duke of	2	(1) 1396
		(1) 1397
Burle, Richard of	3	(1) 1377
		(1) 1380
		(1) 1383
Burley, Sir John	3	(2) 1380
		(1) 1381
Burley, Sir Simon	7	(4) 1384
		(2) 1383
		(1) 1387
Bury, Nicholas	5	(3) 1384
		(1) 1385
		(1) 1394
Calveley, Hugh, captain of Calais [Cavyley]	3	(2) 1378
		(1) 1380
Cantiran, John [Canteran]	2	(1) 1390
		(1) 1391
Carleton, Hugh	1	(1) 1390
Cary, Robert, esquire	4	(2) 1392
		(1) 1393
		(1) 1397
Caryngton, Sir William	1	(1) 1381
Cays, Richard	1	(1) 1390

Champ, Stephen	1	(1) 1393
Chandos, Sir John	1	(1) 1393
Chelmeswyk, Richard, esquire	1	(1) 1395
Cherleton, William of	2	(1) 1378
		(1) 1379
Chetewyn, William, esquire	1	(1) 1379
Cheyne, Sir Alan	1	(1) 1379
Cheyne, Sir John	1	(1) 1394
Churche, William, chaplain	1	(1) 1393
Clanvow, Sir John [Clanvou]	1	(1) 1379
Clanvowe, Thomas, esquire	1	(1) 1394
Clare, Sir John	1	(1) 1379
Clederowe, John	4	(2) 1392
		(2) 1393
Clergy of England	1	(1) 1388
Clifford, Roger, Lord	2	(1) 1380
		(1) 1386
Clifford, Richard	1	(1) 1387
Clifford, Thomas, Lord	9	(1) 1379
		(1) 1382
		(1) 1383
		(2) 1384
		(4) 1385
Clifton, Reginald, chaplain	2	(1) 1381
		(1) 1389
Clinton, Sir William	3	(2) 1380
		(1) 1381
Cobham, John, Lord	2	(1) 1377
		(1) 1380
Coghel, Roger, king's esquire	2	(2) 1381
Cokayn, John	1	(1) 1393
Colbrok, Richard	1	(1) 1396
Colman, Thomas, prior of Launde [Lund]	1	(1) 1380
Constance of Castile, duchess of Lancaster, queen of Spain	2	(1) 1379
		(1) 1380
Corbet, Sir Robert, and Sir Robert Braybrook	1	(1) 1390
Corby, Agnes, one of the damsels of the chamber	2	(2) 1380
Corby, William, esquire	1	(1) 1381
Cork, mayor and commonalty of the city	1	(1) 1392
Corkeby, John	1	(1) 1391
Cotingham, Hugh, clerk	1	(1) 1389
Courtenay, Sir Peter	1	(1) 1383
Courtenay, Sir Philip	1	(1) 1380

Courtenay, William, bishop of London, archbishop of Canterbury	10	(1) 1380
		(1) 1382
		(4) 1389
		(3) 1393
		(1) 1395
Courtenay, William, archbishop of Canterbury and the council	1	(1) 1384
Cratfield, William, abbot of Bury St Edmunds, and convent of	2	(1) 1389
		(1) 1390
Croft, John, esquire	2	(2) 1387
Croft, Richard of	2	(2) 1394
Crophull, Roger, esquire	1	(1) 1392
Crophull, Thomas, esquire	1	(1) 1379
Dacre, William, Lord	1	(1) 1393
Dagworth, Nicholas, Lord	1	(1) 1380
Dallingridge, Sir Edward [Dalyngrigge]	1	(1) 1378
Dancastre, Richard	1	(1) 1392
Darcy, Philip, Lord	1	(1) 1389
Daubrichecourt, Nicholas	1	(1) 1380
Dengaine, Katherine, Lady	1	(1) 1380
Denys, William	1	(1) 1395
Despenser, Henry, bishop of Norwich	9	(1) 1380
		(5) 1383
		(1) 1387
		(1) 1389
		(1) 1395
Despenser, Henry, bishop of Norwich, and Thomas, Lord Despenser	1	(1) 1394
Despenser, Thomas, Lord	12	(12) 1393
Desseford, William, clerk of king's mother	2	(1) 1379
		(1) 1381
Devereaux, John, Lord, steward	7	(3) 1378
		(1) 1382
		(2) 1392
		(1) 1393
Diss, Walter, confessor of John, duke of Lancaster [Disse]	2	(2) 1381
Dotheley, Alexander [Doley, Bodhly, Dodhly] parson of Frenston [Frenstede]	3	(2) 1390
		(1) 1391
Dyghton, William, king's clerk	1	(1) 1380
Dymock, Thomas [Dymmok]	1	(1) 1389
Dyneley, Robert	1	(1) 1380

Edmund of Langley, earl of Cambridge, duke of York	29	(2) 1377
		(3) 1378
		(1) 1381
		(1) 1382
		(1) 1383
		(2) 1384
		(1) 1389
		(2) 1395
		(9) 1396
		(7) 1397
Edmund, duke of York, and Hugh de Audley, earl of Gloucester	1	(1) 1391
Elmham, Sir William	3	(1) 1379
		(1) 1380
		(1) 1389
Elvet, John	1	(1) 1391
Elys, Sir William	1	(1) 1390
Erghum, Ralph, bishop of Salisbury [Ergham]	2	(1) 1378
		(1) 1384
Erpyngton, Sir Thomas	2	(1) 1394
		(1) 1396
Exton, Nicholas	29	(1) 1384
		(20) 1387
		(6) 1389
		(1) 1390
		(1) 1394
Felbrigg, George, esquire	5	(1) 1380
		(1) 1388
		(2) 1389
		(1) 1395
Felbrigg, Robert [Felbrigge]	2	(1) 1396
		(1) 1397
Felbrigg, Sir Simon	5	(1) 1394
		(1) 1395
		(2) 1396
		(1) 1397
Felde, Richard de la, clerk and John Prophete	1	(1) 1395
Fermer, Lambert	4	(2) 1387
		(1) 1391
		(1) 1392
Ferrers, Robert	5	(3) 1379
		(2) 1380
Folgame, John	1	(1) 1391
Fordham, John, bishop of Durham, bishop of Ely	3	(1) 1387
		(2) 1394
Foulmer, John	1	(1) 1390
Fremlyngton, John, esquire [Frennyngham]	1	(1) 1390

Frenton, John	1	(1) 1379
Fulbourn, William	3	(1) 1380
		(1) 1381
		(1) 1382
Fulthorp, William	1	(1) 1393
Garton, Robert, clerk	1	(1) 1391
Gedeneye, John	1	(1) 1389
Gilbert, John, bishop of Hereford, bishop of St Davids	6	(1) 1379
		(3) 1381
		(1) 1385
		(1) 1393
Gisbourn, William	1	(1) 1379
Gloucester, Eleanor, duchess of (Eleanor de Bohun)	11	(7) 1394
		(2) 1395
		(2) 1396
Goderiche, William	2	(1) 1389
		(1) 1394
Godewyk, John	2	(1) 1378
		(1) 1379
Golafre, John	8	(2) 1387
		(2) 1389
		(2) 1390
		(2) 1391
Gomenys, Anne, Lady	1	(1) 1386
Gourney, Sir Matthew	3	(2) 1379
		(1) 1387
Grenacre, Robert	2	(1) 1387
		(1) 1388
Grene, Sir Henry	1	(1) 1380
Grene, William	1	(1) 1393
Grey, Eleanor, Lady	1	(1) 1381
Grey, Reynold, Lord, Lord Lestrange	2	(1) 1380
		(1) 1391
Guelders, William, duke of [Gueldres]	4	(3) 1392
		(1) 1393
Haddam, John	1	(1) 1390
Hales, Edward	1	(1) 1386
Halsale, Gilbert	1	(1) 1392
Hampton, Richard, king's esquire	4	(1) 1379
		(1) 1380
		(1) 1383
		(1) 1384
Harewell, John, bishop of Bath and Wells	2	(1) 1377
		(1) 1379
Harington, Nicholas, Lord [Haryngton]	1	(1) 1385
Harliston, Sir John	1	(1) 1379

Harpele, William, esquire	3	(1) 1380
		(1) 1381
		(1) 1382
Harper, William, king's minstrel	1	(1) 1397
Hastings, Hugh	2	(1) 1380
		(1) 1381
Hastings, Sir Ralph [Hastyng]	1	(1) 1394
Hawberk, Sir Nicholas [Hauberk]	2	(1) 1391
		(1) 1393
Haverford, friars preachers of	1	(1) 1394
Hawkwood, Sir John [Haukwode]	1	(1) 1379
Hay, John	1	(1) 1380
Hemingford, Nicholas, clerk [Hemingford]	1	(1) 1395
Henry Bolingbroke, earl of Derby, duke of Hereford	24	(1) 1380
		(1) 1387
		(7) 1388
		(6) 1389
		(2) 1391
		(2) 1392
		(1) 1393
		(1) 1394
		(1) 1395
		(2) 1397
Henry Bolingbroke, earl of Derby and Thomas Holand, earl of Kent	1	(1) 1397
Hereford, Mary, countess of (Mary de Bohun)	2	(1) 1378
		(1) 1379
Herlyng, John, usher of the chamber	2	(1) 1378
		(1) 1380
Hilton, John	1	(1) 1393
Hilton, Reginald, clerk, controller of the king's household	4	(1) 1378
		(1) 1379
		(1) 1380
		(1) 1384
Hoo, Eleanor	1	(1) 1393
Hoo, Sir William	1	(1) 1389
Horbury, William, clerk	1	(1) 1386
Hore, John	1	(1) 1395
Houghton, Sir Henry	1	(1) 1393
Household, certain of	1	(1) 1389
Hulton, Reginald, controller of household	1	(1) 1379
Hungerford, Sir Thomas	1	(1) 1380
Hunt, Laurence, groom of chamber	1	(1) 1387
Hunt, William, yeoman	1	(1) 1391

Huntingdon, Elizabeth, countess of (Elizabeth of Lancaster)	2	(2) 1393
Huntingdon, Elizabeth, countess of, and Lady Trivet	1	(1) 1393
Huntingdon, John Holand, earl of	12	(1) 1378
		(3) 1379
		(3) 1381
		(1) 1381
		(1) 1382
		(1) 1383
		(1) 1388
		(1) 1397
Ikelyngton, John, parson of St Andrews	1	(1) 1393
Isabella of France, queen	4	(1) 1389
		(1) 1396
		(1) 1397
		(1) 1398
Joan of Kent, princess of Wales, king's mother	31	(2) 1377
		(7) 1378
		(5) 1379
		(3) 1380
		(4) 1381
		(5) 1383
		(3) 1384
		(1) 1385
		(1) 1392
Joan of Kent and the rector of Asherugge	1	(1) 1379
Joce, John	1	(1) 1379
Joce, William, esquire	1	(1) 1383
John of Gaunt, duke of Lancaster	62	(2) 1377
		(3) 1378
		(2) 1379
		(21) 1380
		(7) 1381
		(1) 1383
		(1) 1384
		(2) 1390
		(15) 1393
		(5) 1396
		(3) 1397
John of Gaunt, duke of Lancaster, and the bishop of London	1	(1) 1382
John of Gaunt, duke of Lancaster, and the bishop of Salisbury, treasurer	1	(1) 1393
Kent, Alice, countess of (Alice Holand)	2	(1) 1384
		(1) 1389
Kent, Thomas Holand, earl of	6	(3) 1380
		(1) 1382
		(2) 1390
Kirkeby, John, clerk	1	(1) 1396

Knolles, Sir Robert	1	(1) 1379
Kyrkeby, John	1	(1) 1391
Kyrkestede, Henry	1	(1) 1384
Lakenheath, Sir John [Lakenheth]	3	(2) 1388
		(1) 1389
Lambard, Walter, clerk	1	(1) 1386
Lambe, John, esquire	1	(1) 1379
Langeley, prior of friars preachers	1	(1) 1393
Latimer, Sir Thomas [Latymer]	1	(1) 1379
Latimer, William, Lord [Latymer]	1	(1) 1380
Lee, Sir Walter atte	2	(1) 1380
		(1) 1386
Legh, Peter	3	(1) 1386
		(2) 1392
Lescrope, Walter	2	(2) 1394
Leycestre, Henry of, herald	1	(1) 1390
Lincoln, John of, clerk	2	(1) 1390
		(1) 1394
Litelbury, Sir John	1	(1) 1394
Lodelawe, John	1	(1) 1378
Lodewyk, Margery, damsel of king's mother [Ludwyk]	3	(1) 1380
		(1) 1390
		(1) 1393
Lofwyk, John	2	(2) 1391
Lokton, William	1	(1) 1391
Lombard, Walter, clerk	1	(1) 1386
London, citizens of	1	(1) 1385
Loutrell, Sir Hugh	1	(1) 1390
Lovel, John, banneret and Sir William de Thorp	1	(1) 1379
Ludengton, William	1	(1) 1391
Luttelton, Thomas	1	(1) 1380
Lyngeyn, Ralph	1	(1) 1379
Lyons, James	1	(1) 1380
Lyons, Sir Richard	1	(1) 1380
Macclesfeld, John [Maclysfeld]	7	(1) 1390
		(3) 1391
		(3) 1392
Mallore, Antekin	1	(1) 1381
March, Edmund Mortimer, earl of	1	(1) 1378
March, Philippa, countess of (Lady Mortimer)	3	(3) 1378
March, Roger Mortimer, earl of	3	(1) 1393
		(1) 1393
		(1) 1394

March, Roger Mortimer, earl of and William Arundell	1	(1) 1394
Marchant, Stephen	1	(1) 1391
Mareshall, Roger, esquire	2	(1) 1391
		(1) 1394
Martyn, Thomas, clerk	1	(1) 1394
Maudeleyn, John, servant	1	(1) 1390
Maxfeld, John	1	(1) 1391
Medelton, Robert	1	(1) 1391
Melreth, Thomas	1	(1) 1391
Menhir, John, clerk	2	(1) 1389
		(1) 1390
Mercer, Peter, notary	1	(1) 1391
Merssh, John, abbot of Missenden	1	(1) 1393
Merston, Thomas, prior of Kenilworth	1	(1) 1389
Metford, Richard, bishop of Chichester and Lady de Mohun	1	(1) 1394
Meyner, John, clerk	2	(1) 1385
		(1) 1389
Midelton, John, master, king's physician	2	(1) 1387
		(1) 1399
Mille, Walter atte	1	(1) 1381
Mohun, Guy, bishop of St. Davids	1	(1) 1398
Molyns, Margery, Lady	1	(1) 1392
Monketon, Nicholas, servant	3	(2) 1390
		(1) 1392
More, Thomas, treasurer to queen Anne	1	(1) 1390
Moreaux, Thomas of [Murrieux]	2	(1) 1377
		(1) 1379
Morice, Nicholas, abbot of Waltham	1	(1) 1379
Morriers, Alan	1	(1) 1379
Murrieux, Blanche	1	(1) 1383
Neuport, Andrew, serjeant	2	(1) 1389
		(1) 1391
Neville, Alexander, archbishop of York and Robert de Conyngeston	1	(1) 1384
Neville, Elizabeth [Willoughby]	1	(1) 1383
Neville, John, Lord	1	(1) 1378
Neville, Ralph son of John, Thomas son of Roger, Lord of Clifford	1	(1) 1379
Neville, Sir William	2	(2) 1388
Neville, Sir William and William Walsham	1	(1) 1383
Non, Edmund, esquire	2	(1) 1383
		(1) 1386

Norfolk, Margaret, countess of	6	(2) 1379
		(3) 1380
		(1) 1381
Norfolk, Thomas Mowbray, duke of, earl marshal, earl of Nottingham, [Moubray]	18	(2) 1383
		(1) 1384
		(2) 1389
		(1) 1390
		(2) 1391
		(3) 1393
		(3) 1394
		(1) 1395
		(2) 1397
		(1) 1398
Norfolk, Thomas Mowbray, duke of, earl marshal and Percy, Thomas of, steward of household	2	(2) 1393
Northumberland, Henry Percy, earl of	53	(8) 1377
		(1) 1378
		(2) 1379
		(2) 1380
		(3) 1381
		(1) 1382
		(2) 1383
		(2) 1384
		(3) 1385
		(4) 1386
		(2) 1387
		(3) 1388
		(3) 1389
		(3) 1390
		(4) 1393
		(1) 1395
		(2) 1396
		(5) 1397
		(2) 1399
Norton, Henry, esquire	1	(1) 1391
Oudeby, John, clerk	2	(1) 1392
		(1) 1393
Outeberd, Reymunda	1	(1) 1379
Overton, John, esquire	2	(2) 1393
Oxford, Agnes de Vere, countess of, duchess of Ireland	7	(1) 1391
		(1) 1393
		(3) 1396
		(1) 1397
		(1) 1399
Oxford, Agnes de Vere, countess of, duchess of Ireland and earl marshal, earl of Nottingham	1	(1) 1394

Oxford, Aubrey de Vere, earl of	4	(1) 1379
		(1) 1380
		(1) 1381
		(1)1384
Oxford, Philippa, countess of (Philippa de Vere)	1	(1) 1385
Oxford, Robert de Vere, earl of, duke of Ireland	7	(1) 1378
		(1) 1383
		(1) 1384
		(4) 1387
Pakngton, William	3	(1) 1378
		(1) 1379
		(1) 1384
Par, Sir William	4	(1) 1380
		(1) 1390
		(1) 1391
		(1) 1393
Parys, Eleanor	1	(1) 1379
Parys, John	2	(2) 1388
Parys, Robert of	1	(1) 1390
Pauyle, Sir John	1	(1) 1386
Payn, Richard	2	(1) 1392
		(1) 1393
Paynel, Ralph	1	(1) 1379
Pembroke, Elizabeth, countess of	2	(2) 1383
Percy, Hugh	1	(1) 1380
Petevyn, Thomas	1	(1) 1380
Peytevyn, John, esquire	1	(1) 1380
Ploufeld, Roger, esquire	1	(1) 1387
Pope [Urban VI]	1	(1) 1380
Portugal, queen of	1	(1) 1393
Poynings, Isabel, lady of [Isabel Grey]	6	(1) 1388
		(1) 1390
		(1) 1392
		(3) 1393
Prat, John	1	(1) 1392
Prittlewell, John, esquire	1	(1) 1390
Prophete, John, clerk	1	(1) 1390
Pull, Sir John	1	(1) 1393
Pyle, John, esquire	1	(1) 1379
Radyngton, Sir Baldwin	2	(2) 1380
Radyngton, John	2	(1) 1395
		(1) 1397
Ralph, son of John	1	(1) 1379
Ramesey, Ralph, esquire	1	(1) 1386

Rammesey, Adam, esquire	5	(1) 1379
		(2) 1380
		(1) 1389
		(1) 1391
Rauf, Walter, esquire	1	(1) 1390
Read, Robert, bishop of Waterford and the bishop of Worcester	2	(1) 1394
		(1) 1395
Redman, Matthew	2	(1) 1379
		(1) 1394
Redman, Richard	2	(1) 1394
		(1) 1396
Reede, Ralph	1	(1) 1381
Repyngton, Ralph, clerk of kitchen	1	(1) 1394
Rigmaydyn, William, esquire	1	(1) 1390
Roches, Sir John	1	(1) 1389
Roger, John	1	(1) 1392
Ronclyff, Guy	1	(1) 1391
Ronhale, Richard, master, king's clerk	1	(1) 1385
Roos, John	1	(1) 1385
Roos, Thomas, Lord	2	(1) 1381
		(1) 1386
Rosselyn, Nicholas	1	(1) 1391
Roughton, Richard	1	(1) 1385
Roughton, Thomas, friar minor, king's orator, confessor of the earl of Oxford	2	(1) 1384
		(1) 1386
Rous, Robert	1	(1) 1379
Rushook, Thomas, bishop of Llandaff, king's confessor	6	(1) 1379
		(1) 1380
		(1) 1381
		(1) 1384
		(2) 1385
Rutland, Edward of Langley, earl of	40	(1) 1389
		(1) 1390
		(4) 1391
		(6) 1392
		(17) 1393
		(7) 1393
		(2) 1394
		(2) 1395
Rutland, Edward, earl of and Henry de Percy	1	(1) 1393
Ryther, Henry	1	(1) 1392
Ryvere, William, esquire	2	(1) 1389
		(1) 1390

St Pol, Maud, countess of, Lady Courtenay, king's sister	4	(1) 1378
		(1) 1379
		(1) 1380
		(1) 1390
St Pol, Waleran, count of	4	(1) 1390
		(2) 1391
		(1) 1393
St Werburgh's, abbot and convent of	1	(1) 1397
Salisbury, Elizabeth, countess of (Elizabeth Mohun)	7	(1) 1380
		(1) 1383
		(1) 1384
		(1) 1387
		(1) 1390
		(1) 1393
		(1) 1397
Salisbury, William Montacute, earl of	3	(2) 1385
		(1) 1389
Salle, Robert	1	(1) 1377
Sarnesfeld, Margaret	3	(2) 1391
		(1) 1392
Sarnesfeld, Nicholas [Sharnesfeld]	3	(1) 1378
		(1) 1380
		(1) 1381
Scrope, Richard, bishop of Coventry and Lichfield	2	(1) 1390
		(1) 1391
Segrave, Sir Hugh	4	(1) 1378
		(1) 1381
		(1) 1383
		(1) 1384
Seintcler, Adam	2	(2) 1390
Seys, Sir Diggory	1	(1) 1388
Shaldeburne, Thomas, servant of spicery	2	(2) 1387
Shawe, Richard, clerk	1	(1) 1396
Sheffeld, John, esquire	2	(1) 1389
		(1) 1390
Shelle, Thomas	1	(1) 1391
Shepeye, John, clerk	1	(1) 1384
Skernenge, John	1	(1) 1391
Skipwith, William	1	(1) 1379
Skirlawe, Walter, bishop of Durham	2	(1) 1379
		(1) 1393
Slake, Nicholas	2	(1) 1387
		(1) 1392
Spencer, Richard king's servant	1	(1) 1396
Spridlington, William, bishop of St Asaph	3	(2) 1377
		(1) 1379

Stacy, John	2	(1) 1379
		(1) 1380
Stafford, Hugh, earl of	8	(3) 1378
		(1) 1379
		(1) 1380
		(2) 1384
		(1) 1386
Stafford, Philippa, countess of (Philippa of Beauchamp)	1	(1) 1379
Stafford, Thomas, earl of	7	(1) 1387
		(2) 1388
		(3) 1389
		(1) 1390
Stanhope, Elizabeth	1	(1) 1383
Stanley, Sir John	3	(1) 1391
		(1) 1392
		(1) 1393
Stapilton, Brian	2	(1) 1384
		(1) 1389
Stapulton, Alice	1	(1) 1387
Stathum, Ralph	1	(1) 1392
Stathum, William	1	(1) 1391
Stirkeland, William	1	(1) 1390
Stokes, Alan, king's clerk	2	(2) 1382
Stout, Thomas, king's servant	3	(2) 1394
		(1) 1395
Stratton, John	1	(1) 1381
Strauley, Hugh	1	(1) 1380
Stuklay, Thomas	1	(1) 1392
Suffolk, Michael de la Pole, earl of	9	(1) 1379
		(2) 1380
		(1) 1381
		(2) 1382
		(2) 1387
		(1) 1388
Suffolk, Michael de la Pole, earl of, and earl of Salisbury	1	(1) 1380
Suffolk, William Ufford, earl of	3	(1) 1378
		(1) 1379
		(1) 1380
Sully, John	2	(1) 1379
		(1) 1381
Surrey, Thomas Holand, duke of	5	(5) 1399
Swynbourn, Thomas	1	(1) 1391
Syglem, Sir Roger	1	(1) 1388
Talbot, Gilbert	1	(1) 1379

Thomas of Woodstock, duke of Gloucester, earl of Buckingham	7	(2) 1380
		(1) 1381
		(2) 1382
		(1) 1386
		(1) 1397
Thornebury, Sir John	1	(1) 1388
Tidmann, king's surgeon	1	(1) 1390
Timworth, John, abbot of Bury St Edmunds, and convent of	3	(2) 1386
		(1) 1388
Tiryngton, William, king's servant	1	(1) 1395
Tombler, Guy	1	(1) 1391
Trailly, Sir John	1	(1) 1379
Tresilian, Sir Robert	2	(1) 1382
		(1) 1385
Treverbyn, John, esquire	1	(1) 1391
Trivet, Elizabeth, Lady	4	(2) 1393
		(2) 1394
Trivet, Sir Thomas [Tryvet]	4	(1) 1379
		(2) 1385
		(1) 1387
Troubrugge, John	1	(1) 1392
Trumpyngton, Roger	1	(1) 1379
Tudmann, Daniel	1	(1) 1390
Tylioll, Peter	1	(1) 1388
Upton, Walter	1	(1) 1387
Ursewky, Sir Robert	2	(1) 1387
		(1) 1390
Ursewky, Walter	1	(1) 1390
Urswyk, Sir Robert	2	(1) 1386
		(1) 1390
Vache, Philip	2	(1) 1378
		(1) 1379
Vaghan, Hamo	1	(1) 1389
Vale, Geoffrey	1	(1) 1388
Veer, Richard	1	(1) 1389
Venour, John	1	(1) 1389
Verdon, John, esquire	1	(1) 1384
Vernon, Sir Ralph	1	(1) 1387
Vienne, abbot of the Irishmen of, in the duchy of Daustry	1	(1) 1395
Wake, Thomas	1	(1) 1378
Wakefield, Henry, bishop of Worcester	3	(1) 1384
		(1) 1387
		(1) 1392

Waldby, Robert, bishop of Aire, bishop of Sodor, archbishop of Dublin, bishop of Chichester, archbishop of York	13	(4) 1389
		(3) 1390
		(1) 1391
		(1) 1392
		(1) 1394
		(1) 1396
		(2) 1397
Waldby, Robert, bishop of Aire and Alphonso of Dene	1	(1) 1390
Walden, Roger, king's secretary	2	(1) 1393
		(1) 1396
Walleran, Alice, a poor woman	1	(1) 1383
Waltham, Adam	1	(1) 1379
Waltham, John, bishop of Salisbury	3	(1) 1379
		(1) 1390
		(1) 1392
Waltham, John, bishop of Salisbury and earl marshal and earl of Huntingdon	1	(1) 1391
Walton, Thomas, clerk	2	(1) 1379
		(1) 1384
Walworth, William	1	(1) 1378
Warde, Henry	1	(1) 1379
Warwick, John, esquire	1	(1) 1394
Warwick, Thomas Beauchamp, earl of	11	(1) 1378
		(1) 1379
		(4) 1380
		(1) 1384
		(2) 1385
		(1) 1386
		(1) 1388
Watford, Stephen, esquire	1	(1) 1392
Wetherlay, Thomas	2	(1) 1391
		(1) 1392
Whenewell, John, gaoler	1	(1) 1388
Willoughby, Joan Lady (Joan Holand)	1	(1) 1396
Willoughby, Robert, Lord	2	(1) 1387
		(1) 1388
Wiltshire, Sir John	3	(1) 1387
		(2) 1389
Wilton, John, yeoman of the chamber	2	(1) 1390
		(1) 1392
Winchcombe, Tideman, bishop of Worcester [Robert Tydman]	3	(1) 1396
		(2) 1397
Wodecrofte, Thomas, yeoman	1	(1) 1387
Wodehous, John, chamberlain	1	(1) 1384
Wolforton, William	1	(1) 1393

Worcester, Thomas Percy, earl of	12	(2) 1377
		(1) 1378
		(1) 1379
		(2) 1383
		(1) 1384
		(1) 1391
		(4) 1393
Worthe, Blanche	1	(1) 1391
Worthe, Sir John	3	(1) 1379
		(1) 1387
		(1) 1389
Wrotham, John	1	(1) 1392
Wrottesley, Henry	1	(1) 1377
Wrottesley, Sir Hugh	1	(1) 1377
Wyke, John	1	(1) 1385
Wykeham, William, bishop of Winchester, and bishop of St Davids and earl of Northumberland	1	(1) 1389
Wykmor, Roger, esquire	1	(1) 1390
Wylton, John, yeoman of chamber	1	(1) 1393
Yerdeburgh, John, clerk	2	(1) 1377
		(1) 1379
York, Isabella, duchess of, countess of Cambridge	7	(1) 1381
		(1) 1382
		(1) 1384
		(4) 1385
Zouche, Hugh de la (Souche)	1	(1) 1397
Zouche, William	1	(1) 1387
	1337	

BIBLIOGRAPHY

Manuscript Sources

London, British Library

Cotton Charters
MS Harley, 4292

London, The National Archives

C 1	Court of Chancery
C47	Chancery Miscellanea
C 49	Chancery and Exchequer: King's Remembrancer
C 61	Gascon Rolls
C 66	Chancery: Patent Rolls
C 67/26–44	Chancery: Supplementary Patent Rolls
C 71	Scotch Rolls
C 81	Chancery: Warrants for the Great Seal
C 144	Chancery: Criminal Inquisitions
C 237	Chancery: Bails on Special Pardons
C 266	Chancery: Cancelled Letters Patent
CHES 2	Chester, Palatinate: Exchequer of Chester: Enrolments
E 101	Exchequer: King's Remembrancer: Various Accounts
E 401	Exchequer: Receipt Rolls
E 403	Exchequer of Receipt: Issue Rolls and Registers
E 404	Exchequer of Receipt: Warrants for Issues
HO	Records created or inherited by the Home Office
JUST 1	Justices Itinerant, Assize and Gaol Delivery Justices
JUST 3	Justices of Gaol Delivery, Gaol Delivery Rolls and Files
KB 9	King's Bench: Crown Side
KB 27	King's Bench: Plea and Crown Sides: Coram Rege Rolls
KB 145	Court of King's Bench: Crown and Plea Sides: Recorda and Precepta Recordorum Files
SC 1	Special Collections: Ancient Correspondence
SC 8	Special Collections: Ancient Petitions
SP	State Paper Office

Bibliography

Printed Sources

Primary Sources

Alighieri, Dante. *The Divine Comedy*, trans. A. Mandelbaum. London, 1995

Bémont, C., ed. *Rôles gascons, 1290–1307*. Paris, 1906

Bernard of Clairvaux. *Annuntiatione Beati Mariae, Sancti Bernardi Opera*. Ed. J. Leclerc and H. Rochais. 8 vols. Rome, 1957

Bliss, W. H. and J. A. Twemlow. *Calendar of Entries in the Papal Registers Relating to Great Britain and Ireland: Papal Letters, 1198–1484*. London, 1893–1960

Block, K. S., ed. *Ludus Coventriae or the Plaie Called Corpus Christi*. EETS OS 120. Oxford, 1922

Bolland W. C., ed. *The Eyre of Kent: 6 & 7 Edward II, A.D. 1313–1314*. Selden Society 24. London, 1909

Brewer, J. S., J. Gairdner and R. H. Brodie, eds. *Letters and Papers, Foreign and Domestic, Henry VIII*. 21 vols. London, 1862–1932

Brinton, Thomas. *The Sermons of Thomas Brinton, Bishop of Rochester (1373–1389)*. Ed. M. A. Devlin. Camden Society, 3rd series 85. London, 1954

Burgess, G. S., trans. *Two Medieval Outlaws: Eustace the Monk and Fouke Fitz Waryn*. Cambridge, 1997

Calendar of Chancery Warrants Preserved in the Public Record Office, A.D. 1244–1326. London, 1927

Calendar of Charter Rolls. London, 1916

Calendar of Close Rolls. London, 1914–27

Calendar of Patent Rolls. London, 1895–1909

Capgrave, J. *The Chronicle of England by John Capgrave*. Ed. F. C. Hingeston. RS 1. London, 1858

Caulibus, John of. *Meditationes Vitae Christi*. Ed. F. X. Taney, A. Miller and C. M. Stallings-Taney. Asheville NC, 2000

Cawley, A. C., ed. *Wakefield Pageants in the Towneley Cycle*. Manchester, 1958

Chaucer, Geoffrey. *The Riverside Chaucer*. Ed. L. D. Benson. 3rd edn. Oxford, 1987

Child, F. J. ed. *English and Scottish Popular Ballads*. 5 vols. New York, 1965

Clarke, M. V. and V. H. Galbraith, eds. 'Chronicles of Dieulacres Abbey, 1381–1403'. 'The Deposition of Richard II'. *Bulletin of the John Rylands Library* 14 (1930), 164–70

Coss, P. R., ed. *Thomas Wright's Political Songs*. Cambridge, 1996

Dobson, R. B., ed. *The Peasants' Revolt of 1381*. 2nd edn. London, 1983

Dobson, R. B. and J. Taylor, eds. *Rymes of Robyn Hood: An Introduction to the English Outlaw*. London, 1976

Eccles, M., ed. *The Macro Plays: The Castle of Perseverance; Wisdom; Mankind*. EETS OS 262. London, 1969

Fitzherbert, Anthony. *La graunde abridgement collect par le iudge tresreuerend Monsieur Anthony Fitzherbert*. London, 1565

Flaherty, W. 'The Great Rebellion in Kent of 1381 Illustrated from the Public Records', *Archaeologia Cantiana* 3 (1860), 65–96

Francis, W. N., ed. *The Book of Vices and Virtues*, EETS OS 217. London, 1942

Froissart, Jean. *Froissart: Chronicles*. Ed. G. Brereton. Harmondsworth, 1978

Froissart, Jean. *Chroniques de J. Froissart*. Société de L'Histoire de France. Ed. G. Raynaud. 15 vols. Paris, 1869–1975

Galbraith, V. H., ed. *The Anonimalle Chronicle*. Manchester, 1927

Given-Wilson, C., ed. *Chronicles of the Revolution, 1397–1400*. Manchester, 1993

—— *The Parliament Rolls of Medieval England*, ed. C. Given-Wilson *et al.*, CD-ROM. Leicester, 2005

Gower, John. *Confessio Amantis*. Ed. R. A. Peck. 2nd edn. Kalamazoo, 2006

Gransden, A., ed. *The Chronicle of Bury St. Edmunds 1212–1301*. London, 1964

Grosseteste, Robert. *Le Chateau d'Amour*. Ed. J. Murray. Paris, 1918

Haas, E. and G. D. G. Hall, eds. *Early Registers of Writs*. Selden Society 87. London, 1970

Hale, Matthew. *The Prerogatives of the King*. Ed. D. E. C. Yale. Selden Society 92. London, 1976

Hall, G. D. G., ed. *The Treatise on the Laws and Customs of the Realm of England commonly called Glanvill*. London, 1965

Hall, H., ed. *The Red Book of Exchequer*. RS 99. London, 1896

Harvey, B. 'Draft Letters Patent of Manumission and Pardon for the Men of Somerset in 1381'. *EHR* 80 (1965), 89–90

Harvey, E. R., ed. *Court of Sapience*. London, 1984

Hathaway, E. J., P. T. Ricketts, C. A. Robson and A. D. Wilshere, eds. *Fouke Le Fitz Waryn*. Anglo-Norman Text Society. Oxford, 1975

Haydon, F. S., ed. *Eulogium Historiarum Sive Temporis*. RS 9. London, 1858

Hector, L. C. and B. F. Harvey, eds. *The Westminster Chronicle 1381–1394*. Oxford, 1982.

Herrtage, S. J. H., ed. *The Early English Versions of the Gesta Romanorum*. EETS ES 33. London, 1879

Holthausen, F., ed. *Vices and Virtues: A Soul's Confession of its Sins with the Reason's Description of the Virtues*. EETS, OS 89, 159. London, 1888, 1921

Horstman, C., ed. *Charter of the Abbey of the Holy Ghost, Yorkshire Writers*. London, 1895

Horwood, A. J. and L. O. Pike, eds. *Year Books of the Reign of Edward the Third, Years XI–XX*. RS 31. London, 1883–1911

Immaculate, Sister Mary, C. S. C., ed. 'The Four Daughters of God in the Gesta Romanorum and the Court of Sapience'. *Publications of the Modern Language Association* 57 (1942), 951–65

Kimball, E. G., ed. *The Shropshire Peace Roll, 1400–1414*. Shrewsbury, 1959

Klinefelter, R. A. ed. 'The Four Daughters of God: A New Version'. *Journal of English and German Philology* 52 (1953), 90–5

Knight, S. and T. Ohlgren, eds. *Robin Hood and Other Outlaw Tales*. Kalamazoo, 1997

Knighton, Henry. *Knighton's Chronicle, 1337–1394*. Ed. G. H. Martin. Oxford, 1995

Langland, William. *Piers the Plowman, William Langland*. Trans. J. F. Goodridge. London, 1966

—— *The Vision of Piers Plowman*. Ed. A. V. C. Schmidt. London, 1995

Love, Nicholas. *The Mirour of the Blessed Lyf of Jesu Christ*. Ed. L. R. Powell. Oxford, 1908

Luard, H. R., ed. *Annales Monastici*. London, 1864–9

Luders, A., T. E. Tomlins, J. France, W. E. Taunton and J. Raithby, eds. *Statutes of the Realm, 1101–1713.* 11 vols. London, 1810–28

Lumby, J. R., ed. *Chronicon Henrici Knighton.* RS 92. 2 vols. London, 1889–95

Lydgate, John. *Life of Our Lady.* Ed. J. A. Lauritis, R. A. Klinefelter and V. F. Gallagher. Philological Series 2. Pittsburgh, 1961

Maidstone, Richard. *Concordia: The Reconciliation of Richard II with London.* Ed. A. G. Rigg and D. R. Carlson. Kalamazoo, 2003

Martival, Roger. *The Registers of Roger Martival, Bishop of Salisbury, 1315–30.* Ed. C. R. Elrington. Canterbury and York Society 58 (1972)

Maxwell-Lyte, H. C. *Calendar of Chancery Warrants Preserved in the Public Record Office, A. D. 1244–1326.* London, 1927

—— *Historical Notes on the Use of the Great Seal in England.* London, 1926

Memoranda Rolls. London, 1968

Morris, R., ed. *Cusor Mundi.* EETS OS 57, 59, 62, 66, 68, 69, 101. London, 1874–93

Nichols, F. M., ed. *Britton.* 2 vols. Oxford, 1865

Nicolas, N. H., ed. *Proceedings and Ordinances of the Privy Council of England.* 7 vols. London, 1834–7

Palmer, W. H. and H. W. Saunders, ed. *Documents Relating to Cambridge Villages.* Cambridge, 1926

Peñafort, St. Raymond of. *Summa de Poenitentia.* Farnborough, 1967

Peter Cantor. *Summa de sacramentis et animae consilis. Analecta mediaevalia Namurcensia.* Louvain, 1957–67

Phillipps, S. M., ed. *State Trials: or, A Collection of the Most Interesting Trials, Prior to the Revolution of 1688.* London, 1826

Raine, J., ed. *Sanctuarium Dunelmense et Sanctuarium Beverlacensis.* Surtees Society 5. Durham, 1837

Ralph of Coggeshall. *Radulphi Abbatis de Coggeshal Opera quae supersunt curante Alf. Jhno. Dunkin, nunc primum edita.* Noviomago, 1856

Richardson, H. G. and G.O. Sayles, eds. *Fleta,* Selden Society 72, 89, 99. London, 1955–84

—— *Rotuli Parliamentorum Anglie hactenus inediti, 1279–1373.* Camden Society, 3rd series 51. London, 1935

Riley, H. T., ed. 'Annales Ricardi Secundi et Henrici Quarti'. *Johannis de Trokelowe et Henrici de Blaneforde, monachorum S. Albani, necnon quorundam anonymorum chronica et annales, regnantibus Henrico Tertio, Edwardo Primo, Edwardo Secundo, Ricardo Secundo, et Henrico Quarto.* RS 28. London, 1866

Roberts, E. A. *Edward II, the Ordainers and Piers Gaveston's Jewels and Horses, 1312–1313.* Camden Miscellany 15. 1929

Rolle, Richard. *The Pricke of Conscience.* Ed. R. Morris. Philological Society 6. Berlin, 1863

Roskell, J. S., L. S. Clark and C. Rawcliffe, eds. *The House of Commons 1386–1421.* 4 vols. Stroud, 1993

Rymer, T., ed. *Foedera, Conventiones, Literae et Cujuscunque Generis Acta.* Record Commission edn. 3 vols. in 6 parts. London, 1816–30

Sajavaara, K., ed. *The Middle English Translations of Robert Grosseteste's Chasteau d'Amour.* Memoires de la Société Néophilologique de Helsinki 32. Helsinki, Société Néophilologique, 1967

Sayles, G. O., ed. *Select Cases in the Court of King's Bench*. 7 vols. Selden Society 55, 57–58, 74, 76, 82, 88. London, 1936–71

Scott-Stokes, C. and C. Given-Wilson, ed. *Chronicon Anonymi Cantuariensis: The Chronicle of Anonymous of Canterbury 1346–1365*. Oxford, 2008

Sellers, M. ed. *York Memorandum Book II*. Surtees Society 125 (1914)

Sharpe, R. R., ed. *Calendar of Letter Books of the City of London*. 11 vols. London, 1899–1912

Skeat, W. W. ed. *The Tale of Gamelyn*. Oxford, 1884

_____ *The Vision of Piers Plowman by William Langland*. EETS OS 67. London, 1877

Sparvel-Bayly, J. 'Essex in Insurrection, 1381', *Transactions of the Essex Archaeological Society*, n.s. 1 (1878), 205–19

Storey, R. L. 'Index to Pardon Rolls'. Unpublished typescript, The National Archives

Stow, G. B., ed. *Historia Vitae et Regni Ricardi Secundi*. Philadelphia, 1977

Taylor, J., ed. *Kirkstall Abbey Chronicles*. Publications of the Thoresby Society. 1952

Thomas Becket. *The Correspondence of Thomas Becket, Archbishop of Canterbury, 1162–1170*. Ed. A. J. Duggan. Oxford, 2000

Thorne, S. E., ed. *Bracton on the Laws and Customs of England*. 4 vols. Cambridge MA, 1968–77

Traver, H. The *Four Daughters of God*. Philadelphia, 1907

Usk, Adam. *The Chronicle of Adam Usk 1377–1421*. Ed. C. Given-Wilson. Oxford, 1997

Walsingham, Thomas. *Chronicon Anglie 1328–1388*. Ed. E. M. Thompson. RS 64. 1874

—— *Gesta abbatum monasterii Sancti Albani*. Ed. H. T. Riley, 3 vols. RS 28. London, 1867–9

—— *Historia Anglicana 1272–1422*. Ed. H. T. Riley. RS 28. 2 vols. London, 1863–4

—— *The St. Albans Chronicle: The Chronica maiora of Thomas Walsingham, vol. 1, 1376–1394*. Ed. J. Taylor, W. R. Childs and L. Watkiss. Oxford, 2003

William of Auxerre. *Summa aurea omnia*. Paris, 1980–5

Williams, B., ed. *Traison et Mort: Chronique de la Traison et Mort de Richard Deux Roy Dengleterre*. London, 1846

Wright, T., ed. *Political Poems and Songs*. RS 14. London, 1859–61

Secondary Sources

Alford, J. A. *Piers Plowman: A Glossary of Legal Diction*. Cambridge, 1988

Armitage-Smith, S. *John of Gaunt*. London, 1904

Aston, M. 'Corpus Christi and Corpus Regni: Heresy and the Peasants' Revolt'. *P&P* 143 (1994), 3–47

Baker, J. H. *An Introduction to English Legal History*. 3rd edn. London, 1990

Baldwin, A. P. *The Theme of Government in Piers Plowman*. Cambridge, 1981

Barron, C. M. 'Chivalry, Pageantry and Merchant Culture in Medieval London'. *Heraldry, Pageantry, and Social Display in Medieval England*. Ed. P. R. Coss and M. H. Keen. Woodbridge, 2002. pp. 219–41

—— 'The Tyranny of Richard II'. *BIHR* 41 (1968), 1–18

Beattie, C. 'Single Women, Work and Family: The Chancery Dispute of Jane

Wynde and Margaret Clerk'. *Voices from the Bench: The Narratives of Lesser Folk in Medieval Trials*. Ed. M. Goodich. New York, 2006. pp. 177–202

Beattie, J. M. *Crime and the Courts in England, 1660–1800*. Princeton, 1986

Bellamy, J. G. 'Benefit of Clergy in the Fifteenth and Sixteenth Centuries'. *Criminal Law and Society in Late Medieval and Tudor England*. Ed. J. Bellamy. Gloucester, 1984. pp. 115–72

———— *Crime and Public Order in England in the Later Middle Ages*. London, 1973

———— *The Criminal Trial in Later Medieval England: Felony Before the Courts from Edward I to the Sixteenth Century*. Stroud, 1998

———— *The Law of Treason in England in the Later Middle Ages*. Cambridge and New York, 1970

Bennett, M. 'Edward III's Entail and the Succession to the Crown, 1376–1471'. *EHR* 113 (1998), 586–90

———— *Richard II and the Revolution of 1399*. Stroud, 1999

Berman, H. J. *Faith and Order: The Reconciliation of Law and Religion*. Atlanta, 1993

Bird, W. H. B. 'The Peasant Rising and the King's Itinerary', *EHR* 31 (1916), 124–6

Bloch, M. *The Royal Touch: Sacred Monarchy and Scrofula in England and France*. Trans. J. E. Anderson. London, 1973

Brockman, B. A. 'The Law of Man and the Peace of God: Judicial Process as Satiric Theme in the Wakefield Mactacio Abel'. *Speculum* 49 (1974), 699–707

Brooks, N. 'The Organisation and Achievement of the Peasants of Kent and Essex in 1381'. *Studies in Medieval History presented to R. H. C. Davis*. Ed. H. Mayr-Harting and R. I. Moore. London, 1985. pp. 247–70

Brown, A. L. 'The Authorisation of Letters under the Great Seal'. *BIHR* 37 (1964), 125–55

———— *The Governance of Late Medieval England, 1272–1461*. London, 1989

Bryant, W. N. 'The Financial Dealings of Edward III with the County Communities, 1330–60'. *EHR* 83 (1968), 760–71

Buck, M. 'Reform of the Exchequer, 1313–1326', *EHR* 98 (1983), 241–60

Bynum, C. W. *The Resurrection of the Body in Western Christianity, 1200–1336*. New York, 1995

Cam, H. M. 'The Evolution of the Mediaeval English Franchise', *Speculum* 32 (1957), 427–42

Carpenter, C. 'Introduction: Political Culture, Politics and Cultural History'. *The Fifteenth Century IV: Political Culture in Late Medieval Britain*. Ed. L. Clark and C. Carpenter. Woodbridge, 2004. pp. 1–20

———— *Locality and Polity: A Study of Warwickshire Landed Society, 1401–1499*. Cambridge, 1992

———— 'Political and Constitutional History: Before and After McFarlane'. *The McFarlane Legacy: Studies in Late Medieval Politics and Society*. Ed. R. H. Britnell and A. J. Pollard. Stroud, 1995. pp. 175–206

———— *The Wars of the Roses: Politics and the Constitution in England, c.1437–1509*. Cambridge, 1997

Chew, H., and M. Weinbaum, eds. 'The London Eyre of 1244'. *London Record Society* 6 (1970)

Clanchy, M. T. *From Memory to Written Record, England 1066–1307*. 2nd edn. Oxford, 1993

Coleman, J. *English Literature in History 1350–1400: Medieval Readers and Writers.* London, 1981

Collette, C. P. 'Joan of Kent and Noble Women's Roles in Chaucer's World'. *Chaucer Review* 33 (1999), 350–62

—— *Performing Polity: Women and Agency in the Anglo-French Tradition, 1385–1620.* Turnhout, 2006. pp. 99–121

Cox, J. C. *The Sanctuaries and Sanctuary Seekers of Medieval England.* London, 1911

Crook, D. *Records of the General Eyre.* London,1982

—— 'The Later Eyres'. *EHR* 97 (1982), 241–68

Davies, J. C. 'Common Law Writs and Returns, Richard I to Richard II'. *BIHR* 26 (1953), 140–1

Davies, R. G., and J. H. Denton, eds. *The English Parliament in the Middle Ages.* Manchester, 1981. pp. 34–87

Davies, R. R. 'Richard II and the Principality of Chester, 1397–9'. *The Reign of Richard II: Essays in Honour of May McKisack.* Ed. F. R. H. Du Boulay and C. M. Barron. London, 1971. pp. 256–79

Davis, N. Z. *Fiction in the Archives: Pardon Tales and their Tellers in Sixteenth-Century France.* Cambridge, 1987

Dillon, J. *Geoffrey Chaucer.* London, 1993

Dodd, G. 'A Parliament Full of Rats? *Piers Plowman* and the Good Parliament of 1376'. *Historical Research* 77 (2004), 1–29

—— 'Getting Away with Murder: Sir John Haukeston and Richard II's Cheshire Archers'. *Nottingham Medieval Studies* 46 (2002), 102–18

—— *Justice and Grace: Private Petitioning and the English Parliament in the Late Middle Ages.* Oxford, 2007

Doig, J. A. 'Political Propaganda and Royal Proclamations in Late Medieval England'. *Historical Research* 71 (1998), 253–80

Duffy, E. *The Stripping of the Altars: Traditional Religion in England c. 1400–c. 1580.* London, 1992

Duggan, A. J. *Thomas Becket.* London, 2004

Dunn, A. *The Great Rising of 1381: The Peasants' Revolt and England's Failed Revolution.* Stroud, 2002

—— 'The Rising of 1381 in Suffolk: Its Origins and Participants'. *Proceedings of the Suffolk Institute of Archaeology and History* 36 (1988), 274–87

—— 'The Social and Economic Background to the Rural Revolt of 1381'. *The English Rising of 1381.* Ed. R. H. Hilton and T. H. Aston. Cambridge, 1984. pp. 9–42

Edwards, J. G. '"Confirmatio Cartarum" and the Baronial Grievances in 1297'. *EHR* 58 (1943), 147–71

—— '"Justice" in Early English Parliaments'. *Historical Studies of the English Parliament.* Ed. E. B. Fryde and E. Millar. Cambridge, 1970. vol. l. pp. 280–97

—— 'The Parliamentary Committee of 1398'. *EHR* 40 (1925), 316–28

Eiden, H. 'Joint Action against "Bad" Lordship: The Peasants' Revolt in Essex and Norfolk'. *History* 83 (1998), 5–30

Faith, R. 'The "Great Rumour" of 1377 and Peasant Ideology'. *The English Rising of 1381.* Ed. R. H. Hilton and T. H. Aston. Cambridge, 1984. pp. 43–73

Ferster, J. *Fictions of Advice: The Literature and Politics of Counsel in Late Medieval England.* Philadelphia, 1996

Fowler, K. A. 'News from the Front: Letters and Despatches of the Fourteenth Century'. *Guerre et société en France, en Angleterre et en Bourgogne, XIVe–XVe siècle*. Ed. P. Contamine, C. Giry-Deloison and M. H. Keen. Lille, 1991. pp. 63–92

Francois, M. 'Note sur les lettres de remission transcrites dans les registres du tresor des charters'. *Bibliotheque de l'Ecole des Chartres* 103 (1942), 317–24

Freeman, J. '"And he abjured the realm of England, never to return"'. *Freedom of Movement in the Middle Ages: Proceedings of the 2003 Harlaxton Symposium*. Ed. P. Horden. Donington, 2007. pp. 287–304

Fryde, E. B. 'Parliament and the French War, 1336–40'. *Essays in Medieval History Presented to Bertie Wilkinson*. Ed. T. A. Sandquist and M. R. Powicke. Toronto, 1969. pp. 250–69

—— *Peasants and Landlords in Later Medieval England c.1380–c.1525*. Stroud, 1996

—— *Studies in Medieval Trade and Finance*. Ed. E. B. Fryde. London, 1983

Fryde, N. *The Tyranny and Fall of Edward II*. Cambridge, 1979

Gabel, L. C. *Benefit of Clergy in England in the Later Middle Ages*. Northampton MA, 1928–9

Gauvard, C. *'De grace especiall': crime, état et société en France à la fin du Moyen Age*. 2 vols. Paris, 1991

—— 'Résistants et collaborateurs pendant la guerre de Cent ans: le témoignage des lettres de rémission'. *Actes du 3e congrès national des sociétés savantes (Poitiers, 1986: section d'histoire médiévale et de philologie, 1: la 'France anglaise' au moyen âge*. Paris, 1988

Giancarlo, M. 'Murder, Lies and Storytelling: The Manipulation of Justice(s) in the Parliaments of 1397 and 1399'. *Speculum* 77 (2002), 76–112

—— *Parliament and Literature in Late Medieval England*. Cambridge, 2007

Gillespie, J. L. 'Richard II's Cheshire Archers'. *Transactions of the Historic Society of Lancashire and Cheshire* 125 (1974), 1–35

Given-Wilson, C. 'Adam Usk, the Monk of Evesham, and the Parliament of 1397–8'. *Historical Research* 66 (1993), 329–35

—— 'Royal Charter Witness Lists 1327–1399'. *Medieval Prosopography* 12 (1991), 35–93

Goheen, R. B. 'Peasant Politics? Village Communities and the Crown in Fifteenth-Century England'. *American Historical Review* 96 (1991), 42–62

Goodman, A. *John of Gaunt: The Exercise of Princely Power in Fourteenth Century Europe*. London, 1992

—— *The Loyal Conspiracy: The Lords Appellant under Richard II*. London, 1971

Gransden, A. *Historical Writing in England 2, c. 1307 to the Early Sixteenth Century*. London, 1982

—— 'The Robin Hood Ballads', *Poetica* 18 (1984), 1–39

Green, R. F. *A Crisis of Truth: Literature and Law in Ricardian England*. Philadelphia, 1999

—— *Poets and Princepleasers: Literature and the English Court in the Later Middle Ages*. Toronto, 1980

Green, T. A. 'A Retrospective on the Criminal Trial Jury, 1200–1800'. *Twelve Good Men and True: The Criminal Trial Jury in England, 1200–1800*. Ed. J. S. Cockburn and T. A. Green. Princeton, 1988

—— *Verdict According to Conscience: Perspectives on the English Criminal Trial Jury, 1200–1800*. Chicago, 1985

Grummitt, D. 'Deconstructing Cade's Rebellion: Discourse and Politics in the Mid Fifteenth Century'. *The Fifteenth Century VI: Identity and Insurgency in the Late Middle Ages*. Ed. L. Clark. Woodbridge, 2006. pp. 107–22

Hadwin, J. F. 'The Last Royal Tallages'. *EHR* 96 (1981), 344–58

———— 'The Medieval Lay Subsidies and Economic History'. *Economic History Review*, 2nd series 36 (1983), 200–17

Hamil, F. C. 'The King's Approvers'. *Speculum* 11 (1936), 238–58

Hamilton, J. S. 'Charter Witness Lists for the Reign of Edward II'. *Fourteenth Century England I*. Ed. N. Saul. Woodbridge, 2000. pp. 1–20

Hanawalt, B. A. *Crime and Conflict in English Communities 1300–1348*. Cambridge MA, 1979

Hanawalt B. A. and Reyerson, K. L., eds. *City and Spectacle in Medieval Europe*. Minneapolis, 1994

Harding, A. 'Revolt Against the Justices'. *The English Rising of 1381*. Ed. R. H. Hilton and T. H. Aston. Cambridge, 1984. pp. 165–93

Harriss, G. L. *King, Parliament and Public Finance in Medieval England to 1369*. Oxford, 1975

———— 'Medieval Doctrines in the Debates on Supply 1610–1629'. *Faction and Parliament: Essays on Early Stuart History*. Ed. K. M. Sharpe. Oxford, 1978. pp. 73–104

———— 'Political Society and the Growth of Government in Late Medieval England'. *P&P* 138 (1993), 28–57

———— 'The Commons' Petitions of 1340'. *EHR* 78 (1963), 625–54

———— 'The Dimensions of Politics'. *The McFarlane Legacy: Studies in Late Medieval Politics and Society*. Ed. R. H. Britnell and A. J. Pollard. Stroud, 1995. pp. 1–20

———— 'The King and his Subjects'. *Fifteenth-Century Attitudes: Perceptions of Society in Late Medieval England*. Ed. R. Horrox. Cambridge, 1994. pp. 13–28

Harvey, I. M. W. 'Was There Popular Politics in Fifteenth-Century England?' *The McFarlane Legacy: Studies in Late Medieval Politics and Society*. Ed. R. H. Britnell and A. J. Pollard. Stroud, 1995. pp. 155–74

Haskett, T. S. 'Conscience, Justice and Authority in the Late-Medieval English Court of Chancery'. *Expectations of the Law in the Middle Ages*. Ed. A. Musson. Woodbridge, 2001. pp. 151–63

———— 'County Lawyers? The Composers of English Chancery Bills'. *The Life of the Law: Proceedings of the Tenth British Legal History Conference, Oxford 1991*. Ed. P. Birks. London, 1993. pp. 9–23

———— 'The Medieval English Court of Chancery'. *Law and History Review* 14 (1996), 245–313

Hay, D. 'Property, Authority and the Criminal Law'. *Albion's Fatal Tree: Crime and Society in Eighteenth Century England*. Ed. D. Hay, P. Linebaugh, J. Rule, E. P. Thompson and C. Winslow. London, 1975. pp. 17–64

Hershey, A. H. 'The Earliest Bill in Eyre: 1259'. *Historical Research* 71 (1998), 228–32

Hewitt, H. J. *The Organisation of War Under Edward III 1338–62*. Manchester, 1966

Hill, M. C. 'King's Messengers and Administrative Developments in the Thirteenth and Fourteenth Centuries'. *EHR* 61 (1946), 315–28

———— *The King's Messengers, 1199–1377: A Contribution to the History of the Royal Household*. London, 1961

—— 'The King's Messengers in England, 1199–1377'. *Medieval Prosopography* 17 (1996), 63–96

Hill, R. M. T. 'Fund-Raising in a Fourteenth-Century Province'. *Life and Thought in the Northern Church, c.1100–c.1700: Essays in Honour of Claire Cross*. Ed. D. Wood Studies in Church History, Subsidia 12. Woodbridge, 1999. pp. 31–6

Hilton, R. H. *Bond Men Made Free*. London, 1973

Hobsbawn, E. J. *Bandits*. 2nd edn. London, 1985

Holmes, G. *The Good Parliament*. Oxford, 1975

Holmes, G. A. 'The Rebellion of the Earl of Lancaster, 1328–9'. *BIHR* 28 (1955), 84–9

Holt, J. C. *Magna Carta*. Cambridge, 1965

—— *Robin Hood*. 2nd edn. London, 1989

Honeycutt, L. L. 'Intercession and the High-Medieval Queen: The Esther Topos'. *Power of the Weak: Studies on Medieval Women*. Ed. J. Carpenter and S. McLean. Urbana, 1995. pp. 126–46

Hunnisett, R. F. 'The Late Sussex Abjurations'. *Sussex Archaeological Collections* 102 (1964), 39–51

—— *The Medieval Coroner*. Cambridge, 1961

Hurnard, N. D. *The King's Pardon for Homicide Before A.D 1307*. Oxford, 1969

Hyams, P. 'What did Edwardian Villagers Understand by the Law?' *Medieval Society and the Manor Court*. Ed. Z. Razi and R. M. Smith. Oxford, 1996. pp. 69–102

Innes, J., and J. Styles, 'The Crime Wave: Recent Writing on Crime and Criminal Justice in Eighteenth-Century England'. *Rethinking Social History*. Ed. A. Wilson. Manchester, 1993. pp. 201–65

Jones, W. R. 'Bishops, Politics, and the Two Laws: The *Gravamina* of the English Clergy 1287–1399', *Speculum* 41 (1966), 209–45

Jusserand, J. J. *English Wayfaring Life in the Middle Ages: XIVth century*. Trans. L. T. Smith. 4th edn. London, 1961

Justice, S. *Writing and Rebellion: England in 1381*. Berkeley, 1994

Kaeuper, R. W. 'An Historian's Reading of the Tale of Gamelyn'. *Medium Aevum* 52 (1983), 51–62

—— 'Royal Finances and the Crisis of 1297'. *Order and Innovation in the Middle Ages: Essays in Honour of J. R. Strayer*. Ed. W. C. Jordan, B. McNab and T. F. Ruiz. Princeton, 1976. pp. 103–10

—— *War, Justice and Public Order: England and France in the Later Middle Ages*. Oxford, 1988

Keen, J. A. *The Charters of Christ and* Piers Plowman: *Documenting Salvation*. Oxford, 2002

Kellogg, A. L. and L. A. Haselmayer, 'Chaucer's Satire of the Pardoner'. *Publications of the Modern Language Association* 66 (1951), 251–77

Kesselring, K. J. 'Abjuration and its Demise: The Changing Face of Royal Justice under the Tudors'. *Canadian Journal of History* 34 (1999), 345–58

—— *Mercy and Authority in the Tudor State*. Cambridge, 2003

Kessler, H. L. and J. Zacharias, *Rome 1300: On the Path of the Pilgrim*. New Haven, 2000

King, P. *Crime, Justice and Discretion in England, 1740–1820*. Oxford, 2000

———— 'Decision Makers and Decision-Making in the English Criminal Law, 1750–1800'. *Historical Journal* 27 (1984), 25–58

Kipling, G. *Enter the King: Theatre, Liturgy and Ritual in the Medieval Civic Triumph.* Oxford, 1998

———— 'Richard II's Sumptuous Pageants and the Idea of the Civic Triumph'. *Pageantry in the Shakespearian Theatre.* Ed. D. M. Bergeron. Athens GA, 1985. pp. 83–103

Lacey, H. 'Grace for the Rebels: The Role of the Royal Pardon in the Peasants' Revolt of 1381'. *Journal of Medieval History* 34 (2008), 36–63

———— '"Mercy and truth Preserve the King": Richard II's Use of the Royal Pardon in 1397 and 1398'. *Fourteenth Century England IV.* Ed. J. S. Hamilton. Woodbridge, 2006. pp. 124–35

Laynesmith, J. L. *The Last Medieval Queens: English Queenship 1445–1503.* Oxford, 2005

Lea, H. C. *A History of Auricular Confession and Indulgences in the Latin Church.* New York, 1968

Leland, J. L. 'Unpardonable Sinners'. *Medieval Prosopography* 17 (1996), 181–95

Lunt, W. E. *Financial Relations of the Papacy with England, 1327–1534.* Studies in Anglo-Papal Relations during the Middle Ages 2. Cambridge MA, 1962

McKisack, M. *The Fourteenth Century, 1307–1399.* Oxford, 1959

McLane, B. W. 'Juror Attitudes toward Local Disorder: The Evidence of the 1328 Trailbaston Proceedings'. *Twelve Good Men and True: The Criminal Trial Jury in England, 1200–1800.* Ed. J. S. Cockburn and T. A. Green. Princeton, 1988. pp. 51–2

Maddern, P. C. *Violence and Social Order: East Anglia 1422–1442.* Oxford, 1992

Maddicott, J. R. 'Magna Carta and the Local Community', *P&P* 102 (1984), 25–65

———— 'Poems of Social Protest in Early Fourteenth Century England'. *England in the Fourteenth Century: Proceedings of the 1985 Harlaxton Symposium.* Ed. W. M. Ormrod. Stroud, 1986. pp. 130–44

Marx, C. W. *The Devil's Rights and the Redemption in the Literature of Medieval England.* Cambridge, 1995

Michaud, H. *La Grande Chancellerie et les ecritures royals au seizieme siecle (1515–1589).* Paris, 1967

Middleton, A. 'The Idea of Public Poetry in the Reign of Richard II'. *Speculum* 53 (1978), 94–114

Miller, J. ed. *Dante and the Unorthodox: The Aesthetics of Transgression.* Waterloo ON, 2005

Minnis, A. J. and P. Biller, ed. *Handling Sin: Confession in the Middle Ages.* Woodbridge, 1998

Musson, A. *Medieval Law in Context: The Growth of Legal Consciousness from Magna Carta to the Peasants' Revolt.* Manchester, 2001

———— *Public Order and Law Enforcement: The Local Administration of Criminal Justice, 1294–1350.* Woodbridge, 1996

———— 'Second "English Justinian" or Pragmatic Opportunist? A Re-Examination of the Legal Legislation of Edward III's Reign'. *The Age of Edward III.* Ed. J. Bothwell. York, 2001. pp. 69–88

———— 'Social Exclusivity or Justice for all? Access to Justice in Fourteenth-

Century England'. *Pragmatic Utopias: Ideals and Communities, 1200–1630.* Ed. R. Horrox and S. Rees-Jones. Cambridge, 2001. pp. 136–55

——— 'Turning King's Evidence: The Prosecution of Crime in Late Medieval England'. *Oxford Journal of Legal Studies* 19 (1999), 467–79

——— 'Twelve Good Men and True? The Character of Early Fourteenth-Century Juries'. *Law and History Review* 15 (1997), 115–44

Musson, A. and W. M. Ormrod, *The Evolution of English Justice: Law, Politics and Society in the Fourteenth Century.* Basingstoke, 1999

Neville, C. J. 'Common Knowledge of the Common Law in Later Medieval England'. *Canadian Journal of History* 29 (1994), 461–78

Nicholson, R. G. *Edward III and the Scots: The Formative Years of A Military Career, 1327–1335.* Oxford, 1965

Ormrod, W. M. 'Agenda for Legislation, 1322–c. 1340'. *EHR* 105 (1990), 1–33

_____ ' "Fifty Glorious Years": Edward III and the First English Royal Jubilee'. *Medieval History*, n.s. 1 (2002), 13–20

_____ 'In Bed with Joan of Kent: The King's Mother and the Peasants' Revolt'. *Medieval Women: Texts and Contexts in Late Medieval Britain. Essays for Felicity Riddy.* Ed. J. Wogan-Browne, R. Voaden, A. Diamond, A. M. Hutchison, C. M. Meale and L. Johnson. Turnhout, 2000. pp. 277–92

_____ *Political Life in Medieval England, 1300–1450.* Basingstoke, 1995. pp. 39–60

_____ 'Robin Hood and Public Record: The Authority of Writing in the Medieval Outlaw Tradition'. *Medieval Cultural Studies: Essays in Honour of Stephen Knight.* Ed. R. Evans, H. Fulton and D. Matthews. Cardiff, 2006. pp. 57–74

_____ 'The King's Secrets: Richard de Bury and the Monarchy of Edward III'. *War, Government and Aristocracy in the British Isles c. 1150–1500: Essays in Honour of Michael Prestwich.* Ed. C. Given-Wilson, A. Kettle and L. Scales. Woodbridge, 2008. pp. 163–78

_____ 'The Language of Complaint: Multilingualism and Petitioning in Later Medieval England'. *Language and Culture in Medieval Britain: The French of England c.1100–c.1500.* Ed. J. Wogan-Browne, with C. Collette, M. Kowaleski, L. Mooney, A. Putter and D. Trotter. York, 2009.

_____ 'The Peasants' Revolt and the Government of England'. *Journal of British Studies* 29 (1990), 1–30

_____ 'The Personal Religion of Edward III', *Speculum* 64 (1989), 849–77

_____ *The Reign of Edward III.* Stroud, 2000

_____ 'The Trials of Alice Perrers'. *Speculum* 83 (2008), 366–96

_____ 'The Use of English: Language, Law, and Political Culture in Fourteenth-Century England'. *Speculum* 78 (2003), 750–87

_____ 'Who Was Alice Perrers?', *The Chaucer Review* 40 (2006), 219–29

Ormrod, W. M., G. Dodd and A. Musson, eds. *Medieval Petitions: Grace and Grievance.* York, 2009

Owst, G. R. *Literature and the Pulpit in Medieval England.* 2nd edn. London, 1952

——— 'The Origins of the Legal Profession in England', *Irish Jurist*, n.s. 11 (1976), 126–31

Palmer, R. C. *English Law in the Age of the Black Death 1348–1381: A Transformation of Governance and Law.* Chapel Hill NC, 1993

Parsons, J. C. 'The Intercessionary Patronage of Queens Margaret and Isabella of

France'. *Thirteenth Century England VI*. Ed. M. Prestwich, R. H. Britnell and R. Frame. Woodbridge, 1997. pp. 145–56

—— 'The Queen's Intercession in Thirteenth-Century England'. *Power of the Weak: Studies on Medieval Women*. Ed. J. Carpenter and S.-B. MacLean. Urbana, 1995. pp. 147–77

Parsons J. C. and B. Wheeler, ed. *Medieval Mothering*. London, 1996

—— 'Chaucerian Confession: Penitential Literature and the Pardoner'. *Medievalia et Humanistica*, n.s. 7 (1976), 153–73.

Paulus, N. *Indulgences as a Social Factor in the Middle Ages*. New York, 1922

Pearsall, D. A. 'Chaucer's Pardoner: Death of a Salesman'. *Chaucer Review* 17 (1983), 358–64

—— 'Interpretative Models for the Peasants' Revolt'. *Hermeneutics and Medieval Culture*. Ed. J. Gallacher and H. Damico. New York, 1989. pp. 63–70

____ *The Canterbury Tales*. London, 1985

Petkov, K. *The Kiss of Peace: Ritual, Self and Society in the High and Late Medieval West*. Leiden, 2003

Plucknett, T. F. T. *A Concise History of Common Law*. London, 1956

—— 'Impeachment and Attainder'. *TRHS*, 5th series 3 (1953), 145–58

—— 'Parliament'. *The English Government at Work, 1327–1336. Vol. 1. Central and Prerogative Administration* (Mediaeval Academy of America Pubn, 37). Ed. J. F. Willard and W. A. Morris. Cambridge MA, 1940

Pollard, A. J. *Imagining Robin Hood: The Late-Medieval Stories in Historical Context*. Abingdon, 2004

Pollock, F. and F. M. Maitland, *The History of English Law before the Time of Edward I*. 2 vols. Cambridge, 1911

Powell, E. 'After "After McFarlane": The Poverty of Patronage and the Case for Constitutional History'. *Trade, Devotion and Governance: Papers in Later Medieval History*. Ed. D. J. Clayton, R. G. Davies and P. McNiven. Stroud, 1994. pp. 1–16

—— 'Arbitration and the Law in England in the Later Middle Ages'. *TRHS*. 5th series, 13 (1983), 49–67

—— 'Jury Trial at Gaol Delivery in the Late Middle Ages: The Midland Circuit, 1400–1429'. *Twelve Good Men and True: The Criminal Trial Jury in England, 1200–1800*. Ed. J. S. Cockburn and T. A. Green. Princeton, 1988. pp. 78–116

—— *Kingship, Law and Society: Criminal Justice in the Reign of Henry V*. Oxford, 1989

—— 'Law and Justice'. *Fifteenth-Century Attitudes: Perceptions of Society in Late Medieval England*. Ed. R. Horrox. Cambridge, 1994. pp. 29–41

—— 'Settlement of Disputes by Arbitration in Fifteenth-Century England'. *Law and History Review* 2 (1984), 21–43

____ 'The Administration of Criminal Justice in Late-Medieval England: Peace Sessions and Assizes'. *The Political Context of Law: Proceedings of the Seventh British History Conference*. Ed. R. Eales and D. Sullivan. London, 1987. pp. 49–59

—— 'The Restoration of Law and Order'. *Henry V: The Practice of Kingship*. Ed. G. L. Harriss. Oxford, 1985. pp. 53–74

Powell, E. *The Rising in East Anglia in 1381*. Cambridge, 1896

Powell E. and Trevelyan, G. M., ed. *The Peasants' Rising and the Lollards*. Cambridge, 1899

Powicke, F. M. *The Thirteenth Century, 1216–1307*. 2nd edn. Oxford, 1991

Prescott, A. 'London in the Peasants' Revolt: A Portrait Gallery'. *London Journal* 7 (1981), 125–43

——— '"The hand of God": The Suppression of the Peasants' Revolt of 1381'. *Prophecy, Apocalypse and the Day of Doom: Proceedings of the 2000 Harlaxton Symposium*. Ed. N. Morgan. Donnington, 2004. pp. 317–41

Prestwich, M. C. *Documents Illustrating the Crisis of 1297–8 in England*, Camden Society, 4th series 24. 1980

——— 'Gilbert de Middleton and the Attack on the Cardinals, 1317'. *Warriors and Churchmen in the High Middle Ages: Essays Presented to Karl Leyser*. Ed. T. Reuter. London, 1992. pp. 179–94

——— 'Parliament and the Community of the Realm in Fourteenth Century England'. *Parliament and Community*. Ed. A. Cosgrove and J. I. McGuire. Belfast, 1983. pp. 5–24

Pugh, R. B. *Itinerant Justices in English History*. Exeter, 1967

Putnam, B. H. *The Place in History of Sir William Shareshull*. Cambridge, 1950

——— 'The Transformation of the Keepers of the Peace into the Justices of the Peace, 1327–1380'.*TRHS*, 4th series 12 (1929), 19–48

Rampton, M. 'The Peasants' Revolt of 1381 and the Written Word'. *Comitatus: A Journal of Medieval and Renaissance Studies* 24 (1993), 45–60

Rawcliffe, C. 'English Noblemen and their Advisers: Consultation and Collaboration in the Later Middle Ages'. *Journal of British Studies* 25 (1986), 157–77

——— 'Parliament and the Settlement of Disputes by Arbitration in the Later Middle Ages'. *Parliamentary History* 9 (1990), 316–42

Réville, A. *Etude sur le Soulèvement de 1381 dans le Comtés de Hertford, de Suffolk et de Norfolk*. Paris, 1898

Richardson, H. G. 'John of Gaunt and the Parliamentary Representation of Lancashire'. *BJRL* 22 (1938), 175–222

——— 'Tancred, Raymond, and Bracton'. *EHR* 59 (1944), 376–84

Richardson, H. G. and G. O. Sayles, *The English Parliament in the Middle Ages*. London, 1981

Rigby, S. H. *English Society in the Later Middle Ages: Class, Status and Gender*. Basingstoke, 1995

Rigg, A. G. *A History of Anglo-Latin Literature, 1066–1422*. Cambridge, 1992

Roskell, J. S. *Parliament and Politics in Late Medieval England*. London, 1981

Rothwell, H. 'The Confirmation of the Charters, 1297'. *EHR* 60 (1945), 16–35

Rubin, M. *Corpus Christi: The Eucharist in Late Medieval Culture*. Cambridge, 1991

Saul, N. *Richard II*. London, 1997

Scattergood, V. J. 'The Tale of Gamelyn: The Noble Robber as Provincial Hero'. *Readings in Medieval English Romance*. Ed. C. Meale. Cambridge, 1994. pp. 159–94

Schulz, F. 'Bracton and Raymond de Peñafort'. *Law Quarterly Review* 61 (1945), 286–92

Shaffern, R. W. 'Learned Discussions of Indulgences for the Dead in the Middle Ages'. *Church History* 61 (1992), 367–81

Shannon, E. F. 'Medieval Law in the Tale of Gamelyn'. *Speculum* 26 (1951), 458–64.

Sharpe, J. A. *Crime in Early Modern England, 1550–1750*. 2nd edn. London, 1998

Smith, D. M. and V. C. M. London, eds. *The Heads of Religious Houses: England and Wales*. Cambridge, 2001

Steel, A. *The Receipt of the Exchequer, 1377–1485*. Cambridge, 1954

Stephen, J. F. *History of the Criminal Law of England*. 3 vols. London, 1883

Stokes, M. *Justice and Mercy in Piers Plowman*. Cambridge, 1984

Stones, E. L. G. 'The Folvilles of Ashby Folville, Leicestershire, and their Associates in Crime'. *TRHS*, 5th series 7 (1957), 117–36

Storey, R. L. *The End of the House of Lancaster*. London, 1966

Strohm, P. *Hochon's Arrow: The Social Imagination of Fourteenth Century Texts*. Princeton, 1992

—— *Politique: Languages of Statecraft between Chaucer and Shakespeare*. Notre Dame, 2005

—— *Social Chaucer*. Cambridge MA, 1989

Stubbs, W. *The Constitutional History of England in its Origin and Development*. 3 vols. Oxford, 1875

Sumption, J. *Pilgrimage: An Image of Medieval Religion*. London, 1975. pp. 236–42

Swanson, R. N. 'Indulgences at Norwich Cathedral Priory in the Later Middle Ages: Popular Piety in the Balance Sheet'. *Historical Research* 76 (2003), 18–29

—— 'Indulgences for Prayers for the Dead in the Diocese of Lincoln in the Early Fourteenth Century'. *Journal of Ecclesiastical History* 52 (2001), 197–219

—— *Religion and Devotion in Europe, c. 1215–c.1515*. Cambridge, 1995

Tait, J. 'Did Richard II Murder the Duke of Gloucester?' *Historical Essays by Members of the Owens College, Manchester*. ed. T. F. Tout and J. Tait. Manchester, 1902. pp. 193–216

Thompson, E. P. *Whigs and Hunters: The Origins of the Black Act*. New York, 1976

Thornley, I. D. 'Sanctuary in Medieval London'. *Journal of the British Archaeological Association*, 2nd series 38 (1932), 293–315

—— 'The Destruction of Sanctuary'. *Tudor Studies Presented to Albert Frederick Pollard*. Ed. R. W. Seton-Watson. London, 1924

—— 'The Sanctuary Register of Beverley'. *EHR* 34 (1919), 393–7

Tout, T. F. *Chapters in the Administrative History of Medieval England*. 6 vols. Manchester, 1920–33

Traver, H. 'The Four Daughters of God: A Mirror of Changing Doctrine'. *Publications of the Modern Language Association* 40 (1925), 44–92

Tuck, A. 'Thomas, Duke of Gloucester (1355–1397)'. *Oxford Dictionary of National Biography*. Oxford, 2004. online edn, May 2007

Tuck, J. A. 'Nobles, Commons and the Great Revolt of 1381'. *The English Rising of 1381*. Ed. R. H. Hilton and T. H. Aston. Cambridge, 1984. pp. 194–212

—— *Richard II and the English Nobility*. London, 1973

—— 'Richard II's System of Patronage'. *The Reign of Richard II: Essays in Honour of May McKisack*. Ed. F. R. H. Du Boulay and C. M. Barron. London, 1971. pp. 1–20

Valente, C. *The Theory and Practice of Revolt in Medieval England*. Aldershot, 2003

Verduyn, A. J. 'The Commons and the Early Justices of the Peace under Edward III'. *Regionalism and Revision: The Crown and its Provinces in England, 1250–1650*. Ed. P. Fleming, A. Gross and J. R. Lander. London, 1998. pp. 87–106

—— 'The Politics of Law and Order during the Early Years of Edward III'. *EHR* 108 (1993), 842–67

Vincent, N. 'Some Pardoners' Tales: The Earliest English Indulgences'. *TRHS*, 6th series 12 (2002), 23–58

Walker, S. K. 'Rumour, Sedition and Popular Protest in the Reign of Henry IV'.
P&P 166 (2000), 31–65
────── *The Lancastrian Affinity 1361–1399*. Oxford, 1991
Walker, S., M. J. Braddick and G. L. Harriss, eds. *Political Culture in Later Medieval
England; Essays by Simon Walker*. Manchester, 2006
Wallace, D. *Chaucerian Polity, Absolutist Lineages and Associational Forms in England
and Italy*. Stanford, 1997
Warren, W. L. *King John*. New York, 1961
Watts, J. *Henry VI and the Politics of Kingship*. Cambridge, 1996
────── 'Looking for the State in Later Medieval England'. *Heraldry, Pageantry, and
Social Display in Medieval England*. Ed. P. R. Coss and M. H. Keen. Woodbridge,
2002. pp. 243–67
────── 'Public or Plebs: The Changing Meaning of "the Commons", 1381–1549'.
Power and Identity in the Middle Ages: Essays in Memory of Rees Davies. Ed. H.
Pryce and J. L. Watts. Oxford, 2007. pp. 242–60
────── 'The Pressure of the Public on Later Medieval Politics'. *The Fifteenth Century
IV: Political Culture in Late Medieval Britain*. Ed. L. Clark and C. Carpenter.
Woodbridge, 2004. pp. 159–80
Waugh, S. L. 'The Profits of Violence: The Minor Gentry in the Rebellion of 1321–2
in Gloucestershire and Herefordshire'. *Speculum* 52 (1977), 843–69
Wedgwood, J. C. 'John of Gaunt and the Packing of Parliament'. *EHR* 45 (1930),
623–5
Wilkinson, B. 'The Authorisation of Chancery Writs under Edward III'. *Bulletin of
the John Rylands Library* 8 (1924), 107–39
────── *The Chancery under Edward III*. Manchester, 1929
Wilks, M. J. 'Royal Patronage and Anti-Papalism from Ockham to Wyclif'. *Wyclif:
Political Ideas and Practice*. Ed. A. Hudson. Oxford, 2000. pp. 130–53
Wogan-Browne, J., N. Watson, A. Taylor and R. Evans, eds. *The Idea of the Vernac-
ular: An Anthology of Middle English Literary Theory*. Exeter, 1999
Wood, D. *Clement VI: The Pontificate and Ideas of an Avignon Pope*. Cambridge, 2003
Wright, T. 'On the Popular Cycle of the Robin Hood Ballads'. *Essays on Subjects
Connected with the Literature, Popular Superstition, and History of England in the
Middle Ages*. Ed. T. Wright. London, 1846. pp. 164–211
Zutshi, P. N. R 'Collective Indulgences from Rome and Avignon in English Collec-
tions'. *Medieval Ecclesiastical Studies: In Honour of Dorothy M. Owen*. Ed. M. J.
Franklin and C. Harper-Bill. Studies in the History of Medieval Religion 7.
Woodbridge, 1995. pp. 281–97

Unpublished Theses

Eiden, H. '"In der Knechtschaft werdet ihr verharren …": Ursachen und Verlauf
des englischen Bauernaufstands von 1381'. Unpublished PhD thesis, Trier,
1995
Janecek, T. J. 'The Parliament of Heaven'. Unpublished PhD thesis, University of
Illinois, 1975
Kesselring, K. 'To Pardon and to Punish: Mercy and Authority in Tudor England'.
Unpublished PhD thesis, Queens University, ON, 2000

McCune, P. 'The Ideology of Mercy in English Literature and Law 1200–1600'. Unpublished PhD thesis, University of Michigan, 1989

Prescott, A. J. 'Judicial Records of the Rising of 1381'. Unpublished PhD thesis, University of London, 1984

Verduyn, A. J. 'The Attitude of the Parliamentary Commons to Law and Order under Edward III'. Unpublished DPhil thesis, University of Oxford, 1991

INDEX

Note: For the names of those who acted as intercessors for pardon throughout the period 1307–1399, please see the alphabetical lists in Appendix 4, i–iii.

Kings and their immediate families are indexed under first name; nobles are indexed under the titles they held up to 1399.

YORK MEDIEVAL PRESS: PUBLICATIONS

God's Words, Women's Voices: The Discernment of Spirits in the Writing of Late-Medieval Women Visionaries, Rosalyn Voaden (1999)

Pilgrimage Explored, ed. J. Stopford (1999)

Piety, Fraternity and Power: Religious Gilds in Late Medieval Yorkshire 1389–1547, David J. F. Crouch (2000)

Courts and Regions in Medieval Europe, ed. Sarah Rees Jones, Richard Marks and A. J. Minnis (2000)

Treasure in the Medieval West, ed. Elizabeth M. Tyler (2000)

Nunneries, Learning and Spirituality in Late Medieval English Society: The Dominican Priory of Dartford, Paul Lee (2000)

Prophecy and Public Affairs in Later Medieval England, Lesley A. Coote (2000)

The Problem of Labour in Fourteenth-Century England, ed. James Bothwell, P. J. P. Goldberg and W. M. Ormrod (2000)

New Directions in later Medieval Manuscript Studies: Essays from the 1998 Harvard Conference, ed. Derek Pearsall (2000)

Cistercians, Heresy and Crusadse in Occitania, 1145–1229: Preaching in the Lord's Vineyard, Beverly Mayne Kienzle (2001)

Guilds and the Parish Community in Late Medieval East Anglia, c. 1470–1550, Ken Farnhill (2001)

The Age of Edward III, ed. J. S. Bothwell (2001)

Time in the Medieval World, ed. Chris Humphrey and W. M. Ormrod (2001)

The Cross Goes North: Processes of Conversion in Northern Europe, AD 300–1300, ed. Martin Carver (2002)

Henry IV: The Establishment of the Regime, 1399–1406, ed. Gwilym Dodd and Douglas Biggs (2003)

Youth in the Middle Ages, ed. P. J. P Goldberg and Felicity Riddy (2004)

The Idea of the Castle in Medieval England, Abigail Wheatley (2004)

Rites of Passage: Cultures of Transition in the Fourteenth Century, ed. Nicola F. McDonald and W. M. Ormrod (2004)

Creating the Monastic Past in Medieval Flanders, Karine Ugé (2005)

St William of York, Christopher Norton (2006)

Medieval Obscenities, ed. Nicola F. McDonald (2006)

The Reign of Edward II: New Perspectives, ed. Gwilym Dodd and Anthony Musson (2006)

Old English Poetics: The Aesthetics of the Familiar in Anglo-Saxon England, Elizabeth M. Tyler (2006)

The Late Medieval Interlude: The Drama of Youth and Aristocratic Masculinity, Fiona S. Dunlop (2007)

The Late Medieval English College and its Context, ed. Clive Burgess and Martin Heale (2008)

The Reign of Henry IV: Rebellion and Survival, 1403–1413, ed. Gwilym Dodd and Douglas Biggs (2008)

Medieval Petitions: Grace and Grievance, ed. W. Mark Ormrod, Gwilym Dodd and Anthony Musson (2009)

St Edmund, King and Martyr: Changing Images of a Medieval Saint, ed. Anthony Bale (2009)

Language and Culture in Medieval Britain: The French of England c. 1100–c. 1500, ed. Jocelyn Wogan-Browne et al. (2009)

York Studies in Medieval Theology

I   *Medieval Theology and the Natural Body*, ed. Peter Biller and A. J. Minnis (1997)

II *Handling Sin: Confession in the Middle Ages*, ed. Peter Biller and A. J. Minnis (1998)

III *Religion and Medicine in the Middle Ages*, ed. Peter Biller and Joseph Ziegler (2001)

IV *Texts and the Repression of Medieval Heresy*, ed. Caterina Bruschi and Peter Biller (2002)

York Manuscripts Conference

Manuscripts and Readers in Fifteenth-Century England: The Literary Implications of Manuscript Study, ed. Derek Pearsall (1983) [Proceedings of the 1981 York Manuscripts Conference]

Manuscripts and Texts: Editorial Problems in Later Middle English Literature, ed. Derek Pearsall (1987) [Proceedings of the 1985 York Manuscripts Conference]

Latin and Vernacular: Studies in Late-Medieval Texts and Manuscripts, ed. A. J. Minnis (1989) [Proceedings of the 1987 York Manuscripts Conference]

Regionalism in Late-Medieval Manuscripts and Texts: Essays celebrating the publication of 'A Linguistic Atlas of Late Mediaeval English', ed. Felicity Riddy (1991) [Proceedings of the 1989 York Manuscripts Conference]

Late-Medieval Religious Texts and their Transmission: Essays in Honour of A. I. Doyle, ed. A. J. Minnis (1994) [Proceedings of the 1991 York Manuscripts Conference]

Prestige, Authority and Power in Late Medieval Manuscripts and Texts, ed. Felicity Riddy (2000) [Proceedings of the 1994 York Manuscripts Conference]

Middle English Poetry: Texts and Traditions. Essays in Honour of Derek Pearsall, ed. A. J. Minnis (2001) [Proceedings of the 1996 York Manuscripts Conference]

Manuscript Culture in the British Isles

Design and Distribution of Late Medieval Manuscripts in England, ed. Margaret Connolly and Linne R. Mooney (2008)